Visualizing
FASCISM

JULIA ADENEY THOMAS AND GEOFF ELEY, EDITORS

Visualizing FASCISM

The Twentieth-Century Rise of the Global Right

Duke University Press | *Durham and London* | 2020

Designed by Julienne Alexander / Cover designed by Matthew Tauch
Typeset in Minion Pro and Haettenschweiler by Copperline Books

Library of Congress Cataloging-in-Publication Data
Names: Eley, Geoff, [date] editor. | Thomas, Julia Adeney, [date] editor.
Title: Visualizing fascism : the twentieth-century rise of the global right /
Geoff Eley and Julia Adeney Thomas, editors.
Description: Durham : Duke University Press, 2020. |
Includes bibliographical references and index.
Identifiers: LCCN 2019023964 (print)
LCCN 2019023965 (ebook)
ISBN 9781478003120 (hardback : acid-free paper)
ISBN 9781478003762 (paperback : acid-free paper)
ISBN 9781478004387 (ebook)
Subjects: LCSH: Fascism—History—20th century. | Fascism and culture. |
Fascist aesthetics.
Classification: LCC JC481 .V57 2020 (print) | LCC JC481 (ebook) |
DDC 704.9/49320533—dc23
LC record available at https://lccn.loc.gov/2019023964
LC ebook record available at https://lccn.loc.gov/2019023965

This publication is made possible in part by support from
the Institute for Scholarship in the Liberal Arts, College of
Arts and Letters, University of Notre Dame.

CONTENTS

INTRODUCTION

A Portable Concept of Fascism

JULIA ADENEY THOMAS

Gustave Courbet's painting *Burial at Ornans* caused outrage when it was exhibited at the Paris Salon of 1850–51 because it depicted ordinary people at an
ordinary funeral. Instead of using artist models in sentimental, allegorical, or
heroic guises, Courbet (1819–77) had persuaded the mourners attending his
own great-uncle's burial to pose for his monumental ten-by-twenty-two-foot
canvas. Aghast critics recognized a revolution when they saw one, and Courbet proved them right—not only artistically by overturning Romanticism for
Realism, but also politically by playing a leading role in the Paris Commune
of 1870, an action that led to his imprisonment and ultimate exile to Geneva.[1]
As Courbet's notoriety shows, in the nineteenth century the mere act of representing common people had a radical edge allied with liberal democratic,
socialist, or anarchist movements. However, by the twentieth century the
assumption that "the people" and "the Left" might be rough synonyms in
art and in politics crashed against a new form of right-wing populism that
claimed the people for itself. As historian Peter Clarke observes, "the novelty
of Fascism was to politicize the masses from the right."[2]

Right-wing populism's novelty created a problem when its proponents
tried to promote their politics visually. Fascism upended the Left's exclusive
claim to represent the people, but rejected its artistic experiments with form

and subject matter. It discarded the traditional Right's elite aesthetic tastes, but required a glorious vision of the nation. In short, fascism awkwardly visualized itself as neither avant-garde nor traditional, while poaching from both camps. It therefore confronted an unprecedented challenge when it came to self-depiction. It needed to create a new visual repertoire that avoided the leftist taint of high modernism and socialist realism without seeming to capitulate to a rarified culture borne aloft by old aristocratic or new oligarchic tastes. How fascists around the world met—or, indeed, failed to meet—this aesthetic challenge is the focus of this volume.

This book approaches the question of how fascism was visualized in two complementary and connected ways: as a global phenomenon and as an aesthetic phenomenon. Both themes are interwoven throughout the essays. Here in the Introduction, I explore each theme separately before introducing my synthesis of the two—a portable concept of fascism. I then go on to delineate specific traits common to the global practice of visualizing fascism and end by underscoring the novelty of the twentieth-century rise of the global Right, a phenomenon impossible before colonial capitalism, socialism, and nation-states emerged.

Global Fascism

In arguing for fascism as a worldwide phenomenon, our work explores the rise of the Right during the interwar years as it emerged transnationally. This global approach is now possible because of new scholarship on interwar and wartime Asia, particularly Japan, that begins to balance previous research weighted heavily toward Europe.[3] Indeed, until very recently fascism may have seemed European simply because Europe was the place historians studied most intensively (outside their home countries), not only in the United States, Canada, and Britain but also in Japan.[4] Our deepening understanding of Japan and its Asian imperialism is critical to grasping the transnational nature of the rise of the Right.[5] It is now possible to argue, as literary scholar Alan Tansman does, that "Japan's confrontation with modernity was coeval with Europe's." As Tansman observes, "the social, economic, and cultural conditions that gave birth to European fascism were also shared by Japan, and the solutions, through the state's imposition of mythic thinking that extolled natural bonds of blood and demanded devotion and sacrifice of the individual to the state, nation, or lineage, backed by coercion at home, in the name of domination of peoples of poorer bloodline abroad, made Japan one among other fascist nations."[6] In this volume, then, Japan figures prominently alongside the other Axis powers.

As Asia comes more sharply into focus, it also becomes clear that fascism is not best understood by creating particularistic models that focus on single nations or by abstracting a Eurocentric version of the populist Right and applying it elsewhere. Three reasons support this contention. First, the forces of capitalism and imperialism operated globally. As Ethan Mark argues, envisioning the Second World War as a conflict among European nation-states and excluding Asia has created a "pervasive scholarly blind spot" about the degree to which "fascism was itself determined within a broader, long-term global context of competing imperialisms."[7] The excesses of capitalism, resting on uneven relations of power within and among nations, dissolved the bonds of communities at all levels and sowed despair and resentment around the world. Everywhere this led to similar reactions, including fascist tendencies.

Second, better communication and faster travel increased the speed at which desires, discontents, and, especially for our purposes, aesthetic repertoires were shared. For instance, modernist designs deployed by artists in the Soviet Union and in liberal democracies also figured on the cover of Shanghai's fascist monthly *Qiantu* [The future], as Maggie Clinton shows in chapter 1. Beginning in the 1920s, regular airmail routes carried letters, publications, and news of all sorts, spreading ideas and innovative graphics like wildfire. People traveled more, too. By 1937 Britain's Imperial Airways advertised its flight from Hong Kong to London as taking a mere ten days as opposed to a month by sea, although only the very rich could afford such dizzying velocity. Most ocean-crossing travelers still embarked on ships, as did a mission of Italian Blackshirts who visited Japan in the spring of 1938.[8] A year earlier, Nazi film director Arnold Fanck (1889–1974) had also made the journey to Tokyo. So impressed was Fanck by actress Hara Setsuko (1920–2015) that he teamed up with Itami Mansaku (1900–1946) to cast her as the star in their coproduced film *The New Earth* (the Japanese version was titled *Atarashiki tsuchi* and the German version, *Die Tochter des Samurai*). The film ends with a celebration of Japan's takeover of Manchuria. Such collaborations would obviously have been impossible a few decades earlier. Speed and connections were central to developing fascist visual tactics.

Along with the forces of capitalism and communication, the third factor that compels a new understanding of global fascism is the key role colonies played as sites for producing right-wing populism. The importance of this factor has emerged only recently, in part because of revised understandings of German and Italian colonialism.[9] Work on Japanese colonialism has also heightened awareness of these "offshore" arenas for negotiating nationalism. Particularly in Asia, where Western and Japanese colonialism clashed, these negotiations became murky and complex. In some cases—such as that of Indian leader Subhas Chandra Bose (1897–1945), who allied himself with the Nazis and the Japanese against British imperialists, or Indonesian leader Sukarno (1901–70), who briefly allied himself with the Japanese in opposition to Dutch imperialism—the fascism of the colonized was opportunistic, a means to obtain national independence.[10] In other cases, the fascist vassals willingly mimicked their overlords. As Bertrand Metton demonstrates in his essay on Slovakia, after the Nazis colonized Eastern Europe, Slovaks created organizations and publications that paralleled German counterparts: the Hlinka Youth organization for the *Hilterjugend* and magazines including *Nová Mládež* for the New Youth, *Slovenská* for girls, and *Vlca* (Wolf Cub) for boys. As in Germany, Slovaks produced a vibrant national myth to replace stale right-wing conservatism.[11]

In still other cases, colonies served as places where settlers developed their own iteration of fascism. Examples include the fascination with whiteness in Namibia, which Lorena Rizzo explores in chapter 6, and greater support for the fascist party in the Dutch East Indies than in Holland, as Ethan Mark shows in chapter 8. Likewise, in the 1930s, fascist ideas and institutions were fostered in Manchuria and then exported from this colony back to Japan, as Paul Barclay argues in chapter 2, building on the work of historian Janis Mimura.[12] These three factors—capitalism, modern communication, and colonies—generated the pulsing, angry networks that propelled fascism globally.

In short, fascism did not have a single place of origin—not even Italy. Its birth certificate is held in the archives of many nations, and it grew up as a transnational traveler, a denizen of late-night railroad stations and neon-lit hotels. Historian Reto Hofmann rightly describes it as emerging through "a complex interplay between ideas both local and global."[13] Thus the essays here extend beyond Italy, Germany, and Japan to Taiwan, Korea, Manchuria, China, and Indonesia in the East, and to Holland, Spain, Slovakia, southern Africa, and the United States, in order to suggest that the allure of the Right was almost universal.[14] Fascism was a transnational phenomenon.

Aesthetics of Fascism

In order to show fascism as a global phenomenon, this volume emphasizes its aesthetic strategies. I approach fascism as an aesthetic phenomenon both in the sense of using beauty to mask modernity's pain and in aestheticism's root sense of "perception." How is it possible for something as immaterial and invisible as "the nation" to be seen as the fount of all truth? Looking at photography, the graphic arts, monuments, architecture, and cinema can help answer this question.[15] It may at first seem eccentric for historians, as most of us are, to abandon analyses based on texts alone and focus instead on the changing visual repertoires of fascism, but this approach provides several benefits. As Ruth Ben-Ghiat notes, "The visual not only communicates in ways written documents cannot; it can also enrich the field of historical research by leading us to new subjects and lines of inquiry that often have scant traces in the written and oral historical records."[16] The visual also helps liberate us from mired national debates by revealing how easily aesthetic styles and modes of public commemoration slip across borders. Awareness of this aesthetic dynamism undermines the conventional geographical boundaries that persist among historians and that have truncated our understanding that fascism's heightened nationalism was a product of globalization.

A further value of *seeing* fascism in action is that using visual evidence shows just how permeable the borders were not only among right-wing movements and nations, but also between fascism and antifascism. Visualizing fascism is part of visualizing mid-twentieth-century mass society in general, no matter what sort of politics that society claimed. The final essays in this volume, by Nadya Bair (chapter 10) and Claire Zimmerman (chapter 11), demonstrate how anti-fascist work made during the war was recast from a different perspective afterward. The shared aesthetic repertoire of fascist, communist, and liberal democratic states becomes truly apparent only when viewed transnationally and across time. In other words, by actively *looking* at the rise of the global Right, we can perceive just how powerfully visual sensations can bind people to nations, but also how fragile the alliance between any artistic style and any particular politics became by the 1930s. I will return to the question of defining fascism's aesthetic later. My point here is that this volume's global and visual approaches reinforce one another as we strive to see the rise of the interwar Right in all its complexity. Some studies have stressed the global nature of fascism and others have concerned themselves with the aesthetics of fascism in a single nation. This volume is the first to fuse global and visual approaches to propose a new way of understanding fascism's strategies.

Five Propositions toward a Portable Concept of Fascism

The result of combining the global and the visual is a concept of fascism that is no longer confined to any particular nation. Nor is it restricted to the decades after World War I with its particular crisis of capitalism. This volume argues instead that the fascist ideologies and visualizations that emerged during the interwar period are maverick enough to reemerge in similar circumstances whenever people become alienated not only from the traditional Right but also from liberal democratic and left-wing alternatives. When understood in this way, fascism—defined primarily by its ideological energies rather than by parties and institutions—remains a danger. I call this a "portable concept of fascism." It travels across space and time and is useful in analyzing places where fascist movements failed as well as places where fascist regimes were established. This portable concept of fascism is the volume's primary theoretical contribution. It rests on five propositions, outlined below, that culminate with fascism's use of visual culture.

First and foremost, fascism cannot be safely consigned to the past. It is not the antiquarian phenomenon that Hugh Trevor-Roper insisted it was when he told us that fascism "began in 1922–23 with the emergence of the Italian fascist party . . . came of age in the 1930s when 'fascist' parties sprang up throughout Europe . . . [and] ended in 1945 with the defeat and death of two dictators."[17] I wish Trevor-Roper had been correct. If fascism could be confined to those actions and those years, it could be dispensed with as an unfortunate but discrete episode. Like hoopskirts, it would have no contemporary allure. However, as my coeditor Geoff Eley rightly argues in *Nazism as Fascism*, the reason for studying fascism is, "above all, to help with the urgency of our present discontents."[18] Today's "political dynamics easily threaten the kind of crisis where a politics *that begins to look like fascism* might coalesce."[19] Our current discontents are manifold and magnified most especially, I think, by the pressures of climate change creating refugees and of transnational neoliberalism producing ever-greater inequality. Fascism defined by heightened nationalism, perpetual warfare, and reactionary fear of enemies—real or imagined—cannot be relegated to the dustbin of history.

Second, fascism is the product of *political* crisis in *modern capitalist* states. All three terms—"modern," "capitalist," and "political"—are important. The modernity of fascist states used to be disputed, but most scholars now agree that neither "backwardness" nor "late development" nor a "feudal mind-set" explain the energetic assertion of organic unity between a regime and its people. Premodern regimes were manifestly uninterested in including "the people" as active agents within the polity; only with the rise of modernity does this change. In fact, the consensus today is that Italy and Germany did not become fascist because they were *not* modern states; they became fascist because they were.[20] The same is true for Japan.[21] Ethan Mark and historian Rikki Kersten have elegantly summarized the debates over whether Japan was fascist, ultimately siding with Japanese scholars such as Yoshimi Yoshiaki who are committed to the rubric of "fascism." They do so because it places developments in Japan within global history rather than treating them as sui generis outliers, as Japan's nationalist ideologues like to claim.[22]

To this shared modernity must be added capitalism or at least a strong capitalist sector within the economy. Along with many others, sociologist Mark Neocleous argues point-blank that fascism is "generated by modern industrial capitalism."[23] Here too the Japanese empire is not an Oriental outlier. Although its economy weathered the 1929 economic collapse better than the European and American economies, growing at a rate of 5 percent throughout the 1930s, tensions in its dual economy between tenants and landlords, and between industrial workers and large corporate conglomerates called *zaibatsu*, echoed economic struggles elsewhere. Finally, there is the issue of politics. Producing fascism required not only a crisis of capitalism but also political disarray. Leadership proved timid and self-interested.[24] In Eley's words, "fascism prospered under conditions of general political crisis, in societies that were already dynamically capitalist (or at least possessed a dynamic capitalist sector), but where the state proved incapable of dispatching its organizing functions for the maintenance of social cohesion."[25] It took colossal political failure to clinch the deal, enabling fascist regimes to emerge from fascist movements.

These three factors—modernity, capitalist crisis, and political ineptitude—all existed in Italy, Japan, and Germany where the state became fascist. But fascist movements could emerge without all three factors being present. Surveying the interwar world, Reto Hofmann argues, "Recognizable fascist movements were springing up seemingly everywhere, its members donning a rainbow of shirts—white in Syria, green in Egypt, blue in China, orange in South Africa, gold in Mexico. Politically, Hitler took office in Germany in 1933; in China, Chiang Kai-shek launched the New Life Movement (1934) to counter socialism, liberalism, and democracy; two years later, Spain's Francisco Franco staged a military coup with the support of the right-wing Falange movement."[26] To understand the rise of the global Right, both fascism's victories and its defeats need to be brought into focus. This volume considers places where fascism foundered—China, Holland, and Namibia—as well as places where it triumphed.

The third proposition of my "portable concept of fascism" is that violence is key to propelling the dissolution of civility and governability. Words become blows. Yet, as Ruth Ben-Ghiat notes, "after an initial period of public violence meant to close off other political options and frighten people into submission, fascist governments often sent those agents of violence offstage." They turned to other means for subduing dissent and interpolating the fascist.[27]

Fourth, as Mark Neocleous argues, "fascism is first and foremost an ideology."[28] For some, fascist ideas lack systematicity and should therefore be dismissed, but an ideology need not be logical or even coherent to be effective. Among fascism's main targets, after all, are rationality and the conception of politics as the arena where clearly articulated positions can be expressed and differences negotiated with the help of political parties and representative state structures. Indeed, fascism's success seems to stem largely from its ideological vagueness and mystification of power. Amorphous evocations of national spirit inspire people precisely because they lacked rigor and form, and therefore they cannot be countered by reasoned appeals or expert analysis of probable consequences. Emotions such as wounded pride and resentment can be channeled against "enemies" within and without, bringing new meaning to life and to sacrificing that life for the nation. Gender politics is central to fascist ideology. As women gained a faltering toehold in the public sphere, reactionary fear and a sense of emasculation was assuaged by bouts of manly chest-thumping and by relegating women to the roles of wives and mothers. Compelling ideological gestures pointing to the vitalist energy of youth, the comforts of naturally sanctioned belonging, and the necessity of righteous wars in a hostile world helped mask the paradoxes and tensions of economic and political failures at home. As Eley indicates, it is "vital to reinstate the importance of fascist ideology, not just as the critical dissection of fascist ideas in the programmatic and philosophical senses, as interpretative readings of key texts, or as the analysis of the fascist outlook, but by studying the nature of the fascist popular appeal."[29]

Fifth and finally, visual presentations of fascist ideology were crucial precisely because the "message" of the graphic arts, images, collages, movies, monuments, and pageantry was elusive and emotive. Stylized typefaces on magazine covers could gesture toward a vibrant future without specifying policies. Posters depicting the tender love of a mother for her child could evoke traditional gender roles and the warmth of "home" while deflecting questions about military deaths, missing neighbors, and raining bombs. Photographs of Hitler at the Berghof in the Bavarian Alps or paintings of an incandescent Mount Fuji floating against a red sun celebrated nature while obscuring the military's depredations on natural resources. Although the visual was vital to fascism, our essays show that fascist aesthetics had no essence, no exclusive medium, and no invariable set of visual tropes. The elusive and emotive qualities of fascism's mystical message coalesced no more in visual form than in philosophical form. In some ways this is a disappointment. If all we had to guard against were black shirts and mass rallies illuminated by the antiaircraft searchlights of the 1934 Nuremberg rally, resistance would be far easier. We find instead an array of visual efforts to bind the national community and to heal history's wounds. Fascism's visual tactics were effective because they were diverse, opportunistic, and incoherent.

Many of us associate fascism with the "spectacle" so prominent in Walter Benjamin's analysis. We think immediately of Mussolini's March on Rome, Hitler's Nuremberg rallies, and Japan's 1940 celebration of the supposedly unbroken 2,600-year reign of the imperial family. Such orchestrated public rallies are central to Eley's essay in chapter 3. But spectacle was not the only, or even the most crucial, way in which fascism tried to abolish the distance between the state and its subjects. Images of particular leaders whose heightened presence (and even their incantatory absence) made them magnets for popular desire were important as well; these photographs served almost as a form of mesmerism, replacing democracy's painstaking processes.[30] The challenge of portraying a leader was to make him simultaneously transcendent and yet accessible, which is a difficult thing to do, as Lutz Koepnick makes clear in his analysis of Heinrich Hoffmann's photographs of Hitler as an outdoor reader posing in the mountains (chapter 5). In chapter 4, Ruth Ben-Ghiat explores not only films focusing on Mussolini but also those moments at mass rallies when the camera turned to capture the crowd's response. As Ben-Ghiat observes, when the crowds appeared stone-faced and silent, sounds of cheering were added, using the roar of acquiescence to blot out the vision of passive resistance. Viewers were encouraged to see enthusiasm with their ears. Finally, as the majority of our essays show, fascism was most often brought home at the level of the people's everyday activities through photographs, photomontages, etchings, and graphics in magazines and tourist pamphlets, and through the architecture and monuments intended to glorify the dead from Amsterdam to Manchuria. The most striking feature of most fascist art in many of these formats is not its ecstatic hyperbolism but its banality.

In short, fascism brought into view mass spectacle, awkwardly posed leadership, and people's daily lives, but these visual tropes never added up to a coherent aesthetic. Fascist art was caught in its own paradox. On the one hand, like the avant-garde movements of the early twentieth century, it sought to "redistribute the sensible" (in Jacques Rancière's phrase) across society, and yet unlike the avant-garde, it also sought to contain and control the sensible within the purview of the nation.[31] The result was often hackneyed—thin whitewash with a dash of menace.

Fascism's Counter Aesthetic

Fascism in the 1920s, '30s, and '40s never crystallized a defined aesthetic. In the brief heat of that quarter-century, fascism's aesthetic tactics were driven by political necessity rather than concern for art-making per se. Moreover, fascism resisted drawing attention to modes of *representation* either in politics or in the arts precisely because it wished to *present* the unity of nation and people as unmediated. Indeed, the new Right's attack on the traditional Right, liberalism, and the Left unmoored it not only from political and philosophical history but also from art history. Embedded in no particular lineage and without a past, fascist aesthetics had no reservoir of visual gestures and subject matter to draw from. Without an idiom of its own, it operated as magpies do, stealing bits and pieces for ragtag presentations. The result, I argue, was a counter aesthetic constituted primarily in opposition to tradition of all kinds, to individuality, to universalism, and even, it could be said, to art itself as a mode of representation. Let me expand briefly on each of these three reasons—functionality, resistance to acknowledging representation, and being unmoored from the history of art and design—to explore why the fascist aesthetic is so incoherent and yet so effective.

First and foremost, the visual manifestations of fascism vary *because* they were functional. Fascist visuality was instrumental, manipulative, and "propagandistically" conceived. Under the watchful eyes of movement activists and regime censors, its primary purpose was to promote unity, suppress individuality, defend hierarchy, model discipline, and still dissent. If we understand the aesthetics of fascism not as an ontological category with a particular style, medium, and subject matter, but instead as a dynamic *function* dedicated to producing heightened and uncontested allegiance, it makes sense that fascist aesthetics would be flexible, varied, and changeable. It had to respond to the immediate needs of the movement or regime. In Italy, for instance, during the long years under Mussolini, the film industry, which had initially celebrated the glories of the new state with hard-hitting political messages, gradually accommodated light entertainment and even domestic comedies.[32] In Germany, in preparation for the 1933 election, as Lutz Koepnick shows, Hitler's official photographer Heinrich Hoffmann (1885–1957) altered his presentation of Hitler from the wildly gesticulating leader of the famous 1927 series to the empathetic, morally upright man presented in the 1932 *Hitler wie ihn keiner kennt* (The Hitler nobody knows). In the Japanese empire, as Paul Barclay demonstrates, memorial towers to the "loyal dead" from the turn of the century were made to look like ones built in the 1930s, despite their different styles, through "etchings, magazine illustrations, tourist brochures, and postcard renderings that made them look 'all of a piece' as the Japanese state sought to impress loyalty upon its subjects." Fascist aesthetics slipped from grandeur to sentimentality, from monumentality to kitsch, from the classical to the futuristic, calibrated for immediate circumstances. Instead of visualizing a fascist essence, the essays herein visualize fascism's operations within the body politic.

But the variability, shallowness, and opportunism of fascist aesthetics arise not from its propagandistic function alone. Fascism also resisted one of the core concepts of artistic and political practice: representation. I discuss this further in chapter 7, but let me make the case briefly here. The act of representation in philosophical terms rests on the understanding that a gap, however small, exists between the entity anterior to cultural and political formations and that entity's appearance within them. Political theory proposes rule-governed representative government as a means to give people a mediated voice in decision-making. Fascism, on the other hand, insists that the tedious political operation of representing and negotiating interests can be discarded since national unity leaves no gap between the people and their nation. In a similar manner, fascism mistrusts concern for artistic representation. This is one reason why fascist governments were leery of modernist aesthetic theories and experimentation, discrediting them as decadent precisely because they were self-reflective. Artistic fascination with the relationship between artifice and reality spawned heady debates over how art might represent reality. For instance, cubists experimented gleefully with various ways of suggesting light, speed, and point of view. Their defiance of old conventions heightened the viewers' perception of the canvas as an aesthetic interpretation of the world. Surrealists investigated how landscapes of the psyche could be made visible. Modernists, such as photography critic Ina Nobuo in Japan, insisted that even the camera, far from producing an exact copy of the world, transformed it through framing, exposure, and printing techniques. In other words, attention to the constraints and possibilities of representation made clear that art was not an automatic act of mimesis.

Fascism resists acknowledging that representation lies at the heart of politics and art because representation is an act of mindful artifice always open to reexamination. There is nothing natural about it. As such, it raises the specter of competing forms and interests that might not dissolve in the lukewarm bath of ethnic unity and national greatness. To acknowledge representation is to admit the necessity of reflecting on means and ends. In this regard, it is intriguing, as Lutz Koepnick tells us, that "no photograph ever shows Hitler looking at photographs"—an act at once too self-reflexive and too indexical.[33] Fascism, in short, committed itself ideologically to overcoming all forms of alienation; it promised not a *better* form of representation but unity and natural wholeness without the need for mindful mediation. Its antirepresentational drive was part of its claim to authenticity.

The third reason why fascism never achieved a positive aesthetic was this: it was unmoored from a genealogy of aesthetic production. Defying all that came before and yet rejecting conscious aesthetic experimentation, fascism was reduced to stealthy borrowing from many periods in order to clothe its menace in visually palatable forms. Fascist images referenced many ancient worlds—from classical Greece in the opening moments of Leni Riefenstahl's 1935 *Triumph of the Will* to Jōmon-era (10,000–300 BCE) artifacts shared between Korea and Japan.[34] Etruscans, Romans, and Vikings adorned the mausoleum that avowed Dutch fascist Johan Bastiaan van Heutsz Jr. erected for his father, who had been governor-general of the Dutch East Indies. The fascistic faction of the Chinese Nationalist Party combined the Zhou dynasty (1046–256 BCE) military emblems of archer and chariot with modernist lettering to convey their appreciation of Confucianism as the basis for class-harmonious nationalism without any of Confucianism's "feudal remnants."[35] With this sort of artistic and ideological mishmash, fascism attempted to forge a past that would anchor its claim to a glorious future while simultaneously obliterating history as a resource for understanding difference and change.

But the borrowings were not only from ancient repertories. Bourgeois ideas of art, such as pictorialism (a photographic idiom mimicking painting), and avant-garde elements usually associated with Soviet realism and constructivism were also wielded in fascism's favor.[36] In envisioning the present and the future, fascism's counter aesthetic emerged in a number of ways. The desire to annihilate individuality (despite lauding heroes) turned people into "ideal national types" such as "the youth" depicted on the cover of the December 1941 issue of *Nová Mládež* in Slovakia and in subsequent issues of that journal, as Bertrand Metton explains in this volume. Another ideal type was "the nurse," which was found on the cover of Japan's July 1938 *Shashin shūhō*.[37] Foreign elements, places, and people figured only within the hierarchies dominated by the home nation and not as equal yet distinctive elements of a common humanity. Finally, a deep-seated misogyny sentimentalized women's traditional roles and depicted motherhood in the service of the state, although femininity retained culturally specific aspects, as shown in historian Andrea Germer's comparison of visual propaganda in *Nippon fujin* (The Japanese woman) and NS *Frauen-Warte* (NS women's outlook), the major Nazi women's magazine.[38] In short, fascist artists, designers, architects, stone carvers, and photographers sought to build a visual bulwark against "history's disquiet" without having a visual history to draw upon.[39] The result was a grab bag of incoherent styles.

The end of the war did not clarify the relation between artistic styles and political ideologies. At the end of this volume, we turn the question of visualizing fascism on its head and ask how antifascism was visualized and what became of it when hostilities ceased. As the essays by Nadya Bair on photographer Robert Capa and Claire Zimmerman on American architect Albert Kahn demonstrate, wartime work that was resolutely antifascist could lose its political charge by being reframed. Bair argues that Robert Capa's intensely left-wing political photography in Spain during the 1930s was reinterpreted as apolitical humanism by the 1950s and as "concerned photography" in the 1960s—a legacy that lingers today. This transformation produces a paradox. On the one hand, Capa is crucial to our understanding of the Spanish fight against fascism, and on the other, because his work has been depoliticized (in part by his own self-promotional activities), Capa's legacy obscures our understanding of fascism. The result with Capa's work, as with the famous *Family of Man* exhibition curated by Edward Steichen at MOMA and traveling the world from 1955 to 1963, is that what had been explicitly political art, at least at its inception, was reduced to an anodyne humanism that rejected politics as part of the human condition.

An even more dramatic fate befell the legacy of Albert Kahn (1869–1942), who had inspired modernist architects in Europe and worked for America's war effort until his death. After the war, architectural historian Henry Russell Hitchcock transformed Kahn's industrial buildings. Originally conceived as enlightened, welcoming places of work, Kahn's modern egalitarian spaces were recoded by Hitchcock as "retrograde, obsolete, and developmentally stunted" bureaucratic monuments akin to the Nazis' public buildings.[40] This transposition of Kahn's architecture from the cutting edge of democratic hope to emblems of dark, despotic power was achieved, Zimmerman argues, through the power of photography. During the postwar period, the camera remediated these buildings, placing them in a completely different visual history. Kahn's buildings, like Capa's photographs, no longer served as examples of politicized, antifascist art. Not only were the visual repertoires of left and right remarkably fungible during the war, but politically committed art could be stripped of its politics quite quickly and inserted into alternative narratives, as Bair and Zimmerman show.

Conclusion

Pankaj Mishra's recent *Age of Anger* attempts to give fascism—and contemporary discontent—a deep history. "A particular *climate* of ideas, a structure of feeling, and cognitive disposition" centered on ressentiment can, he claims, be traced back to Jean-Jacques Rousseau and the eighteenth-century critique of the Enlightenment.[41] Anger due to the unmet promise of individual and collective empowerment emerged, suggests Mishra, over 250 years ago. According to Mishra's narrative, this anger links malcontents, from the alienated Genevan author of *The Social Contract* to Gabriele D'Annunzio (the Italian ultranationalist) and ultimately to 9/11 terrorists and beyond. What Mishra misses by casting his net so widely is the extraordinary novelty of mass right-wing radicalism in the early twentieth century.[42] The particular form of anger that in this volume we call "fascism" arose not two and a half centuries ago but rather only after World War I, when the partial failures of liberal democracy and capitalism became globally apparent. The equality of political and economic opportunity promised to men had not entirely materialized, yet some women were beginning to enjoy marginally improved conditions. Wealth was being created through capitalism, but was distributed unequally. This toxic combination of political, economic, and male humiliation became politically potent when opportunistic leaders cultivated grievances to fuel their rise to power and deliberately added national humiliation and fear to the mix. Instead of a modernity founded on individualism and egalitarianism, a new modernity of ecstatic unity was promised, one resting on political and gendered hierarchies, autarkic economies, and national pride regained through aggression.

As these essays show, the media tactics this novel form of politics deployed were aesthetically underwhelming because their shallow functionality lacked both historical resonance and theoretical concern for representation. The result was a visual hodgepodge, both traditional and futuristic, local and international. In the first half of the twentieth century, as Clinton observes, "fascist symbolics emerged from place-specific struggles while also applying globally circulating tropes."[43] By contrast, in the nineteenth century, when Courbet painted the townspeople at his great-uncle's funeral, he was speaking both within and against an artistic tradition that had institutional and theoretical backing within European, and particularly French, culture. In Courbet's day, this specific aesthetic history allowed *Burial at Ornans* to be seen as radical, as he wished it to be seen: elevating ordinary people against established elites and replacing Romantic glory with dignified ordinary reality. Seventy years later, Courbet's revolution was reversed. Ordinary people would be radicalized from the Right and glory asserted in defiance of reality. Fascism, constituted primarily through negation, lacked a single visual rhetoric of its own, but that lack of aesthetic distinctiveness was not a detriment to its utility. Indeed, right-wing populism seems to have been all the stronger for its undisciplined eclecticism of style and its grab bag of motifs. Its protean qualities made opposition all the more difficult, and it could travel the world more freely. Indeed, it could be argued that fascism's visual farrago perfectly matched its political requirements.

Notes

1 For a full treatment of Courbet, see T. J. Clark, *Image of the People: Gustave Courbet and the 1848 Revolution* (Berkeley: University of California Press, 1973).

2 Peter Clarke, "The Century of the Hedgehog: The Demise of Political Ideologies in the Twentieth Century," in *The Future of the Past: Big Questions in History*, ed. Peter Martland (London: Pimlico Press, 2002), 116.

3 The richness of this English-language scholarship is indicated by the following far-from-complete list: Annika A. Culver, *Glorify the Empire: Japanese Avant-*

Garde Propaganda in Manchukuo (Vancouver, BC, Canada: UBC, 2013); John W. Dower et al., *The Brittle Decade: Visualizing Japan in the 1930s* (Boston: Boston Museum of Fine Arts, 2012); Mark Driscoll, *Absolute Erotic, Absolute Grotesque: The Living, Dead, and Undead in Japan's Imperialism, 1895–1945* (Durham, NC: Duke University Press, 2010); David C. Earhart, *Certain Victory: Images of World War II in the Japanese Media* (Armonk, NY: M. E. Sharpe, 2008); Andrea Germer, "Visible Cultures, Invisible Politics: Propaganda in the Magazine *Nippon Fujin*, 1942–1945," *Japan Forum*; Andrea Germer, "Visual Propaganda in Wartime East Asia—The Case of Natori Yōnosuke," *The Asia-Pacific Journal* 9:20 (2011), https://apjjf.org/2011/9/20/Andrea-Germer/3530/article.html; Andrea Germer, "Artists and Wartime Agency: Natori Yōnosuke—A Japanese Riefenstahl?," *Contemporary Japan* 24, no. 1 (2012): 21–50; Christopher Goto-Jones, *Political Philosophy in Japan: Nishida, the Kyoto School and Co-Prosperity* (New York: Routledge, 2005); Christopher Goto-Jones, *Re-Politicising the Kyoto School as Philosophy* (New York: Routledge, 2008); Christopher P. Hanscom and Dennis Washburn, eds., *The Affect of Difference: Representations of Race in East Asian Empire* (Honolulu: University of Hawai'i Press, 2016); Harry Harootunian, *Overcome by Modernity: History, Culture, and Community in Interwar Japan* (Princeton, NJ: Princeton University Press, 2000); Daniel Hedinger, "Universal Fascism and Its Global Legacy: Italy's and Japan's Entangled History in the Early 1930s," *Fascism* 2 (2013): 141–60; Daniel Hedinger, "The Spectacle of Global Fascism: The Italian Blackshirt Mission to Japan's Asian Empire," *Modern Asian Studies* 51, no. 6 (2017): 1999–2034; Peter B. High, *The Imperial Screen: Japanese Film Culture in the Fifteen Years' War, 1931–1945* (Madison: University of Wisconsin Press, 2003); Reto Hofmann and Daniel Hedinger, eds., "Axis Empires: Towards a Global History of Fascist Imperialism," special issue, *Journal of Global History* 12, part 2 (July 2017); Reto Hofmann, *The Fascist Effect: Japan and Italy, 1915–1952* (New York: Columbia University Press, 2015); Eri Hotta, *Japan 1941: Countdown to Infamy* (New York: Alfred A. Knopf, 2013); Rikki Kersten, "Japan," in *The Oxford Handbook of Fascism*, ed. R. J. B. Bosworth (Oxford: Oxford University Press, 2009), 526–44; Yuko Kikuchi, ed., *Refracted Modernity: Visual Culture and Identity in Colonial Taiwan* (Honolulu: University of Hawai'i Press, 2007); Masato Kimura and Tosh Minohara, *Tumultuous Decade: Empire Society, and Diplomacy in 1930s Japan* (Toronto: University of Toronto Press, 2013); Barack Kushnar, *The Thought War: Japanese Imperial Propaganda* (Honolulu: University of Hawai'i Press, 2006); Janis Mimura, *Planning for Empire: Reform Bureaucrats and the Japanese Wartime State* (Ithaca, NY: Cornell University Press, 2011); Janice Matsumura, *More Than a Momentary Nightmare* (Ithaca, NY: Cornell University Press, 1998); John D. Person, "Between Patriotism and Terrorism: The Policing of Nationalist Movements in 1930s Japan," *Journal of Japanese Studies* 43, no. 2 (2017): 289–318; Kenneth J. Ruoff, *Imperial Japan at Its Zenith: Wartime Celebration of the Empire's 2,600th Anniversary* (Ithaca, NY: Cornell University Press, 2010); Sven Saaler and Christopher W. A. Szpilman, eds., *Pan-Asianism: A Documentary History*, vols. 1 and 2 (Lanham, MD:

Rowman and Littlefield, 2011); Chris Szpilman, "Fascist and Quasi-Fascist Ideas in Interwar Japan, 1918–1941," in *Japan in the Fascist Era*, ed. E. Bruce Reynolds (London: Palgrave, 2004), 55–62; Alan Tansman, ed., *The Culture of Japanese Fascism* (Durham, NC: Duke University Press, 2009); Alan Tansman, *The Aesthetics of Japanese Fascism* (Berkeley: University of California Press, 2009); Max Ward, "Displaying the World View of Japanese Fascism," *Critical Asian Studies* 47, no. 3 (2015): 414–39; Lori Watt, *When Empire Comes Home: Repatriation and Reintegration in Postwar Japan* (Cambridge, MA: Harvard University Asia Center, 2009); and Louise Young, *Japan's Total Empire: Manchuria and the Culture of Wartime Imperialism* (Berkeley: University of California Press, 1998).

Four contributors to this volume have added to our understanding of Asian fascism: Paul Barclay, *Outcasts of Empire: Japan's Rule on Taiwan's "Savage Border," 1874–1945* (Berkeley: University of California Press, 2017); Maggie Clinton, *Revolutionary Nativism: Fascism and Culture in China, 1925–1937* (Durham, NC: Duke University Press, 2017); Ethan Mark, "Translator's Introduction," in *Grassroots Fascism: The War Experience of the Japanese People*, ed. Yoshimi Yoshiaki, trans. Ethan Mark (New York: Columbia University Press, 2015); and Julia Adeney Thomas, *Reconfiguring Modernity: Concepts of Nature in Japanese Political Ideology* (Berkeley: University of California Press, 2001). This work builds on important earlier contributions such as those by John Dower, Andrew Gordon, J. Victor Koschmann, Gavan MacCormack, Ryūichi Narita, and Yasushi Yamanouchi.

4 For studies of historians' geographical commitments, see Luke Clossey and Nicholas Guyatt, "It's a Small World after All: The Wider World in the Historians' Peripheral Vision," *Perspectives on History* (May 2013), http://www.historians.org/perspectives (accessed August 22, 2014); and Julia Adeney Thomas, "Why Do Only Some Places Have History? Japan, the West, and the Geography of the Past," *Journal of World History* 28, no. 2 (June 2017): 187–218.

5 Not all scholars of interwar Japan call it "fascist." Angus Lockyer, for instance, makes the interesting argument that the elements of a fascist culture within Japan do not add up to it being a fascist state. See Angus Lockyer, "Expo Fascism? Ideology, Representation, Economy," in *The Culture of Japanese Fascism*, ed. Alan Tansman (Durham, NC: Duke University Press, 2009), especially 279. For other examples of those who dispute this characterization, see endnote 3 in chapter 7 of this volume.

6 Tansman, *The Culture of Japanese Fascism*, 8.

7 Mark, "Translator's Introduction," 8.

8 Hedinger, "The Spectacle of Global Fascism."

9 See, for instance, Shelley Baranowski, *Nazi Empire: German Colonialism and Imperialism from Bismarck to Hitler* (Cambridge: Cambridge University Press, 2010); Sebastian Conrad and Sorcha O'Hagan, *German Colonialism: A Short History* (Cambridge: Cambridge University Press, 2011); Volker Langbehn and Mohammad Salama, eds., *German Colonialism: Race, the Holocaust, and Postwar Germany* (New York: Columbia University Press, 2011); Michelle R. Moyd, *Violent*

Intermediaries: African Soldiers, Conquest, and Everyday Colonialism in German East Africa (Columbus: Ohio University Press, 2014); Bradley Naranch and Geoff Eley, eds., *German Colonialism in a Global Age* (Durham, NC: Duke University Press, 2015); and Ruth Ben-Ghiat and Mia Fuller, eds., *Italian Colonialism* (New York: Palgrave Macmillan, 2005).

10 On the Dutch Indies, see Ethan Mark, this volume.

11 Bertrand Metton, this volume.

12 See the chapters by Rizzo, Mark, and Barclay in this volume. Janis Mimura, in *Planning for Empire*, makes the important argument that fascism developed first and foremost in Japan's colonial hinterlands.

13 Hofmann, *The Fascist Effect*, 3.

14 This list could be expanded to include all regions of the world. For antipodean fascism, see, for instance, David S. Bird, *Nazi Dreamtime: Australian Enthusiasts for Hitler's Germany* (London: Anthem Press, 2013). For South Asian fascism, see, for instance, Benjamin Zachariah, "Global Fascisms and the *Volk*: The Framing of Narratives and the Crossing of Lines," *South Asia: Journal of South Asian Studies* 38, no. 4 (2015): 608–12.

15 Painting, literature, fashion, film, and the performing arts provide equally interesting vantages on the question of visualizing fascism. Limitations of space and the excellence of already existing work argued against including them here. As for film, two of our contributors have written in-depth studies: see Ruth Ben-Ghiat, *Italian Fascism's Empire Cinema* (Bloomington: Indiana University Press, 2015); and Lutz Koepnick, *The Dark Mirror: German Cinema between Hitler and Hollywood* (Berkeley: University of California Press, 2002). See also Erica Carter, *Dietrich's Ghosts: The Sublime and the Beautiful in Third Reich Film* (London: British Film Institute, 2004).

16 Ruth Ben-Ghiat, this volume.

17 Hugh Trevor-Roper, "The Phenomenon of Fascism," in *Fascism in Europe*, ed. Stuart Woolf (London: Methuen, 1981), 19.

18 Geoff Eley, *Nazism as Fascism: Violence, Ideology, and the Ground of Consent in Germany 1930–1945* (London: Routledge, 2013), vi.

19 Eley, *Nazism as Fascism*, 200. Italics in the original.

20 See especially David Blackbourn and Geoff Eley, *The Peculiarities of German History: Bourgeois Society and Politics Nineteenth Century History* (Oxford: Oxford University Press, 1984).

21 As with Blackbourn and Eley for Germany, Harry Harootunian has worked since the 1960s to overturn the trope of prewar Japan as "backward." See his oeuvre, from his earlier essay, "Comment on Professor Matsumoto's 'Introduction,'" *Journal of Social and Political Ideas in Japan* 5, nos. 2–3 (1967), 315–30, to *Overcome by Modernity*.

22 Kersten, "Japan"; and Mark, "Translator's Introduction," esp. 2–5. For a review of the discussions about fascism among Japanese scholars, Alan Tansman's "Intro-

duction: The Culture of Japanese Fascism," in Tansman *The Culture of Japanese Fascism*, is excellent.

23 Mark Neocleous, *Fascism* (Buckingham, U.K.: Open University Press, 1997), xi.

24 Geoff Eley, "What Produces Fascism: Pre-Industrial Traditions or a Crisis of the Capitalist State?," in *Marxist Perspectives on the Weimar Republic and the Rise of German Fascism*, ed. Michael Dubkowski and Isidor Wallimann (New York: Monthly Review Press, 1989), 89; emphasis in the original.

25 Eley, "What Produces Fascism," 88.

26 Hofmann, *The Fascist Effect*, 64.

27 Ben-Ghiat, this volume.

28 Neocleous, *Fascism*, xi. Neocleous argues that this ideology centered on "war, nature and nation."

29 Eley, *Nazism as Fascism*, 207–8.

30 For an analysis of the power of rendering a leader invisible, see Lutz Koepnick's illuminating discussion of Hoffman's photographs of Hitler's audience; the leader himself is not in the images. Lutz Koepnick, "Face/Off: Hitler and Weimer Political Photography," in *Visual Culture in Twentieth-Century Germany*, ed. Gail Finney, 214–34 (Bloomington: Indiana University Press, 2006). For the case of Japan, see Masao Maruyama's analysis of the emperor as an empty center: Masao Maruyama, "The Theory and Psychology of Ultra-nationalism," in *Modern Japanese Politics*, ed. and trans. Ivan Morris (Oxford: Oxford University Press, [1963] 1969), 1–24.

31 For an excellent discussion of the aesthetic revolutions of avant-garde movements from Italian futurism, Russian constructivism, surrealism, muralism, the Situationist International, the American neo-avant-garde, and the Neue Slowenishe Kunst movement, see Aleš Erjavec, ed., *Aesthetics Revolutions and Twentieth-Century Avant-Garde Movements* (Durham, NC: Duke University Press, 2015).

32 See Ruth Ben-Ghiat, "Envisioning Modernity: Desire and Discipline in the Italian Fascist Film," *Critical Inquiry* 23, no. 1 (autumn 1996): 109–44. Lutz Koepnick, this volume.

34 E. Taylor Atkins, *Primitive Selves: Koreana in the Japanese Colonial Gaze, 1910–1945* (Berkeley: University of California Press, 2010).

35 Maggie Clinton, this volume.

36 For Japanese use of Russian constructivism and Socialist realism, see Andrea Germer's work on *Front*, Japan's photography magazine for overseas consumption: Germer, "Visual Propaganda in Wartime East Asia."

37 Ken Domon, "Nurse, Red Cross Hospital, Azabu, Tokyo 1938," *Shashin*, July 8, 1938. *Shūhō* is on the cover.

38 Germer, "Visible Cultures, Invisible Politics."

39 See Harry Harootunian's elucidation of this point in *History's Disquiet: Modernity, Cultural Practice, and the Question of Everyday Life* (New York: Columbia University Press, 2000) and in *Overcome by Modernity*. Neocleous not only stresses

the counter-revolutionary impulses, reactionary modernism, and ideology of fascism but also argues that "fascism obliterates history from politics and fills the space with nature." Neocleous, *Fascism*, 11. I have discussed nature in relation to Japanese fascism in *Reconfiguring Modernity* and in comparison with Germany in "The Cage of Nature: Modernity's History in Japan," *History and Theory* 40, no. 1 (February 2001): 16–36.

40   Claire Zimmerman, this volume.

41   Pankaj Mishra, *Age of Anger: A History of the Present* (New York: Farrar, Strauss, and Giroux, 2017), 27.

42   Mishra includes everyone from "Maxim Gorky, the Bolshevik, Muhammad Iqbal, the poet-advocate of 'pure' Islam, Martin Buber, the exponent of the 'New Jew,' and Lu Xun, the campaigner for a 'New Life' in China," along with Brexiters and ISIS. Mishra, *Age of Anger*, 30.

43   Clinton, this volume.

1

SUBJECTS OF A NEW VISUAL ORDER

Fascist Media in 1930s China

MAGGIE CLINTON

In 1933, several issues of the Shanghai monthly periodical *Qiantu* (*The Future*) ran on the cover a vibrantly colored image of an archer atop an ancient chariot.[1] The archer, depicted in red against a blue, gray, and white background, drives his chariot beneath a blazing red sun. He aims his arrow at the masthead characters "*Qiantu*," which are printed in a geometric typeface. Archery and charioteering—two of the six arts scholars had been required to master during the ancient Zhou dynasty (1046–256 BCE)—are represented here in a modernist idiom. The image conjures a lapsed Confucian scholarly ideal conjoining physical and mental agility and suggests the forceful leap required in the present to connect China's militarily formidable past with a bright new future (figure 1.1). Evincing a simultaneous yearning for a bygone age and one yet to come, China's national rebirth appears here as a "thrust towards a *new* type of society," building "rhetorically on the cultural achievements attributed to the former, more 'glorious' or healthy eras" rather than suggesting a desire to return to the dynastic past as such.[2] Such Janus-faced glances toward both past and future were recurrent themes in 1930s periodicals circulated by Chinese Nationalist Party (Guomindang [GMD]) factions known as the "Blue Shirts" and the "CC Clique."[3] Deploying an image such as this through mass

1.1 Cover of *Qiantu* [*The Future*] 1, no. 8 (1933).

media entailed staking a position in local political struggles, demonstrating that the GMD stood at the forefront of history by simultaneously embracing key aspects of modern life and respecting native traditions.

Throughout the 1927–37 Nanjing decade, during which the Nationalist Party, under Chiang Kai-shek, ruled China as a de facto one-party state from the city of Nanjing, the technocratic CC Clique and militaristic Blue Shirts orchestrated state violence known as the White Terror. They waged this terror with the conviction that the national development agenda GMD leader Sun Yat-sen had developed before his death in 1925 constituted the only suitable revolutionary path for China to follow. Their objections to capitalism and liberal democracy, to class struggle and gender equality, were leveled with a sense of themselves as revolutionary vanguards empowered to eradicate people and ideas that blocked China's national rebirth. Blue Shirt and CC Clique activists had trained as soldiers and engineers at schools in China, the U.S., the USSR, and Japan; they had come of age participating in debates about science, democracy, and the status of Confucianism in the modern world; and they had sharpened their political views amid mass mobilizations in the southern Chinese port city of Canton during the early 1920s. In antagonistic dialogue with Chinese Communists—with whom the GMD formed a tenuous, Soviet-backed alliance from 1923 to 1927—these militant young nationalists grew adamant that the true agent of China's revolution was not the proletariat or peasantry, but the class-harmonious nation bound by a native Confucian culture. After orchestrating the 1927 coup led by Chiang Kai-shek and assuming positions of state power, they remained preoccupied with differentiating both their national-revolutionary agenda from what they regarded as Communism's vulgar materialism and their interest in Confucianism from that of conservative "feudal remnants" who clung to preindustrial ways of life. With these opponents, among others, in mind, Blue Shirt and CC Clique theorists distilled Confucianism into a "national spirit" that anchored national belonging across time and space. And with this spirit animating a strong state-led program of industrial development, they believed they could defeat all legacies of imperialism and restore the nation to its rightful position of worldly strength.

This chapter addresses two aspects of the visual culture that Chinese fascists—that is, the men who composed the Nationalist Party factions known as the Blue Shirts and the CC Clique—generated during the Nanjing decade.[4] First, it examines imagery, including cover art, photo collages, and cartoons, that they deployed in their periodicals. Although scholars still typically regard modernist aesthetics to have been the province of China's interwar commercial advertisers and political left wing, they were also embraced by men who railed against the former's Western sycophancy and condemned the latter as criminals alienating China from its cultural roots; indeed, the fascists killed them on these grounds.[5] As elsewhere, the visual repertoires favored by China's interwar left and right were markedly similar. Both used angular typefaces, industrial motifs, and geometric forms to underscore the futuristic thrust of their respective political agendas. Both also resuscitated indigenous iconographies, in particular flat-planed textile and woodblock patterns, in ways that made familiar the social estrangement that their modernizing agendas otherwise spelled.[6] The fact that Chinese fascists claimed this imagery as their own—and attempted to invest it with particularly nationalist meanings—gives us clues to the ways in which fascist symbolics emerged from place-specific struggles while also applying globally circulating tropes.

Second, this chapter addresses the significance of the fact that fascists in China tried and failed to harness and restrict the meanings of this shared visual language. Their ultimately unsuccessful efforts highlight the degree of state power necessary to enforce particular ways of representing and seeing. Jeffrey T. Schnapp observed that in Italy, fascists managed to generate a kind of "aesthetic *overproduction*—a surfeit of fascist signs, images, slogans, books, and buildings—in order to compensate for, fill in, and cover up [fascism's] unstable ideological core."[7] By the time invading Japanese troops forcibly uprooted the Nationalist government in Nanjing in 1937, the large quantity of new visuals produced by Chinese fascists had hardly succeeded in crowding out—let alone overwhelming—other claims to popular attention. They did, nevertheless, try, and it is in their vociferous attempts to do so that we can discern how an effective state monopoly on representational practices is key to rendering a fascist visual culture identifiable as such.

An integral aspect of the fascist political project was that of remolding the masses to be capable of appreciating these new practices—that is, of understanding the kinds of struggle that they were supposed to disclose, spur, and preclude. It was necessary to transform "ways of seeing" and forcibly restrict fields of vision.[8] Reflecting on the entwined relationship between visual imagery and viewing subjects, Stuart Hall and Jessica Evans succinctly observed how "meaning is constituted not in the visual sign itself as a self-sufficient entity, nor exclusively in the sociological positions and identities of the audience, but in the articulation between viewer and viewed, between the power of the image to signify and the viewer's capacity to interpret meaning."[9] In the case of fascist movements and regimes, Hall and Evans's insight suggests the imperative to account for how new visual repertoires were created over time and in a complex, uneven relationship with the forging of new viewing subjects. As China's fascists well understood, images such as the aforementioned archer-charioteer on the cover of *The Future* likely held little resonance beyond coastal cities subject to imperialist influence; they were perhaps more illegible than inspiring to much of China's rural, preindustrial population. Chinese fascists therefore made a concerted effort to endow the Chinese populace with new ways of understanding and experiencing the world via sweeping social movements such as the New Life Movement, launched in 1934 by the Nationalist military as it expunged Chinese Communists from their rural base areas, and by marshalling modern technologies such as film for specific ends. The fascists on whom this chapter focuses embraced technologies of mechanical reproduction and the visual forms that echoed them, seeking to circumscribe their meanings and cement them to a collectivist struggle for national rebirth. That the aspirations of fascists in China far outstripped their ability to realize them—which would have been all but impossible given the limited and fractured sovereignty of the Nationalist state on the eve of World War II—underscores the importance of state power in shaping the politics of a given set of visual practices.

Fascist Media and Machine-Age Aesthetics

After the Nationalists proclaimed their new state in 1928, fascist groups (the CC Clique and what came to called the "Blue Shirts" after 1932) expanded their power within the party's civilian and military ranks. While they organized and staffed the secret services responsible for the White Terror, they also became active in the media, over which they fought to exert total state control. CC Clique and Blue Shirt media endeavors included magazine, book, and newspaper publishing, radio broadcasting, and film production. These groups also opened bookstores in major cities across China. They attacked what they regarded as degenerate and divisive influences, compensating for the state's limited censorship capabilities by terrorizing individuals deemed to be responsible for such influence, and they attempted to saturate the public with their own political writings, cultural theory, and short fiction.[10] Following various initiatives from the late 1920s onward, at the 1935 Fifth Party Congress a state committee formed to coordinate and police cultural production on an all-China scale.[11] This committee marked the culmination of debates that had taken place within party ranks—and in antagonistic dialogue with Communists and other leftists—concerning what constituted a properly nationalistic work of art or literature, and attempted to officially delegate what fell within and outside such bounds. Despite these efforts, however, and even though the Nanjing government had already criminalized the propagation of ideas deemed "detrimental to the People's Revolution," the regime's actual jurisdiction remained limited geographically, and it had little control over the kinds of works disseminated through the colonial concessions.[12] Thus factors beyond the government's control consistently hampered nationalist efforts to police what Chinese citizens were allowed to view.

With a keen sense of the importance of controlling the media, the CC Clique made their first organized forays into publishing in the late 1920s with daily papers and monthly magazines, and by establishing bookstores in major cities.[13] By the time the CC Clique launched their flagship magazine *Cultural Construction* (*Wenhua jianshe*) in October 1934, they had the financial and technological resources to print high-quality photo spreads and specialized typefaces. Likely spurred by CC Clique leader Chen Lifu's interest in the ways in which cinema could help mold senses of national belonging (discussed below), and by the emerging trend in Chinese publishing of synchronizing graphic design with written content, *Cultural Construction* attempted to convey visually the GMD's capacity to simultaneously defend native traditions and modernize all aspects of national life.[14] Each of *Cultural Construction*'s three dozen or so monthly issues was frontloaded with photographs and typefaces that exuded the harmonization of China's enduring Confucian spirit with the nation's material progress. While the magazine's covers showcased traditional handicraft patterns and ancient seal designs, each issue's twenty-odd pages of pictorial front matter placed these designs in the context of a world on the cusp of a second cataclysmic war, during which the Chinese nation would either revive or perish. Photographs of China's dynastic art treasures and engineering marvels ran quickly into photo spreads of new domestic construction projects and global advances in science and technology. Readers were also presented with laudatory pictures of technology that enhanced the government's capacity to wage war, and with pictures of technological applications of the art deco styles then popular in Shanghai's hotels, cabarets, and department stores. Photographs showcasing the "streamlined style" of an art moderne airplane and the U.S. Union Pacific Streamline Express train, for instance, communicated that the CC Clique approved of this popular style as long as it served a strictly delineated nationalistic purpose (figure 1.2). In turn, such aerodynamic forms visually expressed the kind of rationalized efficiency that CC Clique leaders desired to foster within society at large.[15] Tactically, pictorial pages such as these reinforced their overall push for Confucian-based national unity under the direction of a powerful developmentalist state.

To this end, *Cultural Construction*'s visuals underscored the life-or-death necessity of national cohesion under powerful GMD leadership. While articles stressed Confucianism's enduring emphasis on prioritizing collective needs above individual interests and obeying state authority, photo collages reinforced this message in numerous ways. For example, a 1935 news pictorial

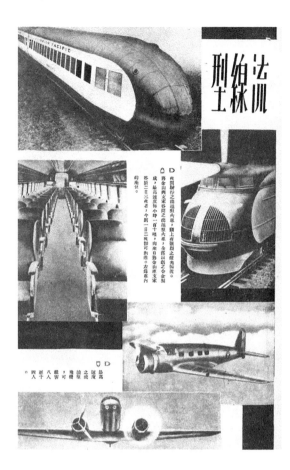

1.2 "Streamlined Forms." Late art deco trains and planes featured in *Wenhua jianshe* [*Cultural Construction*] 1, no. 5 (1935).

on the Italy-Ethiopia conflict—one that was closely followed in the Chinese media for its connections to China's struggle with Japan over Manchuria—depicted mass organization and emboldened state authority in a time of crisis. Here we see a portrait of Benito Mussolini angrily shaking his fist superimposed on a tightly organized mass of Italian troops mobilizing for war (figure 1.3). These images of Mussolini and Italian troops are positioned above paired images of Haile Selassie and Ethiopian soldiers. The collage as a whole simultaneously conveys the discipline that a strong-willed Mussolini had imposed on his people, the upper hand that Italy had quickly established over Ethiopia, and the latter's relative military disorganization. While these collages referenced the imperial-Italian context that Ruth Ben-Ghiat addresses

1.3 "International News" (page 1 of 2). Photos of the Italian invasion of Ethiopia, featured in *Wenhua jianshe* [*Cultural Construction*] 2, no. 1 (1935).

in chapter 4 in this volume, Italian aggression toward Ethiopia had specific meanings in interwar China. China's fascists simultaneously admired Italy for its ability to unite and exert military strength, and they identified with Ethiopia as a victim of imperialist aggression, failed by the League of Nations.[16] The top half of this pictorial signaled a future aspiration and the bottom, a present reality, underscoring the message that militarized national unity was of even greater importance for countries subject to imperialism, such as China and Ethiopia. In key respects, such still images resonated with what Susan Sontag, deriving her notion of fascist aesthetics from Leni Riefenstahl's film oeuvre, called a "characteristic pageantry: the massing of groups of people; the turning of people into things; the multiplication of things and the grouping of people/things around an all-powerful, hypnotic leader figure or force."[17] But in China's case, the nation's failure to organize around a leader posed a threat that referred, in one way or another, to the damage Euro-American imperialism had wrought and to Japan's escalating territorial demands. In this sense, while fascists the world over decried threats to the nation posed by internal and external enemies and clamored for unified struggle against them, how such enemies were construed and depicted inevitably depended on historical context.

The violence that the CC Clique perpetrated in the name of creating a disciplined, synchronized polity was only intermittently visible in magazines such as *Cultural Construction*. Violence, by contrast, was foregrounded and celebrated in periodicals produced by the military-based Blue Shirts. After the Blue Shirts were founded in 1932, they quickly launched various media outlets, actively circulating their plans for a reborn China in books, newspapers, and magazines.[18] Like the CC Clique, Blue Shirts were also enthusiastic about cinema's propagandistic powers, but for tactical reasons their most concerted media interventions took the form of print, which was cheaper to produce and circulated readily to areas without electricity.[19] In terms of titles and design, some of these publications, like the Nanjing-based newspaper *China Daily* (*Zhongguo ribao*), were indistinguishable from the many mainstream papers that the Blue Shirts sought to edge out of circulation. Others such as *Iron and Blood Monthly* (*Tiexue yuekan*), *Sweat and Blood Weekly* (*Hanxue zhoukan*), *Mopping-Up Thrice Monthly* (*Saodang xunkan*), and the *Future* (*Qiantu*) readily announced the militancy of their content. The 1933 archer-charioteer cover of the *Future*, for instance, conveyed the fusion of China's ancient military advances with the industrial era; the *Future*'s more prosaic covers still took care to frame each issue's table of contents with abstract designs and innovative typefaces (figure 1.4). Meanwhile, military magazines such as *Saodang* (*Mopping Up*) and *Jingcheng* (*Absolute Sincerity*) favored more organic forms but likewise celebrated battlefield martyrdom and heroic encounters with death. Illustrations featured in these magazines reinforced Blue Shirts' decisions to live soldiering lives, showcasing what they were fighting for and the forces and behaviors that they struggled against. Communists' base and ulterior motives (banditry, mayhem, and sexual indulgence) were favored themes, underscoring the legitimacy and necessity of violently eliminating them from the national scene. So too were Japanese predations in north China, as seen in a cartoon of Japanese settlers feasting on a Chinese corpse, published in a 1937 issue of *Sweat and Blood Weekly* (figure 1.5).[20]

1.4 Cover of *Qiantu* [*The Future*] 1, no. 3 (1933).

Blue Shirt magazines typically foregrounded concerns common to fascist movements around the world. Many images that circulated in their pages were, at the same time, indistinguishable from those that simultaneously appeared in popular, nonpartisan Chinese lifestyle periodicals such as *Liangyou* (*The Young Companion*), and their design schemes echoed those in magazines concurrently produced by China's embattled left wing.[21] For instance, covers and pictorial spreads similar to those in *Sweat and Blood Weekly* featuring Chinese athletes in exertive poses could be found in all manner of periodicals at the time. By the 1930s, those across the Chinese political spectrum shared pride in tempered, athletic bodies, which often took on connotations of eugenic success. In this regard, the text that framed an image continued to impart necessary information for understanding its message, because the wider sociopolitical context that might have otherwise shaped the meaning of a given image remained highly contested. Images be-

1.5 "Human Calamity in North China." Cartoon by Gao Longsheng, *Hanxue Zhoukan* [*Sweat and Blood Weekly*] 8, no. 20 (1937): 373.

came "fascist" when fascists operationalized them, deploying them for specific ends. As Nadya Bair highlights in chapter 10 with respect to the Left and Right in Spain, in the 1930s China's sharply polarized political factions battled over similar visual repertoires, in particular those that had come to be seen as avant-garde. Moreover, both the Far Left and the Far Right were closely attuned to commercial trends and to the popular purchase, especially in Shanghai, of industrial-inspired styles. In the years leading up to Japan's 1937 invasion of China, neither end of the political spectrum succeeded in affixing a particular repertoire to their own political project or divesting it of other possible meanings.

Yet it was hardly accidental that fascists in China deployed certain kinds of visuals. They did so not simply because some European and Japanese fascists already favored them, but rather because the visuals seemed to convey most effectively the dynamics of revolutionary restoration. While China's fascists touted themselves as defenders of China's ancient Confucian culture, it is important to recognize that they were not particularly interested in revitalizing art forms that had been popular during dynasties past. Media such as ink-and-brush painting were not, they believed, sufficient for inspiring the Chinese populace to participate in a totalizing project of national regeneration. Rather, to borrow a phrase from Maria Gough, they "promoted especially those arts that shared with modern industrial production its primary condition of technological reproducibility, such as graphic design, photomontage, photography, and cinema."[22] These were "consonant with the emphasis on mechanization and acceleration" that animated their visions of a revolutionized China, which were modeled by turns on the efficient capitalist firm and the rationalized military.[23] Such forms more precisely captured the ethos of following orders and streamlining efficiency associated, in their view, with the nation's presently waned Confucian spirit. As Julia Thomas noted in the introduction regarding the malleability of notions of "national spirit," China's fascists could and did insist that their aesthetic preferences readily accorded with China's national spirit, rather than with any particular traditional artistic form or sensibility. The national spirit and the visual forms that effectively expressed it were what the fascists declared them to be.

If the demands of these Nationalist Party factions for revolutionary restoration were forged in increasingly volatile local and global contexts riven by class-based and anti-imperialist activism, the factions' aesthetic preferences were also informed by the military and technical training that they had received in China and overseas. The cc Clique and the Blue Shirts were on different sides of the Nationalist Party's thin civil-bureaucratic and military divide—the cc Clique comprised mostly civilian bureaucrats, whereas the Blue Shirts were soldiers—but the highly militarized nature of the nationalist state and the two groups' shared anti-Communist developmentalism spelled a distinct convergence between their hierarchically rationalized aspirations for a reborn China.[24] They favored industrial-inspired visual styles that seemed to best capture history's acceleration, and they wanted to reorder Chinese society in a streamlined fashion. They rejected the class strife promised by Communism and the atomization encouraged by Western liberalism, and for state-led industrial and infrastructural development grounded in interclass cohesion and coordinated action. At the same time, they worked to ensure that the population at large would understand this political program in intended ways. Colonial treaty ports from which China's fascists emerged, such as Shanghai and Canton and the surrounding regions, were in key respects worlds removed from rural hinterlands. As much as fascists celebrated primordial national unity, they understood that most of the nation still had to be taught the importance of streamlined efficiency, and self-sacrificial pa-triotism. They wanted the art deco–inspired graphics and laudatory photo-graphs of technologies such as airplanes that circulated in their magazines to be read and understood in particular ways. People also had to be taught how not to *mis*read modern imagery as if it permitted individualistic con-sumerism or pointed toward a nationless, Communist-governed future. To this end, fascists worked to police ways of seeing as much as they sought to police what could be seen.

New Frames of Reference

As indicated above, when thinking about the ways in which Chinese fascists tried and failed to craft a new order, it is necessary to stress that, although the Nationalist regime claimed for itself most of the territory that had be-longed to the Qing dynasty, vast stretches of this territory remained beyond its jurisdiction. Regions bordering French Indochina, British India, and the recently consolidated USSR were for all intents and purposes independent. Japan formally claimed the vast northeastern region of Manchuria after 1931, whereas areas of the rural southwest were effectively controlled by the Chi-nese Communist Party. Equally significantly, areas within the Nationalists' territorial jurisdiction, including the wealthiest and most developed sections of Shanghai, remained autonomously governed by various colonial powers, which made it impossible for the Nationalists to effectively control cultural production and distribution. A distinctive visual culture had emerged, in Shanghai in particular, since the late nineteenth century—one that mani-fested the innumerable global currents present there, from Hollywood films to the art deco building designs of the sojourning Hungarian-Slovak ar-chitect László Hudec.[25] The fascist response to this colonial conundrum of compromised sovereignty involved redoubling force against tendencies that seemed to block the nationalists' recuperation of sovereign control and hence China's path to national rebirth. They did not seek to return China to a time before movies and motorcars but instead to revive an ancient spirit of unity, domesticating what they regarded as healthy aspects of modern life and di-vesting these aspects of imperialist associations. This required remolding the Chinese population in a manner that made them perceive and engage with modern life, especially as it had emerged in Shanghai and other coastal cities, in disciplined ways, and likewise controlling what the population was able to perceive in the first place. But the gap remained enormous between the desired future and the existing present situation, and it seemed to widen further as local and global crises mounted over the course of the 1930s.

One index for gauging the amount of time and degree of state strength required to construct and control a coherent visual landscape appears in the 1993 documentary *The Wonderful Horrible Life of Leni Riefenstahl* (released in the U.S./English language in 1998). Partway through the film, Riefenstahl, by then a nonagenarian, is shown erupting in anger at her interviewers for having the gall to speak in the same breath about the results of her first and second attempts to film a Nazi Party congress. The first, *Victory of Faith* (1933), she protested, was not to be considered in the same league as her iconic second film of a party congress, *Triumph of the Will* (1935), whose choreography of enthralled masses, a lionized and individuated Hitler, and surging phalanxes of soldiers soon set a kind of global standard for what fascism in power allegedly looked like. Contextualizing Riefenstahl's misgivings about the first film, the English-language narrator of *Wonderful Horrible Life* explained that "with amateurish shots of Hitler and rather elementary camera angles, *Victory of Faith* is perhaps understandably a film Riefenstahl is very reluctant to talk about. . . . Not only was the camera work shoddy, but the organization of the event itself [i.e., the 1933 Party Congress] seemed uncharacteristically chaotic. The Nazis had not yet learned how to march like Nazis."[26] The narrator thus indicated that neither Riefenstahl's paradigmatic cinematic representation of fascism-in-power nor the Nazis' own self-orchestrations yet measured up to what either would become in time.

This exchange highlights the importance of understanding fascist visual cultures as works in progress. It also reveals the importance of a given regime's capacity to associate certain representational forms and ideas with itself. As Schnapp indicated in the earlier quote regarding how Italian fascists ultimately generated a kind of "aesthetic overproduction," effectively harnessing certain forms or overcompensating for whatever jumble of messages they sent (comfort amid estrangement, stillness amid dynamism, the ancient amid the modern, empowerment in submission, etc.) required a formidable degree of state power. The continued appearance in Nazi Germany, for instance, of entertainment films that were not overtly propagandistic was possible precisely because they circulated within what had quickly become an "entirely hierarchical cultural domain" transformed via "mechanisms of coercion whereby Nazi ideology asserted its dominance across all sociocultural fields, including film" and thus either shored up, or at the very least did not threaten, the integrity of the larger Nazi agenda.[27] Fascists in China never gained enough strength to secure a state monopoly on representational practices, effectively flood the landscape with materials they deemed to be properly nationalistic, or remold how people would perceive and experience these materials. Hollywood films screened in the colonial concessions, such as Clyde Bruckman's *Welcome Danger* (1929), with its racist depiction of San Francisco's Chinatown, were certainly protested and denounced, but the discourse surrounding such imported films could not effectively saturate the population for reasons already noted.[28]

The most determined effort Chinese fascists made to transform popular ways of seeing was known as the New Life Movement (NLM), which the Blue Shirts launched in the inland city of Nanchang in 1934 and the CC Clique and many other groups soon theorized and promoted. The NLM aimed to instill new subjectivities among the Chinese population and to remold it into a regimented national mass. The movement's purpose centered on imbuing the nation with militantly organized productive capacities in preparation for total war and for realizing Sun Yat-sen's program of state-directed industrialization.[29] In a nod to the engineering and military training of the men who devised it, the NLM had a distinctly top-down view (from officers' and managers' perspectives) of the social world. It used militaristic and productivist metaphors interchangeably to speak about the social world: workers were soldiers in an industrial army, soldiers were expected to be as punctual as workers bound by factory whistles, and household management was conceived in terms of battlefield violence. Such directives sought to foster people who understood themselves as dutiful soldiers and workers who voluntarily obeyed commands because doing so was in the best interest of the national collective and would hasten the arrival of a renewed national future. Via campaigns to militarize, aestheticize, and "productivize" everyday life, the minds and bodies of Chinese citizens would become accustomed to the temporal rhythms of mechanized agricultural and industrial work and to being constantly prepared to mobilize against domestic and foreign enemies. One promoter called this process "*zhengqihuayi*": "to organize and remake as one," or "to make uniform" in the sense of calibrating weights and measures.[30] As in a scientifically managed factory or a rationalized military, everything would be rigidly organized and maximally efficient.

New Life Movement events bombarded participants with images of dynamic progress while also interpellating them as Confucian subjects for whom a reborn future would arrive if and only if they performed their proper social roles, and if they accepted the limited range of meanings the state permitted them to perceive in an otherwise anarchic swath of modern signifiers. The movement worked to delimit what could be perceived and by whom. It shined the light of the state into novel spaces such as cabarets and movie theaters—spaces that novelists, left-wing activists, and the masses themselves were concurrently interpreting in very different ways. The NLM sought to penetrate into the deepest recesses of popular consciousness and to render political opposition an unnatural, nonnational, non-Confucian stance. As *The Future* editor Liu Bingli put it, "revolution must enter into people's hearts, consciousness and unconscious life . . . it must permeate the entirety of the life process."[31] Conceiving of daily life as alternately a battlefield and a worksite filled with insubordinates and Luddites, the NLM aimed to keep everyone's eyes trained on a streamlined and efficient future. The rationalized Confucianism that the NLM invoked was central to this process, as it provided a seemingly natural ground for national cohesion amid an unprecedented state effort at social engineering. Jettisoning in the name of efficiency and following orders the socially reciprocal mandates that were intrinsic to dynastic Confucian schemas, NLM Confucianism aimed to foreclose the omnipresent possibility that people would question state directives, look where they should not, and then take unauthorized action. The more intensely people identified with their assigned social roles, the less likely they would be to act unpredictably, and the less likely they would be to notice anything but what they were told to notice. This aimed to "depotentialize areas of struggle" that the GMD itself had ridden to power, turning popular energies against sanctioned enemies when the timing was deemed right.[32]

This intense reconfiguration of ways of being and seeing would, among other things, prime the population to receive state propaganda in intended ways. In this context, NLM champion and CC Clique leader Chen Lifu began to explore film as an ideal medium for fostering new perceptions of the nation while enlightening the masses out of their alleged backwardness. It could simultaneously help alter and saturate perception. In 1933, Chen wrote an extensive treatise on film's capacity to overcome national alienation by presenting Chinese audiences with images of themselves hitherto denied by imperialist domination of China's silver screens.[33] In a self-determining fashion, Chinese-made movies should present the nation's own history and own scenarios. Yet whereas Chinese film studios currently took on this task by churning out martial arts and fairytale films—which Chen noted competed admirably with higher-budget and technically savvy foreign imports—the films that Chen envisioned would present realistic, nationalistic, and spiritually uplifting stories. In a complementary manner, newsreels could be used to publicize state-sponsored development projects, particularly those that required massive organization and labor participation. Successfully harnessing the medium of film would enable fellow nationals to experience their connections to one another in new ways and to collectively envision the nation's past, present, and future precisely as party leaders desired they would.

According to Chen's plan, China's new national cinema would "dramatize the process of nationalist revolution."[34] This meant enabling people to see and hear the nation and its history in new ways—to feel it in their hearts and be moved to sacrifice for it. "Films must not only satisfy people's senses of sight and sound," Chen explained, "they must also move the people's mind-spirit, stimulate their morality and wisdom, spur them to improve their behavior, and increase their knowledge."[35] This entailed showcasing the differences between Eastern and Western civilizations as well as China's national uniqueness.[36] Film should make "China's native old morality"—values of loyalty and filial piety, benevolence, good faith, and peacefulness—"manifest before the eyes of the audience, bolstering their beliefs, stirring their adoration, and providing them with direction."[37] The cooperative thrust of this effort masked distinct social hierarchies within the nation. Newsreels propagating state reconstruction efforts, Chen suggested, could help mitigate "bad habits of laziness, increase the enjoyment [that people] feel in productive labor, and give them bodily experience of the construction of a new country."[38] Although the population writ large needed to acquire a higher level of scientific knowledge, Chen noted that only a select few would actually proceed to become scientists, devoting their minds to "great causes" and other things that "the masses need [not] appreciate."[39] Because the average person did not have time to study science, "we can select materials for them, edit them into scripts, capture them on camera, edit this into movies, present them everywhere and allow the masses amid their enjoyment to absorb into their lives beneficial experiences and knowledge."[40] So powerful was this new technology that it could facilitate the enlightenment of "this mass of ignorant people" who "do not yet even clearly know themselves."[41] Limited electrification was a stumbling block, but film itself could broaden popular appreciation of electricity, as well as of machinery and how it is used.[42] Although cinema could not "rectify the chaos of modern China" of its own accord, Chen made a strong case for the value of cinema in sufficiently altering popular consciousness to make wide-scale industrialization possible and to spur people to perform new kinds of labor without seeking to alter social relations in any unauthorized way. The revolution would gain a recognizable narrative—one that was appreciated as uniquely Chinese.

According to film scholar Laikwan Pang, both the Left and Right in China seized upon film as a political instrument at roughly the same time, in the early 1930s.[43] Cinema had been introduced to China in 1896, just a year after its debut in Paris, and the first Chinese-made film appeared by 1905.[44] Amid the emergence of a domestic studio and star system, it is estimated that "between 1896 and 1937, five thousand or more foreign films, most of which were from Hollywood, were shown in China. Eight American film companies . . . established distribution systems" there.[45] When organized political parties turned their attention to capturing its powers in the early 1930s, the Right had the political upper hand. Chen Lifu's CC Clique spearheaded efforts to rid the film industry of leftists, establishing censorship guidelines by the late 1920s and, by 1935, a state organ whose role was explicitly to control film production.[46] Meanwhile, Blue Shirt vigilantes compensated for the state's limited capacities on this front, ransacking the Left-leaning Yihua Film studio in 1933.[47] Indeed, fascists' recourse to direct violence—such as assassinating media figures who would not abide by state censorship guidelines— signaled not only how far they were willing to go to control the flow of information but how far they were from doing so effectively.

The 1937 occupation of eastern China by Japan, and the ultimatums Japanese occupiers put to Anglo-American imperialists after the Pearl Harbor attack in December 1941, transformed the country's media landscape once again. Throughout the preceding decade of Nationalist rule, the existence of spaces beyond nationalist jurisdiction undermined the party's capacity to create a new national frame of reference. The Nationalist regime certainly had the will to foster and enforce particular ways of seeing, but it lacked the power. Even if the Nationalists had been able to inundate domestic media spheres with favorable magazines and films, they did not garner the corresponding state strength to eliminate unfavorable works from view or to control the discourse surrounding them, as was largely the case in Germany, Japan, and Italy. The Nazis' notorious staging of exhibitions of degenerate versus healthy art in 1937 is a telling demonstration of such power. Much as the Nationalists attempted to do, these exhibitions drew clear lines between art deemed beneficial for the nation and that which was harmful. While the authorial and formal properties were consistent among the artworks included in each respective show, ambiguous selection criteria nevertheless rendered paramount the context in which the exhibitions were staged.[48] They were mounted in an environment that the Nazis had otherwise saturated with reinforcing messages regarding what they approved and disapproved. Moreover, the context was one in which contending counterdiscourses had been effectively silenced and criminalized. However much fascists in China wanted to convince fellow nationals of the degeneracy of Shanghai's jazz clubs and foreign movie theaters, they did not effectively control the discourse around them. They certainly made concerted efforts to do so, however, and readily compensated for state weakness by waging direct violence against alleged national enemies.

Conclusion

Erica Carter summarized how "it is discursive production around the film text that ultimately determines its broader socio-cultural location: its class position, as articulated through debates on high versus mass culture, its relation to audiences, its modes of spectatorship, its relevance to state politics, and/or to revolutionary movements for political change."[49] This observation helps us to see the importance of a given state's ability to regulate the discourse around a set of objects and practices, to shape what each means and could possibly mean. It further helps us understand how a wartime Japanese aesthetic of quietude and perseverance—richly described in this volume by Julia Thomas in her analysis of photographs (chapter 7) and by Paul Barclay in his analysis of imperial monuments to Japan's war dead (chapter 2)—can make sense alongside a dynamically energetic Riefenstahl film or a futurist sculpture as recognizable components of a global fascist visual culture. Formal properties mattered, but they perhaps mattered less than how they were operationalized. In all cases they were put in the service of virulent nationalisms pitted against overlapping sets of enemies, seeking similar reconfigurations of state and society, and with shared conceptions of historical temporality. They also made use of and referenced technologies of mechanical reproduction that imperialism and colonialism had rendered global by the early twentieth century, attempting to restrict what these technologies could mean and do. The key to its coherence, or to compensating for its incoherence, was effective policing.

When formulating plans for a new nationalist culture in China, neither the Blue Shirts nor the CC Clique viewed the revival of dynastic art forms as an end in itself. Reproductions of centuries-old creative works seldom appeared in the pages of their magazines unless they served to highlight future hopes. When they did appear, they were remediated in distinctly modern terms; for instance, photographs of dynastic art and engineering treasures in the pages of *Cultural Construction* suggested the Nationalists' effective suturing of a glorious national past with a radiant new future across the morass of China's chaotic present. Blue Shirt papers such as *The Future* and *Sweat and Blood Weekly* favored abstract graphics, photographs of modern subjects like sports teams, and figurative drawings that were formally distinct from popular cartoon arts of dynasties past. Their literary sections were not filled with Tang dynasty (618–907 CE) poems or Ming dynasty (1368–1644 CE) vernacular fiction; rather, they contained markedly new kinds of stories, plays, and screenplays. By laying claim to modern repertoires, China's fascists self-consciously positioned themselves as anticonservative and as more capable of delivering on promises of modern development than their Communist enemies. By promising to abide by the nation's ancient Confucian spirit, they would modernize China without alienating it from its cultural roots and in the process repossess what imperialists had stolen. Unlike the crassly commercial, degenerate purposes to which popular styles such as art deco were currently put, fascists attempted to delimit their meanings and associate them exclusively with nationalist revolution.

From this perspective, the NLM attempted to make the population capable of perceiving the significance of national regeneration. Bombarding audiences with propaganda, even in the most technologically advanced forms available (film or radio), hardly guaranteed that people would receive its messages in intended ways. The NLM therefore attempted to foster new ways of seeing and to eliminate "the right to look" in unsanctioned directions.[50] The nebulous category "national spirit" served to domesticate technologies with clear imperialist origins, absorbing everything from movies to automobiles into a seamless project of national regeneration and distinguishing China's revolution from projects of national rebirth taking place in Germany, Italy, Japan, and elsewhere at the same time. Still, the GMD's aspiration to control representational practices and modes of reception on an all-China scale had fallen well short of being realized by the time the Japanese Imperial Army invaded eastern China in 1937 and forcibly relocated the GMD government. The state terrorized dissenters in an attempt to compensate for its weakness, but this terror remained insufficient to cogently shape and saturate a visual landscape.

Notes

1 *Qiantu (The Future)* 1, no. 8 (1933), front cover. Parts of this chapter, including the discussion of this particular image, were previously published in Maggie Clinton, *Revolutionary Nativism: Fascism and Culture in China, 1925–1937* (Durham, NC: Duke University Press, 2017).

2 See Clinton, *Revolutionary Nativism*, 5–6; Roger Griffin, *The Nature of Fascism* (London: Routledge, 1993), 47; and Roger Griffin, *Modernism and Fascism: The Sense of a Beginning under Mussolini and Hitler* (London: Palgrave Macmillan, 2007), 2.

3 "CC" is thought to be shorthand for either the last names of the brothers who led the faction (Chen Lifu and Chen Guofu) or for "Central Club."

4 The existence of "cliques" and "factions" within the GMD has long been recognized as a major factor in the regime's overall weakness during the Nanjing decade. Petty power struggles between the CC Clique and the Blue Shirts certainly contributed to this weakness, despite their efforts to get the party, state, and nation to unify behind them. The CC Clique was founded in 1927 and led by brothers Chen Lifu and Chen Guofu. The Blue Shirts, which drew its core members from the first six classes of Canton's Whampoa Military Academy, formed in response to the September 1931 "Mukden Incident." Although the men involved with this secret organization never officially called themselves "Blue Shirts," this is how they became known to Chinese and foreign publics during the 1930s, and how they and their myriad front organizations have been known to subsequent scholars.

5 Leo Ou-fan Lee, *Shanghai Modern: The Flowering of a New Urban Culture in China 1930–1945* (Cambridge, MA: Harvard University Press, 1999); Xiaobing Tang, *Origins of the Chinese Avant-Garde: The Modern Woodcut Movement* (Berkeley: University of California Press, 2007).

6 Scott Minick and Jiao Ping, *Chinese Graphic Design in the Twentieth Century* (London: Thames and Hudson, 2010), 28–41. Compare with covers of the CC Clique magazine *Wenhua jianshe (Cultural Construction)* 1, no. 11 (1935) and 2, no. 1 (1935), among others.

7 Jeffrey T. Schnapp, *Staging Fascism: 18 BL and the Theater of Masses for Masses* (Stanford, CA: Stanford University Press, 1996), 6.

8 John Berger, *Ways of Seeing* (New York: Penguin, 1972).

9 Jessica Evans and Stuart Hall, "What Is Visual Culture," in *Visual Culture: The Reader*, ed. Jessica Evans and Stuart Hall (Thousand Oaks, CA: Sage, 1999), 4.

10 Clinton, *Revolutionary Nativism*, 44.

11 Zhongguo di'er lishi dang'an guan, ed., "Guomindang zhongyang zhixing weiyuanhui wenhua shiye jihua weiyuanhui zuzhitiaolie," *Zhonghua minguoshi dang'an ziliao huibian, diwuji, diyibian, wenhua (yi)* (Nanjing: Fenghuang chubanshe, 1994), 1; Wu Yiping, "Kangzhan shiqi Zhongguo Guomindang de wenyi zhengce jiqi yunzuo" ("The Literature and Art Policy of the Kuomintang, 1937–1945) (PhD diss., National Chengchi University, 2009), 49–57.

12 Legal text quoted from Kuisong Yang, *Guomindang de "lian gong" yu "fangong,"* [*Koumintang: Unity with Communists and Anti-Communism*] (Beijing: Shehui-kexue wenxian chubanshe, 2008), 266. See also Clinton, *Revolutionary Nativism,* 45–51.

13 Zhao Shu, "CC de kuozhang huodong" ["The CC Clique's Expanded Activities"], in *CC Neimu* [*The Inside Story of the CC Clique*], ed. Chai Fu (Beijing: Zhongguo wenshi chubanshe, 1988), 92–95.

14 Lynn Pan, *Shanghai Style: Art and Design between the Wars* (San Francisco: Long River Press, 2008), 97.

15 On the Union Pacific train, see Nicholas P. Maffei, "The Search for an American Design Aesthetic: From Art Deco to Streamlining," in *Art Deco 1930–1939,* ed. Charlotte Benton, Tim Benton, and Ghislaine Wood (Boston: Bullfinch Press, 2003), 361–69. On art deco in China, see Anna Jackson, "Art Deco in East Asia," in Benton, Benton, and Wood, *Art Deco 1930–1939,* 371–81.

16 Maggie Clinton, "Ends of the Universal: Chinese Fascism and the League of Nations on the Eve of World War II," *Modern Asian Studies* 48, no. 6 (2014): 1740–68.

17 Susan Sontag, "Fascinating Fascism," in *Under the Sign of Saturn: Essays* (New York: Farrar, Straus and Giroux, 1980), 73–105. Originally published in *The New York Review of Books*, February 6, 1975, 11, 18.

18 Deng Yuanzhong, *Guomindang hexin zhuzhi zhenxiang: Lixingshe, Fuxingshe, yu suowei "Lanyishe" de yanbian yu chengzhang* [*The Truth about the Guomindang's Core Organizations: The Forceful Action Society, the Renaissance Society, and the So-Called "Blue Shirts"*] (Taipei: Lianjing, 2000), 150; Clinton, *Revolutionary Nativism*, 52–61.

19 Blue Shirts had gained experience with publishing during the May Fourth and United Front periods; leaders such as He Zhonghan were exposed to Soviet propaganda techniques while in the USSR. He Zhonghan xiansheng zhisang weiyuanhui, *He Zhonghan xiansheng shilüe* [*A Biographical Sketch of Mr. He Zhonghan*] (Taibei: He Zhonghan xiansheng zhisang weiyuanhui, 1972), 1.

20 Gao Longsheng, "Human Calamity in North China," *Sweat and Blood Weekly* 8, no. 20 (1937): 373.

21 Paul Pickowicz, Kuiyi Shen, and Yingjin Zhang, eds., *Liangyou: Kaleidoscopic Modernity and the Shanghai Global Metropolis, 1926–1945* (Leiden: Brill, 2013); Tang, *Origins of the Chinese Avant-Garde.*

22 Gough, "Back in the USSR: John Heartfield, Gustav Klucis, and the Medium of Soviet Propaganda," *New German Critique* 107/36, no. 2 (2009): 135.

23 Gough, "Back in the USSR," 135.

24 Clinton, *Revolutionary Nativism*, 30.

25 See Pan, *Shanghai Style*; Michael Knight and Dany Chan, *Shanghai: Art of the City* (San Francisco: Asian Art Museum, 2010); Minick and Ping, *Chinese Graphic Design in the Twentieth Century.*

26 *The Wonderful Horrible Life of Leni Riefenstahl*, dir. Ray Mueller (1993; Berlin: Kino International, 1998, DVD), 0:59–1:02.

27 Erica Carter, *Dietrich's Ghosts: The Sublime and the Beautiful in Third Reich Film* (London: British Film Institute, 2004), 9.

28 Zhiwei Xiao, "Constructing a New National Culture: Film Censorship and Issues of Cantonese Dialect, Superstition, and Sex in the Nanjing Decade," in *Cinema and Urban Culture in Shanghai, 1922–1943*, ed. Yingjin Zhang (Stanford, CA: Stanford University Press, 1999), 188.

29 Deng, *Guomindang hexin zuzhi zhenxiang*, 316.

30 Clinton, *Revolutionary Nativism*, 131–41; Xu Zexiang, "Ruhe jianshe Zhongguo minzu wenhua" ["How to Construct China's National Culture"], *Zhongguo jianshe xiehui huibao* [*Periodical of the Chinese Cultural Construction Association*] 1, no. 4 (1934): 22–24.

31 Liu Bingli, "Xinshenghuo yundong—yige geming fangfa" ["The New Life Movement: A Revolutionary Method"], *Qiantu* [*The Future*] 2, no. 5 (1934): 1.

32 The phrase is from Andrew Hewitt, *Fascist Modernism: Aesthetics, Politics and the Avant-Garde* (Stanford: Stanford University Press, 1993), 134–35, quoted in Mark Antliff, "Fascism, Modernism, and Modernity," *The Art Bulletin* 84, no. 1 (2002): 154.

33 Clinton, *Revolutionary Nativism*, 172–75.

34 Chen Lifu, *Zhongguo dianying shiye* [*The Chinese Film Industry*] (Shanghai: Chenbao she, 1933), 12.

35 Chen, *Zhongguo dianying shiye*, 4.

36 Chen, *Zhongguo dianying shiye*, 7–8.

37 Chen, *Zhongguo dianying shiye*, 9–10.

38 Chen, *Zhongguo dianying shiye*, 18–19.

39 Chen, *Zhongguo dianying shiye*, 23.

40 Chen, *Zhongguo dianying shiye*, 24.

41 Chen, *Zhongguo dianying shiye*, 29.

42 Chen, *Zhongguo dianying shiye*, 32–33.

43 Laikwan Pang, *Building a New China in Cinema: The Chinese Left-Wing Cinema Movement, 1932–1937* (Lanham, MD: Rowman & Littlefield, 2002), 56.

44 Vivian Shen, *The Origins of Left-Wing Cinema in China, 1932–1937* (New York: Routledge, 2005), 12–13.

45 Shen, *The Origins of Left-Wing Cinema in China*, 10.

46 See Xiao, "Constructing a New National Culture"; Clinton, *Revolutionary Nativism*, ch. 5.

47 Pang, *Building a New China in Cinema*, 53.

48 Andrew Calvin, "Delineating a Fascist Aesthetic? Boundary Transgression and the Nazi Degenerate Art Exhibition" (paper presented at the Visualizing Fascism Workshop, University of Michigan, Ann Arbor, MI, June 9–11, 2016).

49 Carter paraphrases Sabine Hake in *Dietrich's Ghosts*, 9.

50 Nicolas Mirzoeff, *The Right to Look: A Counterhistory of Visuality* (Durham, NC: Duke University Press, 2011).

2

FASCISM CARVED IN STONE

Monuments to Loyal Spirits in Wartime Manchukuo

PAUL D. BARCLAY

An Image of the Empire's Last Gasp

According to the Japanese Ministry of Education's last wartime geography textbook, by 1944 the empire had finally integrated the former colonies of Taiwan, Korea, and Karafuto into the *naichi* (home territory) while securing peace and prosperity throughout the rest of Asia. It attributed these accomplishments to Japan's persevering citizenry, sagacious government, and martial prowess.[1] The textbook's intended youth audience may have found such grandiose claims persuasive, but for adult readers at war's end, they must have rung hollow. From their inception in 1903 through the 1930s, the geographies espoused by the Ministry of Education extolled Japan's imperial expansion and waxing global reach by increasing their numbers and types of illustrations of colonized spaces. By 1940, however, they had reversed course.[2] Marking the nadir of the downward spiral of officially sanctioned geography, the last wartime edition of *Secondary Geography* transmitted its confident assessments on flimsy paper, with blurry type and only a handful of shoddily reproduced graphics.[3] Therefore, our imagined adult reader must have wondered how the purportedly world-beating Japanese state, which had until recently projected images of imperial power and success with world-class graphic art, photography, and print media, could have been reduced to publishing such humble and homely textbooks.

As if to justify the deprivation exposed by its material form, *Secondary Geography* explained that the Greater East Asia War (1941–45) was but the latest installment in a defensive struggle against Western expansion, an aggression against Asian peoples that dated back to the 1490s. Japan fought the grueling war against the United States, Britain, and China not only for national survival, but for the sake of Asia—home to 1.2 billion people, over half of humanity. And it was Manchuria that formed the lynchpin of this "Asia" in the Japanese imaginary. *Secondary Geography* regarded Manchuria's 1932 "independence" as a milestone in rolling back Western domination. It also identified Manchuria as the bulwark protecting Korea from the Soviet menace. As a source of raw materials and an arena for emigration, the authors declared that Manchuria was, "in actuality, Japan's continental life-line."[4]

The trope of Manchuria-as-lifeline would have been familiar to our imagined adult reader at war's end, but the image selected to illustrate the Manchuria section of *Secondary Geography* represented yet another departure. Whereas geographies of the more hopeful 1920s and 1930s introduced Japanese youth to Manchuria with pictures of bustling ports, planned cities, and diligent laborers—scenes that would have resonated with metropolitan audiences in any of the world's empire-states—our swansong textbook adorned the "jewel in Japan's imperial crown" with a single etching: a calligraphed masonry tower situated on an empty field silhouetted by darkened clouds. The forlorn structure was simply captioned "Shinkyō's Loyal-Spirit Tower" (figure 2.1).

In contrast to its illustrations of freight trains hauling Taiwanese sugar, tree-felling pioneers reclaiming Hokkaidō, and white-clad Koreans milling about near thatched-roof dwellings, *Secondary Geography*'s "loyal-spirit tower" graphic resisted absorption into the progressive, civilizing-mission discourse typical of Japan's earlier experiments in multilateral imperialism. In this essay, I explain how this dark tower was able to convey, if not distill, a temporally distinct fascist ethos to youth readers in 1940s Japan. My argument here is that fascism in Japan created for itself a deep lineage of sacrifice by erecting towers to the dead, though many of these dead soldiers had lost their lives a quarter of a century before the rise of Japanese fascism. Crucially, there was nothing uniform about the aesthetics of the towers that became known as *chūreitō* (loyal-spirit towers). Instead, what homogenized them in the service of Japan's militarily aggressive state in the 1930s and early '40s were the etchings, magazine illustrations, tourist brochures, and postcard renderings that made them look all of a piece when the Japanese state sought to impress loyalty upon its subjects.

2.1 "Shinkyō's Loyal Spirit Tower." From Monbushō [Ministry of Education], ed., *Secondary School Geography 3 [Chūtō chiri san]* (Tokyo: Chūtō gakkō kyōkasho kabushiki kaisha, 1945), 15. Courtesy of the Hiroshima University Library Digital Textbook Collection Database.

Birth and Transmigration of Loyal-Spirit Towers

By 1945, some 140 "loyal-spirit towers" (chūreitō) had been built in Japan proper, another 10 in Manchuria, 3 in China, and 1 in Singapore.[5] A chūreitō was an ossuary for the cremated remains of those who died during war. These mausoleums were attached to towers of various shapes and sizes and fronted by expansive plazas with Shintō gates. The chūreitō hosted a gamut of rituals, from paying respects to family to exalting the imperial mission en masse on national holidays. Imperial Japan's putative lifeline Manchuria was home to the first and largest of these loyal-spirit towers. The Shinkyō tower achieved particular prominence as the maiden chūreitō (figure 2.1). In addition to receiving tens of thousands of visitors during its brief life span, the Shinkyō tower attained iconic status through graphic reproductions in myriad formats throughout Japan's wartime mediascape.

At thirty-five meters high, Shinkyō's chūreitō towered over Manchukuo's new capital. On November 21, 1934, the behemoth was christened as part of a ceremony to inter the ashes and pray for the repose of General Mutō Nobuyo-shi and over 2,800 "brave soldiers" who died to establish the puppet state. The war to occupy Manchuria started September 18, 1931. The initial invasion was something of an easy task for Japanese armed forces. Indeed, the new state of Manchukuo was announced within months of the first troop deployments, on March 1, 1932. The founding of the state touched off a fresh set of uprisings, however. Japanese forces annexed Rehe to Manchukuo and expanded army zones of occupation south of the Great Wall to buffer the new state, thereby fomenting further Chinese resistance.[6] To house the resultant stream of war dead, the state launched the chūreitō movement in 1934.

Chinese resistance did not end with the 1934 interment of Mutō in Shinkyō, however. Consequently, three more Manchurian towers were built in Harbin (1935–36), Qiqihar (1935–36), and Chengde (1938). Meanwhile, on July 7, 1937, a larger war broke out in the suburbs of Beijing. Now fighting a fully mobi-lized Chinese central government, Japan deployed over 850,000 troops to the continent. At this critical juncture, Japanese army leaders extended the Manchurian chūreitō program to the home islands. While only 140 of 1,500 monuments planned for the home islands were completed between 1939 and 1942, the energetic chūreitō publicity campaigns, subscription drives, and design competitions instilled visions of collective sacrifice, ennobled death in battle, and mobilized the populace for yet more war.[7]

To provide the 1939 chūreitō campaign in Japan with a compelling back-story, publicists repositioned Manchuria's inaugural 1934 Shinkyō chūreitō as a *successor* to a group of five monument complexes built decades earlier to house the remains of those who died in the Russo-Japanese War (1904–5). This chronological sleight of hand elevated a land grab in northeast China, which was initiated by a coterie of disaffected army officers, to the status of a three-decade national crusade for the defense of Asia.

Fascist Imperialism

As fascist-era phenomena, it is fitting that the centrally organized chūreitō movement was launched in Manchuria. Japan did not have a Mussolini or Hitler, so no defining "moment" can attach the emergence of fascism in Ja-pan to a particular event or villain.[8] Broad consensus exists, however, that between 1928 and 1932, a historical conjuncture of global, regional, and do-mestic forces stopped cold Japan's experiment during the Taishō Democ-racy (1912–26).[9] The most infamous plots and assassinations presaging the

1931 invasion of Manchuria were hatched on the Chinese mainland. The so-called Manchurian Incident in turn fueled among the masses a patriotism that abetted a politics of intimidation in Tokyo, spawning a series of national unity cabinets headed by military figures.[10] In other words, Japan's fascist movements did not radiate outward and downward from an apex in Tokyo, but rather gathered steam across a wide geographic expanse. As the chūreitō movement in Manchukuo crested in 1936 with the completion of the Harbin and Qiqihar towers, for example, over 1,400 renegade soldiers launched a bloody coup attempt in Tokyo (see Thomas, chapter 7, in this volume) to usher in a decade of unchecked government-by-decree, political repression, and military adventurism.

Whether the movements to eradicate the sprouts of Japanese liberalism were sufficiently based on the masses to satisfy Eurocentric definitions of fascism, Japan's hard right turn exhibited several of fascism's defining elements.[11] Specifically, the Japanese case featured an antileftist political takeover by right-wing nationalists in the context of liberal capitalism's crisis of representation in the late 1920s and early 1930s. Fascists, as Geoffrey Eley reminds us, implement political agendas with cudgels, guns, and threats rather than through argument, persuasion, and electioneering.[12] It would be difficult to come up with a better characterization of the violent political environment that ruled Tokyo from the early 1930s through the end of the war.

As Louise Young has convincingly argued, the species of fascism that overtook Japan in the 1930s is impossible to disentangle from Japan's imperial projects, especially those on the continent. Rather than separating "wartime abroad" and "oppression at home" as analytically distinct phenomena, Young foregrounds the interplay between events and figures in Manchuria and the home islands. In formulating the concept "fascist imperialism" she identifies "the embrace of Asianism as the loadstar for regional autarky and the New Order in Asia, the mobilization for total war and glorification of the military, and the creation of an empire-wide anti-communist police state, as well as the fetishization of state power and magical thinking about state omnipotence" as its main pillars.[13]

Janis Mimura's study of "techno-fascism" in the 1930s also makes a case for the continental origins of Japanese fascism, with an emphasis on its modernist inflection. Charting the careers of Manchuria-based Japanese technocrats from the 1920s through the postwar era, Mimura demonstrates that employment opportunities and social spaces provided by the South Manchurian Railway Company, the Kwantung Provincial Authority, and the imperial army attracted a variety of misfits, climbers, and frustrated young officers. These techno-fascists were united by an aversion to capitalism, individualism, and liberal politics. For them, war abroad was the key to Japan's spiritual, political, and economic renewal at home. Manchuria was remote enough from the entrenched institutions, ideologies, and networks in Tokyo to serve as a fascist sandbox. After Shinkyō was established as the new capital of Manchukuo in 1934, Mimura argues, the techno-fascist bloc exploited the puppet state's protean administrative structure to make Manchukuo into a proving ground for their version of a "high-performance, 'advanced national defense state.'" In the late 1930s, techno-fascism was exported from Manchukuo to the home islands when Japan's best and brightest took up posts in Tokyo.[14]

Echoing Mimura's work, architectural historians also emphasize Manchuria as a futuristic seedbed, rather than derivative afterthought, for fascist movements. Shinkyō in particular—its city plan, its transportation grid, and its buildings—exhibited an avant-garde "high modernist" sensibility. Japanese architects reinforced a hodge-podge of pan-Asianist ideologies such as "harmony among the five races" or the "kingly way" by capping Shinkyō's colossal public and military structures with neo-Oriental parapets and roofs. In 1933, in conjunction with Japan's departure from the League of Nations, Shinkyō's imperial architects abandoned the practice of building Western-style public buildings in colonial capitals in order to demonstrate Japan's modernity. In a new capital bankrolled with unprecedented state funding for architectural experimentation, a conscious effort to integrate Japanese, Chinese, Mongol, and Manchu motifs into modernist ferroconcrete structures signaled the end of Japan's multilateral imperialism.[15] This pan-Asianist aesthetic is evident in the Shinkyō (figures 2.1 and 2.5), Liaoyang, and Chengde chūreitō.

Nine Foundation Stones for the Advance of Japan's Empire

In 1939, the Baiyushan tower in Port Arthur (Lüshun) displaced the Shinkyō tower as grand progenitor of the chūreitō, at least in the propaganda used to launch the home-island movement. Builders broke ground on the sixty-five-meter-tall lighthouse-shaped monument in 1907 and completed it in November 1909. By the 1920s it drew 100,000 visitors annually to commemorate Japan's great victory over Russia in 1905 (figure 2.2).

Within walking distance of the Baiyushan tower was a mausoleum (*nōkotsushi*), one of five ossuaries built to inter the remains of over seventy

2.2 Baiyushan, or "Lüshun's Manifesting Loyalty Tower," Lüshun, China, 2016. Photograph by Ning Jing. Courtesy of the photographer.

thousand Japanese soldiers scattered across Liaodong's southern peninsula. Completed in 1907, the Lüshun mausoleum was opened to the Japanese public as a site of mourning. The majority of its enshrined souls perished in the devastating (and failed) frontal assaults on Lüshun under the direction of Nogi Maresuke. Nogi's debacle produced some sixty thousand casualties, fifteen thousand of which were fatal.[16] Between 1905 and 1910, four additional mausoleums were built to enshrine Russo-Japanese War dead in Liaoyang, Andong (Dandong), Dalian, and Mukden (Shenyang). The Mukden mausoleum was moved and upgraded in 1925 to better protect remains from flood damage. In its remodeled iteration, which combined a ferroconcrete tower, an ossuary, Shintō gates, and a plaza on a single site, the Mukden complex prefigured the four giant Manchukuo chūreitō of the 1930s.

The numerous Russo-Japanese War monuments that dotted Japan's imperial landscape from 1904 onward had evolved from earlier lithic expressions of war remembrance known as *chūkonhi* (loyal-spirit markers), *hyōchūtō* (manifesting loyalty towers), and *shōkonsha* (summoning spirits shrines). Modern state-sponsored war death ceremonies trace their origins to rites carried out in the Chōshū domain in the 1850s. These underwent several permutations in modern Japan, beginning with rites connected to the Boshin War (1868–69). In the main, Japanese erected monuments for family bereavement, to celebrate battlefield achievements, and to tame the spirits of unsettled ghosts. During the Sino-Japanese War (1894–95), public, state-sponsored funerals were still optional, though they had become mandatory by the Russo-Japanese War (1904–5). However, the memorial landscape after the Russo-Japanese War remained heterogeneous and even contested. Between the conclusion of the Russo-Japanese War in 1905 and the construction of the Manchurian chūreitō in the 1930s, related movements in education, veterans' activism, and state Shintō intervened to broadly and deeply naturalize, even in rural Japan, the concepts of dying for nation and emperor, the notion of fallen soldiers as "military gods," and the acceptance of the state's right to preeminence in memorializing death.[17]

As the culmination of these trends, the Manchurian chūreitō built after 1934 were products of central planning for the purpose of war mobilization. They combined the normally separate functions of commemorating battles, mortuary services, and venerating the nation within single, publicly accessible installations. In addition, these chūreitō, unlike Russo-Japanese War monuments, were built during an ongoing conflict with the expectation that newly dead soldiers would be interred. Nonetheless, despite the radical discontinuities introduced by the chūreitō, the appearance of seamless continuity with the older forms was important to the fascist-era argument for open-ended war fought for increasingly abstract (and unattainable) goals.

The stock phrase "Mongolian-Manchurian life-line" dominated Japanese popular discourse in the 1930s, after Matsuoka Yōsuke (1880–1946), a parliamentarian, diplomat, and South Manchurian Railway executive, adopted it at a January session of the Fifty-Ninth Congress of 1931. This sobriquet implied not only that control over Manchuria was necessary for Japan's preservation, but also that Japan's war to secure it began in 1904. Matsuoka's dictum was an important ideological watershed with world-shaking implications. The notion that the Russo-Japanese War (1904–5) had been fought to defend Manchuria was a minority position at the time of the war itself. In fact, many of Japan's top politicians were willing to barter to Russia a sphere of influence in Manchuria in return for privileged access to Korea in the early 1900s.[18] Nevertheless, student tours to Manchukuo in the late 1930s and early 1940s disseminated Matsuoka's version of Japanese history. The tours, which included stops in Lüshun, Shinkyō, and Harbin, were organized around the fiction that the northern chūreitō near the post-1931 battlefields were historical descendants of the war ruins from 1904 and 1905.[19] Accordingly, after 1938, propaganda adopted a number of graphic devices to link sacrifices on the "plains of Manchuria" in 1905 to the war in China in the 1930s.

The most richly elaborated example, a 1939 series of newspaper articles titled "Immortality on the Manchurian Plain: Nine Foundation Stones for the Advance of Our Empire," sutured the two wars together by means of a fact-filled chart. Its x-axis (place) listed nine putatively commensurate chūreitō in order of completion. The y-axis (time) divided the purported thirty-five-year war into five temporal categories: the Russo-Japanese War (1904–5), the Zhengjiatun Incident (1916), the Siberian Expedition (1918–19), the Kuanchengzi Incident (1919), and finally, "everything since the Manchurian Incident" (1931–39). According to the table's structuring logic, the cost thus paid in Japanese blood spilled on the plains of Manchuria, for the greater good of Asia, had equaled 92,763 souls by May 31, 1939.

It must be emphasized that roughly 83,000 of the 92,783 deaths recorded in this table were connected to the Russo-Japanese War (1904–5). The remainder, about 10,000 (with minor exceptions), occurred after 1932. The lion's share of fatalities, therefore, were distantly related, if at all, to Japan's ongoing war in Northeast China ca. 1939. Moreover, the incidents that bridged the chasm between the September 1905 Portsmouth Treaty that ended the Russo-Japanese War and the September 1931 Mukden Incident that set the stage for the Second Sino-Japanese War in 1937 were local dustups or historical dead-ends. The Zhengjiatun (1916) and Kuanchengzi (1919) Incidents contributed a paltry 32 Japanese fatalities combined, whereas the concurrent Siberian Expedition furnished 118 dead to the grand total. The false equivalencies concealed by this creative accounting in effect elevated minor Taishō-era scrapes to the level of modern Japan's two largest wars, thereby extending the origins of the 1930s China quagmire back to the early twentieth century.

The fascist-era tourism industry reinforced the long-war discourse by featuring the architecturally heterogeneous nine foundation stones in dedicated postcard sets. As playing cards in a deck, the photographed towers—built at different times over a thirty-year span for different purposes and in a variety of architectural styles—were standardized with uniform lithography, lighting, and fonts. While the jackets for these postcard sets label the aforementioned nine foundation stones as chūreitō, the individual Lüshun and Andong postcards within the pack are captioned as *hyōchūtō*.[20] Neither of these two outliers had been remodeled since the 1900s. These souvenir postcard sets thus followed the lead of the home-island chūreitō campaign of 1939 by appending the Andong and Lüshun hyōchūtō to the list of chūreitō towers, probably to better reflect the geography of battlefield tourism around 1940. On the cartographic front, wartime educational materials represented ten chūreitō as outposts in a network of functionally equivalent commemorative structures, suggesting their affinity if not their fungibility.[21]

Loyal-Spirit Towers in Japanese Mass Culture

According to Jonathan M. Reynolds, today's Japanese parliament (the Diet) debuted in 1936 despite decades of debate, planning, and budgeting; it received tepid reviews as an unremarkable example of the internationally circulated "stripped classicist" style of its time. Resembling its counterparts in liberal, communist, and fascist world capitals, the Diet's heavy rectilinear concrete elements sought "to assure . . . citizens of [the state's] strength and durability . . . [with] a building style which was both modern and somehow old" during the global crisis of the 1930s. As Reynolds emphasizes, the 1936 Diet building was also photogenic.[22] This important feature made otherwise immoveable and stolid structures portable and open to redefinition, liberating them from interpretations constrained by environment, function, or even the architect's original intentions.

Indeed, the chūreitō towers had much in common with Japan's parliament building—a mix of old and new and the aura of permanence. Perhaps most signally, however, Manchurian chūreitō were especially fecund sites for producing visual propaganda.[23] Two of them, located in Dalian and Shenyang, shared the Diet building's aversion to curvilinear and decorative elements. In contrast, the Liaoyang, Shinkyō, and Chengde towers accentuated neo-Orientalist motifs, exhibiting continuity with the nativist *teikan yōshiki* (emperor's crown style) movement in 1920s Japan. Two other towers, in Harbin and Qiqihar, took yet another tack: as smooth-faced obelisks, these spires resembled the Wellington Monument in Dublin or the Washington Monument in the United States (figure 2.3).

The fact that such patently nationalistic, death-glorifying, and statist monuments exhibited the full range of contestants from Japan's architectural modernity contests of the early Shōwa period (1926–35) suggests that we should qualify the entrenched view of Shinkyō's neo-Orientalist designs as "fascist architecture." David Buck has usefully highlighted the distinction between commercial and state architecture in Shinkyō after 1933, noting that with the former, grand structures could still include art deco designs and other non-Oriental styles into the mid-1930s.[24] Nonetheless, the Harbin and Qiqihar chūreitō, both completed in late 1936, were forthrightly noncommercial, pan-Asianist in function, and yet clearly Western in form. The synergistic relationship between Manchuria's chūreitō and Japan's fascist turn, in other words, cannot be divined through a visual inspection of the towers' formal properties, but only from their uses in particular times and places.

Drawings, photographs, paintings, and etchings of the Shinkyō chūreitō, in addition to the aforementioned geography textbook, graced notebook covers, tourist maps, coffee-table books, South Manchuria Railway magazine advertisements, and picture postcards.[25] Considering the enormous circulation figures for Japanese dailies and propaganda magazines at the time, photographs and drawings of chūreitō were, from the central government's viewpoint, likely as efficacious as the physical sites themselves.[26]

On the eve of the full-scale land war in China in the summer of 1937, the national daily *Tokyo Asahi Shinbun* printed a photograph of the recently completed thirty-seven-meter-tall chūreitō in Qiqihar. The paper's editors framed the image with a typical description of Manchuria's remoteness, forbidding climate, and crimson sunsets.[27] Invoking the Soviet Union as an existential threat, the article referred to Japanese troops in the northern sector as a "first line of defense." In return for care packages from a Tokyo Elementary School, Japan's stalwart defenders of Qiqihar mailed the children a thank-you card with six hundred photographs of the tomb of fallen heroes in this desolate, frigid land (figure 2.3).[28]

The Cabinet Information Bureau's photographic monthly *Shashin shuhō* also featured chūreitō photographs, whereas its South Manchurian Railway advertisements touted them as main attractions for tourism.[29] A typical one read, "To Manchuria, where the heroic deceased are at rest; in an autumn of full-throttle national mobilization, we pay respects on the ground of our exalted ancestors' spilled blood."[30] In addition, the Shinkyō monument alone spurred at least twenty different picture-postcard designs between 1934 and 1945.[31]

Foot traffic was also central to the propagation of the chūreitō gospel of

2.3 "The War Monument Near Completion," Qiqihar, China. Picture postcard, ca. 1937. Image courtesy of the Harvard-Yenching Library, Harvard University.

collective sacrifice. The Shinkyō chūreitō commanded a prime location, thereby facilitating pilgrimage to the tower from the home islands. The adjoining parade grounds accommodated crowds of up to twenty thousand people.[32] Just after alighting near Shinkyō station, visitors stopped at the tower for an "interesting explanation by a female guide," as one pamphlet put it.[33] A 1940 bus tour ad suggests the flavor of their scripts. It paid homage to the hero of Manchukuo's founding, Kwantung Army Commander Mutō Nobuyoshi. Mutō signed the Japan-Manchukuo accord with Emperor Puyi as Japan's plenipotentiary, commanded operations to annex Rehe in 1933, and died of jaundice while at his post on July 27 of the same year. Mutō's was the first soul to be interred at the Shinkyō monument. His successor Hishikari Takashi, who lent his calligraphy to the tower, is also mentioned, along with the 1,318 who died since the "Manchurian Incident." The ad also reminded tourists of the chūreitō's price tag: 250,000 yen.[34]

A fictionalized set of letters from a school-age Japanese settler to his parents back in Japan captured the Shinkyō monument's intended effects on a more intimate level. Published in 1944, it was marketed as a "tour" of Manchukuo for a youth audience. After visiting Kodama Park (named after a Russo-Japanese War hero), the protagonist approaches the resplendent Shinkyō chūreitō. He comments on its "real Manchurian flavor" and its resemblance to the Qing imperial tombs in Mukden. General Mutō is invoked as the first soldier interred, along with the brave men who fought to secure Manchuria in the battles of Nanling and Kuanchengzi. Seeing its height and its shiny gold roof tiles, and sensing the weight of history, the student feels small. As he takes in the scene, his Manchurian homestay father reminds him that Japanese grave markers can be found in cities, the countryside, and at every small rail station in Manchukuo—reminders of the high price in blood and buried corpses that Japan paid to build such a marvelous country.[35]

Japan's tourist infrastructure, increasingly tilted toward conveying the message of sacrifice, funneled by bus some 38,741 tourists to Shinkyō in 1939 alone. By then, the annual numbers of Japanese visitors to Mukden (Shenyang) and Harbin had reached over a million per year, respectively.[36] The former boasted the most "populous" chūreitō: it housed over 35,000 spirits from the Russo-Japanese War. The latter was Japan's tallest, reaching a height of sixty-seven meters.[37] Manchuria was also a popular destination for school trips in Japan in the late 1930s. In 1938 alone, "213 of these groups, with a total of 14,024 students," took advantage of the 50 percent educational discount to visit Manchukuo. The surviving schedule of the Osaka University of Foreign Languages tour indicates that the stay in Shinkyō, whose route was anchored by the chūreitō and other war monuments, was the longest segment of the itinerary.[38]

"Sunk Costs" and the War without End

The 1931 Manchurian Incident was ostensibly launched in order to protect resident Japanese from the "Chinese bandits" who blew up a section of the South Manchurian Railway. In reality, Kwantung Army officers set the charges themselves. Although Japanese forces were greatly outnumbered in Mukden, they attacked an army that was poorly equipped and under orders to retreat instead of fight back.[39] It was a stretch, therefore, to claim that the gunning down of Zhang Xueliang's troops in the Beidaying barracks was heroic. Nonetheless, the anniversary of the September 18 attack was commemorated in festivals, holidays, and rituals attended by hundreds of thousands of Japanese residents of Manchukuo.[40]

Within two years of the Mukden takeover, Japanese delegates to the League of Nations cemented a link between the rout of Beidaying barracks and seizure of Mukden on September 18, 1931, and the 1904–5 Russo-Japanese War. The delegation's stout defense of Mukden's occupation articulated to an international audience the "sunk cost" argument for open-ended warfare in China:

> Japanese interests in Manchuria differ both in character and degree from those of any other foreign country. Deep in the mind of every Japanese is the memory of their country's great struggle with Russia in 1904–05, fought on the plains of Manchuria, at Mukden and Liaoyang . . . and in the Liaodong Peninsula. To the Japanese, the war with Russia will ever be remembered as a life-and-death struggle fought in self-defense against the menace of Russian encroachments. The fact that a hundred thousand Japanese soldiers died in this war, and that two billion gold yen were expended, has created in Japanese minds a determination that these sacrifices shall not have been made in vain.[41]

It is doubtful, however, that sacrifices made during the Russo-Japanese War were "deep in the minds" of most Japanese in 1933. Famine in the northeast and the recent assassinations of two prime ministers were certainly as pressing for this nation of newshounds—and all the more reason for Kwantung Army authorities to begin constructing the mammoth Shinkyō tower in 1934. The figure of "100,000 dead" in the Russo-Japanese War became a talisman for Japanese pan-Asianists until the end of the war, even though it considerably overshot the known total, even when that number was padded with unrelated deaths from the 1930s.

After all-out war with China commenced in July 1937, Japan lost over twenty thousand soldiers (but killed many more) during the subsequent battle for Shanghai. After committing a massacre of epic proportions in Nanjing in December, the Japanese government presented conditions for cease-fire to the Chinese Nationalists.[42] These conditions included China's formal recognition of Manchukuo as an independent nation (though in reality it was a Japanese puppet state) and a halt to anti-Manchukuo activities. Predictably, Chiang Kai-shek's nationalist government rebuffed these demands. He could not surrender territory that had been under Chinese rule for three centuries. In response, Prime Minister Konoe Fumimarō issued his "non-recognition" declaration of January 16, 1938. The declaration is known in Japanese as "*Kokumin seifu o aite to sezu*," or "the Nationalist Government is no longer [regarded as] an *aite*." To deny a person or party the status of *aite* is to "refuse to deal with, have nothing to do with, ignore, or spurn," which is to say that

Konoe disqualified the ruling Nationalist Party (*Guomindang*) as China's legitimate government. The parties in this land war in the heart of the world's largest nation were thus no longer amenable to negotiated settlement.[43]

The *aite to sezu* posture vis-à-vis China's government in the late 1930s differed from official and popular views of Russia during the earlier war. John Dower's pioneering study of woodblock prints shows that Japanese artists portrayed Russians as people capable of heroism, self-sacrifice, and suffering—in sharp contrast to their dehumanizing portraits of Qing subjects in art of the Sino-Japanese War (1894–95).[44] After the Russo-Japanese War, in June 1908, the Japanese government dedicated a large mausoleum in Lüshun to the Russian dead. Historian Aaron Cohen described the scene: "Officials from both countries celebrated together in an atmosphere of mutual respect and admiration. General Gerngros led a 'hurrah' from Russian troops in honor of the Japanese emperor and his 'excellent' army, while General Nogi and Japanese soldiers cried 'banzai.'"[45] Moreover, the meeting place where General Stöessler surrendered Port Arthur to General Nogi, called the "Suishiei Negotiation Site," was commemorated with a stone monument, preserved historical site, and group portrait, and it was a regular stop on the 1920s "Lüshun Battle Ruins" sightseeing course.[46] Russia was a threat, an adversary, and even a bullying power, but its military commanders and negotiators were regarded, diplomatically and mnemonically, as aite, which means "companion, partner, opponent, rival, or interlocutor."

More importantly, the parity-denying implications of the aite to sezu formulation vis-à-vis China found an analogue in the Japanese citizenry's subordination to the throne. The *chū* in *chūreitō*, after all, stands for "loyalty" to Japan's royal house and imperial bloodline.[47] As Julia Thomas underscores in chapter 7, by the late 1930s, any theory of Japan's political identity that deviated from an organicist conception of the Japanese body politic, centered on the emperor, was considered heterodox and punishable. Thus, as crowds of mourners, tourists, celebrants, and functionaries assembled before the chūreitō, they were diminished before the apotheosized defenders of the family-state—both named heroes such as Mutō and Hishikari, and thousands of anonymous fallen soldiers. If such postures felt forced, wrongheaded, or even silly, doubters could do little to push back effectively.

To put it in another way, if chūreitō discourse had merely abetted the dehumanization of the enemy or the packaging of belligerence as holy war, it could hardly be labeled "fascist." These tactics were operative before the fascist era and have been staples of war mobilization in capitalist, communist, and anticolonial states up to the time of this writing. The chūreitō and the tropes it concretized were agents of fascist culture because they advanced a discourse that blunted, if not eradicated, opportunities to launch coordinated opposition. In imperial fascist regimes—be they Italian, German, or Japanese—civil society collapses along numerous fronts. Their subjects thus destroy, while being robbed of, the means to stop genocidal and self-destructive wars from within.

The Taishō era (1912–26) began with a constitutional crisis sparked by public opposition to the military's overreach into civilian politics. The period also witnessed successful rollbacks of military budgets and a greatly enlarged civil society and electorate. The extent to which the Taishō era can be considered "liberal" has been hotly debated because of repressive measures such as the Peace Preservation Law of 1925.[48] Nonetheless, in 1921, the famous avatar of Taishō Democracy, Yoshino Sakuzō, publicly took exception to "a system . . . which allows anyone to become a god as long as he dies at war, whether he was a libertine or good-for-noting while alive."[49] The following year, a wire service post with a December 9, 1922, Tokyo dateline reported that "the popular swing in Japan against militarism is going to the extreme, so much so that the army is put on the defensive . . . . Objections are being voiced to some of the more prominent and famous monuments commemorating Japanese victories on land and sea. . . . One famous monument in Tokyo, erected to honor a hero of the Russo-Japanese War, is soon to be removed to make way for a street car track."[50] It is hard to imagine such public expressions of skepticism in the mid-1930s, a period characterized by stifling political oppression and a public culture of soldier reverence that shaded into uncritical hero worship.

Technowar, Didacticism, and Censorship

As the bodies from the China quagmire piled up, the literature and paraphernalia promoting chūreitō began to quote precise Japanese casualty totals. Initially, death counts were given in whole numbers. A 1934 newspaper announcing the dedication of the Shinkyō chūreitō provided a figure of "a little over 2800 brave warriors" interred.[51] Kenneth Ruoff quotes a figure of 2,900 for the same monument in his important study of fascist-era imperial culture.[52] These figures do not jibe with subsequent numbers, such as the 1,318 mentioned in the 1940 bus tour ad cited above. More importantly, a new form of numerical reporting was ascending—one that evidenced an obsession with body counts as a measure of the state's investment in securing peace in Asia. Eerily prescient of the U.S. body count mentality in Vietnam in the 1960s, the Japanese thirst for clarity on this front belied the absence of other measurable criteria for progress in the war.[53]

The press release for a mass-interment ceremony on the fifth anniversary of the Mukden Incident, held on September 18, 1936, claimed that 1,569 soldiers who had been killed in action were being memorialized at the Shinkyō, Harbin, Mukden, and Qiqihar chūreitō. General Hishikari Takashi's August 1939 newspaper op-ed, published to whip up support for transplanting the Manchurian chūreitō system to the home islands, put the Shinkyō monument's body count at 1,173 souls. A 1939 newspaper report on the Harbin monument announced that "we have newly welcomed those brave warriors who sacrificed for the foundation of Manchukuo: 522 souls in 1937; 726 souls in 1938; and at the spring ceremony in 1939, we newly welcomed 496 souls from Lieutenants downward for a total 3,523 souls altogether." Each of these examples supplies a precise date to end the accounting period for each statistic.[54] The temporality undergirding these reports was purely actuarial, devoid of reference to strategic or tactical gains during the war. The debt paid in Japanese sweat and blood to secure the peace of Asia was thereby visibly compounded, presumably to accrue interest for the foreseeable future. By one reckoning, the number of deaths since the outbreak of the Manchurian Incident reached 24,141 by its eighth anniversary on September 18, 1939.[55] According to another count dated May 31, 1939, some 9,724 of those killed since September 18, 1931, were enshrined in nine Manchurian chūreitō.[56]

Mukden gave its name to both the largest battle of the Russo-Japanese War (commemorated as a March 10, 1905, event) and the opening battle of the Manchurian Incident on September 18, 1931. It was therefore a pivotal site for the chūreitō movement. Because the revamped tower at Mukden, complete with a large parade ground and Shintō gate, had been in place since 1925, it could host throngs of Japanese residents and soldiers for a ceremony on October 23, 1931, less than two months after the invasion.[57] This date was the national day for summoning the spirits at Yasukuni Shrine and into the 1940s would remain one of two main annual chūreitō ceremonies in Mukden. Millions of imperial subjects across the empire participated, experiencing not only the synchronicity inherent in a militarized ritual calendar, but also near real-time coordination of bodily movements and auditory sensations via radio broadcasts, which had greatly expanded the reach of chūreitō ceremonies in the home islands and in Manchukuo in the 1930s.

The other annual ceremony at the Mukden chūreitō commemorated the last major land battle of the Russo-Japanese War, which became national Army Day (March 10). A series of snapshots from a 1935 celebration, taken by U.S. Vice Consul Gerald Warner, documents a carnivalesque Army Day celebration replete with cross-dressing, exuberant patriotism, and anti-Russian caricatures on floats.[58] Although the proceedings occurred in the shadow of the Mukden chūreitō, celebrants' behavior can easily be imagined as going off script, not unlike the urban crowds described in Andrew Gordon's study of working-class culture during the same period.[59] Accordingly, publishers and censors labored to remind Japanese subjects that chūreitō visits were occasions for revering soldiers and committing spiritually to the ongoing war against China.

One striking example came in the form of a picture postcard (figure 2.4). In counterpoint to the scenes of carnival recorded by Consul Warner's camera, it reminds viewers that the Mukden chūreitō stood in remembrance of Chinese treachery, national peril, and collective sacrifice. The postcard image mashed up a photograph of billowing smoke and destroyed rail track on the South Manchurian Railroad at Liutiaogou with a drawing of the Mukden chūreitō. It explained that the railway explosion that occurred suddenly at Liutiaogou outside of the walled city of Mukden on the evening of 18 September 1931, in due course, became a big event in world history. The Manchurian Incident broke out, and in the blink of an eye, clamors of "let's guard our lifeline to the death" reached high and low and spread like the wind.

Going forth to conquer in faraway lands, our imperial army's might is kindled by righteousness to assure easy victory against overwhelming numbers. On the wide frigid plains of Manchuria's borderlands, and the torrid estuaries of Jiangnan [southern China], precious blood is spilled daily, despite our success in the violent and strenuous fighting. Now, with many difficulties at home and abroad, the establishment of everlasting peace in the Orient rests upon the shoulders of our imperial soldiers.

Using less florid language, the postcard in figure 2.5 instructed visitors in proper comportment at a chūreitō. A pilgrim demonstrates correct and deferential behavior, exhorting, "This is the way you express reverence to the soldiers who fell for the sake of our nation."

A late 1930s ethics textbook for Japanese children in Manchukuo echoed the aforementioned picture postcards, explaining that passersby should face the chūreitō and bow to show thanks for the sacrifices of the soldiers who died so that they could live happily in Manchukuo. The chūreitō section of the primer was preceded by detailed instructions on how to walk, bow, and

2.4 "Mukden Chūreitō and the Manchurian Incident," Liutiaogou, China. Picture postcard, ca. 1931. Image courtesy of the Harvard-Yenching Library, Harvard University.

clap at Shintō shrines.[60]

In addition to the mass ceremonies and didactic texts that strove to keep behavior and ideation regarding the mute chūreitō on track, censorship and photography restrictions helped ensure that alternative imagery, such as that contained in Consul Warner's unpublished 1935 photo album, did not challenge fascist orthodoxy. As the war in China became more severe, restrictive versions of the Fortified Area Laws encroached on the visual culture of battlefield tourism and the depiction of chūreitō. After 1938, all guidebooks, postcards, and albums of scenic spots in the empire's port cities, harbors, ancient battlegrounds, and transportation hubs were stamped with permits from the Fortified Zone Authority Command censors.[61] Late 1930s and early 1940s tourist guides for Manchukuo carefully outline the constraints on photography, commanding tourists to put their cameras away in the fortified zones, which included almost all tourist sites. This combination of censorship and prohibition left officially sanctioned image-producers with a near monopoly on the production of chūreitō iconography.

The model city Shinkyō was built at breakneck speed in 1933 and 1934,

2.5 "War Memorial:
Shinkyō Comics,"
Changchun, China.
Picture postcard, ca.
1940. Courtesy of the
Rupnow Collection.

but as of 1940 the capital remained a half-built construction site because the imperial war effort drained resources.[62] As for the monuments themselves, material shortfalls prompted Army directives for wooden grave markers on the home islands; chūreitō construction in Manchukuo ceased in 1942.[63] Although advocates boasted in 1939 that the chūreitō would stand forever, when the Soviets poured over the border on August 9, 1945, the Kwantung Army had already abandoned the Japanese settlers and their sacred ossuaries to the liberated Chinese and the invading Red Army. In the name of postwar international diplomacy, the government in Tokyo made no effort to trans-ship the charred remains back to the home islands.[64] This ignominious end to the once vaunted "Nine Foundation Stones to Advance the Empire" was well reflected in the 1945 textbook graphic that opens this chapter (figure 2.1). It depicts Shinkyō's darkened tower with no communicants, no crowds. The chūreitō's iconic silhouette may have signaled another round of mass funerals to its war-weary audience, but the black clouds on its horizon suggest that at least a few propagandists in Tokyo had, by the winter of 1944–45, stopped trying to conceal the futility of a strategy that aimed to recover the sunk costs of war by continuing to feed the towers of death.

Notes

1 Published over the course of 1944 and 1945, this three-part text places Korea in Japan's "Western Region," Taiwan in the "Southern Region," and Karafuto in the "Northern Region," while putting the home islands in the "Central Region." Monbusho, ed., *Chūtō chiri ni* (Tokyo: Chūtō gakkō kyōkasho kabushiki kaisha, 1944), 5.

2 My survey of all Ministry of Education geography texts published between 1903 and 1945 indicates a peak in numbers of illustrations for Korea in the late 1920s and a peak for those of Taiwan in the late 1930s. The numbers of illustrations of both colonies precipitously drop in the 1940s.

3 Monbusho, ed., *Chūtō chiri san* (Tokyo: Chūtō gakkō kyōkasho kabushiki kaisha, 1945).

4 Monbusho, *Chūtō chiri san*, 15.

5 Yokoyama Atsuo, "Nihon gun ga chūgoku ni kensetsu shita jūsan-ki no chūreitō," *Nihon kenkyū* 49 (2014): 57–116.

6 Shimada Toshihiko, "Designs on North China, 1933–1937," in *Japan's Road to the Pacific War: The China Quagmire*, ed. James Morley (New York: Columbia University Press, 1983), 11–47; Richard T. Phillips, "'A Picturesque but Hopeless Resistance': Rehe in 1933," *Modern Asian Studies* 42, no. 4 (2008): 733–50.

7 Akiko Takenaka, "Architecture for Mass-Mobilization," in *The Culture of Japanese Fascism*, ed. Alan Tansman (Durham, NC: Duke University Press, 2009), 239.

8 Christopher W. A. Szpilman, "Fascist and Quasi-Fascist Ideas in Interwar Japan, 1918–1941," in *Japan in the Fascist Era*, ed. E. Bruce Reynolds (New York: Palgrave Mcmillan, 2004), 73.

9 "Taishō Democracy" is the term for the period of government by party politicians (instead of the peerage), cosmopolitan urbanity, the emergence of mass readerships, and a culture of political dissent. The Taishō emperor (r. 1912–26) gave his name to this milieu. Richard Sims, *Japanese Political History since the Meiji Renovation 1868–2000* (New York: Palgrave, 2001), 123–28.

10 Tsutsui Kiyotada, ed., *Fifteen Lectures on Showa Japan: Road to the Pacific War in Recent Historiography*, trans. Noda Makito and Paul Narum (Tokyo: Japan Publishing Industry Foundation for Culture, 2016); Louise Young, *Japan's Total Em-*

pire: Manchuria and the Culture of Wartime Imperialism (Berkeley: University of California Press, 1998), 124–29.

11 Szpilman, "Fascist and Quasi-Fascist Ideas," 73–75.

12 Geoff Eley, "What Produces Fascism: Pre-Industrial Traditions or a Crisis of the Capitalist State?," in *From Unification to Nazism: Reinterpreting the German Past*, ed. Geoff Eley (London: Allen and Unwin, 1986), 254–82.

13 Louis Young, "When Fascism Met Empire in Japanese-Occupied Manchuria," *Journal of Global History* 12 (2017): 280.

14 Janis Mimura, *Planning for Empire: Reform Bureaucrats and the Japanese Wartime State* (Ithaca, NY: Cornell University Press, 2011), 41–70; quotation, 70.

15 Nishizawa Yasuhiko, *Nihon shokuminchi kenchikuron* (Nagoya: Nagoya Daigaku shuppankai, 2008), 386–89; Edward Denison and Guangyu Ren, *Ultra-Modernism: Architecture and Modernity in Manchuria* (Hong Kong: Hong Kong University Press, 2016), 53–58, 104–23; David Buck, "Railway City and National Capital: Two Faces of the Modern in Changchun," in *Remaking the Chinese City: Modernity and National Identity, 1900–1950*, ed. Joseph W. Esherick (Honolulu: University of Hawai'i Press, 1999), 82–87; Yukiko Koga, *Inheritance of Loss: China, Japan, and the Political Economy of Redemption after Empire* (Chicago: University of Chicago Press, 2016), 67–71.

16 Edward J. Drea, *Japan's Imperial Army: Its Rise and Fall, 1853–1945* (Lawrence: University of Kansas Press, 2009), 118–19.

17 Naoko Shimazu, *Japanese Society at War: Death, Memory and the Russo-Japanese War* (Cambridge: Cambridge University Press, 2009), 124–42; Akiko Takenaka, *Yasukuni Shrine: History, Memory, and Japan's Unending Postwar* (Honolulu: University of Hawai'i Press, 2015), 23–50, 74–93.

18 Sandra Wilson, "The Russo-Japanese War and Japan: Politics, Nationalism and Historical Memory," in *The Russo-Japanese War in Cultural Perspective, 1904–05*, ed. David Wells and Sandra Wilson (New York: St. Martin's, 1999), 182–88; Haruo Tohmatsu, "From the Manchurian Incident to Japan's Withdrawal from the League of Nations," in Tsutsui, *Fifteen Lectures*, 95–96; Young, *Japan's Total Empire*, 88–92.

19 Yokoyama, "Nihon gun," 71.

20 Two different examples are held in the Harvard Yenching Library Manchuguo Collection (HYLMC).

21 Yokoyama, "Nihon gun," 66–67.

22 Jonathan M. Reynolds, "Imperial Diet Building, National Identity," in *Culture of Japanese Fascism*, ed. Alan Tansman (Durham, NC: Duke University Press, 2009), 271–72.

23 Kishi Toshihiko, *Manshūkoku no bijuaru-media: Postā, ehagaki, kitte* (Tokyo: Yoshikawa kōbunkan, 2010).

24 David Buck, "Railway City," 85; Denison and Ren, *Ultra-Modernism*, 53–58.

25 A large trove of these documents is housed at the Harvard Yenching Library.

These were publicly displayed at the symposium "Harvard Yenching Library New Holdings in Manchukuo History: Needs and Opportunities," May 19, 2016.

26 For national newspaper circulation figures in the 1920s, see Young, *Japan's Total Empire*, 58–61. Japan's largest daily circulated 1.5 million newspapers in 1930, and it was only one among four major national papers. See Gregory J. Kasza, *The State and the Mass Media in Japan 1918–1945* (Berkeley: University of California Press, 1988), 28. Print runs of the Cabinet Planning Board's slickly produced photographic monthly *Shashin shuhō*'s reached a peak of 250,000 issues in 1941. See Taiheiyō sensō kenkyūkai, ed., *"Shashin shuhō" ni miru senjika no Nihon* (Tokyo: Sekai bunkasha, 2011), 51.

27 Young, *Total Empire*, 90–92.

28 "Imon bukurō no o-rei," *Asahi Shinbun* (Tokyo yūkan), May 16, 1937, 4 (in the Kikuzō II Visual Database, accessed June 24, 2016, https://database.asahi.com /index.shtml (hereafter KVD).

29 *Shashin shuhō* issues 8 (April 6, 1938), 61 (April 19, 1939), 101 (January 31, 1940), and 126 (July 24, 1940). Japan Center for Asian Historical Records (JACAR), accessed June 24, 2016, http://www.jacar.go.jp/index.html.

30 Manchurian Railways advertisement in *Shashin Shuhō*, no. 8 (April 6, 1938); JACAR Ref. A06031060300; Kenneth Ruoff, *Imperial Japan at Its Zenith: The Wartime Celebration of the Empire's 2,600th Anniversary* (Ithaca, NY: Cornell University Press, 2010), 130.

31 Based on a survey of the main online digital postcard archives and auction sites, and the collections at the Japan Camera Industry Institute, Tokyo, Japan, and at the Harvard Yenching Library. Thanks to Mari Shirayama, Kuniko McVey, and Ning Jing for providing research assistance. *Zenmanshū meishō shashin chō* (Tokyo: Matsumura Kōbundō, 1937), http://dl.ndl.go.jp/info:ndljp/pid/1207357; *Shinkyō gaikan* (Shinkyō: Taishō shashin kōgeijo, 1939), http://dl.ndl.go.jp/info:ndljp/pid /1112087; Tate Tsunao, *Manshū keikan: shashinchō* (Dalian: Taishō shashin kōgeijo, 1941), http://dl.ndl.go.jp/info:ndljp/pid/1885910. All three volumes are available at the NDL Digital Collection, accessed June 25, 2016.

32 "Shinkyō chūreitō, asu shunkō shiki," *Tokyo Asahi Shinbun*, November 20, 1934, 2 (KVD); "Chūreitō monogatari [part 3: Shinkyō]," *Osaka Mainichi Shinbun*, August 3–14, 1939, in the Kobe University Library Newspaper Clippings Collection, accessed June 24, 2016, http://www.lib.kobe-u.ac.jp/sinbun/e-index.html (hereafter KULNCC); "Manshū kenkoku hasshu nen kyō Shinkyō ni kangeki no dai kōshin zenman wo agete iwau kenkoku setsu," *Osaka Asahi Shinbun*, March 2, 1940 (KULNCC).

33 *Shinkyō yūran noriai jidōsha* (Shinkyō: Shinkyō kōtsū kaisha, 1936), HYLMC.

34 *Kokuto kankō basu annai* (Shinkyō: Shinkyō kōtsū kabushiki kaisha, 1940), HYLMC.

35 Tabata Shūichirō, *Boku no Manshū ryokōki* (Tokyo: Jidō tosho shuppansha, 1944), 98–101.

36 Young, *Japan's Total Empire*, 263.

37 Hishikari Takashi, *Chūreitō monogatari* (Tokyo: Dōwa shūnju, 1942), 77, 111.

38 "A Window into the Early Showa Period: *Shashin Shuhō*: Weekly Photographical Journal, 1938–1945, Railway General Bureau of the South Manchurian Railway Company," JACAR, accessed June 25, 2016, http://www.jacar.go.jp/english /shuhou-english/topics/topics01_02.html.

39 Mark Peattie, "The Dragon's Seed: Origins of the War," in *The Battle for China: Essays on the Military History of the Sino-Japanese War of 1937–1945*, ed. Mark Peattie, Edward Drea, and Hans Van de Ven (Stanford, CA: Stanford University Press, 2011), 66; Haruo, "From the Manchurian Incident," 90; Drea, *Japan's Imperial Army*, 169.

40 Yokoyama, "Nihon gun," 69.

41 Japanese Delegation to the League of Nations, *The Manchurian Question: Japan's Case in the Sino-Japanese Dispute as Presented before the League of Nations* (Geneva, 1933), 31.

42 For details and a general chronology of the China Incident, see Peattie, *The Battle for China*.

43 James B. Crowley, *Japan's Quest for Autonomy: National Security and Foreign Policy, 1930–1938* (Princeton, NJ: Princeton University Press, 1966), 371–77; Rana Mitter, *Forgotten Ally: China's World War II, 1937–1945* (Boston: Houghton Mifflin Harcourt, 2013), 146.

44 John W. Dower, "Throwing Off Asia III," *Visualizing Cultures* (Cambridge: Massachusetts Institute of Technology, 2008), accessed February 11, 2018, http://visualizing cultures.mit.edu.

45 Aaron J. Cohen, "Long Ago and Far Away: War Monuments, Public Relations, and the Memory of the Russo-Japanese War in Russia, 1907–14," *The Russian Review* 69 (July 2010): 394.

46 Harada Keiichi, "Irei no seijigaku," in *Nichi-ro sensō sutadiizu*, ed. Komori Yōichi and Narita Ryūichi (Tokyo: Kinokuniya shoten, 2004), 227.

47 Shimazu, *Japanese Society*, 145.

48 Sims, *Japanese Political History*, 104–15, 123–39.

49 Quoted in Takenaka, *Yasukuni Shrine*, 92.

50 "Popular Opinion in Japan Keen against Militarism," *Democrat and Chronicle* (Rochester, New York), December 10, 1922, 26, archived at Newspapers.com, accessed May 29, 2016, https://www.newspapers.com/image/135625586.

51 "Shinkyō chūreitō asu shunkō shiki," *Tokyo asahi shinbun*, November 20, 1934, 2, (KVD).

52 Ruoff, *Imperial Japan at Its Zenith*, 139.

53 James William Gibson, *The Perfect War: Technowar in Vietnam* (Boston: Atlantic Monthly Press, 1986), 112–17.

54 "Chūreitō monogatari [part 3: Shinkyō] and [part 7: Harbin]," *Osaka Mainichi Shinbun*, August 3–14, 1939, KULNCC.

55 "Sakae no ni-man yonsen hyaku jū-ichi hashira Manshūkoku kenkoku chūreibyō ni hōshi," *Ōsaka Asahi Shinbun*, September 15, 1940, KULNCC.

56 A tenth tower was completed in Hailar in September 1942; little is known about this structure. Yokoyama, "Nihon gun," 69.

57 "Hōten no shōkon matsuri," *Tokyo Asahi Shinbun*, October 27, 1931, 2, KVD.

58 Gerald Warner and Rella Warner, "Gerald & Rella Warner Manchuria Negatives," *East Asia Image Collection* (Easton, PA: Lafayette College, 2012), records 1–50.

59 Andrew Gordon, *Labor and Imperial Democracy in Prewar Japan* (Berkeley: University of California Press, 1991).

60 Eman Hiromichi, *Manshū Jinjō shōgaku sahōsho* (Dalian: Zaiman Nihon kyōikukai kyōkasho henshū-bu, 1940), 14–16.

61 See "Scenic Taiwan Book," *East Asia Image Collections*, record 1, for a detailed account. For one of many clear statements of official policy, see "Script Signed by the Emperor, 1940 Law No. 90 on Amending Fortified Zone Law (Refer to Imperial Ordinance No. 822)," A03022438100, JACAR.

62 Denison and Ren, *Ultra-Modernism*, 131.

63 Yokoyama, "Nihon gun," 63–64.

64 Yokoyama, "Nihon gun," 108–10.

3

NAZISM, EVERYDAYNESS, AND SPECTACLE

The Mass Form in Metropolitan Modernity

GEOFF ELEY

Visualizing Fascism

In Don DeLillo's 1985 novel, *White Noise,* the protagonist, Jack Gladney, a professor in the rural Midwest at the fictitious institution The-College-on-the-Hill, is a specialist in "Hitler studies," a field Gladney is known for pioneering. In tune with the discourse of postmodernism of the time, DeLillo uses this invented academic specialism to convene the novel's interlinked themes, including the addictive properties of mass consumption; the impact of media-driven popular culture on family relations, childhood, and general psychic well-being; the character of contemporary academia and its pretensions; the prevalence of political conspiracy theories; the regenerative potential of violence; and (as a metacommentary informing them all) the relationship between representation and the real. Running through the whole is DeLillo's interest in the Debordian idea of spectacle, itself a primary fascination of the then emergent cross-disciplinary field of cultural studies. The novel strongly suggests, with varying directness across its respective themes, that fascism's emotional power and popular appeal rested in harnessing new technological means and society's ritual and symbolic resources for purposes of cleverly choreographed mass mobilization. The manipulative apotheosis was the Nazi spectacle, which DeLillo encapsulates in the following description early in the book, as Gladney rhapsodizes about his subject: "Close-up jostled shots of thousands of people outside a stadium after a Goebbels speech, people surging, massing, bursting through traffic. Halls hung with swastika banners, with mortuary wreaths and deaths-head insignia. Ranks of thousands of flagbearers arrayed before columns of frozen light, a hundred and thirty aircraft searchlights aimed straight up—a scene that resembled a geometric longing, the formal notation of some powerful mass desire."[1]

DeLillo's description vividly conjures one of our most enduringly familiar images of the Third Reich as it wanted to be seen. By simply googling "NSDAP Nuremberg Rallies," for example, we instantly receive an endlessly cascading array of the kind, showing vast numbers of uniformed, symmetrically ordered, immaculately disciplined, usually male Nazi supporters in anonymously massed ranks, marching or standing, sometimes with arms raised in salute—an embodied perfection of homogeneous collective simultaneity. In the guiding conception behind such massed displays, this perfectly drilled uniformity was intended to symbolize the ideal unity of the nation in a manner that celebrated both the leader's plebiscitary endorsement and his resulting authority. For illustrating the distinctiveness of Nazism's popular appeal, or indeed the self-projection of fascist movements more generally, these are probably the most commonly reached-for visual markers. Yet, when designing posters or choosing illustrations for flyers and magazines, Nazi propagandists themselves were as likely to choose individuated versions of the same messages—the idealized worker, soldier, farmer, mother, family, student, shining young boy or girl—or else an image of violent action, a fist crashing into an opponent's face, for example. A further stock repertoire used caricatures of the Jewish, Bolshevik, Social Democratic, liberal-bourgeois, or other enemy (figure 3.1).[2]

In other words, the Nuremberg Rally and its equivalents were only one element of the purposeful machinery of Nazi visuality. The Third Reich's visual landscape had far more to it than the relatively small number of spectacular massed events per se, however essential these became to the state's ritual calendar. That greater multiplicity of images circulating inside Nazism's visual economy had an impact far beyond what the elaborately stage-managed official spectacle might accomplish. For such rallies, however gigantic, were confined physically in time and space. Their full popular reception presumed varieties of amplification, most obviously via radio, but also via satellite events, print media (newspapers, flyers, posters, pamphlets), photography, and perhaps especially film. Our lasting perception of a Nuremberg Rally has, after

3.1 *The Aryan Family* (undated), print after a painting by Wolfgang Willrich. Copyright BPK Bildagentur/Art Resource, New York.

all, been indelibly shaped by Leni Riefenstahl's artfully contrived documentary of the 1934 rally in *Triumph of the Will* (*Triumph des Willens*, 1935).[3] The event's mobilizing effects, in terms of political excitement, spontaneous identification, and affective solidarity, could be transferred immeasurably more widely than the immediate venue and physical surroundings of the rally itself. Within the overall fields of ideological influence and action managed from Joseph Goebbels's Reich Ministry for Popular Enlightenment and Propaganda, the mounting of these massed spectacles was held mainly distinct, whereas the larger task of producing active popular compliance, in Goebbels's remarkably catholic estimation, knew no boundaries. Schooling, policies for youth, recreation and sports, social work, everything associated with the workplace, family values and domesticity, the behavior of the professions— all were arenas requiring attention, where the Nazi state sought to shape social practices and expectations. The written and spoken word, print and visual media, and cultural policies and the arts were all deployed, consciously and systematically (if not always with the desired consistency), to massage and coerce into existence the active conformity the Nazis wanted.

Here the jump from "movement" to "regime"—a long-standing focus in fascism historiography—had decisive effects. The Nazis had been impressively active in the aforementioned ways before 1933, even without the resources of a state. They were not the first party to perceive the importance of the mass form, whether in stylistics and display or by converting politics into spectacle—even learning some of this from the Left—but they did so on a strikingly new scale by boldly occupying public space. During the electioneering of 1930–32, they blanketed print media and streets with flags, flyers, posters, and badges in a gaudy red-and-black, swastika-adorned visibility; they conveyed youthful energy through every possible type of agitation (marches, parades, rallies, picketing, leafleting), further sensationalized by the SA's (*Sturmabteilung*'s) street-fighting violence; they held 34,000 meetings in the last month of the 1930 election alone. By 1932 such action had already been elaborately choreographed. The April 1932 presidential election saw another bold innovation: Hitler's first publicity-grabbing "Germany Flight" (*Deutschlandflug*), an airborne campaign with no German precedent, used a chartered plane emblazoned with "The Führer over Germany" that crisscrossed the country for twenty major rallies in less than a week, with aggregate audiences a million strong. Hitler repeated this for the various state elections immediately afterward, addressing twenty-five major rallies during April 16–24, ranging from 120,000 in big-city Hamburg to several thousand in small-scale Miesbach in rural Upper Bavaria, where the audience "waited for hours in pouring rain" to hear him speak. For the July national campaign his third "Germany Flight" covered a staggering fifty-three venues. This time the party also used film while distributing fifty thousand gramophone records of Hitler's "Appeal to the Nation."[4]

After power was seized, the technicians of the spectacle worked this into a highly ramified system. With resources of state, the possibilities became incomparably greater: Goebbels acquired a subordinate press, national film studios, and a national broadcasting system; buildings, public arenas, and parade grounds could be commissioned; cities and the entire built environment could be redesigned, technologies harnessed, and centralized budgets deployed. At hand was an elaborate, organized machinery of mobilization, not just for setting people into motion, but for bringing them into deliberately managed public visibility, by materializing them *as* a mass. By these means, the nation and its histories and futures could be reimagined. Citizenship and national belonging could be re-presented through the language of *Volksgemeinschaft*, the community of the people-race-nation. "Germany" itself could be revisualized.

Aesthetics and Politics

In much recent discussion, whether of the Third Reich, Mussolini's Italy, or fascism more generally, this process is conceptualized as the "aestheticization of political life." Most such usage refers to the *Inszenierung* (stage-managing) of political action enabled by the pushing of *Gleichschaltung* (complete coordination and standardization of organized social and political life) into the sphere of cultural expression. Thus, in a drive toward "dedifferentiation and false reconciliation," often mistakenly characterized as "anti-modern," Nazism "infused aesthetics into the political sphere in order to turn life into a unified work of art."[5] The result was a deliberately engineered political stylistics, epitomized not just by the Nuremberg Rallies but still more by the elaborate secondary staging of the surrounding representational excess. Mobilizing the latest technologies of radio, cinematography, light, and sound; organizing masses of people into regimented and ritualized displays of disciplined uniformity; drawing upon rich iconographies, powerfully resonant mythologies, and easily recognizable symbolics, whether well-tried or freshly invented: these were key for the fascist spectacle, all concentrated in the glorified charismatic leader. Politics became subsumed into "a highly ritualized and operatic public sphere" wherein the acclamatory performance of mass political submission followed upon the destruction of the pluralism and procedural negotiations associated with the practice of democracy.[6] The mounting of the fascist spectacle and its intended visual power specifically *replaced* the exchange of views and deliberative civility of the democratic public sphere: "It recast the political as a realm of the beautiful so as to compensate for the costs of modern disenchantment and to suture disenfranchised individuals into an all-encompassing spectacle of homogenization, an aesthetic simulation of community."[7]

The cue has been Walter Benjamin's oft-quoted assertion that "the logical result of fascism is the introduction of aesthetics into political life."[8] An industry of exegesis has gathered around Benjamin's elliptical and aphoristic remarks on this subject, to be found in his brief "Epilogue" to the 1935 essay "The Work of Art in the Age of Its Technical Reproducibility." Thus for Benjamin fascism was a brutally coercive response to the crisis of capitalism and its associated social and political contentiousness, a violent rejoinder to the rise of the masses and the organized challenge of the urban working class, whose impact through the 1918 German Revolution first instigated the Weimar Republic's democratic constitution and then supplied its main defense. Politically, fascism sought to replace the fragmented, mobile, and conflict-ridden openness of society under Weimar with a diametrically contrasting authoritarian frame—one that was centered, rigid, and closed—in a relationship to history conceived as organically finished and whole. In the face of the Left's political challenge, under the late-Weimar political crisis, fascism wanted to immunize the given property relations against reform or attack.[9]

Benjamin's thinking rested on a contrast between "auratic" and "postauratic" art, or the qualities of authenticity and uniqueness of traditional artwork against the commodified circulation of images enabled by the new industrial technologies of photography and cinema and their applications. As a consequence of the latter, the artwork's presumed and reverential authority was lost. "For the first time ever," John Berger argued in one of the earliest commentaries on Benjamin's insight, "images of art have become ephemeral, ubiquitous, insubstantial, available, valueless, free."[10] Against those democratizing effects, Benjamin warned, fascism wanted a restoration. It sought to return the new perceptual openness to the coercively imposed rigidities of order, in an apotheosis of "*l'art pour l'art*." This was in turn linked to an argument about urban modernity (Paris, New York, Berlin) and its transformative consequences for sense perception.[11] Here Benjamin voiced the often seemingly ubiquitous efforts of German intellectuals to capture both the specific qualities of metropolitan life after 1918 and their consequences for how people could live, in their social habits, their psychic composure, and their negotiable forms of everydayness. How, given the challenges of this new environment, should one learn to live in the modern world? Severed from the familiar securities of smaller-scale and readily knowable community living, or "experience" as a lived relationship to dependably known continuities of cultural understanding, people were exposed instead to the constant commotion of city streets: "According to Benjamin, in the age of crowds and automatons, bombarded by images and noises, overwhelmed with chance encounters and glances, we need to put up a 'protective shield' against the excesses of daily shocks hitting us. In this process, our system of perception ends up repressing our senses, deadening them in an 'anaesthetic' procedure, and we lose the capacity for shared meaning." The "alienation of the senses" associ-

3.2 *Berlin: Symphony of a Great City* (*Berlin: Die Sinfonie der Grosstadt*),
by Walter Ruttmann (1927).

ated with this condition of modernity opened a new and distinctive space for politics, one that fascists proved adept at using (figure 3.2).[12]

Parsing this argument requires returning to those pioneering attempts of the 1980s, associated with writers such as Marshall Berman and Stephen Kern, to reopen a discussion of "the modern" and modernity by rehistoriciz-ing their emergence and currency to the late nineteenth and early twentieth centuries.[13] Among German historians, the relevant impact came from the oeuvre of Detlev Peukert.[14] Here the Third Reich's advent and the specificities of Nazi rule were traced back to the unmanageably hypertrophied contradic-tions of modernity under the Weimar Republic, with its "charged atmosphere of social and cultural innovation," its "dreams of reason," and all the result-ing conflicts and insoluble contestation.[15] During the 1920s, Peukert argued, the urgencies of crisis pervaded one sphere after another, including "econom-ics, politics, high culture and mass consumption, science and technology, architecture and city planning, the family and gender relations." Beneath the Republic's protections, he continued, both the cultural experiments of the avant-garde and the progressivist projects of social reform collided with yearnings for a simpler, less hectic, and more reliable way of life, so that under pressures of economic collapse, political polarization, and social disorder, a reach for dictatorship started to become thinkable.[16]

On the one hand, the project-driven imagining of a realizable modernity among the new cohorts of managers and planners, architects and designers, social engineers and social policy experts encouraged an unbounded belief that society could be entirely remade, in effect a utopian wish that social and economic needs would be addressed to a degree that could never actually be satisfied, least of all under the straitened circumstances of fiscal retrenchment after 1929. The *Machbarkeitswahn* ("delirium of makeability") of the heyday of the Republic passed during the freneticism of the succeeding economic and political collapse into anxieties of disorientation. Yet, modernity's inescapable "irritations" hardly ceased to engender the fantasy of wholeness, whose appeal became even radicalized under the societal crisis and its polarizing disorders. Once the Nazis achieved their startling electoral breakthrough in September 1930 and reached a crescendo of success by the summer of 1932, before being hoisted into power in January 1933, that appeal to wholeness acquired material political form, whether by reclaiming "traditions" or through "a 'clean,' frictionless modernity to be achieved by dictatorial political means."[17]

This was what Benjamin meant by "fascist aesthetics as a monolithic space of false reconciliation, as a postauratic renewal of aura."[18] "By demystifying the world," David Crew argues by means of Peukert, "modernity produces a desire for a revitalization of everyday life by a charismatic leader and by irrational appeals to 'new religions'—such as 'race.'"[19] The most successful efforts at concretizing Benjamin's claims—at grounding them in a convincing account of Nazism and its dynamics of organized appeal—have reformulated their conception of modernity in this way, as an argument about Weimar's historical particularities. The Republic emerges as a regime space of social, cultural, and political experiment whose radicalisms provoked an increasingly violent right-wing response. That backlash had many triggers and targets, from the New Woman, the trashiness of popular culture, the flaunting of permissive sexuality, and the visibility of the avant-garde to the political culture of liberal constitutionalism, the legal entrenchment of trade unions, and the militancy of Social Democrats and Communists. The new freedoms simultaneously enabled their opposite: "Modernity constructs new social and cultural forms (i.e. a mass consumerist public) that are politically ambiguous and can be appropriated for dictatorial as well as for 'progressive' political purposes (i.e. the Nazi *Inszenierung der Massen*)."[20]

This is really an argument about the predisposing-cum-generative relation of a certain sociocultural condition of modernity—as modes of intelligibility, as default regimes of perception, as psychic predicament, as sensorium, as both unsettlement and excitation, as both warning and incitement—to the enabling of a certain kind of politics.[21] If we render this more cautiously, then Peukert's approach (and Benjamin's) asks us to consider how the definite political outcome of the 1930s, along with the distinctively fascist publicness of the Third Reich, might be read for their relationship to that cultural condition of modernity. But what, concretely, did the "bringing of aesthetics into politics" mean? My opening gloss on DeLillo's rendering of this into fiction, along with Lutz Koepnick's further explication, seems the most convincing and helpful way of beginning to answer that question. In what follows I point to some of the complications.

Mosse, Gentile, and Political Religion

Here certain affinities exist with arguments about the "sacralization" of politics and "political religion," associated with Emilio Gentile and George Mosse.[22] Invoking the "cult-like" or "quasi-religious" features of the Third Reich's public ceremonial and commemorative calendar, plus some homologies between Nazism's public symbolics, ritual practices, and formal beliefs and those of German Protestantism, this approach reads Nazism's mass appeal for its displaced religiosity, attributing its purchase to a combination of political inventiveness and popular susceptibility during the extremes of the crises of Weimar. Beyond functional and imitative similarities, the most fruitful analyses suggest Nazism's deeper indebtedness to the apocalyptic and salvationist thinking generated by a crisis of German Protestantism in the early twentieth century, which grew ever more radicalized by the traumas of war, military collapse, and revolutionary upheaval. Amid wild talk of spiritual endangerment, darkness, and catastrophe, Nazism offered a redemptive vision of political deliverance based on the leader's charismatic authority, the primacy of the Volksgemeinschaft, and a Manichean drive against the enemies of the race. By addressing the religious disorientation, it sought to capture for itself the primary faculty of faith in the divine—namely, the promise of transcendence—to raise the movement rhetorically *above* politics and sublimate worldly fears in the supreme postulate of the racial struggle for existence and its rewards. This illumines the internal structure of the outlook of ideologues such as Joseph Goebbels, Dietrich Eckert, and Alfred Rosenberg, as well as leading Nazis' salvationist language and the messianic aura imputed to Hitler himself. It makes intelligible the extremes of emotional investment orchestrated around the Nuremberg Rallies and other elements of the Nazi liturgical calendar.[23]

By its excessive formalism and functionalism, however, the sacralization thesis sacrifices historical specificity to an overarching interpretation of the political forms called functionally into life by the conflictual dynamics of modernization as a diffuse macro-historical process. Mosse's version, with its deep cultural indebtedness to his so-called anthropological approach, rests heavily on an argument about the larger political forces of nationalism and mass-political forms seeded by the nineteenth century.[24] Mosse ascribed both the popular breadth of fascism's appeal and the ritualized forms of its plebiscitary orchestration to this ability to draw "for its own purposes" on "the fragments of our Western cultural and ideological past." Fascism succeeded "because it annexed and focused those hopes and longings that informed diverse political and intellectual movements of the previous century."[25]

While originally engaging "the aesthetics of politics" by pioneering the historical treatment of masculinity and sexuality and calling attention to "the myths and symbols that comprised a national liturgy appropriate for national self-representation," Mosse always recurred in this way to a longer-range metatheory of European history, reflecting his own default understanding of Enlightenment-initiated cultural change. Cultural rootedness and "the dialectics of irrationalism" were primary to Mosse's concern.[26] His particular idea of political religion involved essentializing claims about the "hunger for totality" produced by the worries of Europeans in "confronting modernity."[27] But here modernity becomes a far more diffusely transhistorical category than Peukert's (and Benjamin's) more grounded argument about metropolitan life in the 1920s. The particular audacity of the movements of Hitler and Mussolini dissolves into the deeper mists of European time:

> In analyzing a political style which was eventually used for such ugly ends, it may seem odd to begin with a discussion of beauty. But the "aesthetics of politics" was the force which linked myths, symbols, and the feeling of the masses; it was a sense of beauty and form that determined the nature of the new political style. The ugly ends to which this style was eventually used were masked by the appeal of the new politics for a large section of

the population, by its usefulness in capturing their longings and dreams. A concept of beauty objectified the dream world of happiness and order while it enabled men to contact those supposedly immutable forces which stand outside the flow of daily life.[28]

Mosse *does* extend Benjamin in emphasizing the kinds of equivalence that linked Nazism to the mass forms cultural socialism had invented earlier. One unhelpful version of that argument was the conflationist approach of totalitarianism theory, in which Stalinism and fascism are rendered simply the same. Likewise, it is easy enough to invoke the authoritarian dourness of official culture in the post-1945 state-socialist world, with its collectivist uniformities, standardization, limiting morality, and repressive disciplinary power, epitomized in the paramilitary conformities and Boy Scout ethos of the Young Pioneers and other official youth cultures. We might also cite the regimentation of the official Soviet-style sports apparatus, the hostility against sexual dissidence, and the highly gendered languages of Stalinist collectivism. But however uniformly rigidified these state-institutionalized forms were during the 1930s and after, whether in Stalinist, fascist, or wider collectivist versions, the new genres of mass-political action originally had more contingent and dynamically variable meanings in the popular political cultures of the early twentieth century. They came, above all, from the unprecedented post-1918 wave of European democratization and its global anti-colonial equivalents. Rather than the novelties attending the "nationalization of the masses" deeper into the nineteenth century (Mosse's view), they came far more specifically from the popular politics accompanying the revolutionary turbulence of 1917–23. Fascists in Italy, Germany, and more widely certainly invented their own forms of direct-action militancy, collective display, and public intervention based around the heedless paramilitary recourse to physical violence. But they also consciously appropriated the mass forms developed earlier in the socialist tradition (before 1914), while responding with alacrity to the Left's innovations after 1917.

By the 1920s in Germany, in other words, Social Democrats, Communists, and Nazis were all drawing on a rapidly developing common repertoire of organized display and collective mobilization: huge rallies and festivals; public shows of massed discipline and strength; the well-choreographed mass march; the mass gymnastic displays and mass choirs; the development of new rituals; and the orchestration of a distinctive political symbolic. Further, the massed *visual* power defining that repertoire increasingly obscured individual political subjectivities. Sublimating personal desires, effacing individuality, frowning on dissident sexualities, closing down diversity and the latitude for cultural experimentation—all might be found on the Left no less than on the Right. Specifying Left/Right differences is difficult within this emergent arena of spectacular politics. Thus, in Red Vienna, surrounding the opening of the socialist-built Vienna Stadium in July 1931, aggregate crowds of 240,000 watched a mass pageant of the Austrian Socialist Party's history performed by thousands from the movement's cultural organizations, which climaxed with worker-actors toppling "a huge gilt idol-head representing capital from its scaffolding."[29]

Visuality, Monumentalism, and the Faces in the Crowd

Thus, much received wisdom notwithstanding, Nazis did not exactly invent the mass spectacles associated with the Nuremberg Rallies, the 1936 Olympiad, and other efforts at staging the disciplined formations of popular homage and nationalist unanimity. Rather, they drew upon rich antecedents from the 1920s, which the Social Democratic and Communist Parties inventively pioneered. As Nadine Rossol remarks, "in contrast to the common modern perception, the Nazi Party Rallies did not create aesthetically original features. Instead, they combined and expanded, often on an unprecedented scale, well-known elements characteristic of political assemblies."[30] Thus a mode of massed political choreography was already at hand, through which *republican* loyalists had sought to invent "highly disciplined rituals that situated bodies in space—the style of walking, the clothing of the demonstrators, the route of the parade, the sounds of their steps and slogans—to symbolize the unity and strength of the national community."[31] Yet, as the Nazis then showed, these potentials could enhance the public arsenal and performative repertoire of the Republic's enemies too. The mass form in that sense became a site of contestation. As Rossol concludes, "rather than inventing mass spectacles, the Nazi movement brought them under the state's control and eventually abandoned them." Ironically, "the National Socialists showed that the inclusive, spectacular, and representative forms tried out as part of visualizing the republic could be easily extended and reinterpreted to reflect the structure of their own political system."[32]

Fascist monumentalism becomes similarly ambiguous. The Nazi architectural vision seemed distinctive enough in its colossal scale alone. As imagined, this extended from the Nuremberg Party Rally grounds, the Olympic stadium, and the new Reich Chancellery, through a variety of showcase projects across the emblematic cities of the Reich, to the plans for a new Berlin, envisaged to reemerge by 1950 as the new world capital of "Germania." Hamburg was planned to receive the world's tallest skyscraper as the new party regional headquarters, along with the world's largest suspension bridge across the Elbe; Munich's new central rail station would be the world's largest steel-frame structure.[33] One such project actually built was the reconstructed Tempelhof Airport in Berlin, designed by Ernst Sagebiel in the mid-1930s and at the time the largest in the world.[34] Nazi planners happily deployed the modernist techniques and materials of the New Architecture (*Neues Bauen*), if not its aesthetic vision and ethicopolitical *esprit*. Other new technologies were enlisted too. Beginning in August-September 1933, Albert Speer designed a so-called Cathedral of Light to enframe the annual Nuremberg Rally by positioning antiaircraft searchlights at twelve-meter intervals around the Zeppelin Field parade ground and pointing them directly into the night sky. To achieve that effect, he requisitioned the Luftwaffe's entire inventory of 152 powerful searchlights (figure 3.3).[35]

A complex of grand-scale halls, arenas, and assembly grounds covering a site of 4.2 square miles, the Party Rally Grounds in Nuremberg, whose construction was never quite completed, supplied the single clearest example of Nazi monumentalism at work. When filled each year with the regimented ranks of fascist collectivism in motion, the Rally Grounds glorified power as such; they conveyed a morally coercive pedagogy of the state's authority, and they staged the latter as a public drama carefully conceived to overwhelm visual sensibilities.[36] As an organized megaspectacle, the annual Reich Harvest Festival, held on the Bückeberg Hill during 1933–37, was even larger still: likewise overseen by Speer, its initial attendance was half a million, increasing to 1.2 million by 1937. Experientially, these events were certainly multifaceted. But the physical monumentalism of Nazi official architecture—ministries, ceremonial buildings, cultural institutions—was deliberately imposing: the purpose was to intimidate, belittle, overawe. The epitome was the Reich Chancellery, conceived in 1934–35 and built 1938–39, again by Speer: after negotiating a series of entrance rooms (725 feet long) through double doors nearly 17 feet high, visitors approached Hitler's study via the 450-feet-long Gallery of Mirrors, twice as long as its model in the palace at Versailles; the study itself was 4,305 square feet in size (88 feet long, 47.5 feet wide, 40 feet high), intensely laden with promiscuous symbolism (busts, artworks, tapestries, swastikas, eagles, laurel wreaths) and culminating in Hit-

3.3 Photograph of the Nazi rally in the Cathedral of Light, a main aesthetic feature of the Nuremberg Rallies, 1937. Copyright Alamy.

ler's enormous desk (11.5 by 4.6 feet). When aged Czech President Emil Hácha arrived there at 1 a.m. on March 14, 1939, to sign off on the dissolution of his country, "his face red from nervousness and anxiety," he first had to trudge the full length of this building before presenting himself.[37]

Spatially and visually, this was an architecture of belittlement and intimidation, conceding nothing to ambivalence or talking back.[38] But the massed spectacles were more complicated. The photographic record surrounding Nazi celebrations, such as the popular adulation accompanying Hitler's forty-eighth birthday on April 20, 1937, was only deceptively transparent. Did the cheering crowd giving the Hitler salute signify genuine joy, or were the pictures carefully selected and staged? How far was adoration of Hitler's person endorsement for the policies of the regime? Which policies were supported and which not? Who was absent from the crowd and why? These same questions also apply to the organizing ideal of the Volksgemeinschaft, in whose name Nazi spectacles were staged. In the heyday of social history, German historians gave a confident answer: the "people's community" was a mere trick and a "fictitious concept," a projection of bogus unity by the now-triumphal Nazis who declared the divisiveness of Weimar democracy healed. The spectacle was "an aesthetic simulation of community" and a "false reconciliation," in Benjamin's sense.[39] The Volksgemeinschaft may have been "a potent mobilizing agent." But "between the exaggerated pseudo-egalitarian propaganda that claimed to have transcended class, denominational, and political division and the essential continuities in the class structure of Nazi Germany," a huge gap still existed.[40] "What are the reasons," asked Heinrich August Winkler rhetorically, "why we should actually take the Nazi slogans for anything real?"[41]

The big events of the Nazi ritual calendar can be seen too straightforwardly as the vehicles for successful Nazi indoctrination. Readings that rely mainly on the photographic record too trustingly take the visual bombast of Nazi self-representations at face value, accepting that Nazi culture should be identified primarily with "the deindividuating, conformist, and unifying spectacles of Leni Riefenstahl's films and Albert Speer's monumental architecture."[42] In contrast, we need to probe more searchingly into how the impact of the mass spectacle worked its way into the minds and habits of individual Germans, whether they joined in the event directly or partook vicariously from various kinds of distance. For "ideology" existed not only in the explicitly programmatic and dramatically staged doctrinal content of the Nuremberg Rally. It also lurked in the social relations and material practices by which Germans found themselves having to live in an unfamiliar social world after 1933. It was found in the ideas, beliefs, values, prejudices, and assumptions through which people tried to bring meaning and order into their material everyday lives.

The massified character of the spectacle necessarily presumed the multitudinous participation of socially diverse populations, whose personal experience involved complicated mixtures of emotions. Propagation of the Volksgemeinschaft after 1933 was systematic, unceasing, and morally coercive. But joining its appeal could also be emotionally satisfying and socially enjoyable. Ordinary Germans might well embrace "Nazi ideology" as such. But they could also accept Nazi values on a variety of other grounds, including already formed if diffuse patriotic loyalties and anti-Bolshevik fears of disorder, as well as self-interested careerism and material advantage, including the desire for a quiet life and simply to be left alone. Joining the regimented multitude of a Nuremberg Rally or other massed events entailed a very convoluted set of motivations, some consciously chosen, but others externally anticipated or imposed. Joining a rally might well concentrate a person's subjectivity, but only provisionally and doubtless only in part. Being a face in the crowd simultaneously implied a practical self-erasure and a conscious individuality, disappearing into the disciplined and uniform anonymity, on the one hand, yet seeking a satisfying self-validation on the other. What people really did at those official events, and what they took away, would vary immensely, even as their experience undoubtedly converged around certain common ideas and values. Likewise, the event carried very different meanings for the direct participants as against the various categories of immediate spectators, the wider audience listening to the radio, or the broader publics at still further remove, not to speak of the many categories of service laborers who enabled the event even to be staged. Once again, the precise efficacies of the Nazis' intended message will come better into view only if we pursue its effects into the mundane and localized settings of daily life, away from the alarums and excitement of the performance of the spectacle per se.

Here, the evidence of film may help. The earliest historiography of Nazi cinema typically used a dichotomous model of propaganda and society, in which the vast top-down machinery of Goebbels's Ministry acted concertedly *on* German society to manipulate the masses into the desired conformity. In its treatment of filmic content such work was also reductionist, simplifying complex fields of meaning into a straightforward story of indoctrination, even while conceding the entertaining qualities of the vast bulk of the films actually produced after 1933. Thus if the approach presumed one binary opposition between *ideology* and *social context* ("propaganda" and "society"), it also added a second between *ideological indoctrination* and *escapist diversion*, which obscured much of what films actually produced in meanings for the people who saw them. Yet precisely *as* entertainment, films not only filled people's everyday lives by distracting them. They also offered images to frame a private realm of wants—a dreamworld of a better life—in ways that stitched these into the racialized vision of the Volksgemeinschaft. Popular and official culture could thereby be made to work together. Far more than just the regime's propaganda operations, Nazism developed a complex aesthetic program that matched the mass spectacle to the appeals of consumer pleasure and visual enjoyment. In the "seemingly unpolitical spaces of private commodity consumption" and "American-style consumerism," Nazi cinema projected a promise of private satisfactions, "even as it coopted these 'to arrest and rechannel' them."[43] It was in the cinema's space of enjoyment, no less than in the audience for the Nuremberg Rally, that Germans were invited to become good Nazi subjects.

Under its ruthlessly authoritarian and violently coercive terms of rule, the Third Reich's visual environment was both multifaceted and systemically clear. But nor was it lacking in positive appeal. The Nazi Volksgemeinschaft was not just an elaborately constructed propaganda screen or a "beautiful illusion" based on deception and sloganeering that simply disguised repression and preserved social inequalities as before.[44] Workers' rights and collective bargaining may have gone, but the "Beauty of Labor" (*Schönheit der Arbeit*) program of Strength through Joy (*Kraft durch Freude* [KdF]), created under the aegis of the German Labor Front in September 1933, brought real practical benefits into the workplace, from better washrooms and changing facilities, brighter lighting, and more generous space to improved health and safety, longer breaks, and expanded holidays, which increased under the Nazis from an average of only three days to one or two weeks. Even as older forms of collective solidarity and the dignity of labor were being traduced, in other words, new slogans such as "Honor of Labor" (*Ehre der Arbeit*) and "Excellence of German Work" (*Deutsche Qualitätsarbeit*) brought very tangible meanings. KdF also operated sports and fitness facilities; broadened access to previously exclusive pastimes such as sailing, horseback riding, and tennis; discounted tickets for concerts, theaters, and museums; subsidized cinemas and theaters; supported hobbies and adult education; and maximized workers' access to holidays and recreation. As a travel bureau it had some 140,000 employees and by 1939 was running twelve cruise ships, including the custom-built *Wilhelm Gustloff* and *Robert Ley*. By 1938, an aggregated 54 million Germans had passed through its hands; in 1937, inland vacations peaked at 1.4 million tourists, and weekend excursions at 6.8 million; by 1939, 140,000 were taking cruises of the Baltic, North, and Mediterranean Seas.[45]

The balance sheet of popular acceptance of what the Nazis tried to offer was very mixed. In common with other recovering economies in the 1930s, Germany saw certain consumer industries able to flourish: radios, cinema, furniture, and telephones, for example. But the Nazis' grander promise of accessible "people's products" (*Volksprodukte*) never came to much.[46] Although 340,000 orders were placed for the "people's car" (*Volkswagen*), which was announced to great fanfare in 1937, not a single unit ever rolled out of the giant purpose-built plant, which was converted for military production in

September 1939, along with its model city (KdF-City) and planned family housing and amenities.[47] Prora, the intended KdF showcase megaresort, a twenty-thousand-bed vacation complex begun in May 1936 on the Baltic island of Rügen, was likewise never completed but refitted for military use. Yet the potency was in the *promise* of improvement, which was seemingly guaranteed in the Prora resort's imposing comprehensiveness, which combined the *collectivist* sameness of Germans being together with the *personal* pleasures of relaxation. This vision of the future, of a purified Germany beyond the former class divisiveness, in which the body of the nation (*Volkskörper*), healthful and united, purged of its weaknesses and foreign elements, could be strengthened and renewed in the pursuit of wholesome enjoyments was continuously reaffirmed, not just in the visual barrage of the KdF's happy propaganda but in the tangible actualities of the goods it delivered: "Strength through Joy catered to consumer expectations as economic recovery ended unemployment and raised family incomes, recognizing that individual pleasure and autonomy mattered as much as the collective experience of cultural uplift and national renewal. While KdF directed its low-cost, non-commercial consumption toward collective ends, it simultaneously embedded visions of future prosperity in the dream worlds of the present, advertising material 'luxuries' to appeal to its audience."[48]

Any appraisal of Nazi Germany's visual record must take all of these aspects into account. My purpose is not to dispute the attractions of the Volksgemeinschaft or the efficacy of the Third Reich's propaganda, but rather to complicate how their impacts each occurred. Moreover, once we grasp the more insidiously unspoken means by which ideology does its work—in everyday processes, in unexpected places, in personal lives, and in the many semiconscious and unconscious ways through which subjectivities are made—we are unlikely to underplay fascism's popular appeal. Surely the large-scale, extravagant, and systemic propaganda offensives needed to depend on a substrate of ordinary perceptions and quotidian practices. Certainly, through their gargantuan and monolithic scale, Speer's major building projects sought to architecturally stage the fascist will to power. To those already mentioned we may add his design of the German Pavilion for the 1937 World Exposition in Paris.[49] The massed spectacles, no less than this monumental built environment, were meant to dwarf the individual subject while investing the Führer with grandiosity.

Conclusion

These thoughts on Nazi visuality might be taken in various further directions. The "aesthetics of production" and the "beautification of labor," mentioned briefly above, would certainly be one.[50] Representations of *Heimat* (literally, "home") could be another, involving the complex reciprocities joining local and regional rootedness to national identifications in a time of aggressively pursued foreign expansionism. Nazi imperialism—the ideology of *Lebensraum* (living space), the projection of a racialized European "New Order," and the spatial imaginary of the "East"—would be a closely allied third. Yet a fourth could be a visualization of the Jewish enemy, along with the many other categories that the Volksgemeinschaft ruthlessly debarred. Along with the spectacle of the stage-managed massed event, my discussion has focused mainly on the classically modern visual media of film and photography, plus architecture and a redesign of the built environment. But Nazism's visual repertoire also included painting, drama, heroic poetry and myth, dance, monuments, commemorations, museums, exhibitions, and everything involved in memorialization and memory work.

Finally, my discussion deliberately stops short of World War II because with the outbreak of the latter in September 1939, the stakes so markedly changed. The visual landscape was now one of troop movements, weaponry, motorization, and aerial warfare, leading initially to victorious occupation, then apocalyptic retreat, in "the iconography of metalized bodies" joined to "images of death and transfixation."[51] The spectacle moved indoors; after November 1938, no more massed events occurred in the open air. All the war's major speeches, whether by Hitler himself or by Goebbels, including the infamous "Total War" address of February 18, 1943, were interior affairs, delivered invariably in the Berlin *Sportpalast* before audiences of around fourteen thousand. The spectacle was literally unseen, sent by radio over the airwaves (figure 3.4).

But Nazism was nothing if not an imperialism. Only "imperial warfare" could "fulfill the palingenetic promise of national rebirth and racial purification," Koepnick argues, in a politics implacably opposed to Weimar's "political modernity" of conflict, civility, and difference. In 1933, that politics brutally severed the preceding democracy of popular representation while siphoning individual and collective hopes into a new arena of ritualized charismatic redemption. When we describe the fascist spectacle as an effort to

3.4 Goebbel's speech at the Sportpalast in Berlin, February 18, 1943.
Copyright: Bundesarchiv, ID number 183-J05235.

"recast the political as a realm of the beautiful," Koepnick reminds us, we can easily efface these other scenes of mass action, which took brutality, physical violence, destructiveness, and killing as their script: from the repression of 1933–34 through the desecrations and humiliations of *Reichskristallnacht* in 1938 to the mass murdering in the killing fields of the east. These were versions of the spectacle that were not publicly emblazoned across the visual landscape of the official nation, as was the artfully constructed showcase of the Volksgemeinschaft. Nonetheless, they incited and produced records of visualization, circulating privately and furtively in the countless snapshots of ordinary soldiers from the Eastern Front, colonizing the everydayness of intimate life more insidiously, but no less potently, than had the images of Nuremberg. In other words, we should not forget "the distinctive implication of fascist aesthetics in a project of imperial warfare, national purification, and genocide."[52]

Notes

1 Don DeLillo, *White Noise* (New York: Penguin, 1985), 25–26. I was originally brought back to DeLillo's novel by the brilliant treatment in Lutz Koepnick, *Walter Benjamin and the Aesthetics of Power* (Lincoln: University of Nebraska Press, 1999), 1–6.

2 See, for example, Steven Luckert and Susan Bachrach, eds., *The State of Deception: The Power of Nazi Propaganda* (Washington, DC: U.S. Holocaust Memorial Museum, 2011), produced for the exhibition of the same name (January 2009–October 2011).

3 Contemporary access became mediated in turn via Susan Sontag, "Fascinating Fascism," in *Under the Sign of Saturn: Essays*, 73–105 (New York: Farrar, Straus and Giroux, 1980). Originally published in the *New York Review of Books*, February 6, 1975, 11, 18, which appropriately pillories Riefenstahl's reputation.

4 Ian Kershaw, *Hitler 1989–1936: Hubris* (New York: Norton, 1998), 329, 363, 369.

5 Koepnick, *Walter Benjamin and the Aesthetics of Power*, 1.

6 Koepnick, *Walter Benjamin and the Aesthetics of Power*, 187.

7 Koepnick, *Walter Benjamin and the Aesthetics of Power*, 1.

8 Walter Benjamin, "The Work of Art in the Age of Mechanical Reproduction," in Walter Benjamin, *Illuminations*, ed. and with an introduction by Hannah Arendt (London: Collins/Fontana, 1973), 243.

9 Benjamin's thinking about mass-reproduced visuality—photography in particular—channeled wider debates in interwar critical theory about new mass-cultural forms and their relationship to the bases of political life under modernity. Key here was the journalist and critic Siegfried Kracauer (1889–1966), whose 1927 text *Ornament der Masse* was essential context for Benjamin's insight. See Siegfried Kracauer, *The Mass Ornament: Weimar Essays*, ed. Thomas Y. Levin (Cambridge, MA: Harvard University Press, 2005). For brilliant commentary on the cinematic dimension, see Johannes von Moltke, *The Curious Humanist: Siegfried Kracauer in America* (Berkeley: University of California Press, 2016), 93–108, 109–31. See also Kracauer's classic 1947 retrospect, *From Caligari to Hitler: A Psychological History of the German Film* (Princeton, NJ: Princeton University Press, 1966).

10 John Berger, *Ways of Seeing* (Harmondsworth: Penguin, 1972), 32–34.

11 My citation here is to the brilliant compilations of Peter Wollen in *Paris Hollywood: Writings on Film* (London: Verso, 2002) and *Paris Manhattan: Writings on Art* (London: Verso, 2004); also Peter Wollen, "Modern Times: Cinema/Americanism/The Robot," in *Raiding the Icebox: Reflections on Twentieth-Century Culture* (London: Verso, 1993), 35–71.

12 Simonetta Falasca-Zamponi, *Fascist Spectacle: The Aesthetics of Power in Mussolini's Italy* (Berkeley: University of California Press, 1997), 12. In Benjamin's terminology, this is the contrast between two distinct meanings of the English "experience": *Erlebnis* (encountering the random shocks of life) and *Erfahrung* (being able to know life as continuity).

13 Marshal Berman, *All That Is Sold Melts into Air: The Experience of Modernity*

(London: Verso, 1983); Stephen Kern, *The Culture of Time and Space, 1880–1918* (Cambridge, MA: Harvard University Press, 1983).

14 See especially Detlev J. K. Peukert, *Inside Nazi Germany: Conformity, Opposition, and Racism in Everyday Life* (London: Batsford, 1987; published in German in 1982); Detlev J. K. Peukert, *The Weimar Republic: The Crisis of Classical Modernity* (New York: Hill and Wang, 1989; published in German in 1987); and Detlev J. K. Peukert, *Max Webers Diagnose der Moderne* (Göttingen: Vandenhoeck and Ruprecht, 1989).

15 Peukert, *Weimar Republic*, xiii and 273–82; see also Kathleen Canning, "Introduction: Weimar Subjects/Weimar Publics: Rethinking the Political Culture of Germany in the 1920s," in *Weimar Subjects/Weimar Publics: Rethinking the Political Culture of Germany in the 1920s*, ed. Kathleen Canning, Kerstin Barndt, and Kristin McGuire (New York: Berghahn Books, 2010), 2–5.

16 Intervening discussions now carry forward Peukert's argumentation, especially Moritz Föllmer and Rüdiger Graf, eds., *Die "Krise" der Weimarer Republic: Zur Kritik eines Deutungsmusters* (Frankfurt: Campus, 205); Rüdiger Graf, *Die Zukunft der Weimarer Republik: Krisen und Zukunftsaneignungen in Deutschland 1918–1933* (Munich: Oldenbourg, 2008); Rüdiger Graf, "Either-Or: The Narrative of Crisis in Weimar Germany and Historiography," *Central European History* 43, no. 4 (2010): 592–615; Peter Fritzsche, "Historical Time and Future Experience in Postwar Germany," in Wolfgang Hardtwig, ed., *Ordnungen in der Krise: Zur politischen Kulturgeschichte Deutschlands* (Munich: Oldenbourg, 2007), 141–64; and Martin Geyer, "'Die Gleichzeitigkeit des Ungleichzeitigen': Zeitsemantik und die Suche nach Gegenwart in der Weimarer Republik," in Hardtwig, *Ordnungen in der Krise*, 165–87. See also Peter Fritzsche, "Did Weimar Fail?," *Journal of Modern History* 68, no. 3 (1996): 629–56; Peter Fritzsche, "Landscape of Danger, Landscape of Design: Crisis of Modernism in Weimar Germany," in *Dancing on the Volcano: Essays on the Culture of the Weimar Republic*, ed. Thomas W. Kniesche and Stephen Brockmann (Columbus, SC: Camden House, 1994), 29–46; and Kathleen Canning, "The Politics of Symbols, Semantics, and Sentiments in the Weimar Republic," *Central European History* 43, no. 4 (2010): 567–80.

17 David Crew, "The Pathologies of Modernity: Detlev Peukert on Germany's Twentieth Century," *Social History* 17, no. 2 (1992): 321.

18 Koepnick, *Walter Benjamin and the Aesthetics of Power*, 190.

19 Crew, "Pathologies of Modernity," 321.

20 Crew, "Pathologies of Modernity," 321.

21 For the affective registers of Weimar politics and the pertinence of the history of emotions, see Canning, "Politics of Symbols," 577–78; and Manuela Achilles, "With a Passion for Reason: Celebrating the Constitution in Weimar Germany," *Central European History* 43, no. 4 (2010): 666–89.

22 See Emilio Gentile, *The Sacralization of Politics in Fascist Italy* (Cambridge, MA: Harvard University Press, 1996); Emilio Gentile, *Politics as Religion* (Princeton,

NJ: Princeton University Press, 2006); George L. Mosse, *The Nationalization of the Masses: Political Symbolism and Mass Movements in Germany from the Napoleonic Wars through the Third Reich* (New York: Meridian, 1977); and George L. Mosse, *The Fascist Revolution: Toward a General Theory of Fascism* (New York: Howard Fertig, 1999). See also Roger Griffin, ed., *Fascism, Totalitarianism, and Political Religion* (London: Routledge, 2005); and Roger Griffin, "Withstanding the Rush of Time: The Prescience of Mosse's Anthropological View of Fascism," in *What History Tells: George L. Mosse and the Culture of Modern Europe*, ed. Stanley G. Payne, David J. Sorkin, and John S. Tortorice (Madison: University of Wisconsin Press, 2004), 110–33.

23 See especially Claus-Ekkehard Bärsch, *Die politische Religion des Nationalsozialismus: Die religiöse Dimension des NS-Ideologie in den Schriften von Dietrich Eckert, Joseph Goebbels, Adolf Rosenberg und Adolf Hitler* (Munich: W. Fink, 1998); Klaus Vondung, *Magie und Manipulation: Ideologischer Kult und politische Religion des Nationalsozialismus* (Göttingen: Vandenhoeck and Ruprecht, 1994); Richard Steigmann-Gall, *The Holy Reich: Nazi Conceptions of Christianity, 1919–1945* (Cambridge: Cambridge University Press, 2004); Wolfgang Hardtwig, "Political Religion in Modern Germany: Reflections on Nationalism, Socialism, and National Socialism," *Bulletin of the German Historical Institute* (Washington, DC), 28 (spring 2001): 3–27; Jane Caplan, "Politics, Religion, and Ideology: A Comment on Wolfgang Hardtwig," *Bulletin of the German Historical Institute* (Washington, DC), 28 (spring 2001): 28–36.

24 Griffin, "Withstanding the Rush of Time."

25 George L. Mosse, *Masses and Man: Nationalist and Fascist Perceptions of Reality* (New York: Howard Fertig, 1980), 194–96.

26 Steven E. Aschheim, "Introduction," in Payne, Sorkin, and Tortorice, *What History Tells*, 7.

27 Mosse, *Nationalization of the Masses*, 127; "The Aesthetics of Politics" is chapter 2 of the latter (21–46); Gentile uses "hunger for totality" and "confronting modernity" in characterizing Mosse's oeuvre; see Emilio Gentile, "A Professional Dwelling: The Origin and Development of the Concept of Fascism in Mosse's Historiography," in Payne, Sorkin, and Tortorice, *What History Tells*, 56, 58.

28 Mosse, *Nationalization of the Masses*, 20.

29 Helmut Gruber, "History of the Austrian Working Class: Unity of Scholarship and Practice," *International Labor and Working-Class History* 24 (fall 1983): 50–52. See now Nadine Rossol, "Performing the Nation: Sport, Spectacles, and Aesthetics in Germany, 1926–36," *Central European History* 43, no. 4 (2010): 616–38; and Nadine Rossol, *Performing the Nation in Interwar Germany: Sport, Spectacle, and Political Symbolism, 1926–36* (Houndmills: Palgrave Macmillan, 2010).

30 Rossol, "Performing the Nation," 631.

31 Canning, "Politics of Symbols," 577.

32 Rossol, "Performing the Nation," 638.

33 See Jochen Thies, "Nazi Architecture: A Blueprint for World Domination: The Last Aims of Adolf Hitler," in *Nazi Propaganda: The Power and the Limitations*, ed. David Welch (London: CroomHelm, 1983), 45–64.

34 Martin Kitchen, *Speer: Hitler's Architect* (New Haven, CT: Yale University Press, 2015), 33.

35 Kitchen, *Speer*, 35.

36 See Paul B. Jaskot, "Heinrich Himmler and the Nuremberg Party Rally Grounds: The Interest of the ss in the German Building Economy," in *Art, Culture, and Media under the Third Reich*, ed. Richard A. Etlin (Chicago: University of Chicago Press, 2002), 230–56.

37 During the audience with Hitler, Hácha was assaulted by a verbal tirade so ferocious that he eventually fainted. See Ian Kershaw, *Hitler 1936–1945: Nemesis* (New York: Norton, 2000), 170–71.

38 The style of building per se could be quite eclectic. Sagebiel's Air Ministry (1935–36) might well be assimilated into what became the international style, from Albert Kahn's General Motors Building in Detroit (1919) to Hans Poelzig's *IG-Farben-Haus* in Frankfurt (1931). That style traveled transnationally across Josef Stalin's Soviet Union, Benito Mussolini's Rome, and Stanley Baldwin's London. As Speer later claimed, there was nothing specifically national socialist about much of the architecture of the 1930s: "Ideology was apparent in the definition of the commission, but not in the style of its execution." See Albert Speer, *Spandauer Tagebücher* (Berlin, 1975), 202, quoted in Kitchen, *Speer*, 32. For longer-term legacies, see Gavriel D. Rosenfeld, *Munich and Memory: Architecture, Monuments, and the Legacy of the Third Reich* (Berkeley: University of California Press, 2000); Karen E. Till, *The New Berlin: Memory, Politics, Place* (Minneapolis: University of Minnesota Press, 2005).

39 Koepnick, *Walter Benjamin and the Aesthetics of Power*, 1, 190.

40 David Welch, "Nazi Propaganda and the *Volksgemeinschaft*: Constructing a People's Community," *Journal of Contemporary History* 39, no. 2 (2004): 213, n1.

41 Heinrich August Winkler, "Vom Mythos der *Volksgemeinschaft*," *Archiv für Sozialgeschichte* 17 (1977): 485.

42 Scott Spector, "Was the Third Reich Movie-Made? Interdisciplinarity and the Reframing of 'Ideology,'" *American Historical Review* 106, no. 2 (2001): 482–83, citing the argument of Lutz Koepnick, "Fascist Aesthetics Revisited," *modernism/modernity* 6 (1999), 51–73.

43 Spector, "Was the Third Reich Movie-Made?," 483. This is Spector's rendition of the argument in Koepnick, "Fascist Aesthetics Revisited," 52–54.

44 See Peter Reichel, *Der schöne Schein des Dritten Reiches: Faszination und Gewalt des Faschismus* (Munich: Carl Hanser Verlag, 1992).

45 Shelley Baranowski, "Strength through Joy: Tourism and National Integration in the Third Reich," in *Being Elsewhere: Tourism, Consumer Culture, and Identity in Modern Europe and North America*, ed. Baranowski and Eileen Furlough (Ann Arbor: University of Michigan Press, 2001), 216; Shelley Baranowski, *Strength*

through Joy: Consumerism and Mass Tourism in the Third Reich (Cambridge: Cambridge University Press, 2004), 121–22, 135.

46 The "people's radio" (*Volksempfänger*) was an exception: by 1941 almost 75 percent of households had radio sets, up from only 25 percent in 1933. But this was not exceptional to Nazi Germany. Radio was still more extensive in Denmark and Sweden, whereas Norway and France had faster growth from lower starting points.

47 Bernhard Rieger, *The People's Car: A Global History of the Volkswagen Beetle* (Cambridge, MA: Harvard University Press, 2013), 42–91.

48 Baranowski, *Strength through Joy*, 6.

49 "It was dominated by a massive pseudo-Classical tower of ten fluted piers joined by a cornice at the top, towering over all the nearby structures, including the Soviet pavilion, and outdone only by the Eiffel Tower, which stood at the end of the avenue on which the structures were located. Red swastikas glowed at night from the spaces between the piers. Next to the tower, the long, rectangular, windowless main hall projected a monolithic sense of unity to the outside world." See Richard J. Evans, *The Third Reich in Power 1933–1939* (New York: Penguin, 2005), 185.

50 See, classically, Anson G. Rabinbach, "The Aesthetics of Production in the Third Reich," *Journal of Contemporary History* 11, no. 4 (1976): 43–74.

51 Koepnick, *Walter Benjamin and the Aesthetics of Power*, 180–81.

52 Koepnick, *Walter Benjamin and the Aesthetics of Power*.

4

FIVE FACES OF FASCISM

RUTH BEN-GHIAT

"Visualizing fascism" might seem to be an easy endeavor. Most of us can easily conjure mental pictures of the right-wing regimes of the interwar and World War II years. Uniformed men on the march, children performing in sports arenas, the dictator in his uniformed splendor, state-sponsored violence on the street and in disciplinary spaces (prisons, camps, penal colonies) probably figure in this repertoire. One national case may come to mind, or perhaps the differing flags, costumes, and emblems blend into a transnational flow of fascist images. Either way, our quick takes (and those produced by Google and YouTube searches) often settle on two sets of images: the portrait of the leader, and fascism as a mass movement captured through shots of large-scale political spectacle and choreographed bodies.[1]

The mental reflex that defaults to these two poles—the individual and the anonymous crowd—captures an essential truth about the workings and appeal of fascism in its own time. Studies of fascist aesthetics, spectatorship, and ritual bear out the importance of communal activities in shaping the particular sense of togetherness and social cohesiveness such regimes depended on. Paul Corner cites "mass participation in public events" as the defining trait of Italian Fascism, understood as a "popular dictatorship," and this could be extended to many other right-wing regimes. Attending mass rallies, taking part in parades and paramilitary exercises, or even just seeing films with the knowledge that informers were likely present in the theater trained people to subsume their own individuality to that of the collective.

This helped to shape the kinds of subjects who would work toward the social and political goals of the dictatorship. The leader, even if absent, was the binding force at these events. "Losing oneself" in public and sharing adulation of the leader proved to be no small part of fascism's appeal.[2]

This essay argues that when we uncritically rely on this image bank to study fascist regimes we risk replicating fascism's point of view. It asks us to consider other ways of visualizing fascism, and it proposes one: focusing on the anonymous "faces in the crowd" that populate so many fascist photographs and moving images. We cannot draw any firm conclusions about what those unknown people might be thinking—we can never know the inner lives of those caught by fascism's cameras—yet these visages, which are often neglected in analyses of the regime's visual propaganda, deserve our attention nonetheless. They remind us of what these regimes most feared and what their leaders could never fully control: the agency and humanity of the individual, and the everyday that existed apart from, or in spite of, the regime. It is remarkable that fascism's visual archive has had such staying power, to the point of dominating popular views about what dictatorship looked and sounded like, even seventy years after the demise of these regimes. This essay asks us to look at elements that are already present in that archive but that we too often gloss over, and to look again at other kinds of images of the fascist era that we "see," albeit perhaps through the veil of established visual traditions and historiographies. Noa Steimatsky argues that the cinema has long been inspired by "the inexhaustible promise of its human faces to condense and open up clues—true or false—of an inner life, of subjectivity." Historians of dictatorship who seek to know more about those who were caught up in fascism's mass occasions can scrutinize the faces of those who featured in its propaganda to glean clues as well.[3]

Fascist techniques of visualization reflect the mind-set of leaders who consider people in the aggregate, charting history in grand lines and from a top-down perspective. Their states' photographic and film archives excelled at conjuring this collective drive toward a glorious future, producing endless stills and reels of crowds as they enacted Fascism's "wheel of destiny," as Benito Mussolini called it, going where the regime wanted them to go.[4] When the camera does come to rest on a face for more than a few seconds, it is usually for a political reason. Pans of "regional" or "imperial" physiognomies or traditional dress in the context of troop reviews or folkloric performances assert the diversified support for the regime's endeavors. Lingering cameos of faces flushed with joy or otherwise overcome with emotion as they gaze upon the leader reinforce the rewards of submission to his cults of virility and authority. And the continuous feed of loving gazes upon the leader shores up notions of his omniscience and omnipotence. Such close framings of the leader and his masculine proxies in fascist visual propaganda also inculcate ideals of masculinity through intermedial and extracinematic circulations. In his studies of the face, Roland Barthes called attention to "class and social markers effecting facial attitudes and repertoires of expression," as Steimatsky writes, which were then internalized by the public and brought into daily life. Fascist propagandists added to these political and racial markers that led them to single out certain physiognomies and affects. Yet these special faces also end up in the image-flow of a collective march to the future. Time and the cameras stopped only for the face of the one who was directing this fast history while also standing above it; as such, he was already a monument(al)-figure. Under fascism, the leader's was the only political face that viewers were encouraged to duplicate and admire from every angle.[5]

Taking as my case study fascist Italy and its culture of empire, I mine images from a variety of sources: films and photographs of the Istituto Luce (the regime's official image production agency); a photograph taken by an Italian soldier who served in Ethiopia; raw footage of British troops capturing soldiers like him during that empire's demise; and stock photos of the liberation of Italy from Mussolini. Studying the faces therein, I seek to uncover the visual edge of the everyday, the small moments inside big events, as lived by men and women who face the cameras and silently speak to us—if we know how to look and listen. I also reflect on what "visualizing fascism" can mean for historians. For one thing, it raises questions about what sources we privilege to understand the past. It means asking how we can locate history in images, and what the place of images is in history. The former question touches on methodology, whereas the latter engages in historiography. The historical profession still displays a certain reluctance to use images as anything more than supplements to written documents, whether for lack of confidence and training or a bias toward what might be called "proof of the page." These are missed chances to learn what only images can tell us. The visual not only communicates in ways written documents cannot; it can also enrich the field of historical research by leading us to new subjects and lines of inquiry that often have scant traces in the written and oral historical record.

While I'm mindful of the particularities of the photographic medium, I rely here primarily on the writings of scholars who have studied the cinema-history relationship (such as Marc Ferro, Robert Rosenstone, Antoine de

Baecque, Marcia Landy, and Christian Delage) and on my own investigations into the case study of Fascist empire films. This body of work reminds us that images have their own ways of narrating the past, and to hold them to the standards of written historical texts is, in part, to miss the point.[6] Images convey facts but also realms of perception and intuition. The stories they narrate often don't coincide with those the written records of the public sphere convey, nor do they always map onto what the historical and state establishments deem appropriate, interesting, or worthy of narration. Long before the advent of gender and postcolonial studies, for example, the visual record of modern European empires told us just how central indigenous women and relations with them were in the operation of imperial fantasy and of practices of domination on the ground. As Rosenstone has written, the visual can be a valuable font of alternative historiographies that often precede written ones, especially in "societies recovering from totalitarian regimes or the horrors of war."[7]

My essay locates us in the thick of such a regime, during the Italian Fascist occupation of Ethiopia (1935–41) and into World War II. The invasion of a League of Nations member and the massive use of chemical weapons brought international sanctions and the urgent need for image management on a different scale. Starting in 1936, the regime intensified its control of the media and invested heavily in both documentary and feature films on imperial themes. These years allow us to explore what Lutz Koepnick terms "the distinctive implication of fascist aesthetics in a project of imperial warfare, national purification, and genocide."[8] They also highlight the regime's stake in the visual as a means of conquest and governance. The Istituto Luce became a laboratory for visual propaganda, and both the film and political press hosted lively debates about the potential of moving images to transform war journalism and the representation of history. Yet even as cameramen were hailed as paragons of military manhood, the space for their own vision narrowed considerably. Luce's industrial aesthetic required the body behind the camera to all but disappear in the name of a collective and anonymous "eye." Moreover, the fast pace of newsreels and their aim to distill single moments into exemplary mass experiences left almost no room for the expression of individual subjectivity of the kind that might translate into the camera lingering on a particularly expressive face. Thus do the two predominant views of the face in fascist newsreel propaganda mirror the broader figurations of the leader-mass model of power. We have the face of the leader—its composite elements (such as the eyes and jaw) each the subject of visual and textual elaboration—and the cheering crowds seen in rapid pans that leave very little room for individuation.[9]

Mussolini, All-Seeing

In their attention to the mechanics and culture of the image, Fascism's film professionals had a superb teacher: Mussolini, who was Fascism's most prolific generator of images and its most beloved object.

My chosen view of Il Duce may seem odd in an essay about faces, given that his is only partly visible (figure 4.1). The focus, rather, is on his barely clothed body, the camera he peers through, and his scrawled signature. I start with this image as a reminder that processes of visualization begin and end with bodies. It is too easy for dictators' faces to end up as otherworldly objects, ripe for worship as timeless symbols of absolute power—as, for example, in the kind of internet memes so popular among today's alt-right. In fact, at least three bodies haunt every image of the face: the body behind the camera, the body of the subject, and the bodies of its intended spectators. All three of these bodies are invoked in this image, released in 1934 by Mussolini's press office, that depicts him on vacation in Rimini. The autographed card of Il Duce wielding a movie camera conjure his audience while alluding to the image-making process. Mussolini, then at the peak of his international celebrity (it would be tarnished when he invaded Ethiopia), was extremely conscious of all the elements of the stardom equation. Not only was his visage disseminated and plastered all over Italy, but he was a star in America through his regular presence in newsreels and his own syndicated column in William Randolph Hearst's one-thousand-plus publications.[10]

But make no mistake: even as he allows us to gaze undisturbed at his sturdy body, he signals his control of the gaze and the technologies that extend it. Who is he looking at from his boat? His obscured face and prosthetic vision channels a world of state surveillance—informers hidden in the shadows, watching and listening, and policemen looking for the "right" faces—that often had brutal bodily consequences. We are always watching you, Mussolini says, even on the beach in July. It's not surprising that a giant image of him looking through a movie camera, with armed soldiers and black-shirted officials lined up under it, reigned over the inauguration of the Cinecittà movie production complex in 1937.[11]

4.1 Mussolini All-Seeing, Rimini, 1934.

The Face in the Crowd

The mass events that feature so heavily in the repertoire of received images of fascism had a crucial role in the national and international legitimation of such regimes. After an initial period of public violence meant to close off other political options and frighten people into submission, fascist governments often became visible in a different manner. They marshaled crowds of people into public spaces to display approval of the dictator and his proxies and policies. The individual has meaning on these occasions only as part of an aggregate that lends itself to spectacle—a labor no less important than building roads or invading countries. The second face of Fascism, therefore, must be that of the individuals we find when we go into the crowd, in this instance the one assembled in Piazza Venezia in October 1935 to hear Mussolini's announcement of the invasion of Ethiopia (figure 4.2). Italian troops were ready to strike at the Ethiopian border, so the rally was largely performative: the regime wished to show the world that the coming aggression had a popular mandate.[12]

The presence of Luce cameras everywhere at the rally underscored that the participants were "on stage," no less so than Mussolini. In the spirit of the Nazis' blockbuster rally in Nuremberg in 1934, people assembled during the day, giving the press ample time to track their activities. Mussolini delayed his appearance until nightfall. For further dramatic effect, and to let his phrases resonate, silences and pauses composed half of the oration. As always at mass rallies, only a tiny fraction of those present actually saw him. Most looked in the direction of his voice, as transmitted by loudspeakers—those agents of interpellation—or directly at the Luce cameras. Their closed mouths and expressions strongly suggest silence. They are not part of the wild cheering and shouting on the soundtrack later overlaid by the Luce—those after-the-fact sounds of "consent" that become part of the default images of such rightist rallies. Their faces are sober and alert: after all, impending war meant worry about husbands, fathers, and boyfriends being drafted. Or maybe they merely arranged their faces into the neutral expressions that are recommended when one lives in a police state, especially when one finds oneself on camera. The directness of their gazes suggests a calm dignity and reserve. In the midst of a Fascist spectacle announcing that Italians will be sent off to Ethiopia like cattle, they were perhaps reluctant to show the kinds of emotions the state prompted them to have on such occasions. Here, the face is a kind of wall or buffer against the state's intrusions.[13]

In another way, too, these faces in the crowd can help us to "visualize Fascism." Julia Adeney Thomas in chapter 7, this volume, calls attention to the states of unexception that exist during wartime and the many moments that require not rallies and heroics, but quiet fortitude.[14] The faces in this photo, taken on the eve of a military invasion, also anticipate that state of waiting and endurance. Over a million men would be mobilized over the course of the next nine months, and we can imagine that some of these men would be injured, or even dead, one year later. Fascism is nowhere, and everywhere, in these images of the crowd, as it also might have been in the intimate lives of ordinary Italians.

4.2 Faces in the Crowd: Listening to Mussolini, Rome, October 2, 1935. Still from "Adunata!" October 8, 1935, Giornale Luce B0761, Archivio Luce (author's collection).

The Face of Empire

"Ethiopia, 1937" reads the inscription on the back of a photo found in an Italian soldier's album of memories of his service (figure 4.3).[15] We're on the other side of the invasion, in a double sense. The highly asymmetrical Italo-Ethiopian war ended, after nine months, with the May 1936 declaration of Italian victory and the Italian East African Empire, although resistance remained so fierce that the Fascists had to employ more air power for "governance" for the next three years than during the war.[16] The stakes were high for the regime. In Ethiopia, Fascism would demonstrate what its "own" model of colonization really looked like, as Italy's other African colonies (Libya, Somalia, Eritrea) had developed in accordance with the lax racial and population concerns of the liberal era. Fascism's "demographic colonization" foresaw a settler class brought from the metropole and from "Little Italies" all over the world. Luce films (and features) participated in this call for Italian emigrants to "come home" (to Addis Ababa rather than Asti), even as the prospect of a white influx into black Italian Africa led the Fascists to adopt racial laws starting in 1937. These laws criminalized miscegenation and levied fines for fraternalization among the races, which were considered damaging to Italian

4.3 Woman Wearing a
Soldier's Hat, Ethiopia,
1937. Courtesy of Maaza
Mengiste.

"prestige." As oral and other histories of the period make clear, though, this
ideal of a segregationist paradise fell short in practice. Italian men listened
more to the temptations advertised by the song "Faccetta nera" than the dictates that came from Rome. Italian soldiers frequented local brothels (leading
the regime to import white prostitutes to deter them) but also had long-term
relationships with women, and some deserted the military to make a life in
Ethiopia with their companions.[17]

All of these histories surround the image of an Ethiopian woman who
wears the hat of an Italian soldier. Perhaps the hat belongs to the soldier who
took the picture, or to the third party she is smiling at. This female face,
and its absent interlocutors, initiates us into the complexities of colonial re-

lations, which were built on dynamics of intimacy and distance, dependency and domination.[18] Who is this woman? Did the soldier place the hat on her head to stage the picture, or did she do it herself? If so, was it in a spirit of affection or of mockery? The scale of the picture is intimate, almost domestic. She looks down, as though at someone seated close by; a *tucul*, or hut (perhaps hers?), is in the background. The hat is the contrasting element in the picture: seen with the hut and her dress it limns the foreignness and strangeness of the Italian presence in Ethiopia. At the same time, her wearing of the hat enacts the acceptance of the "normality" of the Italian occupation, given that the hat seems to be a familiar, rather than frightening, object for her. The seeming ease of the situation might lead us to assume that this woman is the soldier's lover. Perhaps. The album that holds this image contains plenty of tourist-style pictures and shots of comrades, but no other such intimate photographs with women. Whatever their relationship, the image captures a happy moment, and its female subject escapes from both the ethnographic and eroticizing views of the "black woman as seen by white man" purveyed by fascist propaganda.

And yet it is those highly asymmetrical relations that prevail in the fascist visual archive we have inherited and work with even today. After World War II, as Ruth Iyob has shown, the Italian soldier exited from colonial memory as an agent of violence but remained in play as a libidinal subject. For example, the journalist Indro Montanelli (1909–2001), who denied for years that Italy used chemical weapons in Ethiopia, concurrently boasted on television about buying and then selling a twelve-year-old girl during his wartime military service. The smiling woman in the soldier's hat undoes this strategy. You can't remember me and my beauty, she says to us, without thinking of the military occupation that made this picture possible. The photograph has the status of "imperial debris," to use Ann Stoler's term—artifacts of difficult memory that beg us to pick them up and take a second look.[19]

The Face of Defeat

The Italian soldier came back into the picture as the Fascist empire disintegrated. Italian East Africa had already been lost by the time the Allies launched Operation Compass to drive the Fascists and Nazis out of North Africa. Luce's cameraman filmed the determinant Siege of Tobruk (1941), but this image is from the victor's side. The conquering British shot the outcome of the battle: thousands of Italian soldiers and officers captured. The still in figure 4.4 is from raw footage taken by the British military, some of which was destined for propaganda films that were shown to the public. The intent, as in the prisoner of war scenes filmed by almost every World War II captor, is to demonstrate momentum of the national war machine and boost spirits by showing the enemy cowed and taken from the battlefield. This particular film begins with every soldier's biggest humiliation—disarmament—and continues through the prisoners' transport to makeshift internment camps in Libya and Egypt. Relying on prisoners' memoirs, oral histories, and archival documents, we can suppose that some of these men already knew they might be sent to faraway places (such as India, Australia, South Africa), and that others might have been secretly relieved at their removal from a war going badly. British cameraman had more liberty than Italians to film what interested them, and the film catches a range of individual reactions to the ordeal of capture. A high-ranking officer refuses a body search, his face showing irritation as he swats away the British soldier with a gesture of someone accustomed to the distance that comes with command.[20]

I have chosen to present a moment in which the subject returns the cameraman's curiosity, resulting in sustained mutual regard. In this image the new prisoners crowd in, their differing attire showing how men from diverse military provenances had been thrust into a common fate. Those closest to the camera evince an eagerness and even excitement at being filmed, as though everything else has been forgotten for a moment. In the men behind them, though, one can intuit worry (far right) and perhaps the struggle to process the enormity of capture: Who are these men who will now decide my fate (center)? These candid shots, taken in the first flush of defeat, uncover moments that are forgotten or covered over in simplistic Fascist narratives of military heroism—fighting until death rather than surrender, the many willingly sacrificing for the one—that are kept alive throughout the postwar period, not least by the militaristic images of anonymous troops marching and saluting the leader. And so it's interesting that it's the small scale of human interaction—the scale of face-to-face contact, the spontaneously human moment—that irritates the Fascist film critic Sisto Favre when he laments that Italians were still too "generous" after twenty years of dictatorship. His solution? More displays of cruelty on screen. "The war film, whether as direct documentary or documented dramatic feature, must teach and instill hatred," he recommended in June 1943.[21]

By then the Italian war effort was in shambles. Mussolini would be removed from power by his own Grand Council one month later. Surrender to

4.4 Faces of Surrender: Greeting the Camera, Tobruk, 1941. Still from "The Fall of Tobruk," January 24, 1941, AYY 91. Courtesy of the Imperial War Museum Film and Video Archive.

the Allies, occupation by both Allies and Nazis, and the trauma of civil war were to follow. Yet a new way of seeing had already began to take hold. The future director Alberto Lattuada had authored the manifesto of this new gaze in 1941 with a book of photographs that denounced the consequences of years of internalizing Fascist propaganda's aggressive and dehumanizing gaze and belief that the individual must be sacrificed for the good of the whole: "People have lost *the eyes of love* and can no longer see clearly; they stagger in the obscurity of death. Here are the origins of the disintegration of all values and the destruction and sterilization of conscience: it is a long chain that is anchored at the devil's feet." Lattuada's own eyes of love translated into new images of Fascism: men, women, and children living in penury, selling humble objects to survive. This too was an outcome of Fascism's visual culture, and one that would have important consequences for cinema and photography at the close of the war: the turn away from the triumphal and the exotic to look anew at one's own surroundings and engage with the struggles and poetry of daily life.[22]

Mussolini, Unseeing

Piazza Loreto, Milan, 1945. Mussolini lies on the ground, his eyes unseeing, his face and body battered (figure 4.5). No longer the Leader, he's one of many, a body jettisoned with those of other Fascists after being executed by partisans. His only distinction is a Fascist emblem ironically placed in his lifeless hands. This uncredited image must have been taken soon after Mussolini came down from the scaffolding he had swung from, high above the piazza, so that people who had lived for decades in a context of government-manufactured reality could verify with their own eyes that he was dead. For years, Fascist propaganda had elided the regime's own violence and created a halo of invincibility around the chief persecutor. The display of the corpse was a kind of undoing of that blinded vision, while the actions the crowd took next—battering the inanimate Mussolini almost to a pulp—not only enacted popular revenge but literally defaced him, removing him from his pedestal. The writer Curzio Malaparte, long a worshipper of Il Duce and present at the scene, noted that only Mussolini's eyes had escaped mutilation. "No one had ever looked at the Italians the way he looked at them when he was alive," Malaparte wrote, noting that even in death those eyes retained their almost magical intensity. Clearly, Mussolini would be a troublesome corpse, capable of continuing to orchestrate the leader-crowd dynamic from his grave. Perhaps that's why the new Italian republic took the extraordinary measure of hiding Il Duce's body from 1945 to 1957, refusing to return it to the Mussolini family until that year.[23]

Paradoxically, the quick removal of the defaced Mussolini from sight allowed him to be remembered intact—effacing, as it were, that popular fury. When his name is entered into internet search engines, the resulting images show him at his peak splendor. Yet the knowledge of which bodies took those images, and why, has eroded over time. The digitalization of the Luce archives starting in 2000 counters this loss. Not only does it make Luce's enormous corpus of photographic and nonfiction film propaganda available for study, it allows us to identify images we take as "typical" of Fascism still today as part of official state propaganda, reminding us of what remained off-screen. I've presented these five images to restore some of that context and to bring back into view those who might be dismissed as part of "the mass" that submits to authority. The faces I examine tell a more complicated story, one worth investigating further, for the common denominator of all such

4.5 Mussolini, Unseeing, Milan, 1945. Open Access Stock Footage.

regimes is their dedication to annihilating individuality. They mobilize the visual to teach us not to see. "Visualizing fascism" means taking up these old images with new eyes.

Notes

1 In this essay I use "fascism" for the general phenomenon and "Fascism" (and "Fascist") for the Italian case.

2 Paul Corner, "Collaboration, Complicity, and Evasion under Italian Fascism," in *Everyday Life in Mass Dictatorship*, ed. Alf Lüdtke (New York: Palgrave, 2016), 75–93; Erica Carter, *Dietrich's Ghosts: The Sublime and the Beautiful in Third Reich Film* (London: British Film Institute, 2004); Lutz Koepnick, *The Dark Mirror: German Cinema between Hitler and Hollywood* (Berkeley: University of California Press, 2002); Mabel Berezin, *Making the Fascist Self: The Political Culture of Interwar Italy* (Ithaca, NY: Cornell University Press, 1997); Simonetta Falasca-Zamponi, *Fascist Spectacle: The Aesthetics of Power in Mussolini's Italy* (Berkeley: University of California Press, 1997); Tilman Allert, *The Hitler Salute: On the Meaning of a Gesture* (London: Picador, 2009); Julia Adeney Thomas, chapter 7 in this volume; Geoff Eley, chapter 3 in this volume.

3 Noa Steimatsky, *The Face on Film* (Oxford: Oxford University Press, 2017), 2. I also draw on Jean Aumont, *Du visage au cinema* (Paris: Editions de l'Etoile, 1992); and

Mary Ann Doane, "The Close Up: Scale and Detail in the Cinema," *Differences* 14 (2003): 89–111.

4 Benito Mussolini, "La mobilitazione generale. Discorso del 2 ottobre 1935," in *Scritti e discorsi*, vol. 9 (Milan: Hoepli, 1935), 217–20.

5 Steimatsky, *The Face on Film*, 99, speaking about Roland Barthes, "Visages et figures," *Esprit* 2–4 (July 1953): 1–11; also Ruth Ben-Ghiat, *Italian Fascism's Empire Cinema* (Bloomington: Indiana University Press, 2015); and the reflections on faces and photography under Nazism by Lutz Koepnick in chapter 5 in this volume. On fascist flows of history and time and leaders within them, see the essays in "Fascist Temporalities," special issue of the *Journal of Modern European History* 13 (2015).

6 Robert Rosenstone, *Revisioning History: Film and the Construction of a New Past* (Princeton, NJ: Princeton University Press, 1995); Pierre Sorlin, *The Film in History* (Totowa, NJ: Barnes and Noble, 1980); Marc Ferro, *Cinema and History*, trans. N. Greene (Detroit: Wayne State University Press, 1988); Pasquale Iaccio, *Cinema e storia* (Naples: Liguori, 1988); Antoine de Baecque, *Camera Historica: The Century in Cinema* (New York: Columbia University Press, 2012); Christian Delage and Vincent Guigueno, *Le historien et le film* (Paris: Gallimard, 2004); Marcia Landy, *Cinematic Uses of the Past* (Minneapolis: University of Minnesota Press, 1996). On the Italian case, see Angela Dalle Vacche, *The Body in the Mirror* (Princeton, NJ: Princeton University Press, 1992); and Vito Zagarrio, *L'immagine del fascismo* (Rome: Bulzoni, 2009).

7 Rosenstone, "Introduction," in *Revisioning History*, 5. See Geoff Eley, *A Crooked Line: From Cultural History to the History of Society* (Ann Arbor: University of Michigan Press, 2005), on how what matters to historians and what counts as culture and evidence changes over time.

8 Lutz Koepnick, *Walter Benjamin and the Aesthetics of Power* (Lincoln: University of Nebraska Press, 1999), 80–81.

9 On these debates, see Ben-Ghiat, *Italian Fascism's Empire Cinema*, 62–77.

10 Gian Giacomo Mignone, *The United States and Fascist Italy: The Rise of American Finance in Europe*, trans. Molly Tambor (Cambridge: Cambridge University Press, 2015); Pier Luigi Erbaggio, "Writing Mussolini: Il Duce's Biographies on Paper and on Screen, 1922–1935" (PhD diss., Department of Romance Languages and Literatures, University of Michigan, 2016); Renzo De Felice, *Mussolini il Duce: Gli anni del consenso 1929–1935* (Turin: Einaudi, 2007); Falasca-Zamponi, *Fascist Spectacle*; Luisa Passerini, *Mussolini immaginario* (Rome: Laterza, 1991); Stephen Gundle, *Mussolini's Dream Factory* (New York: Berghahn Books, 2012); and Stephen Gundle, Christopher Duggan, and Giuliana Pieri, eds., *The Cult of the Duce* (Manchester: Manchester University Press, 2013).

11 On informers and the secret police, see Mauro Canali, *Le spie del regime* (Bologna: Il Mulino, 2004); on how they operated in the world of cinema, see Natalia Marino and Valerio Marino, *Ovra a Cinecittà* (Turin: Bollati Boringhieri, 2005).

12 "Adunata!" October 8, 1935, Giornale Luce B0761, Istituto Luce, Archivio Storico. On the Italo-Ethiopian War, see Giorgio Rochat, *Le guerre italiane, 1935–1943* (Turin: Einaudi, 2005); G. Bruce Strang, ed., *Collision of Empires* (London: Routledge, 2013); Giulia Brogini Künzi, *Italien und der Abessinienkrieg 1935/36* (Paderborn: Ferdinand Schöningh, 2006).

13 On such spaces, see Lüdtke, ed., *Everyday Life in Mass Dictatorship*; Luisa Passerini, *Fascism in Popular Memory* (Cambridge: Cambridge University Press, 1987); Michael Ebner, Kate Ferris, and Josh Arthurs, eds., *Everyday Life in Fascist Italy* (London: Palgrave, 2017); Kate Ferris, *Everyday Life in Fascist Venice* (London: Palgrave, 2012).

14 Julia Adeney Thomas, chapter 7 in this volume.

15 I thank Maaza Mengiste, who owns the album and kindly consented to let me publish the image.

16 On the Ethiopian Resistance, see Ian Campbell, *The Addis Ababa Massacre* (London: Hurst, 2017); on the use of aviation, see Giorgio Rochat, "The Italian Air Force in the Ethiopian War (1935–36)," in *Italian Colonialism*, ed. Ruth Ben-Ghiat and Mia Fuller (New York: Palgrave, 2005), 37–46.

17 Fabienne Le Houérou, *L'épopée des soldats de Mussolini en Abyssinie, 1935–1936* (Paris: L'Harmattan, 1994); Mia Fuller, *Moderns Abroad: Architecture, Cities, and Italian Imperialism* (New York: Routledge, 2005). On interracial relationships in the colonies, see Giuliana Barrera, "Mussolini's Colonial Race Laws and State-Settler Relations in Africa Orientale Italiana (1935–1941)," *Journal of Modern Italian Studies* 8 (2003): 425–43.

18 On such colonial dynamics and the ways they find expression in intimate life, see Ann Laura Stoler, *Carnal Knowledge and Imperial Power* (Berkeley: University of California Press, 2002).

19 Ruth Iyob, "*Madamismo* and Beyond: The Construction of Eritrean Women," *Nineteenth Century Contexts* 22, no. 2 (2000): 217–38. On Montanelli's denial of the use of gas in Ethiopia, see Angelo Del Boca, ed., *I gas di Mussolini* (Rome: Editori Riuniti, 2007). Montanelli spoke about his purchase and sale of the adolescent girl to Enzo Biagi on the Rai Tre program "RT-Era ieri," October 13, 2008. Ann Laura Stoler, ed., *Imperial Debris* (Durham, NC: Duke University Press, 2013).

20 "The Fall of Tobruk," January 24, 1941, AYY 91. Courtesy of the Imperial War Museum Film and Video Archive. On the fates of men like these, see Bob Moore and Kent Federowich, *The British Empire and Italian Prisoners of War, 1940–1947* (New York: Palgrave, 2002).

21 Sisto Favre, "Film di guerra," *Lo Schermo* (June 1943).

22 Alberto Lattuada, *Occhio quadrato* (1941), reprinted in *Alberto Lattuada fotografo*, ed. Piero Berengo Gardin (Florence: Alinari, 1982), 15, italics in original. On the transition from Fascist aesthetics to something more humble, see Ben-Ghiat, *Italian Fascism's Empire Cinema*, 243–307.

23 Sergio Luzzatto, *The Body of Il Duce* (New York: Metropolitan Books, 2005).

Margaret Schwartz, *Dead Matter: The Meaning of Iconic Corpses* (Minneapolis: University of Minnesota Press, 2015); "Racconto (di C. Malaparte). Il corpo straziato di Mussolini a Piazzale Loreto e la folla sudicia," Barbaridllo.it, July 20, 2017, http://www.barbadillo.it/67636-il-racconto-di-c-malaparte-il-corpo-straziato-di -mussolini-a-piazzale-loreto-e-la-folla-sudicia/.

5

FACE TIME WITH HITLER

LUTZ KOEPNICK

1

Published in spring 1932, Heinrich Hoffmann's photo album *Hitler wie ihn keiner kennt* (The Hitler nobody knows) transformed Hitler's private life into a matter of public concern. It did not simply showcase the ordinariness of Hitler's existence beyond noisy party rallies and agitated performances, it also silenced rumors about his lifestyle and emphasized his fitness for governing. The book's release date was well chosen, its pictures of Hitler in the mountains hiking, picnicking, or simply relaxing meant to reignite a political campaign presently in disarray.[1] To see Hitler resting his hand on a child's shoulder or enjoying moments of pause amid spectacular landscapes privileged moral authenticity over strategic action; it was to witness an empathetic human who was much more electable than political opponents on the Left and hesitant middle-class voters may have assumed. To learn from Baldur von Schirach's preface about Hitler's vegetarianism and his resistance to both alcohol and tobacco, and to see him easily navigating the divide between the political and the intimate, was to situate the aspiring chancellor as a true embodiment of a future cleansed from the vices of Weimar political culture. Hoffmann's images unlocked the private as a space seemingly void of political conflict, only to convert it into a stage whose apparent ordinariness served eminently political purposes after all.

Hitler's success in 1933 hardly depended on Hoffmann's public relations campaign of 1932. Yet *Hitler wie ihn keiner kennt* certainly brought a preview of coming (fatal) attractions, a blueprint for coupling technological media to political causes without precedent in nineteenth- and early twentieth-century history. *Hitler wie ihn keiner kennt* ran through various reprints and sold more than 400,000 copies over the next ten years. It was complemented by similar volumes such as *Jugend um Hitler* (Youth around Hitler, 1934), *Hitler in seinen Bergen* (Hitler in his mountains, 1935), and *Hitler abseits vom Alltag* (Hitler away from it all, 1937), each selling more than 200,000 copies and outflanking the distribution of photo albums featuring Hitler's role as statesman and commander in chief. It inspired the transformation of Hitler's image into a commodity of first rank, a desirable icon circulating as postcard, wall image, and collectable trading card. It also converted Hoffmann's studio from a local photographer's shop to a full-fledged industrial operation, an image factory that systematically capitalized on Hoffmann's unique access to Hitler and his relative monopoly over the mechanical reproduction of the Führer's face and body.[2] Throughout the 1930s and early 1940s, photographic images of Hitler as a private individual—his love for children, dogs, and the mountains; his need to relax from rigorous work without declining into mere idleness; his eagerness to read books, newspapers, maps, and architectural blueprints—became the stuff of his subjects' dreams. These images vitally enhanced the Nazi choreography of political life, helped brand Hitler's persona, and energized a profitable culture of photographic reproduction that seemed to collapse given boundaries between professionals and amateurs, image makers and spectators.

If scholarship of the 1970s and 1980s was quick to identify (and thereby denounce) aesthetic strategies peculiar to fascism and national socialism, more measured perspectives have prevailed since the 1990s. Rather than seeing Nazi film, architecture, and painting as embodiments of fascist aesthetics, we focus on how aesthetics operated under conditions of fascism, that is, how fascism managed to massage minds and engineer politically useful emotions with the aid of aesthetic materials whose visual appearance may have been unique neither to the 1930s nor to the stages of totalitarian power. Not all products of Nazi film studios, nor even a majority, incorporated the choreography of mass movements, the rituals of messianic leadership and collective submission, infamously captured by Leni Riefenstahl. Monumentalist sculptures à la Arno Breker and neoclassical designs by Paul Troost may have structured how Nazi politics wanted the individual to perceive and navigate public space, but neither Breker's nor Troost's styles were exclusive to the Nazi state, and both were potently present in contemporary democratic societies too. If up until the 1980s Riefenstahl, Breker, and Troost provided signature examples of what Walter Benjamin called the fascist aestheticization of the political,[3] the culturalist turns of the 1990s brought out the heterogeneity at the core of Nazi culture while highlighting many other aspects of art, culture, visual perception, mass media, and aesthetic experience during the 1930s and early 1940s. The notion of fascist aesthetics not only has lost both historical and systematic specificity, it also no longer illuminates the mingling of politics and the aesthetic, of advanced media culture and the representation of power during other periods.

The life and afterlife of Nazi photography, of photographs taken, circulated, and viewed under German fascism, relate oddly to these changes in perspective and evaluation. To be sure, Hoffmann's own visual style of the 1920s and 1930s, when showing Hitler not as a seemingly private citizen but as a statesman molding the body politic like clay, approximated what Riefenstahl's films, Breker's sculptures, or Troost's architecture aspired to accomplish. Although not initially intended for publication, Hoffmann's famous 1927 series of Hitler probing different rhetorical poses sought, as I have argued elsewhere, "to define the political as a self-referential space of ongoing motion in which mesmerizing surface designs, strategic self-performances, and desensitized forms of seeing undid the legacies of bourgeois culture and public debate."[4] In showing Hitler in different postures of leadership, Hoffmann's camera hoped no less than to eliminate some of the dominant binaries of bourgeois life, such as that between authenticity and dissimulation. It invited viewers to become—true to Ernst Jünger's writing on photography and culture—experts in cool conduct.[5] Rather than simply documenting what has often been read as a self-revelatory freak show, Hoffmann's images coupled photographic reproduction to the cause of political mobilization. These images engaged different rhetorics of representation to do away with rhetoric altogether and, like Riefenstahl in the 1930s, recast the real as image, the image as real.

And yet, just as all of Hoffmann's photography between the 1920s and mid-1940s cannot be reduced to a single style, mode, or aspiration, nor can photography under German fascism be described more generally as existing in the singular. There is no particularly fascist way of capturing the world as photographic image; of cropping the image and situating certain elements outside the frame; of triangulating the relationship between photographer, photographed, and viewed; of depicting bodies and objects. With the advent of lightweight cameras in the 1920s, photography became a widespread practice taking many forms. Most of the pictures taken, exchanged, and collected in albums during the 1930s and 1940s, by professionals, hobbyists, and amateurs alike, are commonly indistinguishable, whether in form or even content, from what Germans may have been picturing on either side of the Nazi time. To speak of Nazi photography, of fascist photography, would mislead even more than would identifying a uniquely fascist language of filmmaking, public art, and architecture. Accordingly, the critical discourse about photographic images during the Nazi period emphasizes questions that are often different from those familiar from other art forms and mass media. On the one hand, much writing has concerned the role of amateur and professional photographers in capturing wartime atrocities and genocidal activities, probing degrees of culpability and complicity: How did taking and viewing photographic images, it has been asked, desensitize the perceptions of those committing or witnessing the crimes of national socialism?[6] In perhaps the most rigorous inquiry yet, Georges Didi-Huberman's *Images malgré tout* (2003) extends this line of inquiry to those rare images concentration camp prisoners took to document the horrors of Auschwitz.[7] By learning to look at these images, argues Didi-Huberman, we do justice to photographic acts of resistance and reclaim what was previously declared incommunicable, ineffable, and unrepresentable about camp atrocities. On the other hand, scholars have also devised frameworks to address the massive photographic archive left by amateurs and hobbyists in capturing and commemorating scenes seemingly devoid of politics altogether.[8] Some of this work remains haunted by an older assumption: no picture of ordinariness, of nonpolitical intimacy, taken during fascism can ever be viewed as unpolitical or innocent. But as other recent scholarship argues, rather than leaping directly from the Nazis enjoying their everyday lives to what precisely is *not* shown in the images themselves, we should refocus our gaze on what the image visibly displays. Although many amateur photographers were of course Nazis, the world as viewed and arrested by means of their cameras cannot be reduced to a mere chimera whose sole purpose was to make people *not see* the violence and death Nazis committed in the real world.[9]

Hoffmann's pictures of Hitler in domestic settings are usually read as highly calculated invitations to look away, to forget what fascism was all about. By endowing Hitler's persona with human qualities so as to make people blind to his true nature, they made the political beyond the frame all the more compelling. As the argument runs, whatever we see in them is meant to eclipse what exists beyond the photographic frame, to vacate a space for even more effective operations of propaganda and power; whatever they show leaves no later grounds for viewing them at all, other than to fetishize the icons of Nazi power. By pretending to show something the viewers did not know, Hoffmann's Hitler images deactivated the very possibility of knowledge. They obscured the truth of fascism. No look at what they frame, however rigorous, will ever restore that truth; it will always make us look at the monstrous without seeing it for what it was.

When we abandon a merely representational understanding of photographic imaging and engage these images on their own ground, we find far more in Hoffmann's images of Hitler during the 1930s than critics and historians typically assume. For Hoffmann's images offer no less than a manual of how to think about, see, and circulate photographic images as something that exceeds the representational; a visual set of instructions teaching viewers not to burden photographs with traditional truth claims; a laboratory collapsing presumed differences between the real and the image by redefining a camera's mechanical gaze as the truth and essence of organic vision. Hoffmann's images are deeply paradoxical. They not only train viewers to embrace photographic vision and practice as basic principles of what it means to live in and perceive Nazi Germany, but also seek to persuade the viewer that photography at heart has very little to say and communicate in the first place. While showing Hitler off the beaten track, Hoffmann's images want their viewers to understand that there is nothing to understand when it comes to photography. Far more than simply glorifying Hitler as an honorable and empathetic man, they envision photography as a pervasive modern technology whose principle purpose is to take hold of the everyday, independent of what any individual picture might really be about. Similar to the tweets, Instagram messages, and Facebook communications of our own time, Hoffmann's Hitler—a medium embodying its own message—wants to teach us that we need not read images because, in essence, photographic images are all about doing rather than representing; their task is to shape, transform, and be part of the world rather than merely to picture it.

2

In the early years of the Nazi movement, Hitler was said to base his impact primarily on the aura of his voice and refused any effort to circulate photographic portraits in the public. According to Heinrich Hoffmann's biography, in autumn 1922 Hitler requested $30,000 to have his picture taken and printed in national and international newspapers.[10] In the preface to Hoffmann's *Hitler wie ihn keiner kennt*, Baldur von Schirach described Hitler's early camera shyness as a sign of the agitator's moral authenticity, his refusal to buy into the putative degeneracy of Weimar consumer culture: "To be popular means: to be photographed a lot. Adolf Hitler has always resisted becoming an object of photography. In particular twelve years ago, when his name emerged for the first time from the darkness of anonymity, he was a declared enemy of the camera. Back then, the whole world's illustrated press tried to obtain a picture of the Führer. Without success. In spite of all kinds of monetary offers, Hitler categorically refused to have his picture taken for the sake of reproduction."[11] At once the metaphorical and physical organ of the putatively disenfranchised, Hitler's voice was to serve as the movement's principal medium, not least of all because it seemed to escape the very traps modern technology had set for acts of human communication.

Little of Hitler's reticence about cameras remained when Hoffmann, with *Hitler wie ihn keiner kennt*, embarked on a whole sequence of coffee-table books positioning Hitler as Nazi Germany's foremost object of photography. Hoffmann's images of Hitler's private side have been much discussed, most often perhaps for what they do not show, or conversely, for reconstructing Hitler's circles and hidden levels of access, influence, and command. In what follows, however, I identify four tropes that emerge if Hoffmann's images are viewed at much closer range and our eyes peruse their visual surfaces. It transpires that the effort to *read* these images is deeply paradoxical, given that Hoffmann's photography intends no less than to exceed and displace reading. And yet, whether they feature Hitler's hands, his role as a reader, his unceasing alertness, or his transformation of the privacy of trains and cars into a public stage, all such tropes allegorize how photography can or should move photographers and viewers alike beyond traditional notions of the image. As they present Hitler's sight as a medium to propagate a world in which photographic perception and image making may reign triumphant, all four tropes define the very act of taking pictures as a technique of inhabiting the present. They provide interfaces to the matter of the nation.

Hands. Although rarely the single focus of any particular picture, Hitler's hands figure prominently in the entire series of photo books. They are folded across each other in postures of attentive listening; hold or rest with great care and deliberation on books, newspapers, architectural drawings, and maps; arch over a chair's armrest in gestures of simultaneous relaxation and alertness; lift binoculars to the Führer's eyes in order to fortify his gaze;

sign scraps of paper autograph hunters present to Hitler during car rides through the countryside; and most of all, touch upon the shoulders, cheeks, and heads of children as they cross his path in the crowd or are chaperoned by their parents to meet Hitler one-on-one. To touch one hand with the other, French philosopher Maurice Merleau-Ponty once argued, reveals to us the two dimensions of what he called the flesh: the fact that bodies are both vehicles of (tactile) experience and objects to be touched by others. And yet, "when I press my two hands together, it is not a matter of two sensations felt together as one perceives two objects placed side by side, but of an ambiguous arrangement in which the two hands can alternate in the role of 'touching' and 'touched.'"[12] In Hoffmann's images, Hitler's hands reveal little of this ambiguity. Hitler's hands touch upon his subjects, but such touching in the larger choreography of Hoffmann's images is designed as a one-way street, maintaining distances however proximate Hitler's body may be. Here the hand's touch enchants, energizes, fascinates, commands, arrests, and moves the one being touched, but it does so without ever collapsing the difference, on the side of the toucher, between "touching" and "touched," that is, without ever situating Hitler as the one recognizing the various dimensions of his own flesh. Hitler's hands touch, but they never define him as an object of touch, nor do they ever serve Hitler as vehicles of haptic experience. They disseminate rather than grasp; they radiate outward rather than absorb or appropriate the world.

In *Jugend um Hitler* (1934), Hoffmann presents the viewer with a young woman, eager to catch the Führer's autograph as his automobile passes by (figure 5.1). Her face is in the center of the picture; her hands hold a notepad. Typical of Hoffmann's casual style of framing, referencing an amateur's lack of compositional control to create a sense of documentary authenticity, the image barely shows Hitler's hand at all, relegates it to a small area at the lower left. And yet this hand completely dominates the picture. It reaches into the frame, clasping a pen between thumb and finger. About to leave a mark on the paper, Hitler's hand is in full command of the woman's eyes, riveting her attention to what is about to happen. Hitler's hand is a sight that fascinates, a unique presence that governs space even before it touches upon objects and imparts their singular meaning. It not only animates and seizes the woman's look. It structures and thereby "holds" the entire image, at once defining and transgressing the boundary between the visible and the out-of-frame. Although the woman may have managed to halt the car's movement to gather a handwritten trophy, it is Hitler's hand that arrests viewers and thus precisely

5.1 "Ein Autogramm, bitte!" (*Jugend um Hitler*, 1934).

succeeds in deeply affecting her, in moving the viewer. The pen in Hitler's hand is no different than a finger ready to press a camera's shutter release. It is poised to transform the world into an image, to divide space into zones of visibility and what resides off-frame, all the while defining images—the page of the notepad awaiting the Führer's lasting inscription—as belonging to the very world they capture. As indexical traces of the real, they have a power that energizes reality itself.

Reading. The sheer number of Hoffmann's images showing Hitler as an avid reader is astounding. None of them, however, depicts Hitler with what he required in order to read in the first place—namely, reading glasses—as though the visibility of such devices would question the intensity of his acts of reading, the display of sophistication and intellectual curiosity meant to correct images of Hitler as no more than a shrill agitator ill-suited for the demands of great politics. One of the most famous shows him in civilian clothes turning away from a newspaper and looking directly into the camera, a rather unusual smile—slightly forced—on his face, arms resting on legs as he sits in the grass in some indistinct outdoor location (figure 5.2).

5.2 "Erholung. Abgeschieden von Lärm und Unruhe der Städte ruht hier der Führer auf den großen Wiesen in der Nähe seines Häuschens von den Strapazen des Kampfes aus. Dabei liest er dann die gegnerischen Zeitungen und freut sich über die Märchen, die sie über ihn verbreiten: Sektgelage, jüdische Freundinnen, Luxusvilla, französische Gelder . . ." (*Hitler wie ihn keiner kennt*, 1932).

As so often, Hoffmann's choices of grain and focus obscure what exactly Hitler might be reading; here, as elsewhere, lines of text fuse into solid gray blocks on paper. The caption adds a curious twist. While presenting Hitler in a moment of relaxation and solitude away from the cities' turmoil and his political duties, it identifies his reading material as an enemy newspaper whose "fairy tales" about his persona—"Champagne orgies, Jewish girl friends, luxury mansions, French money . . ."—visibly elicit his amusement. Viewers can glean nothing of this from the image itself. The illegibility of the text in the picture opens up ample space for signification, while Hitler's missing glasses make viewers wonder what exactly produced the amusement in the first place.

Hoffmann's photographs of Hitler as reader, especially when capturing him in natural environments, recall and rework a long pictorial tradition in which reading was encoded as spiritual communication—initially with God, then later as literary exaltation. Reading subtracted the reader from the confines of space and time. It operated as a technique of disembodiment, of unbound absorption. As it connected the subject to something transcendent and invisible, the act of reading divested readers of self-awareness, intentionality, and instrumental reason, of doing something in the first place or being viewed by others in this (non)doing. Although Hoffmann's images work hard to continue this tradition, showcasing moments of absorption as a condition for the possibility of benevolent leadership, they invariably achieve something quite different. Books and newspapers in Hitler's hands mostly figure as mechanisms of embodiment: they situate Hitler in, rather than evacuate him from, the materiality, temporality, and relationality of spatial environments. Here, to read is not to interface the divine or purely poetic or to transport the reading subject to a certain state of obliviousness and unconsciousness, ceding self-awareness and willfulness. It is to anchor the reader's—Hitler's—body in space, to showcase his wondrous ability to inhabit spaces of apparent quiet and solitude amid the busy routines of political leadership, to refuel what it takes to be present rather than immerse himself in what exceeds visibility and tangibility. Hitler's books and newspapers, in Hoffmann's photographs, are objects of the world that enable readers to relish the physical pleasures of holding their covers, turning their pages, sensing their touch, and smelling their scent. Like photographs themselves, they do not lead their users to other worlds altogether but by their physical imprints insert different times and places into the viewer's space. No photograph ever shows Hitler looking at photographs, not simply because self-reflexive gestures would have thwarted the authenticity of the amateur snapshot, but perhaps because Hitler always already reads texts as if they are photographic reproductions, as images that live in the world as much as index it.

Idleness. Hoffmann's famous 1927 images of Hitler probing rhetorical poses tried to counter photography's association with death, its logic of turning fleeting presents into corpses, by turning it on its head. In the name of engineering a viewer whose body could be subsumed coldly to the task of total mobilization, Hoffmann's camera pictured Hitler as a speaker poised to push against and break the frame; a body that could not be contained by the fixity of mechanical images; a presence that eliminated death from reproduction, inscribed temporal flows and dynamics in still images, and thus, in its effort to move and mobilize the viewer, animated photography to become film. In Hoffmann's photographs from the 1930s, little remains of the Hitler whose arms, hands, limbs, and entire torso had once vehemently pounded against the cell of his reproduction. In most of the images gathered in Hoffmann's coffee-table books, to be sure, Hitler's gaze typically fixes on something outside the frame, his physical posture symbolizing his visionary powers. While serving as an object to be looked at, he is rarely shown reciprocating other gazes. Most commonly, he directs existing networks of gazes to what only another picture— hence, an anticipated future—could fully reveal. In addition, he is frequently captured in trains and cars, mobile interfaces rendering his image for crowds of attentive onlookers. On the other hand, pictures rarely show Hitler's body itself in motion, midstride, capturing attention through physical activity as a kinesthetic attraction. In contrast to the 1927 series, Hoffmann's Hitler of the 1930s is a man of calm and composure, no longer rubbing against the frame and trying to beat photography at its own game. He is, in other words, all photograph, compliant with, assimilating to, and embodying what photography as a medium can do best.

Not one of Hoffmann's pictures, even those showing Hitler as a vacationer in "his" mountains in *Hitler in seinen Bergen*, ever presents him simply as being idle, as a slacker, as languid, or in poses of absentmindedness. On the contrary, repose comes with a sharpening of attention, with being alert, thoughtful, and receptive. The Führer's body is never subtracted from the world but situated more firmly in its physical surrounds, recentering things around him. Although Hoffmann's prefaces typically emphasize Hitler's need for stretches of empty time, slowness, and absorption amid the demands of political campaigning and caring for the nation, the images themselves showcase empty time as a time of heightened presence, not of drift but of utter focus and responsiveness. Hitler, the viewer learns, is always "on." Nothing can possibly escape his gaze and awareness.

In one picture, his head tilts downward, right hand holding the chin, eyes fixed on the ground (figure 5.3). The unusual composition has four planes of representation: Hitler in the immediate foreground on the left; some bushes and trees in the midground opening a view onto the background's meadow, trees, and—somewhat surprisingly—a little shrine along a road; and finally a mountain rising majestically in the far background on the right. This is no posture of absentmindedness or absorptive introspection. The image's horizontal spread, planar recession, and perspectival construction suggest something quite other: beyond Hitler's features, screening the contents of his inner eye, lies a mindscape projected onto various planes of visibility. Rather than capturing Hitler in a moment of precarious nonengagement, then, the image actually constructs him as a powerful *metteur-en-scène*. He becomes a godlike conjurer who understands how to translate inner visions into physical realities. He potently directs the very structure of the viewer's looking.

5.3 *Hitler in seinen Bergen*, 1935.

In another photograph, Hitler appears on the terrace of his mountain home watching a boy whose eyes are glued to a telescope, seeing what escapes our own (and Hitler's) view (figure 5.4). Hitler's half-open mouth suggests that he is speaking to his young visitor. The slightly bent posture indicates some urgency, as if encouraging or instructing the boy in the proper use of this technology of vision. In a curiously disjunctive triangle of looks linking Hitler, the boy, and the viewer, with no one's gaze ever reciprocating the other, the photograph places Hitler in all his leisurely repose as the central choreographer of the visible, of a visual field structuring the very modes of possible perception.

In Hitler's universe, these two photographs suggest, visual media are never merely tools for capturing the world in representation. Rather, they produce and provide an entire infrastructure of human existence, a comprehensive environment for, and elemental condition of, being in the world. For Hitler, with idleness this world would implode. It would radically deflate what holds Nazi society together. In Hitler's (re)engineering of the world—as one made *by* and *for* different acts, practices, technologies, and techniques of looking— there is no outside.

5.4 "Wie schön ist die Aussicht vom Haus Wachenfeld" (*Hitler in seinen Bergen*, 1935).

Vehicles. In the early Nazi years, radio was to governance what Twitter is to twenty-first-century political campaigns: it provided a sense of instant connectivity, of seemingly unmediated presence, that cuts across existing boundaries of public and private, the intimate and the political.[13] This archetype of modern communication technologies was at once succeeded and completed by Hitler's use of airplanes during the campaigns in the early 1930s. Before television's mass arrival, yet not so removed from Instagram and other social media of today, air travel propelled Hitler's image speedily around the country, networking distant constituencies into the unified nation.[14] If radios inserted the immediacy of Hitler's voice into the home's interior, airplanes mobilized Hitler's body into ubiquitous visibility. What both media accomplished jointly, however, was to make political leadership seem inevitable and indisputable. So, far from simply re-presenting images and sounds of Hitler to the crowds, they used the capacity of modern media for building worlds and infrastructures to shape, move, and arrest these very crowds in space and time.

In Hoffmann's photo albums, for good reasons, neither radios nor airplanes really move center stage. The former eluded easy photographic reproduction: neither invisible sonic waves nor sound's ability to collapse spatial distance could fit the framing power of photographic images. The latter, on the other hand, still the wondrous spectacle of advanced technology, could scarcely feature Hitler's humble and empathetic side in the way to which Hoffmann's snapshot aesthetic aspired. Yet modern transportation is not entirely foreign to Hoffmann's images of the 1930s. Hitler repeatedly travels the countryside in his Mercedes convertible, dispensing his autograph like a marquee movie star. While the images themselves may not have been deliberately staged, with crowd control and security measures, they each show Hitler's car as a technology of emotional mobilization: a medium powerful enough to wrest individuals from the crowds amassed along the road, a technology allowing Hitler's subjects to meet the Führer in close proximity, a tool wondrously collapsing the very distance and abstraction often associated with modern technological culture. Often, Hitler's car itself barely enters the image; it is present solely through a glimpse of the metallic body. Eliciting affects as a camera does, Hitler's cars articulate the crowd through the very boundaries of the visible; they define the condition for the possibility of seeing (Hitler) without necessarily belonging to the visual field itself. Hoffmann's images of trains, in contrast, show Hitler typically greeting his subjects through a compartment's half-open window. If disparities of height and power are emphasized, they never obviate the staging of the intimate encounters.

Hoffmann's train windows served as interfaces long before the advent of computer screens; they offer a shared boundary between different systems, a material space of interaction where different realities, worlds, and components can touch upon each other. They confer the privilege of face time with Hitler, not simply presenting the Führer as image to the crowd, an object of the look, but reconstituting what we understand as image in the first place, redefining images as meeting grounds of tactile transactions that far exceed the mere exigencies of re-presentation.

In so doing, Hoffmann's cars and trains inscribe the putatively private with what planes and radio were meant to do for public space. Indeed, by tackling the organization of public and private space-time from different ends, they each deliver a powerful reminder: even at its most intimate and private, Nazi visual culture aspired to lodge the public in the private, the private in the public, not simply by flooding its subjects with unprecedented numbers of mechanically reproduced images but also by emancipating image making and viewing from traditional protocols of representation, making them far more than merely media of optical capture and reception. Hoffmann's images of Hitler as private citizen are not *about* Hitler. They explore the conditions of what it might mean to be *in* the image with Hitler. His images were technologies that generate rather than merely depict spaces of wondrous encounters and affective transfers.

3

In his 1933 treatise *Staat, Bewegung, Volk* (State, Movement, People), Nazi legal theorist Carl Schmitt argued that traditional concepts of the image as a vehicle for representing something would not suffice to theorize how the Nazi movement had come to embody leadership in the figure of Adolf Hitler. "Our concept [of leadership] neither requires nor sustains the notion of a mediating image or representative likeness. It originates neither in baroque allegories and representations nor in Descartes's *idée générale*. It is a concept of immediate present and real presence."[15] Hitler, Schmitt intimated, did not simply represent, focus, or serve as an analogue or metaphor of his people, nor was it possible to consider his public image, his body and face, as a symbol, reflection, or projection of what German fascism was all about. Any of this, in Schmitt's assessment, would have continuously enslaved the Nazi era to the legacy of bourgeois culture and political romanticism. True leadership, instead, did without ideas of mediation and representation. It was utterly nonmetaphorical. It collapsed what exile Ernst Kantorowicz would later call the king's two bodies—the body natural and the body politic—into one,[16] presenting Hitler as embodiment of the people, and the people's ongoing movement and mobilization as the energy center of political unity. Hitler was Germany as much as Germany was Hitler. Although his image, in mechanically reproduced forms, penetrated each and every corner of the land, it assumed no less than the qualities of an icon, presenting in material and haptic form what drove and held the nation together, thereby eclipsing bourgeois democracy's frail dedication to imaging rather than doing, mediating and negotiating rather than rendering present.

How much were Hoffmann's 1930s images of Hitler in private a paradoxical attempt to translate Schmitt's philosophy into practice? Although they clearly do not hide their basis in technological reproducibility, Hoffmann's pictures sought no less than to present Hitler as a leader of immediate presentness and real presence, a post-bourgeois politician who no longer appeals to former rhetorics of representation, mediation, and symbolism. To gather youth around him and to bless them with his touch; to refuse the lures of idleness and to embody unfailing alertness 24/7; to use modern vehicles to stage his presence for astonished onlookers—all this eclipsed what images as much as political leaders had once stood for. Hoffmann's images dreamed the dream of no longer being mere images, of remaking themselves into objects that directly acted on and in the world, that empowered and channeled touch, presence, mobility, and movement rather than merely offering ocular and highly mediated interactions with the world. Following Schmitt's understanding of fascism as a fundamental attack on the bourgeois concept of the image, these photographs described a key field of political meaning ordered around their onslaught against the representational and the mediated. Even at their seemingly most private, they unfolded a political mission that many photographs of Hitler in public places, increasingly clichéd and ubiquitous, were no longer able to accomplish.

But rather than turn Hoffmann's images of the unknown Hitler into a mere philosophical issue, a profoundly paradoxical assault on the nature of the image, I conclude this essay by reading photographs of Hitler's hands, his alertness, his relation to printed matter and modern vehicles of transport, in more historical terms: as a concerted effort to train viewers to become photographers in their own right, to define photography as the primary lens for perceiving and inhabiting the realities of Nazi Germany. Seeking to roll back Weimar's modernist forays into *Neues Sehen*, Joseph Goebbels opened the 1933 photography fair in Berlin with the following words:

The photographic image is a visible expression of the height of our culture; we must recognize the value of photography not only for artistic life, but most of all also for the practical existential struggle in its full extent and therefore place photography and the graphic arts into the service of the German issue. We believe in the camera's objectivity and are skeptical about what is mediated through our sense of hearing or written letters. We stand at the threshold of an era which raises unprecedented demands through its community of faith. The human of today—in particular those Germans who were betrayed million-times in all areas of life during those fourteen horrendous years—has begun to be skeptical about news and opinion communicated to them through the ear or the medium of written words. He wants to see things for himself, and given the elevated state of the photographic arts and the illustrated press he has a right to do so. . . . Our modern artificial eye, the camera, has become a faithful witness of our new times. . . . The experience of the individual has become the experience of the *Volk*, and this through the camera alone. . . . In this way, photography fulfills an important political mission these days, to which every German should contribute who owns a camera.[17]

Since the advent of lightweight cameras in the second half of the 1920s, amateur photography in Germany had really taken off, hugely multiplying the number of people eager to capture family snapshots, assemble their images in curated photo albums, take cameras to public events, and document their travels through the countryside. To be sure, the first years of Nazi rule witnessed tremendous conflicts among photo clubs and amateur organizations as they struggled over who could best represent what Goebbels called the new times.[18] Moreover, Nazi authorities sought with alacrity to regulate the taking and circulation of photographic images, notably those of political leaders and party rallies, thereby constraining the desire of amateurs to capture exactly the pictures that "court" photographers such as Hoffmann circulated so proudly. Germans may have demanded the right to look at photographs of things political, but in face of comprehensive legislation they could not take most of them on their own. At the same time, whether or not one needed proper accreditation to direct one's camera at Hitler and his ilk, Goebbels's 1933 speech left little doubt that even amateur photography—the family snapshot, the private moments of detached leisure—served the movement and nation as vigorously as Hoffmann's ever-growing monopoly over reproductions of Hitler's official image. To train one's camera at the new times; to retrain the eye for modern technologies of vision; to allow the presumed objectivity of photographic indexicality to raise individual sight to the level of collective unity; to learn how to frame the real without the mediation of concepts, words, and sounds—all would be no less vital for enrolling the individual in the mission of the nation than would generating reproductions showing Hitler or other Nazi leaders in action. In capturing the familiar and producing memento mori of passing realities, amateur photography could not only picture everyday scenes under the sign of Nazi rule. Its mission exceeded the representational. As it situated common users as both subjects *and* objects of technological reproducibility, photographic practice mobilized the people, engineered affects, and embedded the individual as a picture-taking subject in the community of the Volk, independent of the actual content of individual images, frames, and perspectives. To be a good Nazi, in Goebbels's eyes, was to allow photography to permeate all aspects of existence. It was to see the world through a camera's viewfinder, not in order to distance oneself from the visible, but rather to experience the camera's technological logic as a medium for absorbing the particular into the movement of the whole.

Ten years after Goebbels had envisioned photographic practice as an ideal tool for aligning the individual's experience with the national community, Wolfgang Liebeneiner's wartime feature film, *Großstadtmelodie* (*Melody of a Great City*, 1943), illustrated this political mission paradigmatically (figure 5.5). Ravaged by aerial bombardments and other tolls of war, few may have remembered Goebbels's upbeat vision of 1933, let alone be eager to capture the ruins of everyday life with help of a camera. But the film tells the story of Renate Heiberg (Hilde Krahl), a skilled photographer who leaves the Bavarian countryside for Berlin to become a successful photojournalist. Her zeal for picturing what eludes routine ways of looking initially thwarts her career. Berlin's agitated newspaper editors and readers, she learns, have no time for those patiently aiming their camera at the unseen, the forgotten, the unnoticed. Yet, sticking to her guns while adapting to the tempos, rhythms, and demands of the urban metropolis, she ultimately triumphs as a female photographer in a world mostly dominated by men, taking pictures at public events and capturing decisive moments amid Berlin's restless street life, as well as producing poetic vignettes of everyday activities that escape the artificial eye of her colleagues. If Liebeneiner's film initially enters Berlin as if emulating the legacy of the Weimar avant-garde and *Neues Sehen*—the canted angles, unusual camera locations, moving perspectives, and montage sequences are all quite striking—Heiberg's camera teaches something quite different. It celebrates the power of photography to picture the city—its speed, its mobility and agitation, and the indefatigable activities of its citizens—as a defining environment of life in Germany circa 1943, a quasi-natural habitat charged with poetic energy and unifying force.

Unlike most Nazi entertainment films, whether of the 1930s or 1940s, *Melody of a Great City* explicitly cites political actualities. We hear people greeting each other with "Heil Hitler." We follow Heiberg to political rallies and to a concert of Wagner's music, conducted by no less than Wilhelm Furtwängler. We witness Heiberg taking pictures of architectural landmarks and monumental public art à la Breker, a close-up of her head superimposed onto the objects of her view as she peeks through the viewfinder of her state-of-the-art lightweight camera. In one shot, we even see half of a swastika painted on the tail of an airplane, an icon not really visible in any other feature film

5.5 Stills from *Großstadtmelodie* (dir. Wolfgang Liebeneiner, 1943).

produced in Goebbels's "ministry of illusion."[19] What we do *not* see, though, is any trace of war and aerial bombing, of military mobilization and civilian sacrifice. A one-second shot toward the end gives this absence a weak narrative motivation: a rally for the annexation of Austria locates the film's action *ahead of* World War II. Such temporal displacement hardly masks the film's effort at spatial reordering, however. It celebrates cameras as tools of intense looking, hyperattentive framing, physical mobility, and integrating even seemingly forgotten aspects into the larger picture—all at the cost of *not* allowing us to see what no filmmaker, photographer, actor, or spectator in 1943 Berlin could have escaped. No single image of Heiberg's as captured by Liebeneiner "lies" in any strict sense of the world, even if photographs can be said *not* to tell the truth in the first place.[20]

Photography, as presented by Liebeneiner, cannot but be true, not because it produces images that reveal what spectators may believe or know to be true, but because in essence it is not about representing the real at all. Rather, it depicts the ceaseless efforts involved in seeing the world through a camera's viewfinder. Heiberg's most important accomplishment is not to explore new ways of looking at the real and thereby disclose new insights about the texture of the everyday. Instead, she redefines the world as one produced by and for the camera's modern artificial eye, in which photographic reproduction—its presumed objectivity and indexicality—can collapse the space between the individual and the collective and thereby precisely collapse the very kind of intersubjectivity that permits a lie to be called a lie. True to Goebbels's call of 1933, Heiberg's images are all about doing, not representing. They are about sealing off the visible from the discursive, about evacuating reading altogether from the visible world. They elevate the experience of the individual to the experience of the Volk, and in this way they define the world made by cameras and their photographers, whether in 1938 or 1943, as the shared environment of all experience.

Hoffmann's private pictures, far from merely branding Hitler's nonpolitical side as a site of political and economic utility, offered a medium and manual to turn Germans into Renate Heibergs. Their purpose was not simply to soften and popularize the image of the Führer. It was to train viewers to fancy themselves as photographers in their own right; to reframe the world as if seen through a camera's viewfinder; to embrace photographic practice as a medium of social and political integration, embedding an individual's perspective and action within the fabrics of the whole nation; not simply to *map*, but to *produce* the visible world with the help of modern technology.

5.6 "Auch die Jüngsten wollen ihr Hitlerbild haben" (*Hitler wie ihn keiner kennt*, 1932).

As much as they publicized Hitler as the principal sight/site of visual consumption during the Nazi era, Hoffmann's albums promoted photography as a powerful medium for building worlds and thereby redrawing the line between the private and the public, the intimate and the political altogether.

Hoffmann's images emulated and modeled the rhetoric of amateur photography, of how individual "*Knipser*" (amateur photographers) in particular since the second half of the 1920s had increasingly come to document their lives with the help of snapshots and even to center private activities around the presence of a camera and photographer. As importantly, Hoffmann's images—with their stress on postures of focused alertness; on the pleasures of seemingly unmediated, yet framed looking; on acts of visual transport and wondrous experiences of being touched by the presence of the Führer—sought to shape attitudes and modes of perception that corresponded deeply with how photographic cameras were believed to change the modern subject's being in, and impact on, the world. Although Hoffmann himself surely had no desire to give up on his monopoly to deliver Hitler in the form of a mechanical reproduction, his private images of the Führer aspired to no less than retraining the human sensorium. Their ambition was to enlist the value of photography, of a camera's artificial eye, for the sake of mobilizing the nation; their task was to propagate photography as a mode of action and sensory perception, as a shared form of practice. If properly pursued by each and every German, that practice could do at least as much to consolidate the national community as the experience at a party rally, the formation of the crowd through architectural projects, or the militarization of society at all levels of social interaction. Although the concept of fascist aesthetics may have lost both its descriptive and its critical purchase, Hoffmann's work thus remains emblematic. By means of the above reading we can better understand not only what photography did and aspired to do under conditions of Nazi rule, but also the uncanny echoes today between how fascism and our own image-driven times embed technological media in processes of physical and affective mobilization.

Notes

1 On the branding of the private and domestic aspects of Hitler's persona during and after the 1932 election campaign, see Despina Stratigakos, *Hitler at Home* (New Haven, CT: Yale University Press, 2015), 149–60.

2 On Hoffmann's role as Hitler's photographer, see Rudolf Herz, *Hoffmann und Hitler: Fotografie als Medium des Führer-Mythos* (Munich: Klinkhardt and Biermann, 1994); on the adulation of Hitler's body in general and his face in particular, see Claudia Schmölders, *Hitler's Face: The Biography of an Image*, trans. Adrian Daub (Philadelphia: University of Pennsylvania Press, 2009).

3 Walter Benjamin, "The Work of Art in the Age of Its Technological Reproducibility," in *Selected Writings, Vol. 4: 1938–1940*, ed. Howard Eiland and Michael Jennings (Cambridge, MA: Harvard University Press, 2003), 251–83; also Susan Sontag, "Fascinating Fascism," in *Under the Sign of Saturn: Essays* (New York: Farrar, Straus and Giroux, 1980), 73–105.

4 Lutz Koepnick, "Face/Off: Hitler and Weimar Political Photography," in *Visual Culture in Twentieth-Century Germany: Text as Spectacle*, ed. Gail Finney (Bloomington: Indiana University Press, 2006), 216.

5 Ernst Jünger, "Photography and the 'Second Consciousness': An Excerpt from 'On Pain,'" trans. Joel Agee, in *Photography in the Modern Era: European Documents and Critical Writings, 1913–1940*, ed. Christopher Phillips (New York: Metropolitan Museum of Art/Aperture, 1989), 207–10; Helmut Lethen, *Cool Conduct: The Culture of Distance in Weimar Germany*, trans. Don Reneau (Berkeley: University of California Press, 2002); Brigitte Werneburg, "Die veränderte Welt: Der gefährliche anstelle des entscheidenden Augenblicks: Ernst Jüngers Überlegungen zur Fotografie," *Fotogeschichte* 51 (1994): 51–67.

6 See in particular Bernd Hüppauf, "Emptying the Gaze: Framing Violence through the Viewfinder," *New German Critique* 72 (1997): 3–44.

7   Georges Didi-Huberman, *Images malgré tout* (Paris: Les Edition de Minuit, 2003). See also Ulrich Baer, *Spectral Evidence: The Photography of Trauma* (Cambridge, MA: MIT Press, 2002); and Lutz Koepnick, "Photographs and Memories," *South Central Review* 21, no. 1 (spring 2004): 94–129.

8   For the history of amateur photography, see Timm Starl, *Knipser: Die Bildgeschichte der privaten Fotografie in Deutschland und Österreich von 1880 bis 1980* (Munich: Koehler and Amelang, 1995); Rolf Sachsse, *Die Erziehung zum Wegsehen: Fotografie im NS-Staat* (Hamburg: Philo Fine Arts, 2003); Frances Guerin, *Through Amateur Eyes: Film and Photography in Nazi Germany* (Minneapolis: University of Minnesota Press, 2012); Maiken Umbach, "Selfhood, Place, and Ideology in German Photo Albums, 1933–1945," *Central European History* 48 (2015): 335–65.

9   Guerin, *Through Amateur Eyes*, 11–12.

10 Heinrich Hoffmann, *Hitler Was My Friend*, trans. R. H. Stevens (London: Burke, 1955), 42.

11 Heinrich Hoffmann, *Hitler wie ihn keiner kennt: 100 Bilddokumente aus dem Leben des Führers* (Berlin: Zeitgeschichte-Verlag, 1941), xi.

12 Maurice Merleau-Ponty, *Phenomenology of Perception*, trans. Colin Smith (London: Routledge and Kegan Paul, 1965), 93.

13 See, among many others, David Bathrick, "Making a National Family with the Radio: The Nazi Wunschkonzert," *Modernism/Modernity* 4, no. 1 (January 1997): 115–27.

14 See, among others, Peter Fritzsche, *A Nation of Fliers: German Aviation and the Popular Imagination* (Cambridge, MA: Harvard University Press, 1992), 133–220.

15 Carl Schmitt, *Staat, Bewegung, Volk: Die Dreigliederung der politischen Einheit* (Hamburg: Hanseatische Verlagsanstalt, 1933), 42.

16 Ernst H. Kantorowicz, *The King's Two Bodies: A Study in Mediaeval Political Theology* (Princeton, NJ: Princeton University Press, 1958).

17 Joseph Goebbels, "Eröffnungsrede 'Die Kamera': Ausstellung für Fotografie Druck und Reproduktion, Berlin 1933," reprinted in Sachsse, *Die Erziehung zum Wegsehen*, 319–20.

18 Sachsse, *Die Erziehung zum Wegsehen*, 117–41.

19 Eric Rentschler, *The Ministry of Illusion: Nazi Cinema and Its Afterlife* (Cambridge, MA: Harvard University Press, 1996).

20 Martin Jay, "Can Photographs Lie? Reflections on a Perennial Anxiety," *Critical Studies* 2 (2016): 6–19.

6

SEEING THROUGH WHITENESS

*Late 1930s Settler Photography in Namibia
under South African Rule*

LORENA RIZZO

The Spectre of Fascism in the Colony

This essay chooses settler photography in Namibia in the late 1930s as a point of entry into exploring the problem of fascism's visuality in the colony and to reassess fascism's historical trajectories and transnational interweaving.[1] Although addressing German and Italian fascist endeavors in colonial Africa has occasionally served to decenter and refine historical analyses of fascist aesthetics, such scholarship remains caught in a Eurocentrism that treats the colony as a backdrop for metropolitan fantasy and projection.[2] In contrast, I foreground the question of fascist visualities *in* the colony, more specifically in South West Africa. Ruled by Germany between 1884 and 1915, it later became a South African mandate for more than seven decades until independence in 1990. Thinking about the history of South African segregation and apartheid in terms of fascism has intermittently troubled South African historiography and has gathered momentum more recently in transnational and global inquiries into historical configurations of the Far Right.[3] German and Afrikaner sections of South African and South West African society are considered key vectors of fascist thought throughout the subcontinent, but the process has been commonly understood as a symptom of the brittleness of *whiteness* in a settler society divided by antagonistic imperial, national, and ethnic affinities throughout the interwar period.[4]

The spread of fascism in Namibia during the interwar period and the founding of a local branch of the National Socialist German Workers' Party (NSDAP) in 1928 have generally been attributed to sociopolitical erosion and ethnonational revival among German settlers in the colony.[5] Key to this process was the gradual formation of a myth of discrimination that strategically merged memories of internment and large-scale repatriation after the First World War with German-Afrikaner socioeconomic antagonism and competition over land.[6] A growing sense of exclusion paired with feelings of resentment and cultural marginalization among those who had lost the war and "their" colony created fertile ground for the seeds of national socialist thought. While settlers of German descent had long wavered between assimilating into the South African racial fabric of whiteness and retreating into a politics of reified ethnicity based on *Deutschtum*, political distress intensified amid growing Afrikaner nationalism. Talk of South West Africa's inclusion into South Africa as a fifth province threatened to bury hopes of the colony's return to the German "motherland."[7] During the 1930s, systematic NSDAP propaganda backed by substantial material and human resources from Germany enabled Nazism to permeate every aspect of German sociopolitical life in the colony.[8] While pressure was occasionally applied to individuals and groups who questioned the ideological alignment with the Third Reich and insisted on the colony's self-determination, the spread of a fascist mind-set was facilitated by its shared ground with colonialism, which long nurtured the ideas of a master race and blood and soil ideology.[9] Although it tarried in responding to the fascist threat, the South African administration eventually banned the NSDAP in Namibia in 1934, repatriated most of its leaders, and curtailed German immigration and political organization.[10] Finally, at the outbreak of the Second World War, a thin parliamentary majority overcame Afrikaner-nationalist demands for neutrality, and South Africa joined Britain in the war against Hitler.[11] For many German and Boer settlers, who had traceable links to NSDAP organizations, the war inaugurated yet another period of internment and deportation.[12]

Constrained by the conventions of political history and the racial and ethnic categories shaping the focus on inner-white conflict, Namibian historiography only scratches the surface of fascism's spread during the interwar period. Existing accounts assume a causal relation between Germanness and national socialist sympathies, and thus they fade out deeper lines of class, gender, and generational division within the German settler community.[13] Some of these shortcomings come from neglect of archives that would yield a subtler sense of fascism's sedimentation across the Namibian political and social landscape. Indeed, the sources considered herein are drawn predominantly from national socialist propaganda or from files produced by the South African colonial administration in relation to legitimizing its colonial grip on Namibia and preventing hostile political mobilization.[14] Neglected most, though, is the extent of the sympathy for fascism among the African majority in the region. Although the literature refers to political organizations on the Left and African intellectuals in the diaspora mobilizing against the threat of fascism, no historical research investigates black political, intellectual, and everyday responses to the spread of national socialism in Namibia.[15]

Against this historical backdrop, what can photographs produced at the time tell us about the visuality of fascism in Namibia? With this in mind, how should we read the colonial photographic archive of Namibia during the interwar period? How do images as a historical form complicate received understandings of fascism here? Finally, in a context marked by the embroilment of empire and nation, race and ethnicity, colonialism and fascism, how do we clear an analytical space in which to interrogate historical photographs without straightforwardly conflating ideology and the visual?

Visual Layering

Let us move to the Namibian photographs of Ilse Steinhoff and Anneliese Scherz, professional photographers who operated within colonial and metropolitan visual economies where women of European descent were successfully claiming a share.[16] While Steinhoff's photographic journeys through the former German colonies of South West and East Africa have been taken as an example of Third Reich colonial revisionist propaganda,[17] Scherz's oeuvre, in contrast, has received much less attention, being associated with amateur research in the context of interwar German cultural production.[18] The photography of these two women seems to suggest antagonistic ideological and aesthetic positions. Yet it seems worth exploring whether and how their work, once placed alongside each other, spoke to cultural imaginaries *in the colony itself*, thereby complicating metropolitan articulations of fascist visuality.

Ilse Steinhoff traveled as a photojournalist through South West and East Africa in late 1937 and early 1938. The source of the commission for her travels to the continent remains unclear,[19] but the trajectories of her photographs across various publications and archives, in both Germany and southern Africa, suggest a dynamic of image production, circulation, and consumption that lies partly beyond the axis of the German metropole and its former colonies. Steinhoff's photographs were published in *Illustrierter Beobachter*, the official NSDAP magazine, in 1937 and 1938; they were included in reportages in *Berliner Illustrierte Zeitung* and the more liberal travel magazine *Atlantis*; and they eventually were reused in *Deutsche Heimat in Afrika*.[20] These publications helped situate her images in the photojournalism that had flourished during the Weimar Republic and continued into the period of the Third Reich.[21] Steinhoff belongs conclusively among a number of women professional photographers whose work transcended the framework of temperate colonial desire and moved, after 1933, into the strident ideological framework of colonial revisionism.[22] Yet, unbeknownst to previous commentators, parts of Steinhoff's published *and* unpublished photographic works are preserved today in at least two archival institutions in Germany and South Africa.[23] By linking the photographic holdings of these archives to Steinhoff's published images, we can unearth some less conspicuous facets of metropolitan and colonial image use and circulation, while tracking the images' opportunistic movement into and out of fascist propaganda.[24]

DEUTSCHE HEIMAT IN AFRIKA AND FASCIST AESTHETICS IN SOUTH WEST AFRICA

Deutsche Heimat in Afrika: Ein Bildbuch aus unseren Kolonien was first published in 1939 and again in 1941. It took the reader on a visual journey to African colonies that were boldly declared to belong to Germany and hence part of an extended German homeland. Divided into two sections, the book covered what Steinhoff called "German South West" and "German East" Africa, what were at the time the two mandated territories of South West Africa under South African colonial rule, and Tanganyika under British colonial rule. Both parts of the book were narrated as the photographic diary of a traveler, but their positioning within the ideological frameworks of national socialism and colonial revisionism told surprisingly different stories.

Steinhoff's Namibian photographs are at the center of Willeke Sandler's reading of *Deutsche Heimat in Afrika*.[25] Keeping in mind the possibility of censorship the German Colonial League imposed on images and writings, Sandler notes the centrality of the text-image relationship in the book, along with how Steinhoff deliberately guides her readers' perceptions of the photographs.[26] The captions indeed impose themselves on the photographs, as if concerned with narrowing their semantic instability,[27] and it was the particular configuration of captioned images with the book's focus on key elements of national socialist colonial imaginaries that blended into the revisionist project of Third Reich propaganda with such ease. The South West African colony was presented as a place where fellow Germans secured industriousness and cultural self-consciousness, the actuality of *Deutschtum*, and the values of communal and family life and maintained racial purity while concurrently fostering peaceful relations with a sympathetic colonized population.[28] Sandler continues to argue that it was German colonial women in particular who were given a crucial role in conveying the colony's pervasiveness in mid-twentieth-century German fascist ideology.[29]

Farm life featured prominently in Steinhoff's narrative, and most of the chosen images showed female farmers at work, attending to children and livestock, carrying out domestic activities or overseeing cattle and sheep (figure 6.1). Aestheticizing female domesticity, these images conveyed an affective quality to corporal work, representing it as an expression of the transformative value of colonial women's life.[30] At the same time, an ambiguity in the representation of women's roles in the colony often served as testing ground for female identities.[31] Steinhoff's own African adventure was but one indication of how female subjectivities changed in Germany during the period after World War I. Her aesthetics became more sophisticated in the futuristic framing of colonial women encountered at the forefront of physical performance-cum-technological innovation.[32] Still, celebration of women's modernity and expanded spheres of action remained tentative, and the representational idealization of German settler women seemed to rely less on equality with German men than on its visual and discursive juxtaposition to African women *and* men.[33] Throughout the book, Steinhoff's language, her insidious captioning, repeatedly debased local women and men to objects of cultural curiosity and racial prejudice, thereby cementing the reality of racial difference and the need for civilizing guidance under colonial rule— desirably kept in firm German hands.

Sandler's reading of *Deutsche Heimat in Afrika* concludes with a reference

6.1 Farm Nakusib, Hartmann family, Steinhoff, 1939.

to those photographs, in which Steinhoff made explicit claim to contemporary German presence and the settler community's ideological alignment with national socialism.[34] With one exception, Steinhoff's images showing explicit Nazi posture and insignia all concern youth, depicting boy and girl scouts, schoolchildren, and a school gathering. Although images of youth resonated strongly with key means of Third Reich social mobilization and ideological coordination,[35] the photographs' embeddedness in a series that covered diverse educational institutions in the colony, including mission and vocational schools, seems counterintuitive to mitigating a more straightforward visual narration. The general sparsity of crude fascist visualization in the book seems especially noteworthy: only a few photographs document explicit national socialist iconographies such as the swastika or the Nazi flag. Indeed, Sandler fails to explain why most of Steinhoff's photographs did not sit comfortably with an unambiguous fascist visuality. Still more, what was *fascist* about those few images that did?

Once we move away from implicit charges of fascist aesthetics—that is,

Steinhoff's undoubted national socialist orientation[36]—and cease reading the photographs as signature images for fascism's racial and gender regimes,[37] a different interpretative path can open up that departs from Steinhoff's own narrative and disturbs the photographer's homogenizing gaze. The diversity of image subjects and genres featured in *Deutsche Heimat in Afrika*, then, points to the visual complexity of Steinhoff's photographic engagement with the South West African environment. Indeed, almost half of the book's Namibian photographs are portraits of groups and individuals, and their aesthetic variety eludes any simple blending into ideologically circumscribed categories of race, class, or gender.[38] How, in fact, do we account for the portraits of African women in beautiful attire or African children reading and writing? How can we explain photographs of Africans promenading in the streets of Windhoek, sometimes alongside "whites"? And would these photographs have inevitably incited the fascist vision of an "inferior race" rightfully placed under colonial rule?

STEINHOFF PHOTOGRAPHS IN THE IMAGE COLLECTION
OF THE GERMAN COLONIAL SOCIETY

Steinhoff was quite ingenuous in making her readers believe in the unmediated and sensual character of her photographic work.[39] She claimed that her camera merely documented what she saw during her journey through South West Africa, as though her photographs simply recorded what appeared in front of her eyes. Evoking the medium's realism undoubtedly substantiated the gravitas of German presence in the former colony, and her strategic comments on the risks of camera work lent authenticity to her visual narrative. It was indeed photography's propensity to merge the realistic and the sensual that made the medium so appealing to propaganda, as it enabled audiences to translate the act of *seeing* into one of tangible experience and cognition—of a colonial landscape that remained, in reality, remote.[40] Yet, as much as the programmatic visual account of *Deutsche Heimat in Afrika* was geared toward conflating metropole and colony, and Germany's past and future as a colonial power, it was precisely through the photographs that the colony's presence persisted and formed cracks in the visual architecture of national socialist propaganda. To locate these fissures in Steinhoff's images, we need to consider the archival extensions of her photography.

The photographic collection of the German Colonial Society is suggestive of the process of image selection, exclusion, and inclusion that preceded the publication of *Deutsche Heimat in Afrika*, and of the ways in which the book eclipsed the intricate seriality of photographic production by rendering single photographs as emblematic.[41] The archive likewise provides a subtler sense of Steinhoff's photographic practice *on the ground* and the transitory character of her sojourn and travels. The photographer's South West African journey takes us along a distinctive selection of sites that delineated the space and time of the colony in very particular ways.

When we pay careful attention to the precise locations depicted in the images, we move into the domain of settler topography, the material deposits of white land appropriation, and its photographic consolidation through the medium of landscape.[42] This topographical mapping drew on a double temporality: it used photography to highlight the here and now of white claims to land so that the photographic signification of colonial history naturalized these claims within the framework of settler historiography that had been on the upswing since the 1920s.[43] If anchoring settler subjectivity in the political imaginary of landownership strongly resonated with broader visual configurations of whiteness in southern Africa of the time, then Steinhoff's photographs were decisively engendered by local concerns as well, among them German farmers' assertions of land ownership in relation to settlers of Boer and British South African descent.[44] These become legible in the strategic assortment of the particular farms Steinhoff visited during her journey, a selection almost certainly authored by local travel companions.[45] Figure 6.2 captures the breathtaking vista from the main house on farm Okosongomingo toward the Waterberg massif, an iconic site in the history of the South West African war of 1904–7.[46] In the late 1930s, Okosongomingo and all other farms Steinhoff photographed were among the high-ranking, substantial, and highly capitalized estates owned by some of the most prominent and long-established farmer families of German descent, and Steinhoff's extended archive perpetuated their claim to economic hegemony.[47] But something else percolated through Steinhoff's farm images, particularly once she moved northward to a frontier zone that shadowed out the texture of a consolidating economic and racial order in the colony. The farms Onguma and Nakusib, for example, were situated in close proximity to both the Etosha game reserve and the northern "native reserve" of Ovamboland. The farm owners, the Hartmann and Böhme families, had used the favorable location astutely, building up lucrative transport, trade, and game hunting businesses both under the guise of official authorization and in the more adventurous format of smuggling.[48] Numerous farm photographs taken by Steinhoff inscribed the racialized nature of colonial labor relations and enshrined Af-

6.2 Farm
Okosongomingo.
German Colonial Society
Image Collection,
University Library
Frankfurt.

rican presence on "white"-owned farms as the result of settler benevolence. On the northern frontier and on Nakusib in particular, though, the visual resonances had a further purview into the system of migrant labor that had parasitically spread into Owambo. This system bound men from the northern reserve to year-long contract work on farms and mines across the Namibian colony and beyond.[49]

Migrant labor served as the photographic thread into and across a series of images taken by Steinhoff in and around the Tsumeb copper mine, which returned into the hands of private German financiers in 1936.[50] Here again, her visual language shifted and reenacted more ambitious motifs. Adopting an increasingly modernist tone, her photographs aestheticized German industrial infrastructure by, for example, placing the monumentality and power of Tsumeb's lead furnaces in dramatic opposition to the minuteness and fragility of the miners' bodies. On the other hand, it was on the mines that her camera most clearly faced away from the programmatic and scanned the extractive mining economy on the northern Namibian frontier. The photographs taken in the workers' compound in Tsumeb, for example, might appear as the mere result of the intrusion by a "white" woman into a secluded space for "black" men, but these images also referenced a longer history of control and isolation of contract workers who had been placed under the regime of migrant labor and its biopolitical rationale.[51]

The described conditions of Africans present on farms and in mines pointedly double back on the larger body of photographs included in *Deutsche Heimat in Afrika*. Steinhoff's narrative used images of the local population as evidence for indigenous approval of contemporary economic and future political submission to German colonial rule. The carefully staged photographs of Herero material culture and ritual performance seem to be a case in point. But these images of women in Victorian dress and men in German military uniform also bore the imprint of a subaltern temporality, one that invoked the colonial war and its massive repercussions across African society, while retaining the potential disclosure of forms of embodied memory, collective commemoration, and enactments of historical consciousness, even if the images were eclipsed by the intrusiveness of texts and captions.[52] Against all odds, one is tempted to say that the photographs remained ambiguous and hesitant in the book, but more distinctively in their archival dissemination, where they enabled multiple temporalities to fold into each other and insert the Namibian landscape as a visually constitutive presence. It was the space and time of the colony (not the metropole) that served as the template for the visual positioning of the African subject, thereby disturbing the teleology of Steinhoff's colonial retrieval tuned toward the national socialist imaginary.

STEINHOFF PHOTOGRAPHS IN THE IMAGE COLLECTION
OF THE TRANSNET HERITAGE LIBRARY

The pervasiveness of a colonial representational order, and the movement of Steinhoff's photography into and out of propaganda, gathers further strength through some of her images in an album kept in the archives of the Transnet Heritage Library in Johannesburg.[53] The album extends the scale and scope of Steinhoff's visual topography mapped in *Deutsche Heimat in Afrika* and blends her photographs into a visual survey conducted under the aegis of South African Railways and Harbours (SAR&H). SAR&H was at the time the key commissioner and publisher of photographic images that helped configure the imaginary of an inclusive whiteness grounded in a distinctive notion of landscape to the benefit of an emerging, modern South African nation after Union in 1910.[54] Compared with *Deutsche Heimat in Afrika*, the rail-

6.3 Street in Windhoek, Ilse Steinhoff, from Album 25, Transnet Heritage Library.

way album includes many more portraits of Steinhoff herself, thereby point-ing to the centrality of mobility within the imaginary advanced by SAR&H. By evoking the visuality of "trekking" or being *"auf Pad,"* her photographs forged links with historically embedded repertoires of travel that lent local flavor to SAR&H's growing orientation toward international audiences. Ac-cordingly, her depictions of "natives" as ethnographic curiosity kept their currency once they moved from *Deutsche Heimat in Afrika* into the railway archives and acquired meaning as part of a larger conception of constricted African presence on the land.

The numerous images of the built environment rendered a smooth tran-sition from the transitory image world of trekking into visual solidity. Many of these were not used in Steinhoff's book, as they were no help in visualizing the German cultural imprint on South West Africa's urban landscape.[55] Of-ten focused on railway stations, the street views matched SAR&H's key preoc-cupation with producing a consolidated nation-space marked by the homo-geneity of railway infrastructure and a modern regime of rationalized time.[56] But more importantly, these images disclose rare hints at "white" mobility's "other." Steinhoff had a good eye for the subtleties of *being* in a racially fragmented space. Her backlit male African silhouette in figure 6.3, for example, appears to be lost, misplaced in an urban milieu not his own, his luggage silently marking an unpredictable, disorganized temporality: one that would likely make the man wait for hours, watching cars drive past him, eventually to be removed from the site of futile waiting *and* the sight of "white" urban residents. These streetscapes assured audiences that by the 1930s even the remotest towns in the Namibian colony had become proper white towns and thus desirable travel destinations and residential locations. Once they entered the archives of SAR&H, Steinhoff's images hence became part of an aesthetic exploration that clearly outgrew the narrow confines of national socialist desire and propaganda. Here, her photographs worked toward a copious visual economy that served the constitution of an inclusive white identity grounded in a specific construction of the physical and social environment.[57] Photography along the railway patched the fissures of inner-white division—between settlers of English, Boer, *and* German descent. It articulated what it meant, for all of them, to be white in a future held by South African national and imperial reconstruction.

Anneliese Scherz and the Visuality of Retreat

The problem of photography, sight, and whiteness brings us to the photographic work of Anneliese Scherz, a German who emigrated to Namibia in the late 1930s.[58] The following inquiry proposes a reading of some of the Scherz photographs *alongside* those of Steinhoff in order to determine whether these photographs reveal a different kind of aesthetic negotiation. Using Scherz's photographs to think about the problem of fascism's visuality in the colony might enable insights that trim back the notion of an image world— the domain of German photographic production in Namibia of the time— unambiguously aligned with a particular ideological formation and historical teleology.[59]

Anneliese Scherz moved to South West Africa in 1938, but unlike Ilse Steinhoff, she remained there for almost forty years. Her photographic oeuvre is part of a personal archive containing photographs, correspondence, and manuscripts by herself and her husband, Ernst Rudolf.[60] Attributing single photographs to one individual is often difficult in this archive.[61] The couple's Namibian careers differed to some extent, and Anneliese's training and practice as a professional photographer was ultimately more consistent, a circumstance potentially privileging her authorship.[62] As already mentioned, Scherz's photographs belong to the domain of German cultural work in interwar Namibia, more specifically, the field of semiprofessional visual production and writing. Sections of the wider settler-community—individuals of diverse ethnic descent, social standing, and political *couleur*—were increasingly concerned to establish niches of knowledge production that appealed to South African and metropolitan culture.[63] In a broader context of 1930s settler photography, Scherz's photographs are quite consistent with the broader image economy in terms of both genres and subjects chosen for photographic documentation.[64] Far less obvious is the remarkable visual consonance between Scherz's early South West African images and Steinhoff's travel photography, a convergence partly explicable by the German sociocultural milieu framing both women's entrance into the photographic practice of the time. Still, the shared grounds need further explanation, and although particular photographic subjects surface in both oeuvres, Scherz's photographs clearly adopted a different, less programmatic tone in the visual scanning of the physical and sociopolitical spaces they traversed.

VISUALITY OF RETREAT

Much like Steinhoff's archive, the Scherz collection circles around the space and subject matter of farm life. That Anneliese Scherz was in the process of relocating from Germany to South West Africa, joining her husband for their honeymoon during 1938, allows us to read these photographs for their personal and familial meanings that are intrinsically bound to a politics of sentiment.[65] Indeed, most of the early images were never published, nor were they ever intended for public viewing.

Figure 6.4 is drawn from a series of portraits, photographs of farm interiors and everyday objects taken during the 1938 honeymoon. Many of these speak for an aesthetic sensibility toward family as an emotional space enshrined in transgenerational solidarity, personal affection, and intimate sociality. The moment captured is one of ease and serenity: a man in work wear, interrupting his farming duties to retreat to the cooling shade of the porch, smoking his pipe, gently holding the child in his lap, visibly feeling comfortable. The soft lighting enhances the beauty of the scene—of *a* father lovingly attending to *his* child—while concurrently evoking generic sentimental registers associated with the photographic trope of parental love.[66] Although the man, and many of the photographic subjects in this series, remains unidentified, Scherz's photographs introduce us to individuals, particular men

6.4 Uncaptioned image. S004_107, BAB Scherz Collection from Album Hochzeitsreise 1938.

and women, who inhabit the privacy and intimacy of their family and farm worlds, who appear relaxed, smiling, enjoying the rare moments of rest, the pleasure of a shared meal, *and* the poetics of photographic contemplation. Keeping in mind that the Scherzes had recently arrived in Namibia and Anneliese had before moved among cosmopolitan photographers and artists in a Europe about to descend disastrously into war and fascist terror, the 1938 farm portraits and scenes make photographic homage to the *pastoral*, to the simplicity and beauty of the rural, a visual valorization of a primordial spatiality and temporality embedded in farm work and domestic life that required the camera to approach its subjects with appreciation and respect. The familial and transgenerational cohabitation may also have been a romantic anticipation of the newlyweds' future. But even along these lines, the photographs taken during their honeymoon evoked longer trajectories of aestheticized farm life and its sentimentally charged imaginary.[67] The intimate privacy in the framings of farm and family life, the beauty of the portraits that individualized their subjects, *and* the archival seclusion of these particular images in the Scherz collection aesthetically elude any overt absorption into the political hegemony of late 1930s propaganda, whether in colonial revisionist or national socialist guise. It was indeed the *moment* rather than the *momentous* that asserted itself in the portraits. In this aesthetic language the German-speaking farmers in the community were neither an abstract category comprising individual types nor an essentialized register for the articulation of political—that is, fascist—subjectivity, but rather a visually receding social milieu where the intimacy and privacy of individual positionality could be quietly fathomed. Read alongside, yet in contrast to, Ilse Steinhoff's contemporary work, Scherz's photographs accordingly point toward a rather different sensitivity or state of mind: one that presumably faced the spectre of fascism yet chose to express itself in what might be called a *visuality of retreat*.

HIERARCHIES OF VISUAL PHILANTHROPY

The notion of a visuality of retreat reads the interiority and subjectivity in the Scherz portraits as a counternarrative to the exteriority and objectification of German colonial and national socialist visuality. Yet, although this holds true for parts of the archive, other images reveal the collection's more venturous openings toward the public, the political, and the ideological.[68]

One of these openings comes through a series labeled "Boers on the move" in which the photographic camera left the farmhouse and its immediate surroundings for the open *veld*.[69] The labels for these photographs were quite suggestive in situating their subjects and scenes within a particular sociocultural and pertinently political frame—that of Afrikaner nationalism. As seen in figure 6.5, the photographs of Afrikaans-speaking farmers brought into focus the subjects and objects of a nomadic lifestyle shadowed out by household effects unhandily placed in the open, and usually embodied by women performing domestic work under arduous environmental conditions. Selected material markers of the trek, among them ox wagons, horses, and female garb, further specified the vernacular iconography of Afrikaner historical mythology and folklore.[70] Whether the Scherzes were familiar with the trope of "poor white-ism," which the photographic discourse of poverty and vulnerability among white settlers and farming communities had produced in southern Africa and elsewhere, remains unclear. But the "Boers on the move" series undoubtedly shared representational and aesthetic characteristics with photographs commissioned by the South African Carnegie Commission of 1932 or by the U.S. Farm Security Administration in the 1930s and 1940s.[71] If poor white-ism had become a key theme in the political fabrication of a consolidated white identity in South Africa, then in the Namibian colony it crumbled more along the fault lines of a frail white solidarity pointedly marked by rivalry over land between settlers of German descent and Afrikaner immigrants.[72] Placed against the backdrop of these fraught politi-

6.5 Image from
"'Boers on the move"
series. S004_152, BAB
Scherz Collection,
Hochzeitsreise 1938.

cal complexities, which pitted white solidarity against white sectarianism, Scherz's photographs of impoverished Boer farmers lacked any self-evident programmatic orientation that fueled anti-Afrikaner or partisan articulations of German colonial revisionism. This calls into question the semantic frame imposed on the photographic by the textual—that is, by the label "Boers on the move"—and its privileging of an interwar politics of ethnic difference. Paying attention instead to the camera's focus on *the material*—on the objects, fabrics, and sites of the nomadic—evokes an opening of a different kind. In fact, the question of lifestyles and living standards, based on permanent settlement and meticulously defined requirements for housing, had become normative for a generic understanding of "being white" in Namibia and South Africa in the 1930s.[73] It was this particular materiality of whiteness that endowed the "Boers on the move" series with the quality of *visual philanthropy*, in that it proved sensitive to the everyday normativities of being "white" and thereby ingeniously eclipsed the ways in which it drew less on a politics of ethnic essentialism than on one of colonial racism.[74]

The colonial racial order does indeed resonate across the Scherz archive, but its sedimentation at the level of the visual and even in the single image remains problematic. Pointing to some of the instances in which this collection sheds light on the problem of race and photography implies a de-

6.6 "Eingeborene in
Haribes." S004_160,
BAB Scherz Collection,
Hochzeitsreise 1938.

notative rather than assertive language, as, for example, when we look at
the configuration of a key visual figure, such as the "black farm laborer." As
argued before, the threat of fascism lurking on the colony's political horizon gave pause to the photographic reflection of whiteness. But what was its
bearing—if any—on the camera's framing of blackness?

The figure of the black laborer in this archive emerges first while the camera wandered around the farm and captured unidentified, solitary women
washing linen or fetching water and men stowing away tools and appliances.[75]
The workers' presence in the photographs is silent and unobtrusive, insert-
ing itself almost naturally into the physical environment of farm life. While
aesthetically more sophisticated, farm labor appears in accordance with its
configuration in Steinhoff's photographs. But unlike the latter, the Scherz
archive proves less consistent and gives way to a remarkable framing of African labor, as shown in figure 6.6, where a group of women, children, and one
man lined up in front of Scherz's camera. This photograph has an oppressive
quality in the way it exposes the vulnerability of the black subject's positioning, and the little girl's marvel at the scene proves to be the image's arresting
detail, its intriguing *punctum*.[76] But the semantic contours of this photograph
are outlined most clearly through its archival proximity to the "Boers on the

move" series: it ultimately denotes simply the poverty and precariousness of colonial servitude and raises the question of the relationship of these "other poor" to the visual philanthropy described above. Does the Scherz archive address black poverty in a way that allows for *blackness as vulnerability* to emerge as a shared status with whiteness and accordingly invite the viewer's empathic response?[77] While this possibility is lodged in the photograph itself, it fizzles out in the shallow depth of the farm as a constitutive site of a colonial economy, in which empathy ran against the fact that, for the black subject, labor was the only way out of the poverty it had produced in the first place.

THE SILENT SPECTRE OF FASCISM

What does Scherz's photographic configuration of whiteness as a modality of seeing, and its dialectical counterpiece blackness, tell us about the visuality of fascism in the Namibian colony? In contrast to Steinhoff's photographs, in which the influence of colonial revisionism and national socialism is striking, the Scherz archive is much harder to read. We might understand the Scherzes' *photographic* negotiation of their transition from fascist Germany to colonial Namibia simply as a matter of empire, that is, as the unilateral movement of people and things. Yet, we should likewise pay attention to the ways in which their transition consisted in the remaking of a visual epistemology that was precisely dependent on and engendered by the diachronic formation of fascism across empire.[78] Thinking about Scherz's photographs along these lines has brought to light a visuality of retreat—that is, a renegotiation of photography, ideology, and politics—and a visual philanthropy with its particular notion of whiteness enshrined in seeing blackness. These are but the first components of a late 1930s settler visuality that crisscrossed conventional distinctions between the private and the public, the political and ideological, and was ultimately preoccupied with scraping out what held the promise of persistence. Here the concern was less to make one's choice between the *imperial either-or*—South African incorporation versus German national socialist amalgamation—but more to secure the kernel of a *colonial anyway*, or the material standards of white privilege and a racialized labor regime.

A few archival *casts of fortune* exist though—photographs from the Scherz collection that constitute less elusive evidence for how fascism haunts this archive, even if it does so from the margins. One of them depicts a cryptic assemblage of letters, symbols, and dates engraved on a rock formation.[79] While the image opens up diverse speculative paths into the depth and breadth of love (the heart, the initials) and religion (God and Christian nationalism), our object of reflection here is a swastika engraved in the rock. What caught the attention of Scherz's camera needs explanation: it might have been, of course, mere curiosity, even a sense of inappropriateness in view of a problematic political iconography, that informed the desire to document the site. Yet, other reasons explain why the material visuality of *this* swastika must have spoken to the Scherzes in particular ways, as it bizarrely resonated with one of their key fields of interest—rock art, archaeology—and their media: sketching, drawing, and photography.[80] But how exactly does the photograph visualize fascism, and what does its particular visualization tell us about fascism's presence in the Scherz archive?

The image of an engraved swastika is emblematic because of an intricate ambiguity, which applies first in terms of time as both persistence and decay, of presence and absence, in that the photograph highlights the swastika as an image set in stone, a condition of petrification marking endurance *and* the fragility of power and the force of destruction.[81] Here the image displaces its object, in essence a swastika-as-petroglyph, into an analogy with archaeology and its idiosyncratic temporality, its work of salvage, documentation, and preservation, against disappearance and for the sake of survival.[82] And second, an ambiguity exists at the level of visibility once the photograph brings to light an object that would otherwise have remained out of sight, buried, withdrawn from sensual perception, but would nevertheless claim unlimited visibility and tangibility through its persistent materiality. It is, in short, the described ambiguity of the photograph in terms of presence/absence and in/visibility that qualifies the visualization of fascism in the Scherz archive as a *spectral* one.

Epilogue: The Visuality of Fascism in the Colony

The photographs of Ilse Steinhoff and Anneliese (and Ernst Rudolf) Scherz carried markedly differing meanings in a late 1930s political climate marked by colonialism and nationalism, by ethnic sectarianism and the politics of whiteness, by German national socialism, and by South African imperialism. While Steinhoff's photographs were part of an explicit colonial revisionist and fascist imaginary, the Scherzes' images aligned themselves less obviously with a clear ideological program. Yet, if fascist visuality becomes harder to find in the former, then it seems more insidiously present in the latter. It has appeared in this essay not just through the lens of photography in the colony, but in relation to the colony's spatiality and temporality as they permeate

6.7 Unidentified women, n.p., Steinhoff, 1939.

photographic representation. The relationship between fascism and colonialism is actually an "old" historical problem. Before and after World War II, their mutual complicity was repeatedly addressed in black political thought, whose exponents eventually adopted the fiercer tone appropriate for a world shattered by fascism.[83] Whereas debate over these questions exceeds the histories of photography, the Namibian case study nonetheless confronts us with this problem. My reading of the photographs in the Scherz collection shows them to be deeply embroiled in precisely the desire to establish colonialism as *different*: as an aesthetic order both distinctive to the colony and unrelated to fascism. What were the stakes in making such a distinction? To whom did the distinction between the spectre of fascism and an ongoing colonial order make a difference politically, ideologically, and in terms of vision? Ironically, Steinhoff's *Deutsche Heimat in Afrika* provides a reminder of this (figure 6.7). The photograph itself contains an oddity—the swastika on the roof of a cooling house. But far more importantly, the image invites us to ask, What did the two women see?

Notes

1 Andreas Umland, "Diachronic and Cross-Cultural Comparison: Toward a Better Understanding of International Fascism," *Fascism* 1 (2012): 62–63.

2 George Steinmetz and Julia Hell, "The Visual Archive of Colonialism: Germany and Namibia," *Public Culture* 18, no. 1 (2006): 147–84; Volker Langbehn, ed., *German Colonialism, Visual Culture, and Modern Memory* (New York: Routledge, 2010); Ruth Ben-Ghiat, *Italian Fascism's Empire Cinema* (Bloomington: Indiana University Press, 2015).

3 Brian Bunting, *The Rise of the South African Reich* (London: Penguin, 1964); Howard Simson, *The Social Origins of Afrikaner Fascism and Its Apartheid Policy* (Stockholm: Almqvist and Wiksell International, 1980); Albrecht Hagemann, "Nationalsozialismus, Afrikaaner Nationalismus, und die Entstehung der Apartheid in Südafrika," *Vierteljahrshefte für Zeitgeschichte* 39, no. 3 (1991): 413–36; Hermann Giliomee, "The Making of the Apartheid Plan, 1929–48," *Journal of Southern African Studies* 29, no. 2 (2003): 373–92. And see, more recently, Patrick J. Furlong, "The National Party of South Africa: A Transnational Perspective," in *New Perspectives on the Transnational Right*, ed. M. Durham and M. Power (New York: Palgrave Macmillan, 2010), 67–84.

4 Saul Dubow, "Afrikaner Nationalism, Apartheid and the Conceptualization of Race," *Journal of African History* 33, no. 2 (1992): 209–37; Jeremy Silvester, Marion Wallace, and Patricia Hayes, "'Trees Never Meet': Mobility and Containment: An Overview, 1915–46," in *Namibia under South African Rule: Mobility and Containment, 1915–46*, ed. Patricia Hayes, Jeremy Silvester, Marion Wallace, and Wolfram Hartmann (Athens: Ohio University Press, 1998), 3–49. See also Ethan Mark, chapter 8 in this volume.

5 Brigitta Schmidt-Lauber, *Die abhängigen Herren. Deutsche Identität in Namibia. Interethnische Beziehungen und Kulturwandel* (Münster: Lit Verlag, 1993), 74; Richard Dale, "Reconfiguring White Ethnic Power in Colonial Africa: The German Community in Namibia, 1923–1950," *Nationalism and Ethnic Politics* 7, no. 2 (2001): 75–94.

6 Heinrich Stuebel, "Die Entwicklung des Nationalsozialismus in Südwestafrika," *Vierteljahrsherfte für Zeitgeschichte* 1, no. 2 (1953): 170–76; Robert J. Gordon, "The Impact of the Second World War on Namibia," in "Namibia: Africa's Youngest Nation," special issue, *Journal of Southern African Studies* 19, no. 1 (1993): 149; Martin Eberhardt, *Zwischen Nationalsozialismus und Apartheid. Die deutsche Bevölkerungsgruppe Südwestafrikas 1915–1965* (Berlin: Lit, 2005), 106; Reinhart Kössler, *Namibia and Germany: Negotiating the Past* (Windhoek: University of Namibia Press, 2015), 106.

7 Schmidt-Lauber, *Die abhängigen Herren*, 77; Hagemann, "Nationalsozialismus," 422.

8 Schmidt-Lauber, *Die abhängigen Herren*, 74; Kössler, *Namibia and Germany*, 104; Furlong, "The National Party of South Africa," 70; Eberhardt, *Zwischen Nationalsozialismus und Apartheid*, 283–96.

9 Silvester et al., "'Trees Never Meet,'" 38; Stuebel, "Die Entwicklung des Nationalsozia-lismus in Südwestafrika," 176; Schmidt-Lauber, *Die abhängigen Herren*, 76, 77; Udo Rainer Krautwurst, "Tales of the 'Land of Stories': Settlers and Anti-modernity in German Colonial Discourses on German South West Africa, 1884–1914" (PhD diss., University of Connecticut, 1997), 506; Hagemann, "Nationalsozialismus," 423.

10 Gordon, "The Impact of the Second World War on Namibia," 149–50; Schmidt-Lauber, *Die abhängigen Herren*, 75.

11 See especially Hagemann, "Nationalsozialismus"; and Furlong, "The National Party of South Africa."

12 Schmidt-Lauber, *Die abhängigen Herren*, 78; Stuebel, "Die Entwicklung des Na-tionalsozialismus in Südwestafrika," 176.

13 Silvester et al., "'Trees Never Meet,'" 37; Eberhardt, *Zwischen Nationalsozialismus und Apartheid*, 283.

14 The most comprehensive research based on an analysis of materials produced by NSDAP branches and affiliated German political organizations in Namibia is Eberhardt, *Zwischen Nationalsozialismus und Apartheid*. See also Gordon, "The Impact of the Second World War on Namibia," 150–51.

15 Les Switzer, ed., *South Africa's Alternative Press: Voices of Protest and Resistance, 1880–1960* (Cambridge: Cambridge University Press, 1997), 335; Marc Matera, *Black London: The Imperial Metropolis and Decolonization in the Twentieth Cen-tury* (Oakland: University of California Press, 2015), 96. A few clues can be found in the literature, among them reports of northern Namibian migrant workers singing "Hitler Ote Ya" (Hitler is coming) in 1939 and the rise of "Nazi millenari-anism" among mission-educated black men in the 1930s. See Kössler, *Namibia and Germany*, 105; Wolfgang Werner, "'Playing Soldiers': The Truppenspieler Move-ment among the Herero of Namibia, 1915 to ca. 1945," *Journal of Southern African Studies* 16, no. 3 (1990): 494.

16 Jeremy Silvester, Patricia Hayes, and Wolfram Hartmann, "'This Ideal Conquest': Photography and Colonialism in Namibian History," in Hayes et al., *Namibia un-der South African Rule*, 14. The concept of visual economy was coined by Deborah Poole in her *Vision, Race, and Modernity: A Visual Economy of the Andean Image World* (Princeton, NJ: Princeton University Press, 1997).

17 See H. Stahr, *Fotojournalismus zwischen Exotismus und Rassismus: Darstellungen von Schwarzen und Indianern in Foto-Text-Artikeln deutscher Wochenillustrierter 1919–1939* (Hamburg: Verlag Dr. Kovak, 2004), 324–26; Dag Henrichsen, "'Lees!' Historical Photography, Public Reading Sites and Visuals," in *Posters in Action: Visuality in the Making of an African Nation*, ed. Giorgio Miescher, Lorena Rizzo, and Jeremy Silvester (Basel: Basler Afrika Bibliographien, 2009), 45–57; Willeke Sandler, "Deutsche Heimat in Afrika: Colonial Revisionism and the Construction of Germanness through Photography," *Journal of Women's History* 25, no. 1 (2013): 37–61.

18 Dag Henrichsen, "Teilnachlass E.R. & A. Scherz im Personenarchiv der Basler Af-rika Bibliographien," unpublished library finding aid, Basel, 1990, 5.

19 Stahr, *Fotojournalismus zwischen Exotismus und Rassismus*; and Sandler, "Deutsche Heimat in Afrika."

20 Stahr, *Fotojournalismus zwischen Exotismus und Rassismus*; and Henrichsen, "Lees!," 44fn3.

21 Stahr, *Fotojournalismus zwischen Exotismus und Rassismus*; and Henrichsen, "Lees!," Birthe Kundrus, ed., *Phantasiereiche: Zur Kulturgeschichte des deutschen Kolonialismus* (Frankfurt: Campus, 2003).

22 Stahr, *Fotojournalismus zwischen Exotismus und Rassismus*; and Henrichsen, "Lees!"

23 The collections of the German Colonial Society are kept in the University Library in Frankfurt, accessible online through http://www.ub.uni-frankfurt.de/afrika /bildsammlung.html. On the photographic collection in the Transnet Heritage Library in Johannesburg, see Giorgio Miescher, "Arteries of Empire: On the Geographical Imagination of South Africa's Railway War 1914/1915," *Kronos* 38, no. 1 (2012): 46.

24 On fascism's opportunism as propaganda, see the introduction to this volume.

25 Sandler, "Deutsche Heimat in Afrika."

26 Sandler, "Deutsche Heimat in Afrika," 43.

27 See Roland Barthes, *Image, Music, Text* (New York: Hill and Wang, 1977), 26.

28 See Sandler, "Deutsche Heimat in Afrika," 38; Daniel James Walther, *Creating Germans Abroad: Cultural Policies and Settler Identities in Namibia* (Athens: Ohio University Press, 2002), 55.

29 Sandler, "Deutsche Heimat in Afrika," 48–50.

30 Sandler, "Deutsche Heimat in Afrika," 40.

31 Sandler, "Deutsche Heimat in Afrika," 49.

32 On women in aviation after World War I, see Evelyn Zegenhagen, *"Schneidige Deutsche Mädel": Fliegerinnen zwischen 1918 und 1945* (Göttingen: Wallstein Verlag, 2007).

33 On race and gender in colonial Africa, see Nancy Rose Hunt, Tessie P. Liu, and Jean Quataert, eds., *Gendered Colonialisms in African History* (Oxford: Blackwell, 1997); on the production of German female identity in colonial Namibia, see Walther, *Creating Germans Abroad*, 46ff.

34 Sandler, "Deutsche Heimat in Afrika," 55.

35 See, e.g., Markus Köster, "Hitlers Jugend? Totalitärer Anspruch und zwiespältige Realität," in *Jugend, Wohlfahrtsstaat und Gesellschaft im Wandel: Westfalen zwischen Kaiserreich und Bundesrepublik* (Paderborn: F. Schöningh, 1999), 313–82; and Alessio Ponzio, *Shaping the New Man: Youth Training Regimes in Fascist Italy and Nazi Germany* (Madison: University of Wisconsin Press, 2015), 3–14.

36 Lisa Gates, "Of Seeing Otherness: Leni Riefenstahl's African Photographs," in *The Imperialist Imagination: German Colonialism and Its Legacy*, ed. Sara Friedrichsmeyer, Sara Lennox, and Susanne Zantop (Ann Arbor: University of Michigan Press, 1998), 239.

37 Elizabeth Edwards, *Raw Histories: Photographs, Anthropology and Museums* (Oxford: Berg, 2001), 12.

38 Julia Thomas notes the aesthetic incoherence of fascism more generally in the introduction to this volume.

39 Henrichsen, "Lees!," 46.

40 Julia Adeney Thomas, "The Evidence of Sight," theme issue, "Photography and Historical Interpretation," *History and Theory* 48 (December 2009): 151–68.

41 Christopher Morton and Darren Newbury, eds., *The African Photographic Archive: Research and Curatorial Strategies* (London: Bloomsbury 2015), 2–3.

42 W. J. T. Mitchell, *Landscape and Power*, 2nd ed. (Chicago: University of Chicago Press, 2002), 1–18; Lorena Rizzo, "Faszination Landschaft—Landschaftsphotographie in Namibia," *BAB Working Papers*, 1, 2014.

43 Schmidt-Lauber, *Die abhängigen Herren*, 72.

44 Christo Botha, "The Politics of Land Settlement in Namibia, 1890–1960," *South African Historical Journal* 42, no. 1 (2009): 244–45.

45 Two of these appeared in some of Steinhoff's photographs. On Steinhoff's local travel companions, see Werner Tabel, *Autoren Südwestafrikas: Biographien, Rezensionen und Hintergrundinformationen* (Göttingen: Klaus Hess Verlag, 2007), 388–92.

46 Dag Henrichsen coined the term "South West African War" in his "Pastoral Modernity, Territoriality and Colonial Transformations in Central Namibia, 1860s to 1904," in *Grappling with the Beast: Indigenous Southern African Responses to Colonialism, 1840–1930*, ed. Peter Limb, Norman Etherington, and Peter Midgley (Leiden, Boston: Brill, 2010), 87–114.

47 Correspondence with Dag Henrichsen in March 2016. See also Giorgio Miescher, *Namibia's Red Line: The History of a Veterinary and Settlement Border* (New York: Palgrave Macmillan, 2012), 154; and Botha, "The Politics of Land Settlement in Namibia."

48 In Miescher, *Namibia's Red Line*, see 188–89 and 192–93 for Nakusib and 140 for Onguma. Hence Sandler's reading of the Onguma photographs in *Deutsche Heimat in Afrika* in terms of white poverty is misguided. See Sandler, "Deutsche Heimat in Afrika," 50.

49 See Richard Moorsom, *The Formation of the Contract Labour System in Namibia, 1900–1926* (London: Zell, 1989).

50 Frederic Shaw, *Little Railways of the World* (Berkeley, CA: Howell-North, 1985), 43–45. The mine was closed again by the South African administration in 1940 as "enemy property."

51 See Patricia Hayes, "Okombone: Compound Portraits and Photographic Archives in Namibia," in Morton and Newbury, *The African Photographic Archive*, 180–81.

52 Larissa Förster, Dag Henrichsen, and Michael Bollig (eds.), *Namibia-Deutschland: Eine geteilte Geschichte* (Köln, 2004); D. Henrichsen and G. Krüger, "'We Have Been Captives Long Enough. We Want to Be Free': Land, Uniforms, and Politics

in Herero History in the Interwar Period," in Hayes et al., *Namibia under South African Rule*, 149–74.

53 Album 25—*Swakopmund, Seeheim, Keetmanshoop, Windhoek, Usakos, Ovamboland*, Transnet Heritage Library photographic collection, n.d.

54 Jeremy Foster, "'Land of Contrasts' or 'Home We Have Always Known'? The SAR&H and the Imaginary Geography of White South African Nationhood, 1920–1930," *Journal of Southern African Studies* 29, no. 3 (2003): 657–80.

55 Sandler, "Deutsche Heimat in Afrika"; Henrichsen, "Lees!"

56 Foster, "'Land of Contrasts' or 'Home We Have Always Known'?," 664.

57 Foster, "'Land of Contrasts' or 'Home We Have Always Known'?"

58 A. Scherz joined her husband E. R., who had left Germany in 1934. E. R. Scherz accompanied a family of Jewish exiles, the Loenings, to southern Africa. It is not clear whether Scherz's emigration was politically motivated or more informed by professional prospects or adventurous disposition. Once in Windhoek, the Scherzes lived among a group of German exile and emigrant intellectuals (some of whom were Jewish), who rebuilt their lives in the colony. See Henrichsen, "Teilnachlass."

59 For a more general assessment of the fragility in the relation between aesthetics and fascist politics, see the introduction to this volume.

60 See Henrichsen, "Teilnachlass."

61 See, e.g., Anneliese Scherz, *Menschen aus Südwestafrika/Namibia, 1933–1983: Eine Auslese von Fotografien von Ernst Rudolf und Anneliese Scherz* (Windhoek, Scherz, 1983).

62 Henrichsen, "Teilnachlass," 6–7.

63 Lorena Rizzo, "Between the Book and the Lamp—Interiors of Bureaucracy and the Materiality of Colonial Power," *African Historical Review* 45, no. 2 (2013): 31–51.

64 Henrichsen, "Lees!," 49; Hayes et al., "Photography, History, and Memory," in Hayes et al., *Namibia under South African Rule*, 3.

65 Two albums (S003 and S004) in the Scherz photographs collection are labelled with "Honeymoon" and dated 1938. My phrasing is loosely referring to G. Rose's *Doing Family Photography: The Domestic, the Public and the Politics of Sentiment* (Farnham: Ashgate, 2010), though I do not engage her argument closely.

66 Wendy Kozol, "Madonnas of the Fields: Photography, Gender, and 1930s Farm Relief," *Genders*, no. 2 (1988): 1–23.

67 Marijke Du Toit, "Blank Verbeeld, or the Incredible Whiteness of Being: Amateur Photography and Afrikaner Nationalist Historical Narrative," *Kronos* 27 (2001): 77–113.

68 Similar dynamics fascist visualities moving back and forth between the private and the public are discussed by Lutz Koepnik and Julia Thomas in their contributions to this volume.

69 *Veld* is the Afrikaans term for field or bush.

70 Du Toit, "Blank Verbeeld."

71 See, e.g., Darren Newbury, "The Visibility of Poverty: A Rural Vision of Depres-

sion in the Photographs of the Farm Security Administration," *Visual Anthropology* 8, no. 1 (1996): 1–31.

72 Botha, "The Politics of Land Settlement in Namibia," 242–44.

73 Giorgio Miescher, "Usakos' Urban Past: Traces in the Archive," in *Usakos: Photographs beyond Ruins: The Old Location Albums, 1920s–1960s*, ed. Paul Grendon, Giorgio Miescher, Lorena Rizzo, and Tina Smith (Basel: Basler Afrika Bibliographien, 2015), 28–63.

74 Tiffany Willoughby-Herard, *Waste of a White Skin: The Carnegie Corporation and the Racial Logic of White Vulnerability* (Berkeley: University of California Press, 2015), 2.

75 See, e.g., images S001_106, S003_141, S004_156, S004_157, S004_179, S004_181, and S004_183 in the Scherz photographic collection in the archives of the Basler Afrika Bibliographien.

76 Roland Barthes, *Camera Lucida: Reflections on Photography* (New York: Hill and Wang, 1981), 27.

77 Willoughby-Herard, *Waste of a White Skin*, 9.

78 See the introduction to this volume.

79 The photograph is filed under BAB_ S019_0566, BAB Scherz collection, 1950, probably Erongo.

80 Henrichsen, "Teilnachlass." Documenting archaeological sites became the main long-term professional commitment of the Scherzes and the work they are best known for in the scholarship. See, e.g., E. R. Scherz and A. Scherz, *Afrikanische Felskunst: Malereien auf Felsen in Südwest-Afrika* (Schauberg: M. DuMont), 1974.

81 This draws on Walter Benjamin's notion of petrification as explained in Ann Laura Stoler, "Introduction: 'The Rot Remains': From Ruins to Ruination," in *Imperial Debris: On Ruins and Ruination*, ed. Ann Laura Stoler (Durham, NC: Duke University Press, 2013), 9.

82 Tim Murray, "Introduction," in *Time and Archaeology*, ed. Tim Murray (London: Routledge, 1999), 1–7.

83 R. D. G. Kelley, "Introduction: A Poetics of Anticolonialism," in *Discourse on Colonialism*, ed. A. Césaire (New York: Monthly Review Press, 2000), 19.

7

JAPAN'S WAR WITHOUT PICTURES

Normalizing Fascism

JULIA ADENEY THOMAS

Curiously, Japan's Fifteen-Year War (1931–45) was largely a war without pictures. The extraordinary fact is that few photographs of stirring civic events or genuine military valor appeared in domestic magazines, books, and posters.[1] Although the state demanded ever-greater popular support for the imperial cause, only rarely were people goaded by heroic imagery of national leaders and battlefield bravery. Japan's emperor was nearly invisible and the war itself appeared primarily as a series of choreographed nonincidents and bloodless staged performances. This strange quietness prompted me to revisit the question of whether Japan could be considered fascist because fascism is generally seen as a dramatic break with the past. If fascism requires a charismatic new leader, a self-styled fascist party, and the overthrow of the old government all feverishly celebrated in visual culture, then imperial Japan was not fascist. The Shōwa emperor reigned from 1926 to 1989, the Meiji constitution of 1890 remained in place without amendment until after the war, and no "single mass party along the lines of Hitler's Nazis" arose.[2] Undramatic wartime photography might be seen as underscoring the lack of rupture in Japan's polity, a lack that has allowed scholars to separate Japan's experience from fascism in Europe.[3]

Nonetheless, I propose that the scholarly stress on overt, sudden institutional change accompanied by dramatic imagery is misplaced as the key to understanding fascism's rise. A model based solely on Italian and German experiences is not universalizable. Japan and Japanese photography show that fascism need not involve *revolution*, but can emerge instead through *redefinition*. Or, to put it another way, the Japanese case demonstrates that a revolutionary transformation of the state can be achieved incrementally as radical right-wing nationalists outside the government compel conservative nationalists within it to embrace their ideas and desires.

Gradually redefining institutions and ideology in the service of heightened nationalism, aggressive war, and naturalized authority can suffocate a liberal democratic society at least as effectively as violent overthrow. Popular dedication to the nation can be aroused by celebrating its eternal glories rather than some new vision of collective glory. Redefinition also has the tactical benefit for fascists of not signaling a decisive moment when their power grab can be contested.[4] If we understand fascism in this way, it becomes possible to see how it can emerge *through* established state institutions *without* overturning them. When fascism arises without a radical break and, as happened in Japan, in reaction to the challenge posed by ultraright factions (*uyoku*) claiming to be more patriotic than their patriotic leaders, those in power stress continuity as a means of stabilizing their authority.[5] This velvet-gloved fascism is perhaps the most difficult form to guard against because no obvious moment of contestation arises; no emergency compels action; no crisis crystallizes dissent. In depicting a polity without change and a war without pictures, Japanese photographs help us to understand this insidious right-wing infiltration. Where better to see an event that wishes to efface its eventfulness than in a still image?

Here I explore three aspects of Japan's war without pictures. First, I consider the "imperial fascism," in Andrew Gordon's phrase, that arose in response to more radical right-wing demands for direct imperial authority in the early 1930s and culminated in the February 26 (1936) Incident. Second, I survey the military-authorized images portraying the expanding war in Asia without battles or blood. Third, I show that official censors worked through the government-sponsored photographers' guild to undermine photography's prerogative to represent reality and its capacity to convey artistic expression. As a result, photography became stranded in a no man's land between reality and representation with no claim to truth of any kind, neither conveying facts nor expressing the photographer's aesthetic vision. Photography's critical capacities were effectively neutralized.

These three approaches to Japan's war without pictures help us to place the events there in relation to fascism elsewhere, making visible the similarities. As Gordon makes clear, much in Japan echoed Italian and German fascism: "economic crisis, intense polarization of left and right, intense conflicts in industrial workplaces and rural society, and murderous right-wing terror. In each case a perception took root among intellectuals and the political elite that a cultural malaise gripped the nation. Fear spread that established gender roles were breaking down. Elite and popular opinion in each case held that Anglo-American power blocked the nation's legitimate international aspirations to empire."[6] But unlike Italy and Germany, Japanese military, bureaucratic, and capitalist elites remained in charge through these revolutionary changes. Their fascism through redefinition required that the energies transforming the nation be absorbed within a larger vision of national continuity. Real change, a true revolution, a "state of exception" (in Nazi legal scholar Carl Schmitt's phrase) occurred, but it was coded as nonrevolutionary, as a "state of unexception." Photography was used to mask change, not reveal it.

Revolution by Redefinition

Those of us in love with words—and I count myself among them—sometimes forget the art of looking. So, first I want simply to look at an image I take to be emblematic of Japanese fascism (figure 7.1). We see here a winter scene at dusk, or perhaps at dawn. There are three partial figures and the suggestion of a fourth. All seem to be men; two wear fedoras and the third, the figure to the right, wears something like a bowler hat. They look tensed against the cold. All have their backs to us and face a snowy field, which has the characteristics of Japanese public parks with their uninviting swards and semicircular garden-edging. The old, hand-lettered sign warns visitors that there's no throughway. Uncharacteristic of Japanese parks are the looping strands of barbed wire along what might be a street curb. A couple of moveable wooden barricades off to the right side also hint that trespass would be unwelcome, but these are hardly formidable deterrents.

Formally, the composition of the image reinforces the tension of the men's bodies. What attracts my notice time and time again (in the Barthesian way of the *punctum*) is the awkward angle of the man's foot to the right. I wonder if he is turning to go, tired of watching, or if he is bracing himself against some unseen threat. The indefiniteness of that posture is echoed by the ambiguity of the bowed tree trunk melding with the human figure on the left, like

7.1 Kuwabara Kineo, *Kōjimachi-ku, Babasakimon, Ni ni roku jiken tōji, 1936*
(At the time of the February 26 Incident, Babasakimon, Kōjimachi-ku, 1936).
Courtesy of Kuwabara Kineo.

something out of Ovid. There too, a shoe is silhouetted. These shapes, along with the slight tilt of the massive figure closest to the camera, respond uneasily to the twin discs of sun and stop sign. These circles form the enigmatic double center of the composition. They are both light and dark, the celestial symbol of the sun-descended emperor and the quotidian symbol of state authority. It is tempting to push the symbolics even further and toy with the idea that the emperor is represented by a distorted sun, enlarged on the horizon by the atmosphere's thickness, or by a false sun that hasn't yet risen but is reflected upward, or even by a mirage created by the photographer's lens.[7] In any case, this uncommanding center of sun and sign, at odds even with itself, barely holds the composition together. The tension among the off-kilter points of interest threatens to dissolve the image's perilous compositional balance. This photograph makes me hold my breath, waiting for movement.

Of all the tens of thousands of photographs made during Japan's Fifteen-Year War, why choose this one as exemplary? I do so because I think it helps us understand the nature of Japanese fascism despite its lack of overt political content: it *shows* us tension, rather than illustrating what we already know about political clashes through texts. I want to treat the image itself—this one and others—as a source of knowledge, as a locus for producing understanding, not a means of illustrating an understanding achieved through other media. Ultimately I will fail at this. We cannot do without words, but we can do more without them than we recognize. In this case we see little that is readily identifiable as violent or militaristic. The park might be a construction site; no massed crowd gathers; no one seems to be in charge. Tension hovers in the air, reinforced by the composition, but *nothing is happening*. It is this seeming noneventfulness that I want us to see first and foremost: the tense quiet of this image, the way it teeters between centripetal and centrifugal energies.

If I now move to words and give you the name of the photographer, Kuwabara Kineo (1913–2007), and the title of the photograph, "At the time of the February 26 Incident, Babasakimon, Kōjimachi-ku, 1936," we leave the image as image and begin to create the linguistic net that pulls this still into the linearity of narratives and arguments. The "*ni-ni-roku jiken*," or February 26 Incident, was an uprising of the *kōdōha* (Imperial Way Faction) of the Japanese army hoping to overwhelm the ostensibly more moderate *tōseiha* (Control Faction).[8] It was not the first outbreak of radical right-wing groups. Assorted *uyoku* organizations had left a bloody trail, assassinating government and business leaders, since the May 15 Incident of 1932 and the Blood Pledge Corps (Ketsumeidan) killings of the same year. But the February 26 Incident was in many ways the culmination of extragovernmental ultranationalism.[9] A group of more than 1,400 soldiers seized control of downtown Tokyo and executed several high-ranking government officials, including Finance Minister Takahashi Korekiyo (1854–1936), who had cut military spending; Lord Privy Seal Saitō Makoto (1858–1936), who had served as an admiral, as governor-general of Korea, and as prime minister; and the moderate Inspector General of Military Education Watanabe Jōtarō (1874–1936). They also attacked, wounded, and killed others. Prime Minister Okada Keisuke (1868–1952) barely escaped with his life when the hapless revolutionaries mistakenly murdered his brother-in-law instead of him.[10] After this slaughter, the insurrectionary officers then called for a Shōwa Restoration in which the Shōwa emperor would take direct military control and establish a glorious era for imperial Japan.[11] The immediate response was muted. Martial law was declared, but the uprising was not instantly suppressed. For three days, Tokyo held its breath.

The rebels, with their distrust of the leftist tendencies of the urban working class, made no attempt to spark popular enthusiasm in Tokyo or to contest the prohibition against publications written by soldiers.[12] No pamphlets were disseminated, and the radio station went unmolested.[13] In fact, as Yoshimi Yoshiaki argues, "people felt a strong antagonism toward the young officers who had perpetrated the February 26 incident and toward the army authorities who used them in an attempt to secure hegemony."[14] Eventually, after a three-day wait, when no backing came from imperial, financial, or naval circles, the mutineers were labeled as such and other armed forces were brought in to quell them.[15] Nineteen of the young officers, along with civilian ideologue Kita Ikki (1883–1937), whose writings had inspired them, were executed on August 19, but most soldiers were simply reassigned to other units.[16] Had this group succeeded, Japan might have experienced something more akin to the revolutionary fascisms of Italy and Germany. Instead, the state simultaneously moved to crack down on these extreme patriots *and* became more extreme in its aims, embracing the renegades' hopes as their own.

Kuwabara's photograph reveals three qualities that would help define the nonrevolutionary fascism in Japan after 1936. First, the photograph's lack of a strong central focus suggests the lack of a strong leader. The sun, an imperial symbol, is distant, decentered, and mediated by a stop sign. The Shōwa emperor likewise rarely took center stage. A barely visible public presence, he seldom appeared in person or in photographs. Even the government's official magazine, *Shashin shūhō* (Photographic weekly report), published only thirty-five different photographs of Hirohito in the long years between 1937 and 1945.[17] Second, Kuwabara's image displays the tensions between centrifugal and centripetal forces in its composition, echoing the contending impulses pulling at the polity even as its rightward tilt became more pronounced. Third, the photograph's hesitant figures embody the position of the people. They appear wary but susceptible to the general atmosphere just as Japanese subjects would ultimately embrace imperial fascism as it slithered into place after the February 26 Incident. In showing us these qualities, Kuwabara lets us *see* Japanese fascism taking hold of power.

The February 26 Incident marks the defeat of the fascist movement in Japan, but not the defeat of fascism.[18] The elites harnessed its revolutionary impulses by redefining the state. That redefinition had been several years in the making, most notably with the 1935 *tennō kikansetsu jiken*, or "Emperor Organ Theory" incident, when the standard interpretation of the Meiji Constitution was overthrown. What happened was this: the aging legal scholar Minobe Tatsukichi (1873–1948), serving in the House of Peers, was verbally and physically attacked for supposedly having committed lèse-majesté because he had taken the position—one perfectly unobjectionable in previous decades—that the emperor was an "organ of the state" and thus part of its constitutional framework.[19] Minobe was vanquished, attacked by right-wing thugs, wounded, sent to the hospital, and dismissed from public life by the radical Right and its media allies. Their victory elevated the emperor above the constitution, transcending yet embodying the nation. This new version of the polity helped inspire the February 26 revolt, appealing to the emperor to assert his authority directly, freeing himself from his advisers. In response, the elite within military, bureaucratic, and industrial circles defended their own authority by suppressing the uprising while channeling its revolutionary energies through a redefined state. In so doing, they managed to have both worlds—a new order and an old order simultaneously—with themselves in charge.[20] Continuity was the grounds of their legitimacy, even while they perpetrated dramatic change. The crucial point here is that Japan's imperial fascism arose in reaction to liberal democracy, left-wing socialist and communist efforts, *and* the Far Right revolutionaries at home in an increasingly tense international atmosphere.[21]

War's Indecisive Moments

Visualizing this stealthy fascism required different measures from those used by revolutionary fascist regimes. Take, for instance, mass spectacle. The challenge confronting the Japanese leadership was similar to that of Mussolini and Hitler in "funneling the energies of a glorified national body (whether the *Volk* or the Yamato race) into a quest for military hegemony, autarchic economic empire, and an antidemocratic, hierarchic new political and economic order at home," as Andrew Gordon argues, yet Japan's efforts were encoded as emanations of an immutable empire.[22] Instead of celebrating the recent advent of the fascist nation, Japan celebrated political continuum. This difference is clear when we compare national celebrations by the three Axis powers. In Italy, Benito Mussolini (1883–1945) opened with great fanfare the "Exhibition of the Fascist Revolution" in 1932 to mark the tenth anniversary of his nation's heroic rebirth. Likewise, Adolph Hitler (1889–1945) descended from the clouds in the Nuremberg Rallies to mark Germany's new era. Italy and Germany glorified new beginnings. By contrast, in 1940, Emperor Hirohito presided over commemorations of the twenty-sixth centennial of the Empire of Japan marking the 660 BCE descent of Jimmu, grandson of the sun goddess Amaterasu. As Kenneth Ruoff says, "The ancient nature and fundamental continuity of Japan's polity, however imagined this narrative of nation might have been, was the dominant theme in the 2,600th anniversary celebrations."[23] Huge rallies in Tokyo cheered the ceaseless state, not its birth.

Visually, Japan's New Order (*shin taisei*) was made continuous with its ancient past even in mundane ways.[24] A wartime cigarette package, for instance, displayed Jimmu, the mythical first emperor, with rounded legs modeled on *haniwa*, the burial statuary from the *kofun* era (third to the sixth century CE), surveying a map of the Asian continent on which red marks Japan's expanding dominion.[25] Time is collapsed. All eternity—mythical, archaeological, and contemporary—is on show on a pack of smokes.

Under the cover of this hallucinatory continuity, the Japanese polity was transformed. The Diet became peripheral. Independent organizations of workers, tenant farmers, women's rights groups, businesses, political parties, and professional associations (including photographers) were dissolved. People were linked to the state and the emperor through vast, expanding state-sponsored networks such as the Imperial Rule Assistance Association working through neighborhood associations (*tonarigumi*), the Greater Japan Women's Association, and the Greater Japan Imperial Rule Assistance Youth Corps. Beyond the home islands, the Second Sino-Japanese War, sparked by the Marco Polo Bridge Incident (Rokōkyō Jiken) on July 7, 1937, unleashed horrors of astounding magnitude offstage; in 1941, the Pacific war erupted with attacks on America and European allies. Yet despite this eventfulness, the Japanese polity had to be seen as noneventful so as to override any moment of resistance from the Left, from liberals, and from the ultraright.

The political imperative of "fascism through redefinition" posed particular challenges for Japanese photographers. Talented and technologically astute as they were, they were still beholden to a relatively new medium that could claim no primal association with the Japanese archipelago.[26] Moreover, this medium, through the mechanism of the camera, extracts particular moments and fixes them on film. In other words, instead of purveying eternity in the way that stone carvings might, cameras underscore the play of time, with each photograph "a clock for seeing."[27] A medium dedicated to "the decisive moment" was not ideal for conveying the sense that nothing was happening.[28]

Yet Japanese photographers took seriously their patriotic duty within the new order—their *shin taisei ni okeru shashinka no ninmu*, as noted photography critic Ina Nobuo (1898–1978) called it—and overcame photography's alliance with temporality. Insistently, through subject matter, framing, and printing techniques, they found ways to harmonize the instant with forever-ness.[29] Even in the contingent and action-filled arena of the battlefield, time was stilled. The government, especially the Cabinet Information Bureau (Naikaku Jōhō Kyoku), sought to direct photographers in this patriotic ef-fort through sponsorship, informal guidance, some overt censorship, and the creation of a photographers' guild to which all had to belong. Well-known photographers were commissioned by the military to tour battlefields. Name-less military photographers provided images for the illustrated press. In Janu-ary 1941, the riot of photographically illustrated publications was reduced to a small, manageable number both to conserve resources and to orchestrate patriotism through greater guidance and control.

The results were war images of astonishing quietude. The photographs sent back to the home islands from military units on the continent seldom celebrated gallantry, glory, exceptional courage, fortitude, high emotion, or war's bracing demands. They rarely depicted or even referenced actual fight-ing; the enemy was usually completely out of sight; and the photographer himself almost always remained at a distance from his subjects. If our mea-sure of successful war photography is the dramatic work of antifascist pho-tographer Robert Capa (1913–54) or Soviet photojournalist Dimitri Balter-mants (1912–90), then Japanese war photographers failed. Theirs was a style of image-making dedicated, or so it would seem, not to the decisive moment but to the *in*decisive moment. Although it was not literally a war without pic-tures, Japan's war appeared as a dampened, dull affair.

For instance, during an official mission to occupied Manchuria in 1940, Kuwabara Kineo made Japanese troops look almost like lost boys on a scouting trip (figure 7.2). The bedraggled line of marchers appears to have no particular goal. Moreover, the troops' awkward postures are emphasized by the awkward distance between them and the camera. Another example from the same army-sponsored propaganda tour also shows the troops standing in a haphazard line at a remove from the camera, this time facing the photographer while a frisky puppy digs in the muck in the foreground. In contrast to Robert Capa's famous dictum, "If your picture isn't good enough, you're not close enough," Kuwabara withdraws from his military subjects, standing far enough back to transform his war photographs into landscapes. The army commissioned and approved Kuwabara's photographs, publishing them in *Manshū Shōwa ju-go nen* (Manchuria 1940), despite the fact that they make no effort to depict individual heroism, the consequences of Japan's invasion in 1931 that led to its exit from the League of Nations, or the creation

7.2 Kuwabara Kineo, *Manshu Showa Ju-Go Nen* [Manchuria in Showa 15 (1940)] (Tokyo: Shōbunsha, 1974), 189. The caption reads "159 Kokyōton tetsudō-airo-mura ken [Near the railroad depot village of Kokyoton]."

159 顧郷屯鐵道愛路村付近

of the new puppet state of Manchukuo, nominally under Puyi, the last Qing emperor. In fact, they were valued *because* they show eventlessness. Nothing much is happening at the edge of empire.[30]

This distanced stance was also adopted by embedded, unnamed military photographers whose images appeared in authorized general-interest magazines. For example, the February 11, 1942, issue of *Asahi gurafu* published two shots of troops trailing through in the snow (figure 7.3). Both the top and bottom images have a rhythmic elegance, like calligraphic strokes on rice paper. Both use distance to fuse the thin lines of the patrolling army with the vast wilderness of ice and snow. Here too troops become landscape, and national goals merge with nature. Compared with the commercial energy radiating

7.3 *Asahi gurafu*, no. 973 (July 15, 1942): 2–3. The caption for the photographs on the left reads, "Special troops advance through a large snowy valley on the island of Attu." On the right is an advertisement for Matsuda lamps, declaring "Matsuda" to be the "Trademark of Choice."

from the advertisement on the adjoining page, the war appears enervated. Given that these photographs depict the start of the grisly Aleutian Islands campaign, their quietness seems insistently at odds with the situation's dramatic dangers. Almost all these men would be dead by year's end.

Calling these images "dull" is not simply my projection onto the past. As I have demonstrated elsewhere, there is no guarantee that our interpretation of a photograph today will resemble the way it was seen at the time it was taken.[31] So, it follows that I have to verify that during the war, Japanese also found such wartime images uninspiring. As far as the evidence shows, they did. For instance, in 1943, the head of the official photographers' guild, Domon Ken (1909–90), pronounced wartime images "boring."[32] Court photographer Ikegami Shirō also recalled the articles and photographs of those years as dull. Reminiscing in 1947, Ikegami wrote, "To tell the truth, it probably wasn't me alone who, two or three years ago, upon seeing a headline of an article on the Imperial Family, didn't feel like reading further. No matter how much honorific language I read, it didn't evoke any reaction at all."[33] Japan's way of visualizing fascism responded to the political exigencies of that state, trying to lull people into complacency about their inevitable war under the aegis of an inevitable state. A dulling "state of unexception" settled over the country.

Neither Art nor Reality: Photography as National Spirit

In 1940, the year leading up to the government's consolidation of domestic photography magazines, a dispute (ronsō) broke out among the ranks of Japanese photographers concerning their duty to the state. At issue was the relation between art as a craft and politics as an imperative. Was it possible to serve both? On the one hand, Ina Nobuo (1898–1978), long a leading critic in the Japanese photography world, argued quite subtly that a photographer could be true both to his craft and to the nation. Serving the regime was not, he said, a matter of merely "communicating" (iu) the right subject matter but a matter of "leading" (michibiku) intellectually, emotionally, and sensually. To lead in this way required a self-aware practice that was cognizant of both method and message, technique and topic. Personal talent and patriotism were not at odds. In making this point, Ina insisted that "the difference between journalism (hōdōsei) and art (geijutsu) is a non-issue."[34] A honed aesthetic was a necessary component of good reportage (hōdōshashin); elevating the nation required a purposive art (mokuteki geijutsu).

Photographer Domon Ken responded with his characteristic bluster to Ina's proposals, accusing the critic of lacking patriotic zeal and "ignoring the superiority of politics over culture."[35] Railing against "theory" (riron), Domon rooted patriotic photography in ethnic identity and passion.[36] Being Japanese, it seems, was enough for a photographer to produce photographs conveying the spirit of Japan (Nippon seishin). "Theory," on the other hand, always requires self-reflection and as such threatens to expose the contingency of the status quo. As other participants in the dispute pointed out, Domon had misread Ina's true patriotism, but government officials overseeing photographic publications shared Domon's insistence on the primacy of ethnicity and his suspicion of mindful craft. Through their efforts, photography was effaced as a self-aware aesthetic practice with the capacity to convey the conditions of empire. Patriotism alone mattered. The distance between image and reality, like the distance between state and subject, was to be ignored for the sake of unquestionable and inevitable unity. All too often, the resulting photograph was a mediocre muddle, neither aesthetic expression nor honest documentation. Even discussing how better techniques might produce stronger, more effective propaganda raised suspicion because it implied contending alternatives and the possibility of choice.

The officials in the Cabinet Information Bureau managed to obfuscate photography's capacities as both art and reportage in several ways: publications dedicated to the discussion of photographic technique were limited, pleas for more deliberately artful propaganda were suppressed, and the government itself sponsored images that turned the war into theater—melodramatic kitsch rather than reality. Below, I describe each of these official efforts to bring photography to heel, making it a pallid expression of national spirit.

First, by government decree in 1940, photography magazines were consolidated, and those dedicated to art photography were either eliminated or absorbed by more prosaic publications. For instance, by January 1941, *Asahi camera* had been forced to incorporate two art photography magazines, *Geijutsu shashin kenkyū* [Art Photography Studies] and *Shōzō shashin kenkyū* [Portrait Photography Studies]. The state apparently had no use for journals that explored varieties of photographic practice. Such mindfulness about the craft of image-making (or anything else for that matter) would suggest that some processes and values were only tangentially related to the *kokutai*. From the government's perspective, it was better not to foster critical capacities revealing that photography's reality effect as just that: an effect. It followed that journals promoting a sophisticated understanding of this medium had to be suppressed. Photographers, of course, continued to use various techniques, but discussion of them largely ceased.

Asahi camera, a magazine for amateur and professional photographers, provides an example of this muddle of art and politics. During the first nine months of 1941, after absorbing independent art photography magazines at the government's behest, *Asahi camera* contained its usual mix of amateur submissions, essays by professional photographers, and advertisements for cameras and other equipment. Then the war began to figure. The October 1941 cover portrayed factory workers in military garb. The November cover depicted tank maneuvers.[37] The December 1941 cover featured a photograph of a naval destroyer as though with foreknowledge of the attacks on Pearl Harbor, Hong Kong, and other Allied outposts (figure 7.4, left). From the perspective of the relationship between aesthetics and politics, the curiosity here is that this image recuperates the pictorialist values of soft focus, distanced landscape, and gentleness. Pictorialism was a style developed in

7.4 On the left, the cover of Asahi camera (December 1941); on the right, Alvin Langdon Coburn, Wapping, 1904. Both images are manifestations of pictorialism.

the West in part to make the case that photography could be an art, and it had great staying power in Japan even after the 1920s, when American and European photographers largely abandoned it. Lenses blurring sharp lines and darkroom techniques manipulating the development of the film underscored the presence of the photographer in the creative process and showed his or her artistic sensibility, or so it was argued. English photographer Alvin Langdon Coburn (1882–1966) was a master of this technique, and indeed one might analyze *Asahi camera*'s depiction of the naval vessel within the tradition exemplified by Coburn. Both compositions stress the calming line of the horizon, enlivened in each case by delicate rigging against an overcast sky. But in wartime Japan, the military photographer who produced this cover shot went unnamed and was certainly not elevated to the status of artist. Here reality was aestheticized through pictorialism's soft focus not to turn it into art but, it would seem, to make artifice and reality indistinguishable.

Pictorialism was not the only photographic technique photographers deployed in support of the state. Modernism also figured; its theatrical lighting, posed subjects, and careful backdrops implied that war was clean and orderly.

Unlike battlefield photographs (figures 7.2 and 7.3), in which soldiers lost their individuality as they merged with the landscape, modernist portraits turned individuals into generic types such as "the nurse" (e.g., Domon Ken's image on the cover of *Shashin shūhō*, July 8, 1938) and "the fighter pilot." Standard categories were repeated frequently. For instance, *Asahi gurafu* was apparently so taken with the idea of an airman posing in a cockpit that they used nearly identical compositions on the covers of both the September 1941 and the March 1942 issues. Both images were probably made during the same photo shoot. These photographs referred to war but were not taken during battle. The nameless man in the cockpit is posed in the role of an airman, but he may not even be in the air force. The abstraction and almost hieratic quality of such photographs turns war into theater, event into melodrama, and blurs the distinction between art and reality. Mostly, though, published pictures were dull.

Eventually, even Domon Ken became restless in response to the repetitive imagery, the tired techniques, and the lack of innovation. In 1943, while serving as head of the official photographer's guild and thus a figure of some importance, he wrote an article attacking the government's aesthetic complacency, especially with its twelve official graphic magazines targeting populations in the Greater East Asia Co-Prosperity Sphere (*Daitōa kyōeiken*). In "Taigai senden zasshi ron" (A Discussion of International Propaganda Magazines), Domon, as was his wont, did not mince his words. This essay, excised from his postwar collected works and hard to find, decries the government-sponsored journals for committing several grievous visual sins such as displaying "petit-bourgeois taste," imitating Soviet montage, copying an "outdated French graphic style," and being otherwise "ridiculous." Poorly edited and visually dull, they fail as propaganda, reeking instead of "blatant menace" and "cultural vanity" arising from a lingering inferiority complex in relation to the West—or so Domon declares.[38] In order for these publications to convey confidence in the power of Japan to construct a new Asia, Domon advocates a combination of graphic vitality and "accurate and strong" photojournalism. In other words, Domon advocates precisely the combination of sophisticated, self-aware technique and attention to the realities facing the nation for which he had lambasted Ina Nobuo in 1940.

Domon ends his 1943 diatribe by suggesting that all twelve international publications be replaced by a single magazine, published from Tokyo. Ideally, a younger staff would push old-fashioned editors to secondary positions and direct "a sharp and quick camera eye over the entire Co-prosperity Sphere."[39] The cacophony of languages used in the current publications in an attempt to reach colonized peoples would be replaced by Japanese only because, after all, Japanese was supposed to become the "common international language within the Sphere."[40] Desirable topics in this substantial new publication, ultimately reaching perhaps "a billion people" in Domon's wild estimation, would be upbeat yet quotidian: "constructive phenomena in political, economic, and cultural realms, heartwarming scenes of the common people at mundane events, and the magnificent mysteries of Nature."[41] Colored photographs and even vivid advertisements for "modern transportation, speedy automobiles, and sweet canned goods" were all part of Domon's recommendations. "Taigai senden zasshi ron" is a bravura performance.

The police, however, did not applaud. Domon was summoned for a day-long interview with the authorities, which cannot have been particularly pleasant.[42] Nothing more came of it, but afterward Domon refrained from further suggestions for radically restructuring Japan's international propaganda efforts. In a way, his day of official admonition has served him well, throwing some postwar scholars off track. They mistakenly adduce—sometimes directly, sometimes by implication—that it was resistance to the war that caused official displeasure, when in fact Domon wanted propaganda of greater skill and sharper truth.[43] The artistic techniques of photography should, he thought in 1943, be better exploited to reveal the value of Japan's great empire. He had come around to Ina's position.

The state had a third tactic for blurring art and reality in photographic images. Along with suppressing periodicals dedicated to craft and disciplining calls like Domon's for aesthetically sophisticated reportage, the Cabinet Information Bureau supported the production of perhaps the most famous wartime photographic image, the staged studio shot titled "Uchiteshi yamamu." This phrase, variously translated as "Continue to Shoot, Do Not Desist," "We'll Never Cease to Fire until Our Enemies Cease to Be," or, more elegantly, "Fight to the Bitter End," quotes Emperor Jimmu's rallying cry during his mythical invasion of the Japanese archipelago to found the empire. Beginning in 1943, this phrase, found in the eighth-century imperial history known as the *Kojiki*, was adopted as the slogan for the annual March 10 Army Day celebrations.[44] As an image, "Fight to the Bitter End" is pure melodrama and verges on kitsch (figure 7.5). Two men (possibly the same model posed twice) pretend to advance upon the enemy's abandoned position with its crumpled American flag. One of them, dressed in a crisply pressed uniform and sporting perfect white teeth, rises to throw a grenade.[45] The poster of this image had a print run of fifty thousand copies, which were distributed across

7.5 An article by Yamahata Yōsuke discussed the production and display of the photomontage "Uchiteshi yamamu" (Fight to the Bitter End, 1943) in *Shashin Bunka* [Photographic Culture] 26, no. 4 (April 1943): 8–9.

Japan in February 1943. For the Tokyo celebration on March 10, the Yamahata Photographic Science Institute, under supervision by the Army Information Bureau, produced a giant mural of 3,559 square feet.[46] This mural was hung from the roof of the Nihon Gekijō (Japan Theater) almost as if to underscore that mere playacting had been substituted for real battle. For all intents and purposes, by 1943, Japan was defeated, but the nation, trapped in its own false dream of an eventless history, could not wake itself to face reality.[47]

The Exceptional State Masked as the State of Unexception

In asking what photography might show us about wartime Japan, this essay has focused on two aspects: first, the marked placidness in the photographic portrayals in domestic magazines of military and civilian action and, second, the obfuscation of photography's techniques of representation and its potential to convey reality. Together, the government and photographers masked not simply particular events but eventfulness itself as a characteristic of Japan's imperial politics in the 1930s and early 1940s. The result of these tactics was a visual diet as bland as sawdust and an incapacity to see the truth of Japan's situation.

When we look at these wartime photographs, we can see the Japanese state as it wished to be seen, but we must not be misled into thinking that these images are benign or merely kitschy just because real strife and destruction are invisible. Looking at a similar phenomenon in film, the esteemed historian John Dower interprets the quietism as propitious: as he puts it, "The films are propaganda first and last, but they contain strains of humanism and even pacifism that bespeak the filmmaker's roots in less militaristic and repressive times and constitute strong legacies to the years following Japan's defeat."[48] I see this phenomenon in photography differently. Japan's war was a war without pictures not *in friction with* state interests but in support of them. Sadly, the images of rolling terrains, atmospheric seascapes, and bloodless battles are not remnants of laudatory popular decency and humanism—as Dower sees them in film—but the manifestation of fascism achieved through redefinition.[49] The type of fascism that slithers into place is hard to guard against, but it is not invisible. We can see it in the quiet stills made by Japanese photographers who turned soldiers into landscapes and models into melodramatic men-at-arms.

Looked at in this way, Japanese wartime photography shows us how we might achieve a new understanding of fascism that does not rely on overt revolution overthrowing liberal democratic institutions. Instead, a state of aggressive nationalism and uniformity can be achieved by gradually and insistently downgrading representation in all its forms: political, economic, and cultural. Without modes of representation and the patterns of thought and action that measure the distance between what is and what might be, conditions are seen as natural and incontestable. The Japanese regime absorbed the energies of the ultraright and redefined itself by undermining civil society, unions, artistic independence, and ultimately democratic processes. This redefined state left people without the means to represent their differences. Japanese photographers served the fascist state by collectively forgoing the imperative to approach their craft as a self-aware practice representing social realities and individual vision. As the velvet-gloved hand of a nebulous, vitalist, counterrevolutionary ideology gradually squeezed the breath out of the pluralistic body politic, the "state of exception" appeared in Japan as a "state of unexception." Inevitability erased eventfulness. Fascism was normalized.

Notes

1   W. Miles Fletcher III discusses the use of the term "Fifteen-Year War" in "The Fifteen-Year War," in *A Companion to Japanese History*, ed. William M. Tsutsui (Hoboken, NJ: Wiley-Blackwell, 2009), 241–42. Recent work on Japanese government censorship makes clear that during the war it frequently relied more on soliciting cooperation than on draconian dictates, and it traces this function into the postwar era. See Hiromu Nagahara's fascinating work on the music industry: *Japan's Pop Era: Music in the Making of Middle-Class Society* (Cambridge, MA: Harvard University Press, 2017). See also Jonathan E. Abel, *Redacted: The Archives of Censorship in Transwar Japan* (Berkeley: University of California Press, 2012) and Kirsten Cather, *The Art of Censorship in Post War Japan* (Honolulu: University of Hawai'i Press, 2012), for a penetrating look at the complex censorship mechanisms of wartime and occupied Japan.

2   Andrew Gordon, *A Modern History of Japan: From Tokugawa Times to the Present* (New York: Oxford University Press, 2009), 213.

3   Many English-language Japan specialists consider wartime Japan to be nonfascist. These include Gregory Kasza, who argues that Japan became a "military-bureaucratic regime," not a fascist one, in *The State and the Mass Media in Japan, 1918–1945* (Berkeley: University of California Press, 1988) and in "Fascism from Above: Japan's Kakushin Right in Comparative Perspective," in *Fascism outside Europe*, ed. Stein Ugelvik Larsen (Boulder, CO: Social Science Monographs, 2001). Peter Duus and Daniel I. Okimoto, "Fascism and the History of Pre-War Japan: The Failure of a Concept," *Journal of Asian Studies* 39, no. 1 (November 1979): 65–79. Others include most of the first postwar generation of scholars: Gordon Berger, Albert Craig, James Crowley, Richard Mitchell, Mark Peattie, Edwin O. Reischauer, Ben-Ami Shillony, and George Wilson. Contemporary scholars of Japan have made the same argument on different grounds. See, for instance, Mark Driscoll's "Fascist Aspects of Modern Japan," an unpublished paper for the "Fascisms Then and Now: Italy, Japan, Germany" conference that argues against Japan as fascist and for "*decolonial totalitarianism* as the best political description for Japan from 1936–1945." Non–Japan specialists who adopt the view that fascism was an exclusively European phenomenon include Robert O. Paxton, *The Anatomy of Fascism* (New York: Vintage Books, 2005); Stanley G. Payne, *A History of Fascism 1914–1945* (Madison: University of Wisconsin Press, 1995) and "Fascisms, Nazism, and Japanism," *International History Review* 6, no. 2 (May 1984): 265–76; and Michael Mann, *Fascists* (Cambridge: Cambridge University Press, 2004).

4   Mark Neocleous "focuses on three concepts central to fascism: war, nature, and nation" in *Fascism* (Buckingham: Open University Press, 1997), xi.

5   John D. Person incisively analyzes the consternation among thought police in the 1930s when they suddenly found themselves confronting not socialists (their sole target in the 1920s) but the radical Right *uyoku*, who denounced police and state officials for insufficient patriotism. See John D. Person, "Between Patriotism

and Terrorism: The Policing of Nationalist Movements in 1930s Japan," *Journal of Japanese Studies* 43, no. 2 (2017): 289–318.

6   Gordon, *A Modern History of Japan*, 201.

7   When the sun is 4° above the horizon, its light passes through an atmosphere more than twelve times thicker than when the sun is directly overhead, which makes the sun look larger as it rises or sets. A "false sun" is created when the sun, still well below the horizon, casts light onto clouds or ice particles, creating the effect of having risen.

8   For a thorough early study of this event, see Ben-Ami Shillony, *Revolt in Japan: The Young Officers and the February 26, 1936 Incident* (Princeton, NJ: Princeton University Press, 1973).

9   Shillony, *Revolt in Japan*.

10 Okada was targeted despite having caved on the "emperor organ theory" debate, declaring along with his cabinet on August 3, 1935, that sovereignty "lies strictly with the Emperor." Quoted in Asahi Shimbun Company, *Media, Propaganda and Politics in 20th-Century Japan*, trans. Barak Kushner (London: Bloomsbury Academic, 2010), 61.

11 "Shōwa" is the reign name for the period during which Emperor Hirohito was on the throne, 1926–89. Calls for a Shōwa Resoration, modeled on the Meiji Restoration of 1868, aimed to clear away all the obstructions to direct divine imperial rule.

12 Rikki Kersten, "Japan," in *The Oxford Handbook of Fascism*, ed. R. J. B. Bosworth (Oxford: Oxford University Press, 2009), 540; Paxton, *The Anatomy of Fascism*, 197–204; Payne, *A History of Fascism 1914–1945*, 336.

13 Kasza, *The State and Mass Media in Japan*, 147. Kasza argues that the rebellious young officers' lack of interest in stirring up popular support for their efforts to topple the advisers around the emperor is evidence that Japan did not experience a fascist movement.

14 Yoshimi Yoshiaki, *Grassroots Fascism: The War Experience of the Japanese People*, trans. Ethan Mark (New York: Columbia University Press, 2015), 42.

15 To quell the Kōdō faction, troops loyal to the *tōsei*, or control faction (a rather loose grouping of like-minded officers), were deployed. The control faction's emphasis on state expansion in Manchuria and China, and alliances with bureaucrats and big business interests, prevailed over the *kōdō-ha*'s interest in domestic, particularly agrarian, reform. Japan's February 26 Incident was comparable in form, though slightly bloodier than, the February 23, 1981, military coup attempted in Spain, where a faction within the army, led by Colonel Tejero, stormed the Cortes, firing weapons but not killing anyone, in an attempt to overturn democracy and "stabilize" the country by instituting military rule. Because of an immediate intervention by King Juan Carlos, who took to the airwaves within hours, and the coup's lack of active support among eleven military governors (all Francoist veterans) in their respective territories, democracy was saved and the myth of "23-F"—that swarms of Spaniards launched themselves immediately into

the streets in its defense—was born. It was actually three days later, once matters had been settled, that Spaniards in the millions celebrated parliamentary democracy in the streets. See Javier Cercas, *The Anatomy of a Movement*, trans. Anne McLean (London: Bloomsbury, 2011), reviewed by Chase Madar, "23-F," *London Review of Books*, September 8, 2011, 30–31. In Spain, putting down the military coup shored up fledgling democracy; in Japan, putting down the military coup shored up other factions within the military and sped up the "incremental shift from party dominance toward military bureaucratic rule" (Kasza, *The State and Mass Media in Japan*, 122).

16 Kita Ikki's most famous statement is *Kokka kaizōan genri daikō* (Outline of a Plan for the Reconstruction of Japan, 1919), reprinted in *Kita Ikki Chosaku shū* (Tokyo: Misuzu Shobō, 1959). For particularly penetrating insight into Kita Ikki's early career, see Christopher W. A. Szpilman, "The Yūzonsha's 'War Cry,' 1920," in *Pan-Asianism: A Documentary History*, ed. Sven Saaler and Christopher W. A. Szpilman (Lanham, MD: Rowman & Littlefield, 2011). For a full biography, see Brij Tankha, *Kita Ikki and the Making of Modern Japan: A Vision of Empire* (Folkestone, Kent, U.K.: Global Oriental, 2006).

17 I rely here on David C. Earhart's extraordinarily detailed and deeply researched *Certain Victory: Images of World War II in the Japanese Media* (Armonk, NY: M. E. Sharpe, 2008), 13. For a capacious analysis of the modern emperor's position, see Takashi Fujitani, *Splendid Monarchy: Power and Pageantry in Modern Japan* (Berkeley: University of California Press, 1998).

18 Maruyama Masao, Japan's leading twentieth-century political theorist, describes the February 26 Incident as follows: "When fascism as a movement is the central consideration, the February Incident is the great dividing line. For this was the occasion that brought the movement of radical fascism from below to an end, and clearly determined that Japan's course towards fascism would not take the shape of a fascist revolution and *coup d'état* as in Germany and Italy." Maruyama Masao, "The Ideology and Dynamics of Japanese Fascism," in *Thought and Behavior in Modern Japanese Politics*, ed. Ivan Morris (London: Oxford University Press, 1969), 33.

19 A clear statement of Minobe's theory appears, among other places, in Minobe Tatsukichi, *Kenpō kōwa* [Lectures on the Constitution] (Tōkyō: Yūhikaku Shobō, 1921). For detail on the emperor organ incident, see Frank O. Miller, *Minobe Tatsukichi: Interpreter of Constitutionalism in Japan* (Berkeley: University of California Press, 1965); Herbert P. Bix, *Hirohito and the Making of Modern Japan* (New York: Harper Perennial, 2001); and Tachibana Takashi, "The Aftermath of the Emperor-Organ Incident: The Tōdai Faculty of Law," trans. Richard H. Minear, *The Asia-Pacific Journal* 11, issue 9, no. 1 (March 4, 2013): 1–21.

20 Earl Kinmouth argues that they had the support of various nonelites such as small-business owners hoping for some of the spoils. Earl H. Kinmonth, "The Mouse That Roared: Saitō Takao, Conservative Critic of Japan's 'Holy War' in China," *Journal of Japanese Studies* 25 (1999): 331–60.

21 I am grateful to Ethan Mark for advising me to stress the international pressures leading to an astronomical increase of Japan's military budget in the wake of the February 26 Incident.

22 Andrew Gordon, *Labor and Imperial Democracy in Prewar Japan* (Berkeley: University of California Press, 1991), 238.

23 For the definitive study replete with detail, see Kenneth J. Ruoff, *Imperial Japan at Its Zenith: The Wartime Celebration of the Empire's 2,600th Anniversary* (Ithaca, NY: Cornell University Press, 2010), 3.

24 Paul Barclay also stresses the value of continuity to the Japanese state in his analysis of the way Russo-Japanese War memorials were grouped with monuments to the more recent dead so that all seemed to have died for the same cause. See Barclay, chapter 2 in this volume.

25 Ruoff, *Imperial Japan at Its Zenith*, color insert 3.

26 For instance, Ina Nobuo worried about the Western origins of camera technology in "Nihonteki shashin geijutsu no kakuritsu e, 2" [Toward the Establishment of Japanese Photographic Art, 2], *Camera Art* 2, no. 6 (December 1940): 248.

27 John Berger argued that "The true content of *a photograph is invisible, for it derives from a play, not with form, but with time.*" Berger, "Understanding a Photograph," in *Classic Essays on Photography*, ed. Alan Trachtenberg (New Haven, CT: Leete's Island Books, 1980), 293. This essay originally appeared in 1974. The idea of a "clock for seeing" is from Roland Barthes, *Camera Lucida: Reflections on Photography*, trans. Richard Howard (New York: Hill and Wang, 1981), 4.

28 The phrase "the decisive moment" is photographer Henri Cartier-Bresson's. See his discussion of this concept in his collected essays, Henri Cartier-Bresson, *Henri Cartier-Bresson: The Mind's Eye: Writings on Photography and Photographers* (New York: Aperture, 2005).

29 Ina Nobuo, "Shin taisei ni okeru shashinka no ninmu" [The Duty of Photographers in the New Order], *Camera Art* 12, no. 3 (September 1940): 85–89.

30 Kuwabara Kineo, *Manshu Shōwa ju-go nen* (Manchuria in Shōwa 15 [1940]) (Tokyo: Shōbunsha, 1974).

31 I make this argument in "The Evidence of Sight," theme issue, "Photography and Historical Interpretation," *History and Theory* 48 (December 2009): 151–68.

32 Domon Ken, "Taigai senden zasshi ron" [A Discussion of International Propaganda Magazines], *Nihon hyōron* 18 (September 1943): 62.

33 Ikegami Shirō, "Tennō to shashin" [The Emperor and Photography], *Shashin Tenbō* 1, no. 1 (January 1947): 30.

34 Ina Nobuo, "Nihonteki shashin geijustu no kakuritsu e, 2" [Toward the Establishment of Japanese-Style Photographic Art, 2], *Camera Art* 12, no. 5 (December 1940), 250. Ina's initial foray into this topic is found in Ina Nobuo, "Shin taisei shita ni okeru shashinka no ninmu" [The Duty of Photographers under the New Order], *Camera Art* 12, no. 3 (September, 1940), 85–89; followed by Ina Nobuo, "Nihonteki shashin geijustu no kakuritsu e, I" [Toward the Establishment of Japanese-Style Photographic Art, I], *Camera Art* 12, no. 5 (November 1940): 193–95.

35 Domon Ken, "Hōdō mango, 3," *Foto Times* 17, no. 10 (October 1940): 52. Others weighed in on this dispute, including critic Watanabe Tsutomu and an anonymous writer using the pseudonym "Tagēru" (presumably Daguerre), accusing Domon of misreading Ina.

36 Domon, "Hōdō mango, 3," 51. See also Domon Ken, "Hōdō mango, 4," *Foto Times* 17, no. 11 (November 1940), for a particularly vehement defense of emotional politics.

37 Having made the decision to attack the Allies despite Konoe's backroom attempts to negotiate an end to the American oil embargo (America had been supplying over 80 percent of Japan's oil needs), the Japanese government seems to have been preparing the populace for an expansion of the war effort.

38 Domon, "Taigai senden zasshi ron," 62.

39 Domon, "Taigai senden zasshi ron," 65.

40 Domon, "Taigai senden zasshi ron," 66. This Japanese was, however, to be written in katakana for beginners rather than the more complicated mixture of kanji, *hiragana*, and katakana in which Japanese is normally expressed.

41 Domon Ken, "Taigai senden zasshi ron," 65.

42 Janice Matsumura's detailed account of the punishment meted out to the staff of *Chūō kōron*, three of whom died the very year of Domon's momentary detainment, demonstrates the dangers of an encounter with the police. Janice Matsumura, *More than a Momentary Nightmare: The Yokohama Incident and Wartime Japan* (Ithaca, NY: Cornell University Press, 1998).

43 See, for instance, Alice Y. Tseng, "Domon Ken's Murōji," in "Pictures and Things: Bridging Visual and Material Culture in Japan," special issue, *Impressions*, no. 30 (March 2009): 114–18.

44 See David Earhart's discussion of the phrase "Uchiteshi yamamu" in *Certain Victory*, 309. Earhart provides a full and fascinating description of the patriotic campaign centered on this image in chapter 9 of *Certain Victory*. By this time the war was all but lost, though Japan's high command pushed on.

45 Earhart points to the use of the same model in a different pose on the cover of *Asahi Camera*, March 10, 1943, 320.

46 A special report on the "Uchiteshi yamamu" campaign was published in "'Uchiteshi yamamu' nao nokoru katate ari," *Shashin shūhō* 262 (March 10, 1943).

47 After the war, photographers and critics continued to argue about the relationship between art and reality in the depiction of wounded veterans begging in the streets. See my "Power Made Visible: Photography and Postwar Japan's Elusive Reality," *Journal of Asian Studies* 67, no. 2 (May 2008): 365–94. Also see Lee K. Pennington, *Causalities of War: Wounded Japanese Servicemen and the Second World War* (Ithaca, NY: Cornell University Press, 2015).

48 John W. Dower, "Japanese Cinema Goes to War," in *Japan in War and Peace: Selected Essays* (New York: New Press, 1993), 35.

49 Ruth Ben-Ghiat, "Envisioning Modernity: Desire and Discipline in the Italian Fascist Film," *Critical Inquiry* 23, no. 1 (autumn 1996): 109–44.

8

FASCISMS SEEN AND UNSEEN

The Netherlands, Japan, Indonesia,
and the Relationalities of Imperial Crisis

ETHAN MARK

Interwar Fascism Viewed from Empire

On July 16, 1943, Edward John Voûte, the Nazi-appointed mayor of Amsterdam, received a letter of complaint from Johan Bastiaan Van Heutsz Jr. Mayor Voûte surely knew who its author was. Van Heutsz's father, former governor-general of the Netherlands Indies Joannes Benedictus Van Heutsz (1851–1924), was the most famous and decorated Dutch military man of modern times, known above all for his successful "pacification" of the ever restive region of Aceh at the turn of the twentieth century. Eight years earlier, a grand monument to mark his memory had been unveiled, with great fanfare, in the southwest of the city and was christened by Queen Wilhelmina herself. Yet Van Heutsz Jr., who made little secret of his Nazi sympathies, was not impressed. With a smug conviction that reflected not only his prestigious familial pedigree but also the confidence of a man convinced that history was finally on his side, he condemned the monument as "weak" and "decadent," unbefitting the image of his conquering imperial warrior father. As such, he wrote, it was in fact the very embodiment of the "weakness" of the prewar Dutch political status quo that had produced it—an indecisive, corrupt system of parliamentary democratic rule that had proven itself incapable of defending the national interest, sold out the empire, and, in effect, brought Nazi occupation upon itself. The monument should be replaced, he insisted, with something more appropriately masculine and martial.[1]

Van Heutsz Jr. left behind his own visual record that makes it easy to imagine what sort of alternative he had in mind. A year before writing to the mayor, he had returned to the Netherlands from an extended tour of Nazi-occupied Russia and published a travelogue entitled *A Viking in Russia* (*Wiking door Rusland*), its cover emblazoned with a Viking warrior with medieval armor, sword, a winged helmet, and a Nazi swastika on his shield, standing against a backdrop of a large "ss" logo. Several months later, Van Heutsz Jr., a medical doctor, volunteered for the *Waffen ss* (the ss military arm) and headed back to the Eastern Front to treat wounded German soldiers, by now in great supply. Subsequently decorated for bravery after his "Viking Panzer Division" escaped Soviet encirclement at Cherkasy in the Ukraine, he died in battle near Munich shortly before war's end. In the meantime, Mayor Voûte, a faithful servant of the Nazis, had taken no action on Van Heutsz Jr.'s request to change the monument. Indeed, he had little incentive to do so: despite their open and avowed loyalty to the Nazi cause, Van Heutsz Jr. and other open supporters of Nazi German rule, such as the Dutch fascist *Nationaal Socialistische Beweging* (NSB), wielded little influence with Voûte's Nazi bosses. Nor were they popular with most of the Dutch population, many of whom viewed them as traitors to the nation.

Although not widely known among the Dutch general public, the story of Van Heutsz Jr. and his letter to the mayor is hardly a secret among scholars of modern Dutch history. On the one hand clearly substantiating the existence of home-grown Dutch fascists, it also serves to illustrate why scholars of fascism and its visual expressions would rarely envision the interwar Netherlands as the most fruitful place to start: whatever his family relation to the Netherlands' most famous colonial military man, in his open devotion to Nazi Germany and to Nazism, Van Heutsz Jr. was an exception to the Dutch rule. Moreover, his problem with the monument was, after all, its *lack* of any fascist aesthetic, which he saw as symbolic of a prewar Dutch political regime also lacking in everything he admired so much in the German one. The period leading up to Nazi occupation had indeed witnessed a continued Dutch commitment to parliamentary democracy and to institutions such as the League of Nations as a civilized and progressive means of settling international disputes, along with an ongoing faith in the possibility of respect for the Netherlands' peaceful neutrality (which had kept it out of the previous world war). Even at the height of its popularity during the depths of the Great Depression in the mid-1930s, the NSB had never managed to attain more than 8 percent of the national vote, and it subsequently lost support as its leader, Anton Mussert, moved to embrace Hitler and his policies of anti-Semitism and racial purity. The stability of Dutch liberal democracy through the thick and thin of this period of crisis—a time when not only Germany and Italy but many other societies in central, eastern, and southern Europe turned decisively toward reactionary authoritarianism—has conventionally resulted in a positioning of the interwar Netherlands at a far remove from fascism.[2] In seeking out fascism in the *Pacific* theater during this period, historiographical and popular conventions would much sooner point us toward the aggressive imperial Japanese than to the peaceful Dutch. Amid a long list of other wartime atrocities they committed against the inhabitants of East Asia, Southeast Asia, and the Pacific, it was, after all, the Japanese who unilaterally invaded the Netherlands East Indies and subjected its Dutch population to a merciless and brutal incarceration many experienced as quintessentially fascist.

Yet looking beyond the conventional equation of interwar Dutch fascism with that of Nazi Germany—an equation that makes fascism in the interwar Netherlands seem reassuringly limited to a fringe group of puppets, opportunists, and ideologues such as Van Heutsz Jr. and NSB leader Anton Mussert—another perspective exists from which emerges an entirely *indigenous* Dutch lineage of interwar fascism far more pervasive and troubling in its influence. It is a lineage whose monuments are still everywhere visible if we only take the trouble to look. That we are not in the habit of doing so is attributable to two ideological force fields whose global grip on the study of the interwar period, and thus also on that of fascism, remains nearly hegemonic: Eurocentrism and nation-centrism. The identity of Van Heutsz Jr. as the son of the Netherlands' most famous colonial general, born and raised in the Netherlands Indies and obsessed with their fate, serves as an essential clue here, though his exceptional Nazi loyalties could also be said to have long served as a distraction convenient to the Eurocentric conventions of the discipline, distracting us from, in a word, empire. For while Van Heutsz Jr. must be thankfully acknowledged as atypical of the interwar Dutch social and political elite in his open *Nazi* sympathies, his anxiety over the fate of a Dutch empire under siege from within and without, his nostalgia for the memory of his imperial strongman father, and his embrace of a fascist worldview as a means of "returning" the Netherlands to the imagined prosperous, orderly, and world-renowned empire over which his father had once presided were all in fact sentiments with a much wider currency.

Rendered invisible in the conventional Euro- and nation-centric story of the Netherlands' World War II is the essential identity of this period as one in which Dutch colonial subjects still vastly outnumbered its citizens. In an increasingly hostile interwar environment that embraced metropole and colony alike, many Dutch citizens were drawn *not* to Nazism as such but to an essentially native, imperial form of fascism as a vehicle for securing their continued imperial privileges or gaining new ones. Viewed not with the internecine rivalries of Europe but rather the global order of empires in mind, the peace-loving, democratic, progressive, liberal Netherlands motherland of the interwar period is thus revealed as rather like the top of an iceberg, whose emergence above the visible surface as such was made possible only by its placement atop a much larger social body groaning underneath the waves: a colonial body riven with social hierarchy, racism, autocracy, militarism, and exploitation—and a place where the Dutchman's position of authority, superiority, and prosperity was forever secure.

During the interwar period and above all amid the crisis generated by the Great Depression, uncontrollable revolutionary forces both within the Kingdom of the Netherlands and around the world began to raise the temperature of the seas in which this imperial iceberg floated: forces from the Left, including rising labor movements critical of the social status quo and anticolonial nationalists who sought an end to empire; and forces from the Right, including the Netherlands' prime imperial competitors, the Japanese, who sought a radical global imperial redistribution. In response, Dutch political, economic, and social elites both in the metropole and in the colony increasingly sought solace in a nostalgic return to the imperial glory days that was in fact something new. The period also witnessed the parallel rise of a Dutch middle-class fascist movement, the NSB, that shared and amplified these domestic and imperial anxieties and antipathies. Domestically, the NSB had an agenda and social composition similar to those of contemporaneous fascist movements in neighboring countries, and as elsewhere in Europe, it stood in ambivalent relation to domestic elites as having shared social and political enemies but also as being a potential political competitor. Its failure to make serious inroads among metropolitan socioeconomic elites ensured that the dominant story of the Netherlands' World War II would be one of fascist failure. Meanwhile, "offstage" in the colonial arena of the Netherlands East

Indies, however, the two streams of Dutch fascism flowed synergistically and powerfully together, revealing a shared imperial progeny and logic. Although it was increasingly politically contested and pushed to the fringes of the public eye in the metropole as the more immediate threat of war within Europe expanded, Dutch interwar fascism thus remained strongest and most visible on the "front lines" of the Netherlands' increasingly besieged Pacific empire.

Thus viewed in a relational and transnational frame that takes in the interwar Netherlands, its Indonesian colony, and its main imperial competitor Japan as an interconnected whole, it is in fact the Dutch interwar empire more than the Japanese one that confronts the viewer with the most obvious and monumental material expressions of fascism. It is these that are therefore the focus of this essay. Carved in stone or cast in metal and emphasizing the masculine military charisma of the individualized imperial ruler, they reflected Dutch fascism's mainly elite and colonial pedigree as quintessentially imperialist, exclusive, and hierarchical. Specifically, the discussion revolves around three distinctive interwar monuments built to honor Governor-General Van Heutsz in colony and metropole in the 1920s and '30s and their subsequent divergent histories: a massive militaristic mausoleum built in 1927 that still stands in Amsterdam's New Eastern Cemetery; a domineering memorial in the center of the colonial capital Batavia, completed in 1932, that surprisingly survived the Japanese occupation but not the transition to an independent Indonesia; and last, a monument erected in the southwest quarter of Amsterdam in 1935, which Van Heutsz's son singled out during the war for its atypical *lack* of a fascist aesthetic. All three were unveiled with equally immense fanfare during the interwar period, but only the last survived into postwar memory.

Such Dutch designs of the interwar years reflected a yearning to freeze imperial hierarchy in place, thereby forever fixing Indonesians as colonial subjects rather than citizens of the Dutch nation. In contrast, visual and other propaganda produced by the Japanese promised the revolutionary destruction of the old Dutch order and its replacement with an Asia revitalized and unified by a common cause and a common culture. Insofar as it emphasized horizontal social unity and inclusion rather than the social hierarchy and distancing of the Dutch model, Japan's call for an "Asia for the Asians" bore immeasurably greater potential appeal and transferability to Japan's colonial populations. But in practice, such promises were contradicted by a Japanese determination to preserve their empire that was no less fierce than that of their Dutch competitors. In Indonesian eyes, the resultant contradiction—the gap between the nation-building that was promised and the empire-building that was delivered—ultimately revealed a Japanese fascist logic no less cruel than that of the Dutch.

Bringing the two together, the following discussion presents a brief history of interwar fascism and its visual expressions in what might be called an Indonesia-centric frame: a look at Dutch and Japanese interwar fascisms and their social logics as revealed in mutual competition over an increasingly resistant colonial location whose resources and population each sought to secure. The attempt has yielded a narrative centered on Dutch fascism and its interwar evolution, with Japan and its wartime alternative arriving and receiving brief attention as a counterreferent relatively late in the story. Such an emphasis reflects not only limitations of space and an Indonesian chronology in which Japan made a relatively late appearance, but also the oft-hidden relational nature of "Japanese fascism" as expressed in how Japan's message necessarily manifested itself in a specifically Southeast Asian wartime context, that is, as a revolutionary alternative to the European imperial order—and European fascism—that had come before. An exploration of these two distinct and competing fascist lineages highlights two inflections of a global phenomenon studies of fascism and fascist aesthetics underemphasize: the complex global relationality between the interwar rise of fascism and the crisis of empire.

Monuments to Imperial Glory and the Fascist Face of the Interwar Netherlands

Fascist monumentality in the interwar Netherlands? As the avowed Nazi Van Heutsz Jr. fulminated, little of this was on offer in the 1935 monument in the southwest of Amsterdam (figure 8.1). Its centerpiece was a female figure clad in toga, mounted upon a large stone base positioned in the middle of a reflecting pool. The figure bore in her hands not a sword but a legal parchment roll: she was a version of the Greek Lady Justice. Behind her stood two small lions, and behind those towered two brick pillars connected high above by an inverted U-shaped metal form with rays projecting outward and upward, suggesting the sun. The pillars and the lions were meant to symbolize metropole and colony, separated by the water below and united by the sun above. Between arched galleries emerging to the left and right appeared a succession of stone-carved pictorials representing the main islands comprising the colonial archipelago, peacefully populated by male and female Indone-

8.1 Unveiling of the Van Heutsz Monument, Amsterdam, 1935. From the photo collection Het Leven (1906–1941), SFA022001389, Het Leven, Spaarnestad Photo.

sian figures and figurines of social status from high to low and in primitively stylized native dress—kings, peasants, and godlike figures—surrounded by products and dwellings associated with each. The image of the conqueror of Aceh himself, however, appeared almost as an afterthought, in virtually two dimensions, on a round metal plaque mounted on the front of the central base. Rather than that of the conquering Viking warrior that Van Heutsz Jr. had in mind, the colonial relationship depicted here was one of a gentle and maternalistic purveyance of civilization.

Since the end of World War II, the Van Heutsz monument in Amsterdam's southwest has remained standing in a relative obscurity reflective of a more general Dutch ignorance of, and discomfort with, the imperial past. For the minority taking an interest in the matter, it has nevertheless remained the nation's best known monument to that past, and as such has been the greatest focal point of public struggles over the meaning of that heritage. For the postwar Dutch Left in particular, the ruthless brutality associated with Van Heutsz's "successes" in bringing to heel the rebellious "outer" provinces of Aceh as well as Bali, Celebes, Sumbawa, Lombok, and elsewhere during his tenure as general and subsequently governor-general (1904–9) made the monument a logical and perennial target of attacks as a symbol of the evils of Dutch imperialism.

Even in his turn-of-the-century heyday, Van Heutsz's capacity for "excesses," yielding "native" casualties in the tens of thousands, were already well known. When news and grisly photographs of the 1904 slaughter of the entire Acehnese village of Kuta Reh trickled into the mother country, pressure mounted for his resignation. He was saved from this fate only by the unyielding support of the young Queen Wilhelmina, who was to remain a die-hard fan of Van Heutsz during his life and after his death.[3] In 1967, amid expanding anti–Vietnam War protests, the Van Heutsz monument was defaced with white paint and even subjected to a failed bomb attack. By 1984, when it was targeted in a second failed bomb attack, the lettering and the plaque of the general had disappeared altogether, never to be recovered.

Over the same decades, however, mainstream historians, military men, and others among the Dutch elite—including a large community of former colonial residents—have more quietly continued to characterize Van Heutsz as a tough but admirable figure who succeeded in unifying the archipelago when all others had failed, also emphasizing that he was not only a conqueror but also a bearer of civilization. It was, after all, under his watch that the colonial regime had responded to long-standing progressive calls for an "ethical policy" toward the "natives" by instituting a system of village schools (albeit also catering to conservatives of the day by insisting that the "natives" foot the bill for the schools themselves). A 2006 essay in the mainstream *Historisch Nieuwsblad* described Van Heutsz as progressive for his day, a man "too practical to be racist."[4] Even today, a prominent infantry regiment of the Dutch Mobile Air Brigade still proudly bears Van Heutsz's name; this brigade was originally formed directly out of units of the defunct Netherlands Indies Colonial Army (KNIL) when the Dutch lost their military bid to hold onto the colony in 1950. It is perhaps not surprising, then, that a committee appointed to restore and rechristen the monument in the early 2000s referred to it as representing the "two faces of Dutch colonialism."[5]

For all the controversy and attention to Dutch colonial history that the Van Heutsz monument has brought to the surface since its unveiling some eighty years ago, the focusing of Dutch attention upon this *particular* monument, and upon the particular colonial history of the man with whom it is associated, is even more remarkable for what it obscures. For all their heatedness and social significance, such debates, and the ideological frame they reinforce, have functioned as a remarkably effective means of detaching and distancing postwar understandings of Dutch colonialism from the immediate late imperial context in which the monument itself was actually produced—that is, from the interwar period. Significantly, this was a period in which Van Heutsz achieved a far greater stature in death than he had ever achieved in life. Among Dutch elites both metropolitan and colonial, it was in fact a period that witnessed a virtual Van Heutsz mania. Properly restored to this context, the monument in Amsterdam's southwest emerges in quite a different light: as only the last in a *whole series* of Van Heutsz statues, busts, and monuments—a veritable avalanche, in fact—erected not only across Amsterdam and the Dutch motherland, but across the length and breadth of the Netherlands Indies as well, during the decade after his death in 1924. Among these, the 1935 monument in Amsterdam's southwest in fact stands out as a striking *exception* to the interwar rule, particular in its pronounced rejection of the fascistic martial, masculine aesthetics upon which Van Heutsz's Nazi son insisted.

From the façade of the Dutch Commercial Company (Nederlandsche Handelmaatschappij) in Amsterdam's city center to the central square of Banda Aceh, capital of the province where Van Heutsz's worst atrocities were committed, busts, figures, and references to Van Heutsz (and other beloved Dutch colonial figures such as East India Company (VOC) founder Jan Pieterszoon Coen), cast in bronze or cut in stone, came to adorn dozens of public spaces across both metropole and colony between roughly 1925 and 1935. Along with the 1935 monument in Amsterdam's southwest, the two largest and most monumental of these arose, respectively, in the east of Amsterdam in 1927 and in the center of the colonial capital of Batavia in 1932. Reflecting the depth of Van Heutsz nostalgia that gripped Dutch economic and political elites during this period, each was funded through massive private donations and christened with overwhelming official fanfare.

When Van Heutsz Jr. wrote to Amsterdam's mayor in 1943 to complain about the "weakness" of the newest monument to his father, he might have indeed pointed to more than just the cover of his own recent pamphlet as an example of an appropriately "strong" alternative. For sixteen years, the model alternative had in fact already existed for all to see: the Van Heutsz mausoleum, constructed as the centerpiece of Amsterdam's New Eastern Cemetery and christened—like the 1935 monument—by Queen Wilhelmina herself (figure 8.2). Van Heutsz's reburial there in July 1927 was conducted with the full honors of a state funeral, and he remains today the only non-

8.2 Reburial ceremony at the Van Heutsz Mausoleum, Nieuwe Oosterbegraafplaats, Amsterdam, 1927. From the photo collection Hat Leven (1906–1941), SFA022001387, Hat Leven, Spaarnestad Photo.

royal recipient of such an honor. Those standing in attendance included an honor guard of the colonial militia (KNIL), which included a sizeable Indonesian representation.

Led by an honorary monument committee whose membership represented the cream of the Dutch political and economic elite, the mausoleum had been financed through donations from a host of national, provincial, and local committees founded across the nation and in the Netherlands Indies upon the retired general's death in Switzerland in 1924.[6] Exhumed and transported to Amsterdam for reburial three years later, the general's coffin and remains were first displayed at a great public ceremony at the royal palace on the Dam Square, from whence they were solemnly paraded some six kilometers to the cemetery. Designed by the modernist "Amsterdam school" architect Jordanus Roodenburgh and carved of great reddish granite blocks by the sculptor Bon Ingen-Housz (1881–1953) of the Hague—both winners of a design competition—the colossal mausoleum suggested the form of a military fortress or an immense battle tank. Its bunker-like entrance was flanked by two supremely muscular, larger-than-life Viking warriors modeled after figures on the Monument to the Battle of Nations christened by Kaiser Wilhelm in Leipzig in 1913.[7] At the mausoleum's rear, flanking a listing of Van Heutsz's military and political titles, stood two more muscular male figures. The soldier to the left of the title list wore a helmet and sported the bundle of wooden rods that symbolized strength and authority in Etruscan and Roman yore, now also the symbol of Mussolini's new regime to the south—the *fasces*. To its right stood Mercury, the Roman god of trade and profit as well as guide to the underworld.

Despite the immensity and extravagance of Van Heutsz's Amsterdam tomb, so much donor money was left over that the committee decided to invest this in two more monuments, one in the colonial capital of Batavia and the other in a second location in Amsterdam. As we have seen, the latter was to become a source of distress for Van Heutsz Jr. The stories of these two monuments reveal the way fascism's course diverged between metropole and colony before and after World War II.

A suitably central location in Batavia had been chosen and work by 1930 was underway. Reflecting the general's sudden public ubiquity as symbolic crystallization of a colonial nostalgia that had only deepened since the Great Depression had set in, one observer noted, with little apparent sense of irony, that "the Van Heutsz Monument Committee chose this location because there is not enough room for such a large monument on the Van Heutsz Boulevard."[8]

The Batavia Van Heutsz Monument was finally unveiled in August 1932 (figure 8.3). The winning design, stunningly executed by Indonesian craftsmen, had been conceived in the Netherlands by the architect Willem Marinus Dudok, famous for his "romantic cubism," in collaboration with sculptor Hendrik van den Eynde.[9] As Van Heutsz's successor Governor-General J. C. De Jonge revealed the monument to the public for the first time, a great crowd of dignitaries and onlookers marveled at its immense and imposing stonework and the unmistakable message of imperial power it projected. The figure of Van Heutsz, his eyes and rigid body both facing firmly forward toward the horizon, stood high on a central pedestal from which emerged, far below and before him, a well-ordered mass of "natives" driven forward by Dutch colonial troops. A great elephant stood in their midst, a "native" guide perched atop him, suggesting the opening of a way through hitherto impenetrable jungle. Other half-naked Indonesians emerged in a relief to Van Heutsz's side, somewhat higher up but still well beneath him, bearing the fruits of their manual labors on their shoulders. Below them appeared Van Heutsz's name

8.3 The Van Heutsz Monument in Batavia, covered in wreaths from its admirers, on the day of its unveiling ceremony in August 1932. From the photo collection Hat Level (1906–1941), SFA022001376, Hat Leven, Spaarnestad Photo.

and dates in office (1904–9) and text that read, "He Created Order, Peace, and Prosperity, and Unified the Peoples of the Netherlands Indies into One."

In a commemoration speech amplified through great loudspeakers that could be "seen from afar" and relayed live to both of the new public radio channels in the European mother country more than ten thousand kilometers distant, De Jonge said of his forerunner Van Heutsz: "He laid a milestone." Echoing the grand words carved into the monument, he continued: "More than ever before, he executed policies that aimed for prosperity, happiness, and development of the land and its people. It is right," he proclaimed, "that he is called an 'Empire builder.' But nevertheless, we must also acknowledge that he was a 'home builder'—builder of the home of the Indies' society that we now inhabit."[10]

The monument's reactionary colonial symbolism was not equally welcomed by all. Days before its unveiling ceremony, the Indonesian Student's Association (PPPI) had convened at their Batavia headquarters—a boarding house that had been rechristened the "Indonesia Building" since the association's founding in 1928—to issue the following statement: "The history of

General Van Heutsz is a history of suffering for the Indonesian people, the people of a subject nation, and Van Heutsz' name is synonymous with the loss of freedom in various territories, causing Indonesia to be the victim of imperialism . . . the construction of a monument to Van Heutsz in these times . . . means the deliberate deepening of a wound in the hearts of the Indonesian people."[11] In the metropole too, plans for a second Amsterdam monument had met with unprecedented resistance from the city council, whose membership now included socialists and even communists determined to prevent another expensive tribute to "a man with blood on his hands." After a long standoff, an uncomfortable, controversial compromise was reached: the conservatives would get "their" monument, and the Left theirs. The latter, a statue of Domela Nieuwenhuis (1846–1919), the founder of the Netherlands' first social democratic party, was unveiled to huge, enthusiastic crowds in the west of the city center in 1931, his provocatively raised arm ending in a clenched fist.[12]

When the monument in Amsterdam's southwest was finally unveiled in 1935, it was greeted with a hyperbolic speech from then prime minister Hendrikus Colijn entirely in keeping with earlier precedent. The hard-liner Colijn, founder of the "Anti-Revolutionary Party" and with a long record of ministerial appointments, had served under Van Heutsz in Aceh in his younger days, also committing atrocities in the name of "pacification." His speech compared the general to no less than "Hannibal, Caesar, and Alexander the Great."[13] Yet as Van Heutsz's son later noted, this time the look of the monument decisively failed to match the martial rhetoric. In subsequent years, a remarkable story emerged as an explanation: Frits van Hall, coauthor of the winning entry in the competition for the monument's design, was in fact a committed communist. A colleague even contended later that the superficial, two-dimensional quality of the Van Heutsz plaque and lettering on the monument had been entirely intentional, attributing to Van Hall the subversive declaration, "replace it with the words 'freedom,' 'merdeka [the Indonesian word for independence],' or 'Indonesia,' and you've got a Statue of Liberty!" Yet the selection committee's choice for such a peaceful, maternal motif seems above all a reflection of the monument's broader formative context: an interwar Dutch political environment in which the critical views of the now-established Left could no longer be simply ignored or suppressed. In its very serenity, the 1935 monument thus revealed the scars of the pitched political battles of the late 1920s that lay behind its construction.[14]

It was no doubt to such unwelcome, "subversive" interwar developments in both metropole and colony that Governor-General J. C. De Jonge alluded in his speech as he unveiled the Batavia monument in 1932—developments that only seemed to be gaining momentum since the recent onset of the Great Depression: "How far away from us Van Heutsz now seems to stand. One might wonder if people would put up with a figure like Van Heutsz nowadays. He was a man of action. Imagine a man of action in these times of so much talk! A man like Van Heutsz in these times where everything is criticized! In these times, when everyone wants to have a say in everything!"[15] For De Jonge and others of his ilk, the colonies at least remained a place where it was still possible to rule with an iron fist, particularly where the "natives" were concerned. Elsewhere in Asia, where anticolonial movements were gathering momentum—places such as British India, the Philippines, China, and Burma—the Anglo-American powers were beginning to opt for a more "constructive" response that combined the suppression of "radicals" with piecemeal, gradualist delaying tactics of compromises and negotiations with "moderate elements." By the late 1930s, within this context, the U.S. and Great Britain had made pledges of greater autonomy and future independence to Burma and the Philippines. But for the Dutch in the East Indies—as with the Japanese in Korea and China during the same period, for example—immense economic and psychological investments in their imperial "jewels in the crown" combined with heightened fears of international instability and economic peril to yield instead a more aggressive and uncompromising stance than ever. The appointment of the hard-liner De Jonge, and his enthusiasm for Van Heutsz, reflected the determination of Dutch elites to make time stand still—or better yet, to make it retreat.

Nowhere was this clearer than in De Jonge's response to Indonesia's fledgling nationalist movement and its charismatic young leader Sukarno. Upon his appointment in 1931, one of De Jonge's first moves was to send Sukarno to prison for a four-year term for "subversive activities." At first, protests from Dutch progressives in both colony and metropole pressured him into releasing Sukarno three years early, but a year later, after publishing the essay "Attaining Indonesian Independence," Sukarno was again arrested. This time De Jonge invoked emergency powers to ship the troublemaker and his right-hand man Mohammad Hatta safely off to unlimited exile on the distant island of Flores. The two would only be released at Japanese hands some eight years later.

Interimperial Competition and the Rise of Japanese Fascism

If the insecurity of the early 1930s found many Dutch looking back nostalgically, many Japanese were looking rather aggressively ahead. Just as the Dutch were unveiling the Van Heutsz monument in Batavia, their Japanese imperial competitors were busy putting the finishing touches on a radical challenge not only to rising Chinese anticolonial nationalism but also to long-standing Euro-American imperial hegemony in Asia: 1932 witnessed the crowning of Pu Yi on the throne of the puppet state of "Manchukuo." Prompted by visions of a "Manchurian lifeline" that would provide land, resources, and military security in a hostile and dangerous post-1929 world—a buffer against the rising threats of Chinese nationalism and Soviet communism, as well as insurance against Western protective trade barriers and anti-immigration policies—the Manchurian invasion was initiated by rebellious factions within Japan's military, but it quickly proved wildly popular among the general public. In Japan, as in places like Germany, where Hitler came to power in 1933, and in Italy, where Mussolini's regime peaked in popularity with its brutal victory over Ethiopia in 1935, interwar yearnings for such a decisive "breakthrough" were feeding dangerous support for a combination of authoritarian politics at home and aggressive imperial expansion abroad.

The social mapping of Dutch and Japanese interwar fascisms alike was complex and varied, but they had important and telling differences. In comparison to Dutch imperial fascism, whose center of gravity lay among its political and economic elites, particularly those with a direct investment in the empire, Japan's interwar fascism was fundamentally more a phenomenon of a frustrated middle class. As such, as much as it shared with Dutch interwar fascism an embrace of a reactionary nostalgia against the revolutionary social challenges and imperial threats of the era, it also had a stronger social revolutionary component. Reflective of their class position, its supporters (heavily represented by younger, low-ranking army officers) often expressed a particular sense of frustration at the persistence of Japan's "old order," a domestic power structure perceived to be dominated at the top by a "semifeudal" political and economic oligarchy from which they felt excluded. They also felt threatened "from below" by the rise of an increasingly restless, politicized, and chaotic "mass society" symbolized by activist workers and audacious modern women. A renovated, unified, virile nation-state—one cleansed of the "Western" scourges of individual and class interests, efficiently implementing and distributing the benefits of technological progress, and regimented and mobilized for battle in the ruthless international struggles of the day—was the only way forward. In combining a call for a "return" to an ancient indigenous morality and spirituality with a leap into a socially and technologically engineered future, along with a critique of the materialism, individualism, and class conflict of capitalism and communism alike as unwelcome "Western" imports, such discourses can be usefully compared with those of fascist Chinese counterparts that Maggie Clinton considers in chapter 1 of this volume.

As in Italy and Germany too, Japan's interwar spokesmen for national renovation saw an expanded and rejuvenated empire as key to the success of their domestic program (an aggressive luxury the Guomindang, relatively politically weak and at the mercy of the much more powerful Western and Japanese imperialists, could hardly afford). But unlike the Germans and Italians, Japan's position as a non-Western empire in a Western-dominated world made both its imperialism and its stance toward anticolonial nationalism more complex. As the crisis of Western modernity deepened and tensions with the Western powers mounted, Japan's "outsider" status as a nonwestern society was increasingly seen as strength rather than weakness: Japan's solution to the interwar crisis would consist of a rejection of "Western" individualism and liberalism and a "return" to its original Asian values. By the same token, interwar Japanese were inclined to sympathize with the anticolonial nationalism of fellow Asians so long as it was directed against Western colonizers. As imperial Japan moved deeper into China, it increasingly proclaimed its struggle as a mission of Asian liberation from Western domination. Where the Dutch sought to increasingly suppress anticolonial nationalism, Japan's spokesmen sought in effect to transcend the inherently conflicting agendas of Japanese imperialism and Asian nationalism by coopting Asian anticolonial nationalism and its appeals within a Japanese imperial framework.

Dutch Fascism from Below:
The Crisis of Empire and the Rise of the NSB

As the Depression continued and the international climate darkened further, mass middle-class-oriented fascist movements gained traction not only in Japan, Germany, and Italy but across the length and breadth of Europe. Mainstream observers in the Netherlands and elsewhere marveled at the "achievements" of Mussolini and Hitler, who seemed to be uniquely successful in quieting unrest, unifying their populations, and strengthening their economies while the rest of the world was losing its way. Less commonly noted is that fascist ideas and movements also enjoyed a particular popularity among colonial middle classes as well as elites in Western Europe's colonies in Asia and Africa. This was fortified not only by particularly strong colonial identification with fascism's racist, social Darwinist worldviews but also by unease at the newfound aggressiveness of anticolonial movements and the fascists' particularly muscular promises to defend against them.

In the Netherlands Indies such sentiments were strengthened further in response to increasing tensions with imperial Japan. Before Japan's expanding war with China raised the military temperature in the region from the late 1930s onward, these tensions were fostered primarily by economic competition, as Japanese businesses and entrepreneurs aggressively sought, in Asian markets, a means of exporting Japan's way out of the Depression. In the early 1930s, cheap Japanese products flooded the Netherlands Indies, and hundreds of small-scale Japanese entrepreneurs set up shops across the archipelago to sell them. Friendly and selling their wares at competitively low prices, these shopkeepers had become popular among the local population. Indonesians often favored them over the ethnic Chinese, who were traditionally seen as economic and social rivals, dominated the lower reaches of the retail economy, and received relatively preferential treatment from the Dutch colonizers. With their own colonial market share severely threatened, the Dutch responded with protectionism. An increasingly militant Japan, which left the League of Nations in 1933 over Manchuria, responded with increasingly militant rhetoric.

Against this ominous backdrop, the Netherlands' own aspiring fascist leader Anton Mussert found no warmer reception than in the Netherlands Indies. When he arrived in Batavia in 1935, his NSB party, founded four years earlier, was the fifth largest in the mother country, having won 8 percent of the votes in the most recent election. But among the Dutch community of the Netherlands Indies, the NSB was the largest political party. In both colony and metropole, the NSB enjoyed considerable support among the unemployed, small-business owners, and low-ranking officials such as the police forces. "At home," at least so long as Mussert's support at the polls remained manageably low, the ruling elite preferred to keep him at arm's length; state employees were prohibited from joining his party.[16] In the Indies, however, Mussert was treated as a guest of state and was twice received with great ceremony by Governor-General De Jonge himself. The highlight of Mussert's colonial visit, avidly filmed and screened in the local cinemas, was his ceremonial wreath-laying at the new Van Heutsz monument.

In an accompanying speech, Mussert hammered upon his qualifications as defender of the empire from unprecedented threats within and without: "Countrymen, any year now could be the last of our existence as a self-sufficient nation. And I say to you, the Indies is practically undefended, and if we lose the Indies—I cannot say it enough—at that moment there will be no possibility for a self-sufficient existence for our people. At that moment, we'll have to become a part of Germany. And no matter how much we might respect our neighbors, that's surely the last thing a real Dutchman would want!" Until 1940, donations from the Dutch colonial community would remain an essential source of revenue for the NSB—a little-known colonial lifeline for Holland's metropolitan fascists.[17]

In both colony and metropole, however, 1935 proved to be the high point of Mussert's popularity. In the mother country, the elite establishment shunned the NSB as radical upstarts, and strong conservative allegiance to the political parties associated with the Netherlands' two main, largely separate religious communities (*zuilen*) of Catholics and Protestants further condemned supporters of the NSB to "outsider" status and even social ostracism. Largely as a result, its support at the polls in 1937 dropped to little more than half that of two years earlier; it would not recover before the Nazi invasion in 1940. While the NSB in the colony clearly enjoyed more open support from members of the social elite, there, as in the Netherlands, a substantial proportion of the NSB's support came from disaffected members of the middle class. In other ways, however, the social composition of the NSB's supporters, the reasons for their support, and the eventual reasons for its decline were all distinctive— and distinctively colonial. For here the majority of NSB party members—some 70 percent—were members of its large mestizo Indo-European ("Indo") community, who comprised some four-fifths of those with official status as Dutch citizens.[18]

The Indo community had come about through centuries of Dutch rule in Batavia and the surrounding areas, and it comprised the core of the traditional colonial ruling elite. In practice, as in other places around the world, closer ties with the Dutch motherland and the increasing influence of social Darwinist, racist thinking in the late nineteenth century meant increasing discrimination against these "mixed bloods" at the hands of the "pure" (*totok*) Dutch. But when the colonial state formalized a system of separate, discriminatory legal codes for themselves, "natives," and "foreign Orientals" at the end of the nineteenth century, most Indos were awarded official Dutch status. However severe the racist attitudes that Dutch colonial elites entertained toward them, in the overriding interest of maintaining the "tranquility" of the colonial status quo, the move was a practical necessity. In a classic act of colonial "divide and conquer," the Indos were thus strategically aligned with the totok Dutch and positioned above and separately from the natives, thereby heightening tensions between them and the latter.

As Indonesian anticolonial nationalism gained strength, for the many Indos for whom the Netherlands Indies was the only imaginable homeland (rather than the Netherlands, let alone "Indonesia"), the NSB's stress on protecting Dutch civilization and the Dutch empire against all such "radical" threats inside and out held a distinctive appeal. NSB membership was also a way of emphasizing one's Dutch cultural identity and loyalty in a colonial environment in which the questioning of both was frequently deployed as a basis for anti-Indo discrimination.[19]

Making such Indo support for the NSB at all possible was the NSB's emphasis on *cultural* purity and national loyalty, rather than *racial* purity, as the prime criteria for membership in the Dutch nation. In this the Dutch fascists of the early to mid-1930s more closely resembled and emulated those in Italy than those in Germany.[20] This situation was to change, however, as Mussert and other NSB leaders increasingly came to identify the party with the Nazis and correspondingly increase emphasis on "Aryan" racial purity and anti-Semitism. Such moves inevitably alienated many Indos from the NSB, and the NSB overall experienced a dramatic decline in its colonial membership during the last years before the war.

After Nazi Germany invaded the Netherlands in May 1940 and the NSB there chose collaboration, the Dutch colonial authorities in the Netherland Indies cracked down on the local NSB as an enemy of the free Dutch state. Yet where Indonesian nationalists were concerned, the continued hard-line stance of the Dutch colonial regime was not easily distinguishable from that advocated by the NSB. It was only in mid-1941, when the great showdown between imperial powers, long predicted by both fascists and the communists, threatened to spread to the Pacific, that the Dutch colonial state actively began to court the support of "moderate" Indonesian nationalist elements. In the meantime the Netherlands had been occupied by Japan's ally Nazi Germany, and Japanese relations with the Dutch and their American allies had steeply declined as a result of ongoing tension over Japan's war in China and related Japanese moves into a French Indochina now controlled by Vichy fascists. In their hour of need, the Dutch belatedly called upon their Indonesian "brethren" to help them defend "their" homeland against the invading Japanese "fascists."

Ambivalent Alternative:
Japanese Fascism and Occupied Indonesia

For Indonesians, to say such Dutch wartime appeals were too little too late would be an understatement. Indeed, it was easy to view such belated Dutch calls for (little) "brotherhood" as nothing really new but merely the other side of the Dutch imperial Janus face that had existed in the form of the "ethical policy" at least since the days of Van Heutsz. While the Dutch sought to identify a common enemy by branding the Japanese as fascists, until now Indonesians' most intimate encounter with fascism had been with that of the Dutch rather than the Japanese variety; democracy, meanwhile, had remained an exclusively Dutch possession.[21] In practice, most Indonesians could therefore be forgiven for harboring a more positive inclination toward the arriving Japanese than the Dutch expected—all the more so given the jaw-dropping power with which the Japanese made their irresistible entry.

On March 9, 1942, Japanese forces conquered Java after a whirlwind campaign lasting just nine days, wresting it, along with the rest of the Indonesian archipelago, from centuries of Dutch colonial domination. Singapore, the "impregnable fortress" of Britain's Asian empire, had fallen ignominiously just weeks before. Japanese, Americans, Europeans, and Southeast Asians were stunned and radicalized by the suddenness of this development and the vastness of its implications. Japan, perennially viewed not only by Westerners but by most Indonesians as little more than a distant, second-class Western copycat, now seemed to have beaten the West at its own game. Indonesians lined the roads to welcome Asia's new leaders, who also proclaimed themselves Asia's liberators; they emphasized the point by hoisting Indonesian flags alongside their own. Not just for Japanese but for Indonesians as well, both past and future seemed suddenly bathed in a new "Asian" light.

It is one of the great ironies of modern imperial history that the "liberation" of Indonesians from the late imperial Dutch brand of fascism thus came at the hands of imperial Japanese, whose own fascistic conviction of their unique "world-historical" racial destiny as Asia's natural-born leaders and liberators, hardened through years of brutal, frustrated aggression against a resistant China and ongoing resentment at Western domination and arrogance, was in turn immeasurably strengthened by their success in this very same act, and by the warm reception they received in response in Southeast Asia. For those who refused to acknowledge their new imperial hegemony—Chinese, Korean resistors, Westerners, communists—the Japanese continued to reveal their most exclusionary and brutal fascist face. But Japanese justification of their Asian mission rested on a critique of a Western hegemony based on imperialism, racism, and capitalism, and they were in desperate need of support from their neighbors. To those who acknowledged their hegemony and shared their enemies, they promised inclusion in an Asian order of blood brotherhood rather than imperialist exploitation, a "return to Asia" comprising both cultural restoration and social renovation.

The result was that the legitimacy and identity of Japan's mission of "liberation" in Southeast Asia was located in a contradictory space, at once fascist and antifascist, imperialist and anti-imperialist, capitalist and anticapitalist, modern and antimodern. This is perhaps the reason that Japanese propaganda imagery in Southeast Asia, like its domestic expressions considered by Julia Adeney Thomas in chapter 7 of this volume, appeared markedly lacking in what might be called a fascist aesthetic—in stark contrast to the aesthetics of the monuments the Dutch erected in a desperate attempt to turn back the imperial clock. Reflecting a fundamentally ambivalent and contradictory Japanese wartime position vis-à-vis its new colonial subjects—and indeed toward the old-fashioned hierarchies of empire itself—Japanese propaganda combined appeals to the imperial and the national that overlapped with and contradicted one another.

As a first step toward building this new Japanese-Asian order, the Japanese sought to undermine remaining symbols of Dutch imperial legitimacy not only through confining the Dutch to prison camps—first men and later women and children—but also by destroying monuments and other points of reference to Dutch colonial power. On April 29, 1942, the eve of mass celebrations of the emperor's birthday some two months after the Japanese arrived, a statue commemorating Jan Pieterszoon Coen, the seventeenth-century founder of Batavia, was toppled, along with the "Amsterdam Gate on Prinsen Street." Yet remarkably, the Japanese chose to leave the Van Heutsz monument standing, electing only to erase the text engraved upon it and to remove the figure of Van Heutsz from view by encasing it in wood (figure 8.4). A Japanese-language newspaper explained that the monument "is considered unique and of artistic merit."[22]

Elsewhere, in propaganda films such as *The Battle of Hawaii and the Malay*

8.4 The Van Heutsz memorial in 1947, showing the Japanese erasure of the lettering and the covering over the figure of Van Heutsz. NFA02: cas-10037-9 (negative), Indonesia Independent collection (photos 1947–1953), Dutch Photo Museum.

Straits (1942), ordinary Indonesians were treated to repeated visual displays of Japanese power, most often in the form of ordinary soldiery mobilized for, and winning, battles in air and on land and sea. Such films were shown in theaters as well as in traveling film screenings throughout the countryside using specially outfitted trucks and portable outdoor screens, a technique that drew upon an Italian fascist model. Later, as the war situation grew more desperate, local propaganda such as the short film *Indonesia Raya*—named after and with a stirring soundtrack comprising the Indonesian national anthem—moved to incorporate Indonesians as active, empowered participants in a similar militarized aesthetic. A series of recognizably typical Indonesian landscapes melted into anonymous, neat ranks of marching, muscle-bound Indonesian paramilitaries. (Although an ongoing Japanese ambivalence toward "arming the natives" could still be read in the soldiers bearing wood-carved rifles rather than real ones!)

Dazzled by Japan's military successes, seduced by such propaganda, and intrigued by the lessons of Japan's experience as a uniquely successful and modern non-Western nation-state, many Indonesians were more receptive to Japan's appeals than was later acknowledged.[23] Sukarno, whom the Japanese freed from years of Dutch-imposed exile, was the most prominent of the many Indonesian nationalists from across the political spectrum who chose to work with the new overlords. In practice, however, the Japanese delivered much less than they had promised. Early hopes that Japan might soon grant Indonesia independence were quickly dashed when both the Indonesian flag and the national anthem were banned "until further notice" in the name of maintaining public order. It was only in September 1944, when the tide of the war had turned decisively against Japan, that Tokyo finally issued a promise of Indonesian national independence, and only then at some undetermined point in the future—a point that had yet to be reached when Japan surrendered to the Allies in August 1945. Like the Dutch before them, the Japanese were little interested in affording Indonesians greater political autonomy, and Sukarno and other nationalist leaders soon grew tired of the fetters imposed on their expression and activities in the name of wartime unity. The mass of Indonesia's population, out of direct reach of such media campaigns, experienced the Japanese and their regime in the impersonal form of increasingly crushing administrative exactions, meted out by Indonesian officials who had little time for or interest in intellectual argumentation. Japan's ever-escalating demands for labor and resources were combined with military-colonial arrogance, ignorance, and oppression that made the former Dutch rulers seem tolerant and brotherly by comparison. By the end of the occupation in 1945, with the colony ravaged and basic necessities in impossibly short supply, even most of the nationalists who had cast their lot with Japan early on had lost faith in them. The negative image of "fascists" in the minds of Indonesians, once dominated by the Dutch, was now more commonly associated with the Japanese.

In the end, the ambivalence of Japanese occupation for Indonesia might well be summed up in the wartime fate of Batavia's Van Heutsz monument: in erasing Van Heutsz's name and tribute and covering up his figure, the Japanese occupiers had succeeded in effacing Dutch authority and the symbols upon which its power and legitimacy were based. But they failed to replace it with anything concrete. Not only did they not have the time to craft and recraft the monumentalization of the dead as they did in Taiwan and Korea, as Paul Barclay shows in chapter 2; in ideological terms too the situation in Indonesia was even more unsettled and precarious. Throughout the occupation, the monument's offer-bearing Indonesians remained, and its soldiers continued to drive them forward to ruin. When the returning Dutch began a new, ultimately futile and devastating war in late 1945 to turn back the colonial clock, the monument remained standing as silent witness.[24] During the

8.5 The Van Heutsz monument in Jakarta in its final days. From the Spaarnestad photo collection.

revolution, nationalist youth covered the Jakarta monument with anticolonial slogans, and in 1953, —four years after that war's end, it was completely destroyed by the newly independent Indonesian government (figure 8.5).

Legacies Seen and Unseen

Long demolished in Indonesia, both the main monuments to Van Heutsz in Amsterdam remain standing today, each highlighting in its own way the ongoing limits and lacunae in the Dutch engagement with the colonial past—above all with regard to the inglorious interwar decades in which the two monuments arose. As noted above, the 1935 monument was a frequent target of postwar protest and vandalism, and by the late 1990s it was commonly recognized that it was in need of a facelift. In 2004, after several years of deliberations involving consultation with historians and interested parties, the city of Amsterdam rechristened it the "Indies-Netherlands Monument,

1596–1949." The first date refers to the Dutch founding of the colonial capital of Batavia by Jan Pieterszoon Coen (the same man whose monument in Batavia had been knocked down by the Japanese, to Indonesian applause, in 1942). The second year marks that in which the Dutch were finally compelled to surrender their colony to an Indonesia whose leaders had in fact declared its independence four years earlier in 1945. A committee member claimed that they had thereby "finally honored [monument co-designer] Van Hall's wishes." Yet contrary to Van Hall's wishes, it was to the colonial "Indies" rather than to an independent "Indonesia" that the monument was renamed, and nowhere did the anticolonial nationalist slogan *"merdeka"* (independence) appear.[25] The compromised new/old naming reflected a twenty-first-century Dutch state and civil society in which colonial nostalgia retained great sway among many of those with the greatest investment in the colonial past—foremost among them the large postcolonial community of former Indies residents and their descendants, along with the Dutch military.[26] The Dutch king attended a ceremony to honor the Van Heutsz Brigade's sixty-fifth anniversary in June 2015, its members proudly clad in colonial-era military attire.

In 2003, with much less fanfare, the Van Heutsz mausoleum was dismantled and removed from its central, commanding position at the entrance to Amsterdam's New Eastern Graveyard. Five years later it was reassembled in a more quiet and secluded location several minutes' walk deeper into the graveyard, among trees, bushes, and, ironically enough, several graves of honored Dutch resistors to Nazi rule during the World War II era. Less ironic, but no less remarkable, is the presence of another grave nearby occupied by the notorious Dutch war criminal Captain Raymond Westerling (1919–87), who, in a manner reminiscent of Van Heutsz two generations before him, oversaw the killing of thousands of Indonesians in campaigns to "restore order" during the war of independence.[27] Westerling was never prosecuted.[28]

Interviewed in 2003 regarding the Van Heutsz mausoleum's planned move to "a less prominent location," the graveyard director insisted that the action was prompted not by the sight of the monument but only by long-standing frustration at the inconvenience of having to lead funeral processions around it on the way to the main hall. Despite the apparent synchronicity of the move with the refurbishing and rechristening of its sister monument to the west, the director denied any connection to "political correctness or any change in the status of the 'pacifier of Aceh'. . . . 'If it had been Johan Cruijff lying there, we still would have moved him.'"[29] A small new signboard planted next to the mausoleum when it was reassembled in its new location in 2008 nevertheless contends that it "tells the story of our changing view of the Netherlands's colonial past . . .[;] designed to honor the general and his military successes, it now reminds us mostly of a dark page of Dutch history." In the single paragraph subsequently dedicated to this history, however, reference is made only to the Aceh War. The history of the interwar period that actually produced the mausoleum—including its multiple fascisms and the imperial relationalities that shaped their distinctive forms—remain hidden in the shadows.

Notes

1 Maurice Blessing, "Jo van Heutsz (1851–1924): Te praktisch om een racist te zijn," *Historisch Nieuwsblad*, March 2006.

2 In his 2004 study *Fascists* (Cambridge: Cambridge University Press, 2004), sociologist Michael Mann divides interwar Europe into three zones: a zone of sturdy parliamentary democracies to the west, a zone of uniform authoritarian regimes to the east, and a "swing zone" in the middle that included Spain, France, and Germany—societies deeply divided between Left and Right, whose ultimate fate was determined, argues Mann, in relation to the depth of their experience with and commitment to parliamentary democracy.

3 During the same period, Van Heutsz's public reputation was further weakened by rumors of an extramarital affair (Blessing, "Jo van Heutsz [1851–1924]").

4 Blessing, "Jo van Heutsz (1851–1924)."

5 "Andere Tijden: Van Heutsz," accessed May 19, 2019, https://anderetijden.nl/aflevering/652/Van-Heutsz. The website of the Netherlands Veterans' Museum at Bronbeek, operated by the Ministry of Defense, maintains that while "the debate about whether he [van Heutsz] was a hero or a villain continues in both the Netherlands and Indonesia . . . partly through his actions, peace, order, and prosperity were attained." "Museum schenkingen: Brokstukken Van Heutszmonument," accessed June 5, 2018, http://www.vriendenvanbronbeek.nl/10%20Schenking2015HEUTZDUDOK.htm.

6 Members of the honorary committee, which was chaired by Prince Hendrik, included Prime Minister Ruys de Beerenbrouck, Ministers of the Colonies and Finance De Graaff and Colijn, all of the queen's commissioners, and the mayors of Amsterdam, the Hague, Rotterdam, and Coevorden. Paul Berendsen, Ginet Gebert, and Coen Tasman, "Nota Inzake Het Van Heutsz-Monument: Held of Houwdegen?" September 23, 1998, accessed May 26, 2016, http://wvi.antenna.nl/nl/ic/vp/atjeh/heutsz/groen2.html.

7 Ewald Vanvugt, "Beknopte iconologie van de koloniale sculptuur in Amsterdam," in *Pluriform Amsterdam: Essays*, ed. Irene van Eerd and Berne Hermes (Amsterdam: University of Amsterdam Press, 1998), 174–75.

8 *Het nieuws van den dag voor Nederlandsch-Indië*, December 12, 1930. After In-

donesian independence the boulevard was named after the Acehnese resistance leader Teuku Umar.

9   Peter Veenendaal, "Van Heutszmonument, Batavia (1932)," accessed June 5, 2018, https://dudok.org/2016/12/13/van-heutszmonument-batavia-1932/.

10 "De Redevoeringen," *De Indische Courant*, August 24, 1932.

11 "Binnenland Van Heutsz en 'Indonesia': Manifest Perhimpunan Peladjar2 Indonesia," *Sumatra Post*, August 22, 1932.

12 Like Van Heutsz, Nieuwenhuis's glory days had actually occurred decades earlier, and his son would remark decades later that such a confrontational revolutionary gesture had never been a part of his father's visual vocabulary. But as with Van Heutsz, the interwar period put its own stamp on his legacy. "Domela in het Westerpark," *Ons Amsterdam* 10 (October 2012): 3.

13 https://www.doorbraak.eu/anti-koloniale-activist-laten-we-ophouden-foute-heren-te-eren/, accessed on May 19, 2019.

14 The young van Hall accepted the commission as his first major project after several other leading progressive artists refused it, including members of the De Kring Society and the most well-known sculptor of the "Amsterdam school," Hildo Krop. Ruud van Haastrecht, "Geef Van Heutsz Monument Ander Doel," *Trouw/De Verdieping*, October 30, 1998.

15 "De Redevoeringen."

16 "NSB was in Indië niet zo omstreden als in Nederland," *Trouw*, August 21, 1999.

17 Paul Verhoeven, "Portret van Anton Mussert," VPRO Documentary, 1969/1970, accessed May 19, 2019, https://www.vpro.nl/speel~WO_VPRO_043128~portret-van-anton-adriaan-mussert~.html.

18 Lizzy van Leeuwen, "Wreker Van Zijn Indische Grootouders: De Politieke Roots van Geert Wilders," *Groen Amsterdammer*, September 2, 2009.

19 See, for example, Lizzy van Leeuwen, "Wreker Van Zijn Indische Grootouders"; and Ann Laura Stoler's classic essay, "Sexual Affronts and Racial Frontiers: European Identities and the Cultural Politics of Exclusion," *Comparative Studies in Society and History* 34, no. 3 (July 1992): 514–51 (later republished in Frederick Cooper and Ann Laura Stoler, eds., *Tensions of Empire: Colonial Cultures in a Bourgeois World* [Berkeley: University of California Press, 1997]).

20 "The Dutch nation is found equally in Europe, East Asia, and the West Indies as a race of the spirit, which absorbs the race of the blood," states an early NSB pamphlet. "We deny anyone the right to bring discord to the nation of the spirit by investigating whether Dutch who are pure in their national feeling have un-Aryan, that is to say Jewish or *Indisch* blood." "Page 26 of Mussert Brochure number 4," quoted in "Een merkwaardig Verbond," *Soerabaiasch Handelsblad*, March 30, 1935.

21 The conservative Dutch interpretation of the Atlantic Charter issued by the Allies in August 1941, which promised postwar the right of self-determination to all countries participating in the conflict, only added fuel to the fire. When pressed by Indonesian *Volksraad* councilman Soetardjo as to whether the Netherlands

intended to honor the charter with relation to Indonesia, the Dutch authorities waffled, asserting their commitment to "democratic principles" while at the same time maintaining that the promise of self-determination did not apply within empires! Bernhard Dahm, *History of Indonesia in the Twentieth Century* (London: Praeger, 1971), 80.

22 *Unabara* newspaper, April 28,' 1942, 2.

23 See, for example, Ethan Mark, *The Japanese Occupation of Java in the Second World War: A Transnational History* (London: Bloomsbury, 2018).

24 While playing well to a Dutch audience inclined to blame the Japanese for destroying the "bond of centuries," Dutch postwar attempts to delegitimize Sukarno as a pro-Japanese "fascist puppet" gained little traction among Indonesians.

25 See "Andere Tijden: Van Heutsz."

26 See, for example, Lizzie van Leeuwen, *Ons Indisch Erfgoed: Zestig jaar strijd om cultuur en identiteit* (Amsterdam: Bert Bakker, 2008).

27 Adding insult to injury for a man who to this day personifies Dutch brutality in Indonesia but retains support in Dutch military circles, an Indonesian text inscribed on the gravestone by Westerling's family reads, "The People Gave You the Title of Just Ruler" (*Rakjat memberi beliau gelar ratu adil*).

28 Although Westerling was never tried, the author of *The Last Typhoon*, a 1992 fictional account of Westerling's atrocities that compared them to those of the ss, was put on trial in Groningen in 1994 for "tarnishing the honour and the good name of Dutch troops." The two were acquitted, but the Ministry of Justice appealed the case; acquittal followed once again in January 1995. See Leonard Doyle, "Colonial Atrocities Explode Myth of Dutch Tolerance," *The Independent*, May 28, 1994.

29 "Graf van Heutsz verplaatst," NRC *Handelsblad*, January 15, 2003.

9

YOUTH MOVEMENTS, NAZISM, AND WAR

*Photography and the Making of a Slovak Future
in World War II (1939–1944)*

BERTRAND METTON

The first independent Slovak state was created in March 1939 in the wake of the Munich agreement and the dismemberment of Czechoslovakia. As the first of what were later to be called "Nazi puppet states," its institutional framework was largely influenced by that of the Nazi tutelary power. In the months that followed, Catholic priest Jozef Tiso, who was the head of the new state, and his political formation, the reactionary-nationalist Hlinka's People's Party, implemented a policy of coordination that mimicked the Nazi *Gleichschaltung* of the mid-1930s: it passed racial laws, outlawed other political formations, and expanded the reach of the People's Party by creating a number of affiliated organizations.[1] The new state's youth organization, the Hlinka Youth, which had been founded a few months earlier in December 1938, was responsible for the physical and ideological training of the country's future generations.[2] As such it was ascribed the fundamental double task of regenerating the Slovak nation according to the new official creed, a mélange of reactionary Catholic ideas embodied by Tiso and a form of Europeanist Nazism championed by the radical wing of the People's Party, and cementing the rebirth of the Slovak nation through its first independent state.[3]

From 1939 until the fall of the regime in 1945, the organization published a series of youth magazines relaying official propaganda among young Slovaks. Carefully crafted photographs quickly replaced the drawn illustrations of the early issues, while at the same time the party's discourse proceeded to a reconsideration of the national narrative: references to a heroic national past came to be superseded by the transformative value of the war on the Eastern Front and by the future of Slovakia in Hitler's Europe. The evidence of these Slovak youth magazines shows the national narrative being redrawn under the pressure of war and militarization. Photographic images and the use of a militaristic aesthetic emulating the Nazi model became means of developing a modernist discourse that exploded the conservative Catholic national narrative in favor of a new political myth turned toward the future.[4] As revealed in the interplay between visual representation and ideology, the images featured in the Slovak youth magazines helped develop political and historical discourses inspired by those of Nazi Germany and fascist Italy.

Evidenced by the power of photographic images in the ideological toolbox of fascism, this Slovak context delivers an interesting perspective on the attempts of fascist publicists during World War II to use photography to produce serviceable ideological materials. Inscribed in those materials were the ideas of rebirth and an alternate modernity that saturated fascist discourses. Some of the main themes discussed in this chapter are also central to the arguments put forth by other contributors to this volume. It is particularly the case of Maggie Clinton's essay on the Chinese fascists' attempts to convey ideas of rebirth and build up mass support through the use of modernist aesthetics (chapter 1). Ethan Mark's chapter on colonial Indonesia also suggests that the processes of identification that framed fascist ideology should be understood as part of metahistorical dynamics that transcended national boundaries (chapter 8). Finally, while Nadya Bair's work on Robert Capa's war photographs provides us with a powerful antifascist counterpoint, it also serves as a reminder that the massive reliance on visual materials was not the exclusive domain of fascist movements, but it nonetheless provided fascist militants and political formations from around the world with a common language that helped frame a unified self-image of power, dynamism, and regeneration (chapter 10).

The Hlinka Youth and Its Propaganda Apparatus

From its inception, the Hlinka Youth organization sought to follow the Hitler Youth's German example: on the basis of one-party rule put into place by Tiso and the People's Party, it incorporated and replaced preexisting youth organizations such as the Sokol and the Slovak scouts.[5] Commander-in-chief Alojz Macek headed the movement, and it was placed under the supervision of the Ministry of Interior and the Hlinka Guard, both under the control of Alexander Mach, one of the leaders of the People's Party's radical faction.[6] As an extracurricular paramilitary organization, the Hlinka Youth's main purpose was to replenish the ranks of the Hlinka Guard with ideologically and physically primed personnel. By 1940, membership was made compulsory for youth between six and nineteen years of age. At the height of its powers in May 1943, it totaled 238,000 members, accounting for over 10 percent of wartime Slovakia's population.[7]

As Slovak Minister of Propaganda from March 1939 to August 1940, Mach vitally steered the modernization of the Slovak propaganda apparatus, drawing heavily on the Nazi model. If Mach conceived the Hlinka Youth as "an autonomous organization for the extra-curricular education of the Slovak Christian youth," its main task was to prepare youths for war and the role Slovakia played in Hitler's new continental order.[8] The education dispensed by the Hlinka Youth, which complemented that received in regular schools, consisted in two hours daily of courses and group activities divided into ideological (national-political education, social education, social health education) and military teachings; the latter became more prominent in the classes for older students.[9]

One of the principal innovations introduced during the first year of the Hlinka Youth and Mach's tenure at the Ministry of Propaganda was the creation of a complete set of youth magazines aimed at Slovak boys and girls during their membership in the organization. The first and most important was *Nová Mládež* (New youth), an illustrated monthly that appeared for the first time in April 1939. It was intended for a large audience of boys and girls between ten and eighteen years of age.[10] The Hlinka Youth also published a magazine for girls, *Slovenská Deva* (The Slovak girl), and another for boys aged six to ten years: *Vlča* (Cub).[11] Both magazines were extensively illustrated and offered their young readers cartoons and activities (crosswords, drawings, or knitting patterns) as well as news pertaining to the organization (summer camps, excursions, meetings with state officials).[12] Starting in September 1939, a fourth magazine was published by Hlinka Youth Headquarters: *Straž* was designed as a text-only organ and think piece for the chiefs and functionaries of the movement.[13]

Toward a Modernized National Narrative

Since the early 1990s and the democratization of Slovakia, historians have mostly focused on the question of the Slovak state's responsibility in deporting Slovak Jews and on the historical figure of Jozef Tiso.[14] This research vitally debunked the attempts by the radical nationalist Right, supported by then prime minister Vladimír Mečiar, to rehabilitate and glorify the figure of Tiso and the legacy of the Slovak state.[15] These works played a significant political role by confronting the reemergence of nationalist myths in the political arena. Yet their specific, albeit justified, focus somewhat obscured the emergence of a new political ideology that effected the fusion of the conservative national narrative of the People's Party with a fascism-inspired, forward-looking vision of the Slovak nation under Hitler's new European order.[16] The ensuing transformation of the national narrative in the Slovak youth press in 1941–44, from Catholic conservatism to fascism, owed much to the increased reliance on photographic images. These carefully crafted and edited images, emulating those in popular Nazi publications such as the youth magazine *Der Pimpf* or the widely circulated illustrated *Signal*, were key in producing a dynamic iconography that gave credence to the new political myth of the future.[17] A fine-grained study of the images that formed the core of a youth magazine such as *Nová Mládež* shows the extent to which the Catholic-national ideology of 1939 and 1940 was superseded by fascist conceptions of the future that promoted the construction of a "new Europe" through Slovakia's support of the Nazi war effort.

The involvement of Slovakia in the Second World War, as part of a "mutual assistance treaty" signed with Nazi Germany in 1939, made this radical discursive and ideological shift possible.[18] In the wake of the invasion of the USSR, in which a Slovak expeditionary force took part, Slovak society and political culture became subjected to an intense military propaganda.[19] The direct link between the Hlinka Youth and the military, through the training of future soldiers for the defense of the Slovak state, made it a primary outlet for official militaristic discourses. In September 1941, as the Axis forces advanced through the Soviet Union, Alojz Macek defined the purpose of the organization as "the organization and fulfillment of the current acknowledged needs concerning extra-curricular education, for the establishment of a new order, of a new life at home and throughout Europe."[20]

Michael Geyer has defined the genuine experience of war in the modern world as a phenomenon that "engulfs everybody, comes from somewhere *out there*—literally and figuratively—and seems to envelop society in all its partial activities and to transcend it. War thus becomes a metahistorical force, everyone participates but no one takes responsibility."[21] For the Slovak state's youth organization, as for that of fascist Italy or Nazi Germany from which it drew inspiration, photography supplied an adequate means for representing this metahistorical dimension of total war. Individual subjects of the photographs, often cast in heroic poses, functioned as the expression of the mass, symbolic characters with which individual readers of the magazines could identify.

Photographic images and simple photomontages, which the Slovak youth press featured extensively during 1941, were used to draw readers into the dramatic events unfolding before their eyes. From images of the Eastern Front's battlefields, of youth in other fascist countries, or of women working in the Hlinka Youth uniform, each young Slovak could make of himself or herself a builder of the new nation, in the present and the future. A transformative experience for society as a whole, the war period seemed to effect a formidable acceleration of time, promising for Slovakia a role in the grand historical scheme of Hitler's European project.[22] Photographic images were also crucial in creating the new historical narrative: as snapshots of a history in the making, they powerfully conveyed the myth of rebirth that framed the fascist conception of self.

Drawings as a Middle Ground between Conservatism and Fascism

In the Slovak state's first year, the visual output of the Hlinka Youth press mostly followed a traditional formula: textual content enhanced by drawings and illustrations. The themes developed in the magazines mostly fit within the Catholic, nationalist, and conservative discourse of the People's Party's ideological platform during the interwar period.[23] The first issue of *Nová Mládež* particularly emphasized the roots of the Slovak nation, its Catholicism, and the accomplishment of the People's Party with a series of articles on the movement's mythical forbears, such as Prince Pribina from Nitra (the

9.1 *Nová Mládež* magazine (published in Bratislava by the Hlinka Youth organization), April 1939, original drawn cover illustration.

first Christian Slavic lord) and the paternalistic figure of Andrej Hlinka, or an article on the Vatican, which was referred to as "the smallest but the greatest state" as an allegorical image of independent Slovakia.[24]

The cover of the magazine's first issue featured a black ink drawing of a Hlinka Youth member in uniform flanked by an eagle bearing a double cross and sitting on three bundled pieces of wood (figure 9.1). The cover's design mixed a traditional aesthetic with a set of references to fascism in the form of the eagle, the bundle, and the slick, tie-wearing, uniformed member of the organization.[25] Yet, the drawing's main focal point was a double cross positioned on the eagle's chest, a centerpiece joining the two wings; the cross is the national emblem of Slovakia and the expression of its Catholicism. In this image, the generic representation of the boy in uniform was placed under the protection of the cross-bearing eagle, a hybrid figure between fascist symbols and the traditional emblem of the cross. The same illustration was used, with different ink colors, for each of the magazine's first three covers. The drawing was loaded with symbols: a trinity comprising the state and the party (the eagle) and Catholicism (the double cross) looking over the emerging Slovak youth (the Hlinka Youth member). Its historicity relied precisely on the presence of these three elements yet somehow failed to render a convincing message of historical and political dynamism.

Photographic images were introduced inside the magazine at the beginning of 1940. By then, the Slovak army had already participated in the invasion of Poland in the autumn of 1939, and the contours of a new historical narrative were being sketched out. The German grip was tightening on Slovak political life, and it was officially ratified when Slovak leaders met Hitler and foreign minister Joachim von Ribbentrop in Salzburg on July 28, 1940.[26] The "Salzburg agreement" ensured that Nazi influence increased in Slovakia via the appointment of Vojtech Tuka as prime minister. A leader of the People's Party's radical wing, Tuka's boundless opportunism, anti-Semitism, and lust for power met Germany's needs for military and economic cooperation.[27] The agreement also introduced a number of German advisers who were responsible for securing German interests in all parts of public life in Slovakia. Among them were experts for the police, for the so-called Jewish question, and for the Hlinka Party and its youth organization.[28]

Visions of Movement in Photographic Images

Although the German advisers' involvement in the Hlinka Youth does not appear explicitly in the archive, they surely contributed to the profound revamping of its press in late 1940 and early 1941. Original, well-crafted photographs particular to each issue replaced the generic drawing of the cross-bearing eagle and Hlinka Youth member that previously adorned the covers of *Nová Mládež*. This new model, which also was used for the children's magazine *Vlca*, borrowed heavily from the Nazi youth magazine *Der Pimpf*. Indeed, the printing patterns with a full-page photograph on the cover and a thick bottom band containing the name of the tutelary organization were strikingly similar.

While the new template retained the cross-bearing eagle, tucked in the top left corner and styled as a medallion, it now relinquished center stage to the photographs. The cover picture for the June 1942 issue of *Nová Mládež* is telling of the iconographic innovations of that period (figure 9.2).[29] It features a group of teenage Hlinka Youth members performing a military salute before

9.2 *Nová Mládež* magazine (published in Bratislava by the Hlinka Youth organization), June 1942 cover, Hlinka bust and Hlinka Youth.

a symbol of Slovak nationalism: a bust of Andrej Hlinka in Ružomberok, the priest-politician's hometown and parish. The interplay between the youths looking to the left at an unknown horizon and the father figure of Hlinka looking benevolently upon them but in the other direction suggest a semantic opposition between past and future, old and new. It not only offers the image of a power transition but also posits two hardly reconcilable conceptions of time and politics: a history anchored in the past, immobile and looking inward on the nation, and another narrative written in the present that frames movement as the precondition for its very existence. Finally, the image also suggests the passage of power from a unique, identifiable figure to a multitude, a nation of future soldiers united under the banner of the Hlinka Youth and the People's Party.

War in the East and a Fascist Way of Life

The outbreak of war against the Soviet Union in June 1941 gave Slovak propagandists ample opportunity to test the appeal of photographic images and a powerful discursive trope with which to historicize the ideological struggle of the Slovak state. The dynamic of war, the physical movement of the Slovak army, served as parables for the inclusion of the country in Hitler's new European order.[30] The years 1941 and 1942 brought a remarkable surge of military imagery to the Slovak Youth press, while the adult press, especially the *Slovak* and *Gardista* newspapers, placed special emphasis on anti-Semitic textual content, as the Hlinka Guard prepared to deport the Slovak Jews.[31] Aestheticizing war in support of a renewed political message remained a crucial prerogative of the Hlinka Youth and its press.

Embracing this turn toward militaristic imagery, the cover of the December 1941 issue of *Nová Mládež* showcased a staged picture of a young man wearing the parade uniform of the organization and carrying a gun among crawling soldiers on the battlefield (figure 9.3).[32] A somewhat unrefined photomontage superimposing an armed character onto a picture of Slovak soldiers at war, this image nonetheless possessed a strong evocative power. The stance of the man in uniform clearly suggests an attitude of defiance vis-à-vis danger, fear, and fate; he stands among men laying on the ground, holding his weapon tightly with two hands. Despite the simplicity of composition, the picture produces a dramatic effect, projecting the reader into the battlefield, almost about to hear the bullets fly.

This image encapsulates the fascist conception of life familiar from Mussolini and Gentile in *The Doctrine of Fascism*: a life based on action, physical and moral courage, duty, and comradeship.[33] In the picture, the Hlinka Youth member rises above the mass of soldiers to symbolize the heroic nature of his personal engagement, a life that, following the fascist creed, relinquished personal pursuits and instead was dedicated to the state and the nation. The significance of war in fascist ideology lies, as Mark Neocleous argues, "in the conjunction of war as an inner experience, as the highest form of political activity, and as the supreme application of modern technology. The subjectivism of the front soldier's experience of annihilation is transformed into the objectivist affirmation of metaphysical-vitalist strength shaped by fate."[34] The Slovak soldier pictured in the photomontage is framed as the embodiment of this attitude toward life.

As the display of such images and photomontages of members of the movement posing in heroic attitudes became the norm on the magazine's cover, the back cover began showcasing the Slovak contingent in actual combat operations in the east. The goal was to create interplay between the staged, fantasized renditions of warfare and real action photographs: if the former projected a much-desired future in which youths could see themselves while reading the magazine, then the latter depicted the present struggle, a necessary stage in attaining political fantasy. The back cover of the December 1941 issue of *Nová Mládež* was an ideal counterpoint to the picture of the standing man (figure 9.4). Entitled "The Slovak Army in the Far East," it featured eight small frames organized around a bigger one showing three soldiers firing a long-range cannon.[35] The smaller images showcased military personnel engaging Soviet troops in the USSR, as well as captured Soviet equipment, with minister and Hlinka Guard leader Alexander Mach visiting troops near the front. When set next to each other, the front and back covers form a diptych bridging the mythical and the real, projecting the magazine's young readers into the heroic life of the new fascist Slovak man.

Photomontage, Modernity, and War

By the time of the Second World War, photomontage was a common image-altering technique. According to Christopher Phillips, Soviet interwar art critic Sergei Tretyakov defined photomontage as a technique in which reality is consciously altered by superimposing two or more images and further transforming them by adding drawings, collages, or text.[36] Building on Tretyakov's definition, Phillips considers montage as a technique validating the changes that had been occurring in industrialized societies since the early twentieth century: "In Germany, in the USSR, and the United States, this (1919–1942) was a period of heightened awareness of being caught up in an epoch of accelerated transformation. This period marked the culmination of a series of irreversible passages: the passage from the seasonal rhythms of a rural society to the frenzied tempo of an urban culture; the passage from national economies based on the land and on artisanal occupations to industrial economies driven by machine technology; the passage from a social life rooted in traditional family life and local communities to larger, more impersonal aggregations of mass society."[37] The rudimentary photomontages featured in Slovak youth magazines lacked the refinement of the Russian constructivists or John Heartfield in Germany, yet they retained the evocative power and historical charge described by Phillips.[38] In the case of *Nová*

9.3 and **9.4** (next page) *Nová Mládež* magazine (published in Bratislava by the Hlinka Youth organization), December 1941, front cover (left) and back cover (right), showing the Slovak army on the Eastern Front.

Mládež, photomontage was used in support of two main themes: warfare and the use of modern technology. It was usually subsumed into a larger visual trope in which modern warfare became a parable for the national community's accession to European modernity.

The relationship between photomontage and technology lies in its ability to elicit and contain "the speed of blur of an experience of modernity, of the everyday assimilation of modern urban and technological imagery."[39] In the particular context of wartime Slovakia, photography gave credence to the modernist political discourse of the Hlinka Youth by drawing a strong connection between speed, politics, and warfare. The purpose of such images as the standing man with the gun was to emphasize the transformative value of the experience of modern warfare, for the individual soldier no less than for the larger national group (figure 9.3). The transition from a reactionary to a fascist discourse was precisely located in the exaltation of war and technology and its ability to create a new, fascist man.[40]

For Paul Virilio, the relation between speed and politics is fundamentally an aspect of modern societies. About warfare in the twentieth century he writes, "Speed is time saved in the most absolute sense of the word, since it becomes human time directly torn from death. . . . Salvation is no longer in flight; safety is in running toward your death, in *killing your* death. *Safety is in assault* simply because ballistic vehicles make flight useless. . . . *From now on, general safety can come only from the masses in their entirety reaching speed*."[41] The combination of photomontage and military imagery in *Nová Mládež* performed an essential task toward creating a fascist discourse by projecting onto the reading youths the perception that salvation could be attained only through voluntary sacrifice. Taking part in Hitler's war was part of the same intellectual logic: Operation Barbarossa was conceived as a preemptive strike against the supposedly inevitable Soviet aggression; it sought to remake history by outpacing time.

The Flying Youth

As the use of deftly arranged photographs and photomontages increased, so did the use of pictures of combat aircrafts as the definitive expression of both speed and modernity. The cover of the May 1942 issue of *Nová Mládež* exemplifies this evolution (figure 9.5).[42] In the foreground of the image, three differently aged boys are putting together a wooden aircraft model. The one on the right appears to be the oldest; he wears a uniform with two crosses on

9.5 *Nová Mládež* magazine (published in Bratislava by the Hlinka Youth organization), May 1942.

the shoulder, indicating his leadership in the organization.[43] Beneath him, a younger member affixes the model's wing to the frame, supervised by the first member. A third boy, on the left side of the frame, holds the model while the others work. Behind this image another picture is superimposed, presenting three Slovak air force fighter planes in tight formation.

The interplay between the boys works on two levels: first, craftsmanship and knowledge are being transmitted from the older boy to the younger ones; second, a clear subjective transposition seems to exist from the model being built in the foreground to the actual aircrafts behind. Here, the training performed in the Hlinka Youth acquires its concrete meaning: apprentices were figuratively transformed into actual combat aircraft pilots. This model-to-reality transposition also bears strong historical implications, erasing the distance in time that separates the boys from their future in the Slovak air force.

Montage is used to transpose the present into the future: time is abridged and the warplane, as the expression of speed and power, endows the young Slovak militants with the substance of their future fascist selves.[44]

Perhaps more so than in a technologically advanced society such as Britain or Germany, using airplanes as a parable of the future would certainly have resonated powerfully with the young Slovak readers of the magazine. For Peter Fritzsche, aviation came to be understood as "the quintessential marker of twentieth century progress[;] the airplane, more so than any other technology, clarified the link between nationalist aspirations and the advent of the modern age. In promising military and economic advantage, and in demonstrating mastery over nature, the airplane emerged as the clearest measure of nations, distinguishing not only European civilization from those of Africa and Asia, but also great powers among the continent's leading states."[45] In wartime Slovakia, a small agricultural country with a paper-thin national narrative, the use of airplanes in propaganda materials was meant to equip youths with an inflated self-image of power and a sense of belonging among the elite of European nations.

The Hlinka Youth and Hitler's Europe

During the Second World War, fascist parties across Europe embraced Hitler's continental rule as a protective bulwark against communism. In France and Belgium, fascist parties such as Jacques Doriot's French Popular Party (PPF), Léon Degrelle's Rexists or Marcel Déat's National Popular Rally (RNP) made participation in Hitler's European Project a centerpiece of their ideological platforms.[46] In east-central Europe, fascist leaders often used Europeanist discourse extensively; they conceived of *Festung Europa* (fortress Europe) as a means for their "backward" countries to board the train of modernity. Horia Sima, leader of the Romanian Legion of the Archangel Michael, saw the Nazi continental order as "a forerunner of today's united Europe, insofar as it allowed the more developed countries to exercise benevolent tutelage over the small nations of the periphery that were struggling to break out of the confining condition of their underdevelopment."[47] In Slovakia, this brand of Europeanist positioning gained traction in the People's Party in 1941 and became one of the pillars of the official discourse. The idea of Hitler's Europe was emphasized with particular diligence in the youth press. The creation of a new Slovak future through the war effort worked hand in hand with the inclusion of the Hlinka Youth and its leaders among the future rulers of the continent, learning their political craft in the Hitler Youth and other fascist youth organizations.

By early 1941, the Hitler Youth and the Italian Youth of the Lictor (GIL) regularly organized sporting events and summer camps, bringing together fascist youth movements from around Europe.[48] In August, when international youth games were held in Breslau, fascist youth delegations from fourteen countries flocked to Lower Silesia for what was to be the first step of the European Youth Association.[49] In Slovakia, the Breslau games represented the first participation of a Slovak state delegation in a significant international event. The Hlinka Youth press produced a series of articles and photograph albums showcasing progress since the beginning of the war.

A first set of photographs from the Breslau games appeared on the back of the November 1941 issue of *Nová Mládež* (figure 9.6).[50] The main frame comprised a silhouette of a Hlinka Youth member standing in front of the Breslau stadium, facing the young athletes parading in tight formation wearing the uniforms of their respective delegations. In the background the stadium stands, overlooked by the typical clock tower of Nazi-era arenas, display rows of spectators forming the "V" of victory and Nazi symbols: swastika-bearing flags, uniforms, and eagles.[51] Crowning the image, three smaller frames show Hlinka Youth leader Alojz Macek meeting with German, Italian, and Croatian officials.[52] At the bottom, slightly wider frames depict the starting line of a race and the Hlinka Youth delegation marching alongside youths from other countries.

Linking the two sets of pictures at the top and the bottom, the main image performs a task similar to that of the Hlinka Youth member with the gun (figure 9.3) and the three model-making teenagers (figure 9.5). The shaded Hlinka Youth character stands in the center of the frame, creating a strong interplay between him and the crowd, the individual fascist man in the making as the emanation of the larger group. As in the two other images, the lone member of the organization, a generic identifiable model, delivers a metaphorical image for individual readers and members of the Hlinka Youth. Such identification mechanisms nurtured in the Slovak state's youth press were essential for the wartime fascist national discourse. Through pictures of the Breslau games, Hlinka Youth members from Bratislava, Nitra, Ružomberok, or the Tatras Mountains found themselves sharing in a larger historical and spatial dynamic transcending the confines of Slovakia. The explosion of the *passéist* national narrative also meant a dramatic reframing of the collective spatial imaginary.[53] Participation in Hitler's Europe occurred at the military level

Z ÚČASTI HLINKOVEJ MLÁDEŽE NA LETNÝCH HRÁCH HJ V BRESLAU OD 24. VIII.—31. AUG. 1941, KDE ZASTÚPENÁ BOLA MLÁDEŽ TEMER CELEJ EURÓPY.

9.6 *Nová Mládež* magazine (published in Bratislava by the Hlinka Youth organization), November 1941.

through the conquest of territories in the east (figure 9.4) but also through international gatherings such as the Breslau games. Multinational camps also expanded in 1942; as the travels of the Hlinka Youth and their contacts with sister movements from fascist countries increased, so did the presence of photographs with a pan-European theme in the pages of *Nová Mládež*.[54]

The sense of belonging to a larger European and global fascist youth community was emblazoned in the eleven frames forming the back cover of the April 1942 *Nová Mládež*.[55] The top part of the page, made up of images depicting a Hlinka Youth trip in the town of Asiago in northern Italy, functioned as a roman photo of the life of Slovak youth leaders in Mussolini's Italy.[56] The pictures provided a detailed outlook on the travels of the Slovak representatives, from their departure in Bratislava to their meetings with "comrades from the new Europe." The bottom half of the page, for its part, comprised exclusively images of the Hitler Youth ("On the life of the Hitler Youth") and of the Japanese Youth ("Learning How to Fly"). Juxtaposing photographs from the Hlinka Youth's travels with others borrowed from the Nazi press effected the inclusion of the Slovak group in the activities of the future leaders of the two most powerful Axis countries. Once again, the arrangement of this photographic set conveyed the newfound emergent power of the Slovak youth via the creation of the new European fascist man. The pan-European and pan-fascist imagery displayed in *Nová Mládež* suggested a recession of national differences before powerful generational sentiment.[57]

Photographs and Fascist Imagery

By the autumn of 1942, the advance of the Wehrmacht and its allies into the USSR was at a standstill. Around the same time, the Slovak youth press sharply increased its militaristic content for what already seemed a prefiguring of the coming debacle. For a short period between summer 1941 and spring 1943, the "new youth" of Tiso's Slovak state were framed as the heroic material for creating the Slovak fascist man. The Hlinka Youth's paramilitary training and participation in the activities of the future fascist leaders helped advance the image of Slovakia as a historically significant entity. The space for cultivating this radically modern forward-looking self-image was opened by deploying photographic images, with their ability to convey movement and physical dynamism. For the Slovak fascists, like their German and Italian godfathers, technology, speed, and war were key to fulfilling the myth of rebirth and the coming of the fascist man.[58] The photographs used in the wartime Slovak youth press testify to this obsession with war. Their fascist imagery composed the visual language of a movement that sought to portray itself as disdainful of the possibility of death.[59] From a conception of time, politics, and the nation steeped in Catholic tradition and turned toward the past, the Slovak state developed, during World War II, a new historical vision based on technology and youth that was meant to find its end point in the foundation of Hitler's Europe. For the small Slavic nation with virtually no history before 1918, participating in the creation of the new continental order amounted to a thorough rewriting of the national narrative. History was written in the present and the future through the deeds of the emerging generation cultivated in the Hlinka Youth. The photographic images displayed in *Nová Mládež*, conceived as historical snapshots, also served as proof that the Slovak national revolution was happening.

Conclusion

By the autumn of 1943, as the course of events irreversibly turned against Nazi Germany and its allies, the Hlinka Youth magazines' editors returned to a more conservative imagery emphasizing old and dignified national figures. This period coincided with a loss of popularity of Vojtech Tuka's fascist government, largely because of its unconditional collaboration with Nazi Germany and the central role it played in deporting Slovak Jews during 1942.[60] The retreat of the Wehrmacht in the east and the rapid advance of the Red Army all but signified the end of Hitler's "New Europe," a notion that had been instrumental in the development of Slovakia's wartime spatial and historical imaginary. The National Slovak Uprising that took place in the summer of 1944 prompted the Nazis to invade the country, and it put a brutal end to the relative independence Tiso and his cronies had enjoyed for a little over five years.

More so than the return to prominence of the conservative faction within the Hlinka People's Party,[61] the reappearance of a traditional nationalist imaginary in the Slovak youth press at the end of 1943 signified the cancellation of the short-lived political horizon opened by German victories in the USSR. From its foray into fascist territory during 1941–43, when modernity, war, and visions of the future formed its backbone, the Slovak historical narrative retreated to a conservative position heralding the glorious figures of the past. In November 1944, a few months before the Wehrmacht's final collapse and the disappearance of Tiso's state, *Nová Mládež* published one of its last issues. The image chosen for the cover was rather unusual: instead of featuring a youthful character in a dynamic, willful attitude, it consisted of a picture of an emaciated Andrej Hlinka in his old days, wearing a clergy shirt and hat.[62]

The cover layout was modified for the occasion, and the tight black and white portrait of the Catholic national hero was framed by a solid black background. The interplay between the magazine's title, set below the picture in white block letters, and Hlinka's image functioned as an obituary: that of the magazine, the Hlinka Youth, the Slovak state, and the boundless power aspirations of the wartime years. The grim quality of this last effort should not overshadow the mastery of the composition and the remarkable ability of the Slovak youth propagandists to create an alternative national discourse during the Second World War. The use of photographic images was instrumental in giving life to a doctored historical narrative that posited the accession of Slovakia to European modernity through its association with Nazi Germany. Considering the significance of national rebirth, youth, and the idea of the new man in fascist ideology, it is not surprising that these cutting-edge materials were primarily used in the People's Party's youth press. The photography of *Nová Mládež* and other youth magazines published by the Hlinka Youth has no equivalent in the propaganda output of the Slovak state. As this essay has shown, photographs were used as a means to create a record of history in the making, snapshots of Slovakia's accession to a larger historical stage. They can serve as the primary material to make a case for the "fascization" of Tiso's Slovak state during 1940–43 and its attempt to remake the country's future by mobilizing the generation that came of age during the Second World War.

Notes

1 On Tiso's life and political career, see James M. Ward, *Priest, Politician, Collaborator: Josef Tiso and the Making of Fascist Slovakia* (Ithaca, NY: Cornell University Press, 2013); and Ivan Kamenec, *Tragédia Politika, Knaza a Človeka* (Bratislava: Archa, 1998). According to Ward, "Tiso placed his hopes for domestic stability, national progress, and social justice in his vision of 'New Slovakia,' a polity that aimed to unify the nation, to make the Slovak 'the master of his house,' and to return god to public life. Enacting 'New Slovakia' often resembled (without always imitating) a Nazi Gleichshaltung" (161).

2 Michal Milla, *Hlinková Mládež 1938–1945* (Bratislava: Ústav Pamäti Národa, 2008), 32.

3 Tiso's main competitors, Vojtech Tuka and Alexander Mach, whose Hlinka Guard sought unsuccessfully to gain the favor of Nazi Germany, headed the Nazi wing

of the Slovak People's Party. As elsewhere, the Nazis managed such internal strife between conservatives and radicals to their own advantage. While Slovaks and other national minorities were given ample constitutional protections in the Federal Czechoslovak Republic (1918–38), the nationalists of the People's Party under Father Andrej Hlinka (1864–1938) drove hard for autonomy and independence, systematically opposing Prague's influence in Slovak domestic affairs. Hlinka had been a forceful opponent of Magyarization before 1914 and the repression of Slovak national traditions by Hungarian state authorities. Tiso and the People's Party used Hlinka to root their movement in a Catholic nationalist tradition. See James Felak, *At the Price of the Republic: Hlinka's Slovak People's Party, 1929–1939* (Pittsburgh: University of Pittsburgh Press, 1993).

4 The importance of the myth of rebirth and the central place of visions of the future in fascist discourses and ideology has been central to Roger Griffin's interpretation of fascism as "Palingenetic ultra-nationalism." As Griffin writes, "fascism's main goal was the total—and totalitarian—transformation of the political, moral and aesthetic culture of the nation to produce a new type of national community and a new type of 'man': a social, political, cultural and anthropological revolution subsumed in the vision of imminent national rebirth (palingenesis)." Roger Griffin, *A Fascist Century* (London: Palgrave, 2008), 50.

5 For the Sokol organization in the Czech lands, see Tara Zahra, *Kidnapped Souls: National Indifference and the Battle for Children and the Bohemian Lands, 1900–1948* (Ithaca, NY: Cornell University Press, 2011). People's Party and Hlinka Guard officials envisaged integrating Slovak scouting into a paramilitary youth organization from October 1938, coming to fruition after April 1939 with the creation of the Hlinka Youth. See Milla, *Hlinková Mládež.*

6 For the Hlinka Guard, the party militia, see Peter Sokolovič, *Hlinková Garda, 1938–1945* (Bratislava: Ústav Pamäti Národa, 2009). Alexander Mach instigated the creation of the Hlinka Guard in 1938 and, upon assuming its leadership in March 1939, orchestrated the wave of violence leading to Czechoslovakia's dismemberment and invasion of the Czech lands by Nazi Germany on March 15, 1939. He served the Slovak state, first as Minister of Propaganda (1939–40), then as Minister of the Interior (1940–44). Under his direction, the Hlinka Guard managed the 1942 deportation of Slovak Jews. See František Vnuk, *Mat' Svoj Štát Znamená Život* (Bratislava: Slovensky Ustav, 1991); Ivan Kamenec, *Slovensky Štát* (Prague: Anomal, 1992).

7 Figures taken from Hlinka Youth internal communication: Slovak National Archives (sna), Fond Hlinková Mládež, box 605–19–2.

8 sna, Fond Hlinková Mládež, box 605–19–2; *Straž* 1, nos. 1–2 (September–October 1939): 18–20.

9 Detailed schemes and programs of the organization (with a complete list of local officials) can be found in the Slovak National Archives: sna, Fond Hlinková Mládež, box 19–5, 25–58.

10 The magazine's circulation was particularly high considering Slovakia's population and the number of youths in the organization: at the beginning of 1941 over 30,000 copies were printed monthly of both *Vlca* and *Nová Mládež*. See Milla, *Hlinková Mládež*, 255.

11 *Slovenská Deva* was published September 1941 through March 1945. During the transition between the Munich agreements and formal Slovak independence in March 1939, *Vlca* was preceded by a less elaborate magazine, *Mlady Slovák* (Young Slovak).

12 Substantial collections of the magazines are available at the University Library in Bratislava.

13 *Straž* 1, nos. 1–2 (September–October 1939).

14 After the fall of communism in 1989, Slovakia became independent on January 1, 1993, via peaceful partition of Czechoslovakia. Ivan Kamenec's groundbreaking *Po Stopách Tragédie*, published in Prague in 1991, decisively demonstrated the Slovak state's responsibility for deporting the Slovak Jews in 1942, thereby countering older right-wing nationalist claims that Jews were protected by presidential exemptions granted to them. James M. Ward later dismantled the myth of presidential exemptions in "People Who Deserve It: Jozef Tiso and the Presidential Exemption," *Nationalities Papers* 30, no. 4 (August 2002): 571–601.

15 In the mid-1990s, revisionist historian Milan Durica's general history of Slovakia offered a positive view of interwar and wartime Slovak Catholic nationalism and especially the figures of Hlinka and Tiso. The book became compulsory school reading under Mečiar's government. Milan Durica, *Dejiny Slovenska a Slovákov* (Kosice: Pressko, 1995). See also Axel Schneider and Daniel Woolf, eds., *Oxford History of Historical Writing*, vol. 5 (Oxford: Oxford University Press, 2011), 259–60.

16 This view was expressed in the first issue of *Straž* by Jozef Kirschbaum, a high-ranking People's Party official who perceived the creation of the Slovak state as "a grant of leadership to the nation" to be realized in the future. *Straž* 1, nos. 1–2 (September–October 1939): 5.

17 *Der Pimpf* was published by Hitler Youth in 1937–45. It targeted members of the *Deutsches Jungvolk* (ten to fourteen years of age) and featured photographs, adventure stories, and reportage by Hitler Youth serving in the war. See Tatjana Schrutke, *Die Jugendpresse der Nationalsozialismus* (Cologne: Böhlau Verlag, 1997), 102; Steven Luckert and Susan Bachrach, *State of Deception: The Power of Nazi Propaganda* (Washington, DC: U.S. Holocaust Memorial Museum, 2009). On *Signal* magazine see Jeremy Harwood, *Hitler's War: World War II as Portrayed by* Signal, *the International Nazi Propaganda Magazine* (Minneapolis: Zenith Press, 2014); Rainer Rutz, *Signal: Eine Deutsches Auslandsillustrierte als Propagandainstrument im Zweiten Weltkrieg* (Essen: Klartext, 2007).

18 The Protection Treaty between Slovakia and Germany was signed on March 23, 1939.

19 For the Slovak army on the Eastern Front see Charles Kliment and Bretislav Na-

kladal, *Germany's First Ally: Armed Forces of the Slovak State, 1939–1945* (Atlgen: Schiffer, 1997).

20 Alojz Macek in *Straž* 3, no. 1 (September 1941): 1.

21 Michael Geyer, "The Militarization of Europe (1914–1945)," in *The Militarization of the Western World*, ed. John Gillis (New Brunswick, NJ: Rutgers University Press, 1989), 78.

22 For Slovak nationalists, acceding to the rank of nation-state broke the spell the Magyar invasion had cast on the nation in the tenth century. Slovakia's mythical ancestors, the Great Moravian Empire of Svatopluk (870–94) and the two missionaries who evangelized his territory, Cyril and Method, were heralded as the original Slovaks before a thousand years of darkness until creation of the Slovak state in 1939. See Stanislav Kirschbaum, *Slovakia: The Struggle for Survival* (New York: Palgrave Macmillan, 2005).

23 See Felak, *At the Price of the Republic*, 39–55.

24 *Nová Mládež* 1, no. 1 (April 1939): 4–8.

25 *Nová Mládež* 1, no. 1 (April 1939).

26 For this "Salzburg conference" and the transition toward national socialism see Jorg K. Hoensch, "Slovakia: One God, One People, One Party," in *Catholics, the State, and the European Radical Right, 1919–1945*, ed. Richard Wolff and Jörg Hoensch (New York: Columbia University Press, 1987), 175–77.

27 On Tuka's role at Salzburg and beyond see Ward, *Priest, Politician, Collaborator*, 211–13.

28 Tatjana Toensmeyer, *Das Dritte Reich und die Slowakei: Politischer Alltag Zwischen Kooperation und Eigensinn* (Paderborn: Fernand Schoeningh, 2003).

29 *Nová Mládež* 4, no. 10 (June 1942).

30 On Hitler's European order see Mark Mazower, *Hitler's Empire: How the Nazis Ruled Europe* (New York: Penguin, 2008); and Peter Fritzsche, *An Iron Wind: Europe under Hitler* (New York: Basic Books, 2016).

31 See Ivan Kamenec, *Po Stopách Tragédie* (Prague: Archa, 1991).

32 *Nová Mládež* 4, no. 4 (December 1941).

33 Benito Mussolini, *Fascism: Doctrine and Institutions* (Rome: Ardita, 1935).

34 Mark Neocleous, *Fascism* (Minneapolis: University of Minnesota Press, 1997), 18.

35 "The Slovak Army in the Far East," *Nová Mládež* 4, no. 4 (December 1941).

36 Christopher Phillips, "Introduction," in *Montage and Modern Life, 1919–1942*, ed. Matthew Teitelbaum (Cambridge, MA: MIT Press, 1992), 28.

37 Phillips, "Introduction," 29.

38 On the importance of photomontage for Russian constructivist artists, see Margarita Tupitsyn, *The Soviet Photograph: 1924–1937* (New Haven, CT: Yale University Press, 1996); and Christina Lodder, *Russian Constructivism* (New Haven, CT: Yale University Press, 1985). For John Heartfield, see Andres Mario Zervigon, *John Heartfield and the Associated Image: Photography, Persuasion, and the Rise of Avant-Garde Photomontage* (Chicago: University of Chicago Press, 2012); David King and Ernest Volland, *John Heartfield: Laughter Is a Devastating Weapon*

(London: Tate, 2015); Sabine T. Kriebel, *Revolutionary Beauty: The Radical Photomontages of John Heartfield* (Berkeley: University of California Press, 2014).

39 Maud Lavin, "Photomontage, Mass Culture, and Modernity: Utopianism in the Circle of New Advertising Designers," in Teitelbaum, *Montage and Modern Life,* 49.

40 On the idea of the fascist man, see Roger Griffin, "*I Am No Longer Human. I Am a Titan. A God!* The Fascist Quest to Regenerate Time," in Griffin, *A Fascist Century,* 3–23.

41 Paul Virilio, *Vitesse et Politique: Essai de Dromologie* (Paris: Galilée, 1977), 31. Original emphasis.

42 *Nová Mladež* 4, no. 9 (May 1942).

43 For the Hlinka Youth organizational structure, see Milla, *Hlinková Mládež,* 238.

44 On aviation as an interwar symbol of power, see Robert Wohl, *The Spectacle of Flight: Aviation and the Western Imagination* (New Haven, CT: Yale University Press, 2005).

45 Peter Fritzsche, *A Nation of Fliers: German Aviation and the Popular Imagination* (Cambridge, MA: Harvard University Press, 1992), 3.

46 Doriot and Déat each began their career on the Left before embracing fascism in the late 1930s. See Robert Soucy, *French Fascism: The Second Wave* (New Haven, CT: Yale University Press, 1986); Kevin Passmore, *The Right in France from the Third Republic to Vichy* (Oxford: Oxford University Press, 2013); Philippe Burrin, *La Dérive Fasciste: Doriot, Déat, Bergery* (Paris: Seuil, 1986). On Degrelle and the Rexist movement during World War II, see Eddy de Bruyne and Mark Rikmenspoel, *For Rex and Belgium: Léon Degrelle and Walloon Political and Military Collaboration, 1940–1945* (Solihull: Helion, 2004); Jonathan Littell, *Le Sec et l'Humide: Une Breve Incursion en Territoire Fasciste* (Paris: Gallimard, 2008). On Fascist Europe in France, see Bernard Bruneteau, *L'Europe Nouvelle de Hitler: Une Illusion des Intellectuels de la France de Vichy* (Monaco: Éditions du Rocher, 2003).

47 Andrew Janos, *East Central Europe in the Modern World* (Berkeley: University of California Press, 2000), 185.

48 See Alessio Ponzio, *Shaping the New Man: Youth Training Regimes in Fascist Italy and Nazi Germany* (Madison: University of Wisconsin Press, 2015), 171–95.

49 Ponzio, *Shaping the New Man,* 181: "Just before the attack on the Soviet Union, Axmann and Von Schirach proposed to create an anti-Bolshevik European association formed by the youth organizations of the Axis states. In May 1941 Axmann (Hitler Youth leader), in Italy on an official visit, got the complete support of Ciano (Italian Minister of Foreign Affairs) and Mussolini for the fulfillment of this project. The Italians agreed to help create a pan-European association that would coordinate the youth of the continent and prepare them for the 'New Order.'"

50 *Nová Mládež* 4, no. 3 (November 1941).

51 On the significance of stadiums and sporting events in Nazi Germany and fascist Italy see Daphné Bolz, *Les Arènes Totalitaires: Hitler, Mussolini et les Jeux du Stade* (Paris: CNRS Éditions, 2008).

52 The fascist Ustaša Croatian regime has often been casually compared to the Slovak state. But the extreme ethnic violence the Croatian state perpetrated against Serbs and Bosnians during World War II distinguishes it from Tiso's Slovakia. See Rory Yeomans, *Visions of Annihilation: The Ustasha Regime and the Cultural Politics of Fascism* (Pittsburgh: University of Pittsburgh Press, 2013).

53 Geoff Eley argues for the significance of a spatial imaginary for the dynamics of Nazi during World War II. See Eley, "Empire, Ideology, and the East: Thoughts on Nazism's Spatial Imaginary," in *Nazism as Fascism: Violence, Ideology, and the Ground of Consent in Germany, 1930–1945* (London: Routledge, 2013), 131–55. See also Paolo Giaccaria and Claudio Minca, eds., *Hitler's Geographies: The Spatialities of the Third Reich* (Chicago: University of Chicago Press, 2016).

54 According to an internal note from the Hlinka Youth Headquarters from 1943, the number and scope of the international manifestations in which the Hlinka Youth took part considerably increased over the years: three youth camps with the Hitler Youth took place in 1940, five events in 1941 (including the Breslau games and trips to Croatia and Austria), and fifteen in 1942 (many of them consisting in binational summer camps organized with the Italian GIL). SNA, Fond Hlinková Mladež, box 605–19–7.

55 *Nová Mládež* 4, no. 8 (April 1942).

56 The Italian GIL was one of the most proactive pan-European wartime youth movements. The Hlinka Youth Asiago trip occurred February 11–20, 1942.

57 On generational sentiment in Nazi Germany, see A. Dirk Moses, *German Intellectuals and the Nazi Past* (New York: Cambridge University Press, 2007).

58 See Roger Griffin, *Modernism and Fascism: The Sense of a New Beginning under Mussolini and Hitler* (London: Palgrave Macmillan, 2007).

59 In an often quoted paragraph of *La Chambre Claire*, Roland Barthes argues that "it is because there is always in it this unavoidable sign of my future death, that each picture, even if it were seemingly the most tightly bound to the world of the living, comes to strike every single one of us, besides any generalization (but not besides all transcendence)." Drawing on photographic templates from Nazi Germany, Slovak photographers and youth press editors sought to bring this latent quality of the medium to the fore and extract the transformative substance of fascist ideology. More so than any other medium at the time, photography, because of its supposed ability to represent reality so accurately and allow viewers to project themselves into the images, was able to express the dynamics of historical time and the flight toward one's own death as expressed in Barthes's theory. See Roland Barthes, *Camera Lucida: Reflections on Photography*, trans. Richard Howard (New York: Hill and Wang, 1981), 97.

60 See Ward, "People Who Deserve It."

61 Ward, *Priest, Politician, Collaborator*, chapters 7 and 8.

62 *Nová Mládež* 7, no. 3 (November 1944).

10

FROM ANTIFASCISM TO HUMANISM

The Legacies of Robert Capa's Spanish Civil War Photography

NADYA BAIR

In February 1953, the photographer Robert Capa was called to the American Embassy in Paris, where his passport was promptly revoked.[1] Born Andre Friedman in 1913, the Hungarian Jewish photographer had spent most of his adult life as an émigré, first in Berlin, then Paris, and finally the United States, where he arrived in 1939. He attained American citizenship in 1946. Later in life he described this trajectory in humorous terms, making light of the rise of fascism that had sent him, like many other Jewish photographers of his generation, into exile time and again: "Due to disagreement with a Mr. Horthy, [Capa] left Hungary at the age of 18 and became a photographer in Germany. In 1933, due to disagreement with a Mr. Hitler, Capa left Germany and found his way to France."[2] But he rarely commented on the later turn of events, when, amid the Red Scare in the United States, an anonymous source had claimed that he was a communist. The naturalized American citizen lost his ability to travel throughout Europe, where he was supposed to be working on assignment for his magazine clients.[3] This sudden turn of events was a blow not only to Capa, but potentially to all of Magnum Photos, the international photo agency that he had cofounded in 1947 in New York, and which now risked being blacklisted as a communist front organization and forced to close. The New York–based Photo League had, after all, been forced to disband in 1951.[4] "It is needless to say that we have to be extremely careful and attach no *camarades* [*sic*] to our free-lancing outfit, because it would be disastrous for both of us," Capa noted in a confidential letter to Magnum's executive editor John Morris after returning from the embassy.[5]

The revocation of Capa's passport may have been connected to his activities in the 1930s. Based in Paris at the time, the photographer had covered the rise of the Popular Front in France and the Spanish Civil War for a number of magazines on the Left, including the French *Vu* and the Communist *Regards*.[6] Between 1936 and 1939, his photographs of the civil war in Spain circulated widely, informing American and European magazine readers about the conflict and earning Capa international fame as a war photographer and documentarian of antifascism in Europe.

By the 1950s, the naturalized American needed to deflect attention away from his early international, Left, and antifascist networks, which had included well-known communists such as Louis Aragon. Aragon had served as editor-in-chief of the communist-run *Ce Soir*, which had briefly employed Capa, and his continued support of Stalinist Russia after World War II made him a particularly undesirable connection.[7] Thinking about how to best present his case against the charges, Capa emphasized his connections with conservative publications in France and enumerated the many patriotically American clients (such as *Life* magazine and the U.S. Economic Cooperation Administration, set up to administer the Marshall Plan) and editors (including Ed Thompson of *Life* and Ted Patrick of *Holiday*) who had published his work during and after Spain.[8] Capa suggested that his defense lawyer in New York ask for an affidavit from Lucien Vogel, the founding editor of the French illustrated magazine *Vu*, which could say that "he knew me well personally, that he took me to Spain first for his magazine, and that to his best judgment I never have been neither a member or other [*sic*]; and we could get the same from Pierre Lazaroff who was at that period of the conservative *Paris Soir* and *Match*, and is now the editor of the very conservative *France Soir*."[9] In a subsequent letter, he insisted, "even when I was involved in so-called political reporting, I never editorialized, and my reporting was human or humorous, never violently political in any direction."[10] Out of necessity, then, Capa depoliticized the meaning of his photographic output and his writing, especially from the Spanish Civil War. The State Department failed to produce enough evidence of Capa's direct involvement in communist activities and soon dropped the case against him.[11]

Within a year of the passport controversy, Capa was dead, having stepped on a landmine in Indochina on May 25, 1954, while covering the retreat of

French forces from the region for *Life* magazine. By many accounts, Capa took the *Life* assignment because he needed the money to pay off the thousands of dollars in legal fees that he had accrued to disprove the State Department's allegations.[12] Colleagues mourned the sad irony of Capa's death in a faraway conflict that had meant little to the photographer, especially in comparison with what they understood as Capa's personal investment in the fight against fascism in Spain and then during World War II.

In a range of exhibitions and publications appearing in the decade after his death, Capa's photographs from Spain became canonized as humanist imagery devoid of ideology. Today, one is hard-pressed to learn about Robert Capa's pictures outside of two framing narratives: one of "concerned photography" and the other the myth of Robert Capa as "The Greatest War Photographer in the World." The former label obscures the historical and political specificity of his images and turns Capa into an apolitical humanist. The latter situates Capa's work exclusively within the project of his adventurous and courageous reporting on international conflicts for the illustrated press, beginning with the Spanish Civil War.

This essay's inclusion in a volume about visualizing fascism invites a different set of questions about Capa's legacy—ones that interrogate Capa's fame and the discourse around his pictures. In particular, this chapter asks: What role have iconic images and legendary photographers played in perpetuating or obscuring certain narratives about the rise of the global Right? How have Capa's photographs shaped memories and analyses of this era, and what can this history teach us about approaching iconic images as historical documents? While Spain is crucial to discussions of fascism and the 1930s, Capa's Spanish war photographs are key to understanding how photography's relationship to politics and history has been narrated at different moments in the twentieth century. Examining the uses and interpretations of Capa's Spanish Civil War imagery from the 1930s to the 1970s means asking how photographs, as material objects, "shape how what happened is remembered, taught, learned, and interpreted."[13]

A War of Images and Print Media

The Spanish Civil War began on July 18, 1936, with a military coup against the democratically elected Republican government, which established a dictatorial regime in Spain from 1939 to 1975 under the leadership of General Francisco Franco.[14] While Germany and Italy covertly provided military aid—especially planes, aerial bombs, and pilots—to Franco, Britain and France, Spain's traditional allies, signed a nonintervention treaty in August 1936, effectively isolating the Spanish Republic.[15] Spain thus became the battleground for people from a range of ethnic, national, and political backgrounds who united against Spanish fascist aggression without the aid of their governments. In the United States, sending aid to Republican Spain became a leading form of American antifascist activism, and it was highest among Eastern and Western European émigrés who had fled the conservative politics and anti-Semitism of their birthplaces.[16] Such émigrés also made up the vast majority of the International Brigades—the army made up of thousands of volunteers from Europe and North America who came to fight in support of the Spanish Republic between 1936 and 1939.

The Spanish Civil War became an international affair not only through such volunteer activism but especially through how its story was told in the press, particularly the illustrated press.[17] Publications at both ends of the political spectrum had recently gained the technical capability to print photographic reports of conflicts as they unfolded, and Spain provided them with a headline story of unprecedented urgency and international relevance. Conservative publications that supported Franco's insurgents included *Le Matin*, *L'Illustration*, *Paris-Soir*, and *Match* in France and the *Daily Mail* and *Illustrated London News* in England.[18] Founded in 1936, the American *Life* claimed neutrality, but its publisher, Henry Luce, was an ardent anticommunist who often showed sympathy toward Franco and Mussolini.[19] Magazines sympathetic to the Republican cause included the French *Vu* and *Regards* and England's *Picture Post*, and they employed a new generation of young, Left-leaning photojournalists, many of whom were Jewish émigrés to France from Eastern Europe. Motivated by their progressive politics and a healthy dose of professional ambition, these photographers flocked to cover the fight against fascism in Spain.

Although the meaning and uses of press images are always inherently flexible and open to manipulation, during wartime in Spain the boundary between news and propaganda became basically nonexistent. Operating in an economy of limited resources and high stakes, the Right and the Left relied on cheaply reproduced photographs to cast blame on the opposite side, and it was not uncommon for publishers across ideological and political boundaries to reprint the same images, photographic layouts, and visual tropes while inflecting them with radically different messages via text.[20] Similar to the case of interwar China, where, as Maggie Clinton demonstrates in chapter

1, artists on the Left and Right drew on the same styles and iconographies, the publishing practices in wartime Spain make it difficult to identify a stable body of imagery aligned consistently with either fascism or antifascism. With the right caption, images of fleeing refugees, distraught mothers and children, rubble, and other signs of violence and destruction could point the finger of guilt at either side. Both sides regularly used these visual tropes with damning texts.

Upon arriving in Paris in 1933, the Hungarian-Jewish Andre Friedman (Robert Capa) met the German-Jewish Gerta Pohorylle (later Gerda Taro) and the Polish-Jewish Dawid Szymin (David "Chim" Seymour), who was already employed as a photojournalist by *Regards*. These photographers took on names that were legible across language barriers and free from Jewish associations in the hope that this would help them to sell their pictures to diverse magazine clients.[21] The three often worked together and distributed their images to the press through the same agents, including Alliance Photo and later through Capa's own studio, Atelier Robert Capa.[22] While these figures crafted their own personas to attract magazine clients, the magazines used them in a similar way, vaunting the photographers' accomplishments in order to increase their prestige and grow their readership. The Spanish Civil War thus helped create celebrity photojournalists, and Robert Capa became the best known of these through magazine publicity. When *Life* used Capa's "Death of a Loyalist Soldier" on July 12, 1937, to lead into a review of the first year of the conflict in Spain, the magazine marveled especially at the photographer's ability to capture the moment. And on December 3, 1938, the *Picture Post* endorsed him, quite simply, as "The Greatest War Photographer in the World." Notably, Capa's celebrity eclipsed Chim's and Taro's role in documenting the civil war for decades.[23]

Photographers, of course, were in the business of selling their pictures to as many clients as possible. Scholars have noted that the variability and expansive framing of Capa's contact sheets from Spain seem purposeful, encouraging picture agencies and magazines to crop, montage, reproduce, and interpret the photographs in different ways.[24] The agents with whom Capa worked, including those at Alliance Photo, printed copies of images that they deemed particularly successful and distributed them quickly and widely, encouraging their use in magazine features, as illustrations for political propaganda, and as promotion for humanitarian aid. In the context of magazines, Capa's images of the events in Spain were presented as news and opinion.

Some of his photographs took on heavy symbolic weight. On December 10, 1936, the cover of *Regards* featured Capa's photograph of a woman standing on a heap of rubble and the words "La capital Crucifiée" (The crucified capital) printed across the bottom half of the image. Her face was gaunt and her skirt was stained; the slippers on her feet and her short jacket suggested that she has no warmer clothes, and she appeared to be immobilized by the sight of destruction. The dramatic word choice cast blame on Franco's cruel betrayal of the city and its inhabitants. The woman was proof that this war was uprooting and shattering lives, but standing on top of the rubble, she was also a symbol of antifascist resilience. Inside the issue, a double-page spread combined seven more photographs by Capa showing life in a working-class area of Madrid that had been hit hard during the bombing of the capital. Frequently overlapping and arranged at slight angles, the photographs contained many debris piles, bundles of intimate belongings, and groups of women and small children who, the captions explained, were the primary victims of the conflict. These repetitive visual details showed the extent of the physical destruction while also conjuring the shock and dislocation Madrid's residents experienced.

One of the photographs from this essay later became the cover of a propaganda pamphlet printed in 1938 in Barcelona, a key publishing center and the center of Catalan culture held by the Republican side during the Civil War.[25] Showing three children sitting on a broken sidewalk with the façade of a shelled-out building behind them, the picture was no longer about the siege of Madrid but rather about the effects of war in general. The title of the pamphlet read, "La guerre en Espagne: barbarie et civilization" (The war in Spain: barbarism and civilization). Like other iconic pictures by Capa, including "Death of a Loyalist Soldier," the photograph was appealing not for its inherent meaning—which is hard to deduce without a caption—but rather for the symbolic implications that could be read into it.[26] The reappearance of such images in international antifascist publications including Ilya Ehrenburg's two-volume *Ispania—No Pasaran!*, released in Moscow in 1936–37, shows that book and magazine publishers worked with a relatively limited set of pictures.[27] Although select photographs traversed long distances and became visible, profitable, and eventually iconic, the vast majority of pictures were filed away, unused and unseen. Such practices helped shape what are now considered the foundational visual tropes of antifascism *and* Capa's work, confined to images of distraught mothers, children, rubble, and refugees.

Death in the Making

In 1938, Capa traveled to New York to visit his mother and brother Cornell, who had already emigrated to the U.S., and to discuss possible work arrangements with editors at *Life* and the Pix photo agency.[28] While there, he also worked with his colleague and mentor, André Kertész, on a book of Civil War photographs. Published by the New York–based firm Covici-Friede as *Death in the Making*, it was intended in part to raise American support for the antifascist struggle in Spain.[29] Like most books published by Covici-Friede, *Death in the Making* had a relatively limited print run, suggesting that the firm prioritized print quality over affordability and extensive sales.[30] At $2.50 per copy (roughly $41 by today's standards), the book required a moderate investment from buyers, who may have been motivated to buy it as a philanthropic act in addition to their interest in acquiring a limited edition of Capa's pictures.

In *Death in the Making*, Capa's self-promotion was inextricably linked with portraying the heroism of the international antifascist coalition in Spain.[31] Although the book featured many photographs by his colleagues Chim and Taro, the book's cover identified only Robert Capa as the author.[32] The images in the volume were uncredited, reflecting the lax standards of attribution at the time as well as the photographers' teamwork. The book thus helped Capa's name become the synecdoche for Spanish Civil War photography.[33]

Death in the Making relied on photography's evidentiary status and implied objectivity—that is, the indisputable fact of the photographer and camera having been there—to present a highly selective accounting of the Spanish Civil War. It opened with enthusiastic crowds of Republican supporters raising their fists in support of the Popular Front and quickly moved to partisan soldiers training and engaging in combat, including in Madrid. The book focused especially on the war's heroes and victims: the farmers turned partisan soldiers, the youth of the International Brigades, the refugees who fled rebel bombs and violent takeovers of Republican-held towns and villages, and the key battles of the war in Madrid and elsewhere. Its most obvious occlusion was the total absence of the fascist side: no photographs of the fascist salute nor Franco himself, which were regular tropes of insurgent publications. In part, this was a question of access. Franco's press office refused entry to correspondents working for the left-wing press. The Battle of Teruel in December 1937, which ended in nationalist defeat, is one of the few instances in which Capa could photograph the insurgent side.[34] As a result, the photo book showed a war against the looming but invisible sceptre of fascism.

Death in the Making also included visual rebuttals of anti-Republican propaganda that used picture sequences that had already appeared in the press, often in the same layouts and to the same ends.[35] During the conflict's early stages, American and European publications reported on a series of church burnings by supporters of the Republican government. Subsequently, the Republic worked to show that it was protecting the Church and religion in Spain (a trope that the insurgents regularly exploited as well). In *Death in the Making*, a five-page section on "Catholics in Bilbao" showed members of the clergy living peacefully alongside members of the Basque militia. Church and hospital scenes showed that priests and nuns were helping the Republic by giving "comfort to the wounded, absolution to the dying and Christian burial to the dead."[36] The sequence concluded with Chim's bird's-eye view of an outdoor mass for Republican soldiers, who fold their hands and bow their heads respectfully. The caption explains that these men would gather early on Sunday mornings, "before the rebel planes came over to spit death along the green hillsides," affirming that Republicans and Catholics could be one and the same, and that both were potential targets of Franco's indiscriminate air raids.

Other images took part in a visual battle over which side could be trusted to protect Spanish art and culture. Five pictures were dedicated to "Safeguarding of the art treasures," including a scene from the Palacio de Liria in which young Republicans help take inventory of Spain's national treasures and prepare them for safekeeping. Also taken by Chim, the photograph was part of a carefully constructed propaganda series that worked against Francoist representations of Republicans as destroyers of the country's infrastructure and religious buildings.[37] For instance, the Francoist five-volume photo album *Estampas de la Guerra*, produced and circulated by Franco's Delegation of Press and Propaganda, devoted ample space to both of these tropes, overwhelming the reader with images of decimated churches and destroyed bridges (figure 10.1). With no visual evidence of Republicans actually carrying out such deeds, the publication relied on scenes of the aftermath to cast blame. On other page spreads, *Estampas* included scenes of its own outdoor masses, presenting Franco's insurrection as a crusade to restore tradition and the authority of the Church.

Toward the middle of the book, *Death in the Making* turns to the war's victims and refugees, which would have been familiar to readers from their previous appearances in the illustrated press. Capa and Kertész selected images of mothers fleeing with children along rural roads, running from aerial

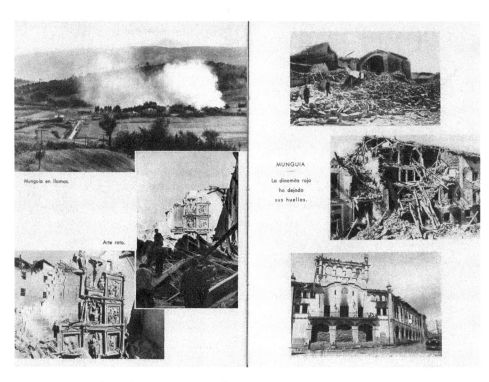

Munguía en llamas.

Arte roto.

MUNGUIA
La dinamita roja
ha dejado
sus huellas.

10.1 Federico de Urrutia, *Estampas de la Guerra*, Album no. 1, *De Irun a Bilbao* (Bilbao: Editora Nacional, 1937). Reproduction courtesy of the Jon Bilbao Basque Library, University of Nevada-Reno Libraries.

bombings in Bilbao, and living in the subway tunnels or rubble heaps of Madrid. Labeled with new captions written by Capa, the images symbolized fascist violence against civilian populations "at their most generalized and universal level" instead of describing the details of specific military campaigns or aerial attacks.[38] In one spread of three images, a mother holds her half-naked child with a firm grasp and seems eager to rush out of the frame; on the right, children walk along a rail track wearing extra layers of clothing, a few holding small parcels. Below, a young man with a child on his back helps an older woman who struggles to keep up. Printed toward the middle of the book, these photographs were labeled as having been taken "On the Road to Malaga," though according to Capa's biographer, Capa made some of them the year prior at Cerro Muriano. The photographer's own sense of iconicity and the news seems to be at play in this captioning decision.[39] Capa understood that the wide reporting on the massacre of refugees by aerial bombardment between Malaga and Almeria in February 1937 had become known as an episode of insurgent ruthlessness. Showing readers the actual images from the episode was less important than using the book to help them recall what they had already heard about Francoist crimes. The pictures likewise contributed to the image of Capa as a valiant war reporter capable of arriving at the scene of action in time and at any price in order to make such events known in the first place.

Death in the Making gave Capa his first opportunity to introduce himself to an American audience. In 1938, he promoted the book at his first exhibition of the same name at the New School for Social Research in New York City.[40] The displaced and financially struggling photographer hoped that his Spanish Civil War images would help generate more assignments in the United States. The book was therefore bound up in the history of fascism on the level of form and material. On the one hand, it created a lasting iconography of antifascism focusing on refugees and partisan soldiers. And as an object, the book is a by-product and material trace of the rise of fascism, which sent photographers, magazine editors, and picture agency directors into exile, challenging them to pick up their work and reinvent themselves on the other side of the Atlantic. In an era when photographers and agents passed through editors' offices, showing samples of recent work with the hope of making a sale or gaining a new assignment, we can imagine *Death in the Making* functioning as a portfolio and a calling card. With the help of publishers and editors, Capa made his first mark in America as a photographer of war and the struggle against fascism.[41]

Concern for Humanity

In the aftermath of Capa's death in May 1954, the photographer's antifascist work began to be reinterpreted, reflecting both Cold War politics and the changing market conditions for photojournalism. Magnum, the photo agency Capa helped found, poured energy into proving that it could remain the premier supplier of images despite losing its most entrepreneurial photographer. As part of this effort, Magnum adapted the rhetoric of humanism in its promotional articles for the industry press. This rhetoric was also being popularized at the Museum of Modern Art through the work of its photography curator Edward Steichen. Humanist photography, Steichen enthused, possessed "a tender simplicity, a sly humor, a warm earthiness, the 'everydayness' of the familiar and the convincing aliveness found only in the best of the folk arts."[42] Magnum suggested that the compassionate and universal spirit of photography on display at MOMA, including the 1955 blockbuster exhibition *The Family of Man*, had likewise driven the photojournalistic efforts of its founder Capa.[43] In a *Popular Photography* feature, the agency's executive editor John Morris explained that Magnum's "reporter-photographers" have a "peculiarly human point of view," which satisfied editors and readers who wished to "understand their confusing world in terms of people rather than propaganda or statistics."[44] Morris frequently used such formulations to suggest that Magnum's photo essays offered a corrective to fascism's manipulation of the media in the years leading up to World War II. Together with Steichen, Morris was part of a larger network of cultural leaders who believed that the mass media could be used to create democratic citizens in postwar America.[45]

Against this backdrop, Capa's pictures from Spain continued to garner attention, and Capa became institutionalized, quite narrowly, as *the* war photographer of the twentieth century—a label that ignored his ample peacetime work, including in color.[46] A year after his death, in 1955, the Overseas Press Club established the Robert Capa Gold Medal to award the "best published photographic reporting from abroad requiring exceptional courage and enterprise."[47] Capa's icons of war—his "Death of the Loyalist Soldier" and D-Day landing photos—were displayed in MOMA's *Memorable Life Photographs* and included in the Missouri School of Journalism's influential list of Fifty Great Photographs.[48] By 1960, such pictures were also seen in art galleries and photography festivals that hosted traveling exhibitions of the photographer's work. *War Photographs—Robert Capa*, organized by his brother Cornell Capa and circulated throughout the U.S., Italy, France, and Japan, surveyed his career through an exclusive focus on his best-known images of war.[49] Capa's work also appeared in the group show *The World as Seen by Magnum Photographers*, organized by Magnum and shown in Japan and the U.S. In that exhibition, Capa was once again represented through his images of war, including "Death of a Loyalist Soldier" and a series of refugee pictures from Spain.[50]

Beginning in the 1960s, Cornell Capa worked to keep his brother's achievements before the public under the new rubric of concerned photography. He did this primarily through the Fund for Concerned Photography (today, the International Center of Photography). The Fund's first and pivotal group exhibition of 1967, *The Concerned Photographer*, brought together the work of seven photographers whom Cornell Capa identified as modeling a "vital concern with their world and times."[51] Four of the photographers—Capa, Chim, Werner Bischof, and Dan Weiner—had recently died on assignment. The other two were André Kertész, representing the earlier generation of "candid photography," and Leonard Freed, particularly known for his for documentary work on black life in America. Placed side by side, their images testified to the photographers' ability to empathize with their subjects and represent the universal aspects of their struggles. Cornell Capa explained that this group of mostly European and Jewish photographers had actually followed in the footsteps of the American documentary photographer Lewis Hine, producing work that showed a "personal commitment and concern for mankind." Without obscuring the contents of his brother's photographs, Cornell Capa did reframe what they meant and why they mattered for the sixties and beyond. The images were now a testament to Robert Capa's humanism (rather than his antifascism) and to the American (rather than European or émigré) school of photography in which he worked.

When the *Saturday Review* devoted two pages to the exhibit on December 9, 1967, under the title "Mutual Concern," the paper offered a loose summary of the issues that had preoccupied photojournalists and the illustrated press to date (figure 10.2). On the right-hand page were three photographs, captioned to emphasize the photographer as author: "Robert Capa—Spain, 1938," "David Seymour ('Chim')—Israel, 1953," and "Leonard Freed—New York, 1963." Capa's photograph showed a woman pausing in a doorway, cloaked in a dark coat and clutching a crying girl with a smooth-faced doll, which offered an eerie contrast to the strained faces of the woman and child. Made in Barcelona in January 1939, this was one of Capa's many Spanish refugee pictures that had circulated in the international press to inform readers of the specific events leading up to their flight and to demonstrate the human costs of the war more generally.[52] Seymour's photograph of a wedding ceremony in Israel—a country that he visited and photographed regularly after 1951—showed a couple standing under a chuppah (ritual canopy).[53] Rifles and pitchforks double as posts, attesting to the makeshift nature of everyday life in the country, while the uncultivated, rolling hills in the background suggest an expansive land, free of other inhabitants. And Freed's picture captures two gleeful children on a city street, the sister holding her little brother up to a fire hydrant's spray. Lighthearted in comparison to Capa's refugees, Freed's picture had also appeared that year in his documentary photo book *Black in White America*. As part of an image sequence exploring white flight and the

10.2 "Mutual Concern," *Saturday Review*, December 9, 1967, 66–67.

rise of black ghettoes, the joyful portrait of childhood also points to the racial tensions that Freed had witnessed all across the country.[54]

These images introduced readers to "concerned" photography while evoking the shifting political issues that had preoccupied Left Jewish cultural figures between the thirties and sixties. During the Cold War, New York intellectuals, authors, and photographers channeled their antifascist politics into new areas of activism that ranged from reclaiming Jewish identity and Zionism to becoming involved in the struggle for racial equality in the U.S.[55] Whereas Capa and Chim took up the former, Freed tackled the latter. Upon seeing *The Concerned Photographer*, Freed said, "suddenly I feel I belong to a tradition."[56] In this case it was Cornell Capa who identified the "tradition" of photographing marginalized and oppressed groups as a mode of social activism and who created a unified narrative about the work of photographers who were predominantly Jewish (yet without mentioning the latter detail).

Given the Red Scare that brought on Robert Capa's passport troubles in 1953, it was perhaps inevitable that by the sixties, the antifascist Hungarian-Jewish Capa would be transformed into the cornerstone of a new tradition of depoliticized yet compassionate photography that had its roots in American documentary practices. "The many awards established in [Robert Capa's] name," the *Concerned Photographer* exhibition catalog explained, "spell out the elements of the tradition: a deep concern for mankind, superlative photography, exceptional courage, and enterprise."[57] The *Concerned Photographer* gallery dedicated to Robert Capa emphasized his work from the Spanish Civil War, World War II, and the 1948 Arab-Israel War. The images were organized thematically by symbolic category: soldiers, mothers and children, refugees, and the aftermath of war. Eschewing chronological order or attention to the historical specificities of each picture or conflict, the exhibit suggested that Robert Capa had a preordained career trajectory and unified oeuvre, whereas the exhibition texts depicted him as a brave combat photographer and a compassionate witness to the plight of civilians. The question of Capa's antifascist, leftist politics was thus suspended and subsumed by other meanings: the formally symbolic and socially engaged aspects of his photography, which could be appreciated in the new museum contexts for photography being created amid the decline of the illustrated press.[58]

Such a shift also informed how scholars and institutions would value Capa's images in the twenty-first century.[59] Today one finds that a 1937 photograph by Capa from Bilbao, a copy of which was acquired by the Metropolitan Museum of Art with the help of Cornell Capa, is lauded specifically for its symbolism and composition (figure 10.3).[60] The picture shows two women running parallel to a sidewalk, the fabric of their skirts flying like their legs. Capa took the picture from the middle of the street, snapping the shutter as the women approached the center of the frame. The first woman appears scared, but her companion smiles slightly. Has she, like the figures on the sidewalk, noticed Capa's camera? The graininess of the image heightens the sense of speed and emotional turbulence in the scene. This aesthetic would become a known feature of Capa's work following the publication of his out-of-focus D-Day photographs in *Life* on June 19, 1944. From the perspective of the institution acquiring the photograph, the graininess is also a sign of authenticity, marking it as a Capa photograph. The Met's text explains: "As a report on a specific conflict . . . this photograph could be found wanting because

10.3 Robert Capa, ["Crowds running for shelter when the air-raid alarm sounded, Bilbao, Spain"], May 1937. © International Center of Photography/Magnum Photos (2635.1992)

of its lack of explicitness. However, the sense of urgency without precise cause, so perfectly captured, makes it a particularly compelling image."[61] While acknowledging that the image is poor historical evidence—we see no perpetrators, no indicators that this is Spain, and no signs of war—the Met focuses instead on the photographer's skill as an artist. What matters, we are told, is that Capa used his camera to capture the dramatic sentiment of the moment. Endowed with new cultural and financial value—as the work of an established author, as an accomplishment in documenting human emotions—this image lives out the fate that both *The Family of Man* and *The Concerned Photographer* exhibitions set into motion at a transitional moment in politics and the photo market.

Legacies

The popularity of Robert Capa's images of civilians running from air raids in the streets of Bilbao also contributed to an understanding of fascism as a European phenomenon. In the 1938 *Death in the Making*, Capa had repre-

10.4 Robert Capa, ["Women running for shelter when the air-raid alarm sounded, Bilbao, Spain"], May 1937. © International Center of Photography/Magnum Photos (2636.1992)

sented the Bilbao raids with a photograph of two women running directly toward him, which he took as he stood on trolley tracks. The picture is similar to the one acquired by the Met in 2005, but it is even grainer and taken from an even closer vantage point. After Capa's death, a tamer and more carefully composed picture began to be published and displayed to represent the same events (figure 10.4). In that photograph, a mother and daughter are crossing a street toward Capa. While the child looks off to the side and tries to keep up, the mother looks up intently, her expression stern and the grip on her daughter's hand firm. The image contains little information about the circumstances, but the woman's upward gaze invites viewers to imagine the sight of planes above them or to hear the sound of the "screaming" bomb blasts in Bilbao that Capa described in *Death in the Making*.

Photography scholars have recently worked diligently to identify when, by whom, and under what circumstances such images were made.[62] This is an important task because photographers such as Capa and Chim often shot similar compositions, and their pictures were often published with contradictory dates or captions. We now have more information about the provenance of these images, but what do they actually teach us about the history of modern conflict? In more than one photo history, one can read that Capa's images of mothers and children are significant because Spain was the *first* conflict before World War II in which civilians were targeted en masse via aerial fire.[63] By extension, Capa's accomplishment was that he was among the first to capture a fascist coalition using a new military technology to target civilians. Yet in the years preceding Capa's work, aerial bombardments of civilians occurred numerous times, including in Ethiopia, Iraq, and China, and they were not only the work of fascist regimes.[64] Nor were aerial bombings the most significant source of the casualties in Spain, which totaled in the vicinity of half a million.[65]

The aerial bombings in Spain *were* the first that could be easily covered, dramatized in the press, and made available through circulation in the years since. Earlier incidents, including the Japanese bombing of Shanghai, were covered in newsreels and with press photographs, but their coverage cannot be compared to the illustrious photo documentation of the Spanish Civil War.[66] Moreover, the details surrounding those earlier events were often repressed or obscured. Italian archives documenting the use of aerial bombs and gas in Ethiopia were closed to researchers in the 1960s and 1970s, and the country formally admitted to these acts only in 1995.[67] During the American occupation of Japan, the country more commonly addressed its aggression against the U.S. as part of Japan's "culture of defeat," and as late as the 1990s, photographic exhibitions deflected attention from Japan's imperial legacy, including the violence carried out against other Asians.[68] In those same decades, Capa's war photographs from Spain were shown widely, traveling to the very countries that were looking away from their own fascist legacies.[69] More recent exhibitions with titles such as *In Our Time* (1989) and *This Is War!* (2007) have also circulated globally, suggesting that Capa succeeded in capturing the most important moments of the twentieth century—themselves deemed significant because they were photographed.

Today, Capa's photographs from Spain continue to be displayed and reprinted by institutions that are invested in Capa's centrality in the history of photojournalism and in the financial value of his work, rather than in a specific and exhaustive history of fascism's rise. Compared with the relative invisibility of other visual histories of fascism and antifascism, the high visibility of Capa's Spain pictures—especially in photo exhibitions and in photo histories—suggests that Capa's work offers *the* way into this chapter of the twentieth century. It would be difficult to understand the visual history of fascism without taking into account Capa's contributions, but neither can one photographer's work stand in for the complexities of that history. Capa's iconic photographs open onto a larger history of the inclusions and exclusions at play in visualizing fascism in the 1930s and in subsequent decades. They invite a look at many more images of the global Right that emerged during the photographer's lifetime, and they should make us question how later generations formulated the significance of those visual legacies around the world.

Notes

1. Robert Capa to Ted Patrick and to John Morris, February 24, 1953, archive of John G. Morris (hereafter AJGM).
2. Robert Capa, self-authored biography, n.d., Magnum Foundation Archive, New York.
3. Richard Whelan, *Robert Capa: A Biography* (New York: Alfred A. Knopf, 1985), 284–89.
4. Mason Klein and Catherine Evans, *The Radical Camera: New York's Photo League, 1936–1951* (New Haven, CT: Yale University Press, 2011).
5. Robert Capa to John Morris, February 24, 1953, AJGM.
6. Bernard Lebrun and Michel Lefebvre, *Robert Capa: The Paris Years, 1933–1954* (New York: Abrams, 2011), 76–85; and Whelan, *Robert Capa*, 83–90.
7. Whelan, *Robert Capa*, 110.
8. Robert Capa to John Morris, February 24, 1953, AJGM; and Robert Capa to Morris Ernst, April 18, 1953, AJGM.
9. Robert Capa to Morris Ernst, March 10, 1953, AJGM.
10. Robert Capa to Morris Ernst, April 13, 1953, AJGM.
11. Whelan, *Robert Capa*, 284–88.
12. Whelan, *Robert Capa*, 295; John Morris, *Get the Picture: A Personal History of Photojournalism* (Chicago: University of Chicago Press, 1998), 155–59; Richard Whelan and Cornell Capa, *Robert Capa: The Definitive Collection* (New York: Phaidon, 2001), 12. Written by friends, relatives, and reverent biographers, such sources have long contributed to mythologizing Capa. Although they are some of the only sources on the details about his life, these texts largely lack footnotes and should be read as critically as the photographs and essays by Capa himself.
13. Catherine E. Clark, "Capturing the Moment, Picturing History: Photographs of the Liberation of Paris," *American Historical Review* 121, no. 3 (2016): 825, 828.
14. A summary of the mountainous scholarship on the Spanish Civil War is beyond the scope of this essay. Still foundational is Hugh Thomas, *The Spanish Civil War* (New York: Modern Library, 2001).

15 By November 1936, the USSR began to supply the Republican side with tanks, drivers, planes, and pilots, albeit without publicly acknowledging its involvement.

16 Peter N. Carroll and James D. Fernandez, *Facing Fascism: New York and the Spanish Civil War* (New York: Museum of the City of New York and New York University Press, 2007).

17 An extensive literature discusses the intertwined political and artistic stakes of the Spanish Civil War, but start with Jordana Mendelson, *Documenting Spain: Artists, Exhibition Culture, and the Modern Nation, 1929–1939* (University Park: Pennsylvania State University Press, 2005), including her bibliography.

18 Caroline Brothers, *War and Photography: A Cultural History* (London: Routledge, 1997).

19 Alan Brinkley, *The Publisher: Henry Luce and His American Century* (New York: Random House, 2010).

20 The same was true of documentary films, which often used stolen footage from the opposite side. Geoffrey B. Pingree, "The Documentary Dilemma and the Spanish Civil War," in *Teaching Representations of the Spanish Civil War*, ed. Neol Valis (New York: Modern Language Association, 2007), 313.

21 John Hersey, "The Man Who Invented Himself," in *Robert Capa, 1913–1954*, ed. Cornell Capa (New York: Grossman Publishers, 1974), 14–18.

22 Whelan, *Robert Capa*, 111; and Michel Lefebvre and Bernard Lebrun, "Where Does the 'Mexican Suitcase' Come From?," in *The Mexican Suitcase: The Rediscovered Spanish Civil War Negatives of Capa, Chim, and Taro*, ed. Cynthia Young (New York: International Center of Photography, 2010), 75–82.

23 The recent discovery of the "Mexican suitcase," which contained rolls of negatives by Capa, Chim, and Taro considered lost for decades, has now made it possible to study the team's collaboration and reattribute work to Chim and Taro. See Cynthia Young, "The Process of Identifying 4,500 Negatives: The Mexican Suitcase Revealed," and Kristen Lubben, "'Reportage Capa and Taro': Collaboration and Uncertainty," in Young, *Mexican Suitcase*, 95–125.

24 Simon Dell, "Mediation and Immediacy: The Press, the Popular Front in France, and the Spanish Civil War," in Young, *Mexican Suitcase*, 39.

25 Jordana Mendelson, *Revistas y Guerra, 1936–1939* (Madrid: Museo Nacional Centro de Arte Reina Sofía, 2007), 342–52.

26 Michael Griffin, "The Great War Photographs: Constructing Myths of History and Photojournalism," in *Picturing the Past: Media, History and Photography*, ed. Bonnie Brennen and Hanno Hardt (Urbana: University of Illinois Press, 1999), 122–57.

27 Ilya Ehrenburg, *Ispania—No Pasaran!* (Moscow: IZOGIZ, 1936 and 1937).

28 Whelan, *Robert Capa*, 128.

29 New Yorkers alone used publications, film screenings, and rallies to raise over $2 million in nonmilitary relief aid for the Spanish Republic. Eric R. Smith, "New York's Aid to the Spanish Republic," in Carroll and Fernandez, *Facing Fascism*, 50.

30 Covici-Friede's specialization in limited-edition books was difficult to maintain

during the Depression and led the firm to publish a second line of pulp novels. "Pascal Covici: An Inventory of His Correspondence at the Harry Ransom Humanities Research Center," Harry Ransom Humanities Research Center, Pascal Covici finding aid, accessed September 1, 2016, http://www.lib.utexas.edu/taro /uthrc/00028/hrc-00028.html.

31 Sally Stein notes that by the time the book appeared, the Republic was suffering heavy losses and that *Death in the Making* was an elegy for both the Spanish Republic and Capa's lover Gerda Taro. Sally Stein, "Close-ups from Afar: Contested Framings of the Spanish Civil War in U.S. Print Media, 1936," in *Magazines, Modernity and War*, ed. Jordana Mendelson (Madrid: Museo Nacional Centro de Arte Reina Sofía, 2008), 117–39.

32 Unlike the cover, the book's title page listed three levels of authorship: "Death in the Making by Robert Capa," followed by "Photographs by Robert Capa and Gerda Taro," and finally "Captions by Robert Capa." Chim was not mentioned.

33 The book also allowed Capa to fold Taro's photography and memory into his own narrative of grief and fame. Kristen Lubben, conversation with the author, April 20, 2016.

34 Richard Whelan, *This Is War! Robert Capa at War* (New York: International Center of Photography, 2007), 62–64; and Young, *Mexican Suitcase*, vol. 2, 294.

35 Juan Salas, "Images at War: Photographs of the Spanish Civil War in New York City," in Carroll and Fernandez, *Facing Fascism*, 123–29.

36 Robert Capa, *Death in the Making* (New York: Covici-Friede, 1938), n.p.

37 Miriam Basilio, "Museums for the People: Chim's Photographs of the Palacio de Liria and the Descalzas Reales," in Young, *Mexican Suitcase*, vol. 2, 66–73.

38 This generalized mode of presenting photographs of violence would be repeated in the aftermath of World War II. Barbie Zelizer, "Holocaust Photography, Then and Now," in Brennen and Hardt, *Picturing the Past*, 101–2.

39 According to Capa's image archive, searchable via http://pro.magnumphotos. com/, some of the images were made in Andalucia in 1936; at least one picture of a refugee captioned as arriving in Almeria was taken in Murcia, over two hundred kilometers away. Whelan comes to a similar conclusion in *Robert Capa*, 110.

40 Lebrun and Lefebvre, *Robert Capa*, 155.

41 Capa went on to photograph World War II for *Life* and published an illustrated and highly embellished memoir of the war titled *Slightly Out of Focus* (New York: Henry Holt, 1947).

42 "Postwar European Photography to Be Shown at the Museum," Museum of Modern Art Press Release 530522–45 (May 27, 1953), accessed March 3, 2016, https:// www.moma.org/docs/press_archives/1720/releases/MOMA_1953_0050_45.pdf ?2010.

43 John Morris, "Magnum Photos, an International Cooperative," *U.S. Camera*, 1954, 110–20; Byron Dobell, "Magnum: The First Ten Years," *Popular Photography*, September 1957, n.p.; David Seymour, "Magnum," Photokina catalog text, n.d. (circa 1956), AJGM.

44 Morris quoted in Dobell, "Magnum: The First Ten Years," n.p.

45 As Fred Turner shows, American cultural leaders during World War II saw Nazi Germany as proof that the mass media could be used to create authoritarian and totalitarian citizens. With the rise of the Cold War, communism became the new source of the totalitarian threat. Steichen's politics in particular could be described as a democratic humanism contra communism. Fred Turner, *The Democratic Surround: Multimedia and American Liberalism from World War II to the Psychedelic Sixties* (Chicago: University of Chicago Press, 2013), 3–5, 181–212.

46 Cynthia Young, *Capa in Color* (New York: International Center of Photography, 2014).

47 Harvey V. Fondiller, "Magnum—Image and Reality," *35mm Photography* (winter 1976), 68.

48 *Memorable Life Photographs* (New York: Museum of Modern Art, 1951); and Magnum Memo no. 194, October 17, 1959, AJGM.

49 Cornell Capa, "Robert Capa War Photographs—Exhibit," May 6, 1961; and Cornell Capa to Magnum, November 17, 1961, AJGM.

50 "The World as Seen by Magnum Photographers," Exhibition Checklist, n.d., AJGM.

51 Cornell Capa, *The Concerned Photographer* (New York: Grossman, 1967), n.p.

52 Although not included in *Death in the Making*, this picture appeared in Cornell Capa, ed., *Images of War: Robert Capa* (New York: Grossman, 1964), on the ten-year anniversary of Robert Capa's death.

53 This photo has been dated to 1952 in Cynthia Young, *We Went Back: Photographs from Europe 1933–1956 by Chim* (New York: International Center of Photography, 2013).

54 Leonard Freed, *Black in White America* (New York: Grossman, 1967).

55 Alan Wald, *Trinity of Passion: The Literary Left and the Antifascist Crusade* (Chapel Hill: University of North Carolina Press, 2007) and *American Night: The Literary Left in the Era of the Cold War* (Chapel Hill: University of North Carolina Press, 2014).

56 C. Capa, *Concerned Photographer.*

57 C. Capa, *Concerned Photographer.*

58 *Collier's* was the first illustrated magazine to close in 1956, followed by *Picture Post* in 1957, the *Saturday Evening Post* in 1969, *Look* in 1971, and finally *Life* in 1972.

59 Susie Linfield, *The Cruel Radiance: Photography and Political Violence* (Chicago: University of Chicago Press, 2010); Peter Baki et al., *Eyewitness: Hungarian Photography in the Twentieth Century* (London: Royal Academy of Arts, 2011); Lebrun and Lefebvre, *Robert Capa.*

60 "Alarm in Bilbao, 1937," Metropolitan Museum of Art, accessed August 4, 2016, http://www.metmuseum.org/art/collection/search/286705/.

61 "Alarm in Bilbao, 1937," Metropolitan Museum of Art, accessed August 4, 2016, http://www.metmuseum.org/art/collection/search/286705/.

62 See Young, *We Went Back* and *Mexican Suitcase*; Horacio Fernández, *Photobooks Spain 1905–1977* (Madrid: Museo Nacional Centro de Arte Reina Sofía, 2014).

63 Linfield, *Cruel Radiance*, 177, 187–88; Russell Miller, *Magnum: Fifty Years at the Frontline of History* (New York: Grove Press, 1997), 29–30; Inge Bondi, *Chim: The Photographs of David Seymour* (New York: Bulfinch Press, 1996), 45.

64 On Italy's aerial bombardments during the 1911–12 Italo-Turkish War see Ruth Ben-Ghiat and Mia Fuller, eds., *Italian Colonialism* (New York: Palgrave Macmillan, 2005). David Omissi, in *Air Power and Colonial Control: The Royal Air Force 1919–1939* (Manchester: Manchester University Press, 1990), shows that the British Royal Air Force repeatedly bombed Iraq, including civilians, between 1920 and 1924. The Japanese bombed Shanghai on January 28, 1932, which led to massive casualties.

65 Approximately 200,000 of the casualties were soldiers who died in battle. Another 200,000 died through acts of violence that used conventional and deliberately antiquated methods that were not documented by journalists. Thousands more perished after Franco's victory, whereas the number of bombing casualties remains contested. Paul Preston, *The Spanish Holocaust: Inquisition and Extermination in Twentieth Century Spain* (New York: Norton and Simon, 2012).

66 "On the Eastern Front," *Popular Mechanics*, April 1932, 535–50.

67 Ben-Ghiat and Fuller, *Italian Colonialism*, 6, 45, n3.

68 John W. Dower, *Embracing Defeat: Japan in the Wake of World War II* (New York: Norton, 2000), 508–20; and Julia Adeney Thomas, "Photography, National Identity, and the 'Cataract of Times': Wartime Images and the Case of Japan," *American Historical Review* 103, no. 5 (1998): 1475–501.

69 *War Photographs—Robert Capa* went to Italy and Japan in 1961, and his work has regularly been shown there since, both in the context of group shows and in solo exhibitions.

11

HEEDLESS OBLIVION

Curating Architecture after World War II

CLAIRE ZIMMERMAN

The similarities between German architecture in the 1930s
and that of the rest of the western world at the same time
seem even more striking to me now than they originally did.

—BARBARA MILLER LANE

"Invisibilizing" Architecture

Within photography's histories, photographic depictions of architecture occupy an ambiguous position.[1] Often used as functional instruments that coupled word and image to disseminate information about buildings, architects,
and clients, they also helped inoculate a humanistic profession from substan-
tive technological change by substituting single images for concrete things.
If a building *looked like* something modern, something traditional, or something ancient in a photograph, its technical aspects were less evident in its
public reception. Building technology and architectural expression, already
separate, were licensed by photography to part completely, recalling Oliver
Wendell Holmes's memorable words about the separation of skins from car-
casses.[2] Added to this disjuncture between image and constructed object,

media tactics could make entire historical fields vanish from discourse about buildings simply by excluding their photographs from magazines, journals, and books. The visual *re*mediation of architecture layers editorial practice on top of image making on top of formal appearance, leaving much of the industry of architecture almost entirely to one side. Yet the economic force of publicity has made photography a powerful agent in determining architectural futures.

What did photographs of fascist architecture *effect*, then, both by presence and by absence, in histories written after World War II? Early national socialist publications depicted the monumental architecture of the new regime in bold compositions deploying visual tropes of the interwar avant-gardes: asymmetrical compositions, raking views, and liberal use of the wide-angle lens.[3] (figure 11.1) Radical visual tropes promiscuously coupled with conservative building style provide just one example of fascism's counter aesthetic, described so eloquently by Julia Adeney Thomas in the introduction to this volume. As the global political goals of the national socialist government emerged, so did national socialist architecture appear to concretize those goals, drawing from other states' increasingly negative critiques of "the word in stone."[4]

Nazi buildings disappeared from much of the international architectural press after 1939. Similarly, historicizing architecture from the U.S. or the USSR also began to disappear, as if spirited away by visual association with the neoclassicism of the new Berlin. As fascist regimes broadcast "stripped classicism" as a house style in the press, so did the architectural profession elsewhere gradually release it. Both moves were part of media tactics largely unrelated to work "on the ground."

Contemporary architectural polemics are, by definition, geared toward future production. Selected narratives of the past strategically influence professional futures. Two caveats integrate photographic architecture into a book on the visual modes of global fascism. First, staged professional photographs of buildings meant for propaganda and trade publications differ fundamentally from photojournalistic images like those by Robert Capa, in which political ideology is often clearly mobilized.[5] In commercial photography of buildings, presumed photographic objectivity often obscures how composition and framing deliver rhetorical messages. Yet it is the success of the photograph *as image*, as much as other information about buildings, that determines the frequency of re-publication after an initial appearance. Readers and writers of images also conflate photographs with "three-dimensional

11.1 Montage of images from Sydney Clark, "Architecture under the Surge of Nationalism," *Arts and Decoration* 50 (May 1939): 39.

images" of carefully designed buildings, *not seeing* the complex tasks that buildings perform, which are invisible in photographs. Two formal tropes thus complicate architectural analysis: building form and photographic form. The latter often takes precedence over the former in historical and critical accounts.[6]

U.S. historian Henry-Russell Hitchcock (1903–87), accomplished reader of architectural photographs, understood this gap between image and object. A steadfast ally of practicing architects, Hitchcock creatively affiliated national socialist, U.S., and Soviet eclectic classicism, using photography to create associations among buildings in which function, political goal, construction technique, and aesthetic address differed fundamentally. Photography helped historians such as Hitchcock jettison a heterogeneous array of buildings for a more singular image of building that had developed in Europe between the wars and was associated with a limited number of architect auteurs. Although a logical way to promote new architecture, this was a dubious way to write the history of the immediate present.

As international-style architecture became the avatar of U.S. imperialism during the Cold War and the beacon of Western capitalism, alternative responses to modernity—some more technologically modern than their external appearance suggested—disappeared from view. Thus we might trace what happened, not when national socialist architectural photographs were made and first published, but rather when they began to disappear, edited out of postwar architectural history for decades. This virtual *Bildverbot*, an editorial iconoclasm, was accompanied by equally striking textual ellipses, as if not seeing the unwelcome image would make it disappear. Miller Lane reopened this chapter of German history in 1968, yet we are slow to probe the impact of fascism on architectural history after World War II.

Using global politics as a fulcrum, postwar modernists of the 1950s and '60s excluded important recent developments from architectural discourse. Industrialization and war had produced radical inventiveness in rapidly built daylight factories and innovations in concrete and steel building technologies prompted by shortages of materials and time. Recognizable visual regimes such as "classicism," "gothic," and "Mesoamerican" clothed buildings that exemplified significant economic and technical efficiencies. Overlooking these developments for a modernist aesthetic program equated with antifascism, the United States began its own campaign for global dominance against the USSR, using media tactics that are surprisingly familiar—as if the success of fascism's counter aesthetic begot the hegemony of Cold War propaganda.

Substituting an abstract aesthetic program historically affiliated with the Left for a historicizing one newly associated with fascism by the likes of Hitchcock, modern architects and critics unwittingly reprised the semantic violence that inhered when building style, or photographic image, became instrument of political ideology, as in global fascist movements. Other essays in *Visualizing Fascism* suggest how images (included or excluded) reveal historical developments with sometimes surprising directness. Here, the absent historiography of fascist architecture reveals an unwelcome postwar legacy, as photographs again obscured as much as they revealed of a new global order advanced through architecture. The genie of dominating ambition could not be contained by the bottle of world peace. Considering eclectic architecture, increasingly invisible in the media as the war passed, opens a complex chapter of North American architectural history, one that begins here a year before the 1933 election in Germany. The intertwining of historiography and professional practice shows the past annexed to the present, retarding any effective "coming to terms" with difficult history.

Hitchcock, 1932

In 1932, Hitchcock co-curated the influential exhibition *Modern Architecture: International Style* at MoMA, bringing to U.S. audiences European architecture along with select North Americans such as Frank Lloyd Wright (1867–1959), and providing a visual narrative for a new way of building.[7] A formalist tour de force, the exhibition included detailed architectural models and photographs closely trained on the buildings they depicted. Two years later, Hitchcock reclaimed an august heritage for twentieth-century architecture in print. His "Romantic Classicism in Germany" focused on architects Karl Friedrich Schinkel (1781–1841), Ludwig Persius (1803–45), and Leo von Klenze (1784–1864) (figure 11.2).[8]

A second essay on Baroque garden design and a third on the city of Potsdam affiliated late eighteenth- and early nineteenth-century romantic classicism with architectural modernism, specifically that of the mid-1920s.[9] This trio of articles appeared in the *American-German Review*, established by the philanthropic, business-oriented Karl Schurz Foundation in 1930 in order to promote German culture to U.S. audiences.[10] In the 1932 exhibition and later articles, Hitchcock steeped modernism in historical precedent, not revolution.[11] Similar shifts of rhetoric in modernist polemics have been noted elsewhere.[12] Historians and critics eager to establish architecture as a patronage art like painting, and to distance major public buildings from the political regimes they embodied, increasingly overlooked modernization processes in favor of historical genealogy. Photographic mediation aided and abetted this aim.

For historians before and after the war, the architectural eclecticism of the second half of the nineteenth century—Lewis Mumford's "brown decades"—interrupted a stylistic evolution from neoclassicism (romantic or "revolutionary" classicism, ca. 1800) to modernism. The stripped classicism of Schinkel's Greek and Roman designs, by contrast, threw a line backward and forward at once, connecting ancient and modern and stabilizing contemporary developments. Hitchcock's articles in the *American-German Review* belong to an entire literature on this topic.[13] In all of these instances, the old authorized the new, bestowing legitimacy and authority on newly produced work, despite implicit conflicts with the revolutionary program of the radical avant-gardes.

Figure 2. ALTES MUSEUM, Berlin. *Karl Friedrich Schinkel*, 1824-28

Romantic Classicism in Germany By HENRY RUSSEL HITCHCOCK, Jr.

IN America the classicism of the early nineteenth century seriously attempted to compress the various functions of architecture within the design formula of the Greek temple. In France also, academic pontiffs such as Quatremère de Quincy demanded of architects an equal submission to an impossible and ridiculous programme. Fortunately neither in America nor in France was the Classical Revival as drastic in application as in intention and the best work paid little attention to the rigid temple scheme.

But if the classical revival was by no means what historians of art, accepting contemporary theories too literally, have made it out to be, it was nevertheless a perfectly definite style whose more or less unconscious rules of purity of structural expression and economy of decoration were as widely accepted as its formal and inapplicable temple programme was scouted. In no country is the true character of the developed Classical Revival clearer than in Germany, although Germany originated few, if any, of the underlying principles which were there

Figure 1. Typical treatments and compositions from Durand's *Leçon d'Architecture* from which the Classic-Romantic movement in Germany derives

SEPTEMBER, 1934   19

11.2 Title page of Henry-Russell Hitchcock, "Romantic Classicism in Germany," *The American German Review*, September 1934, 19.

At roughly the same time, however, traditional architects in Germany laid claim to similar territory. The place of Schinkel in the genealogy of Nazi architecture disrupted the historical claims of Hitchcock and others.[14] The former responded in the *Architectural Forum* with a scathing review of the German contribution to the 1937 World's Exposition in Paris, roundly condemning Nazi architecture and culture policy. Of Albert Speer's oversized exhibition pavilion, Hitchcock wrote, "this is certainly the worst building in Paris" (figure 11.3).[15]

Thus unfolded before World War II a competition for cultural capital that prefigured similar skirmishes during the Cold War, if with different players. For both sides, affiliation with the past was a means to claim legitimacy in the present, an invaluable if intangible justification for "Architecture" in the eyes of clients, publics, and public officials. The authoritative past was also a blind

11.3 "The Paris Exhibition," *Architectural Review* special issue, September 1937, 7.

in the present, one that placed architecture on a historical continuum while simultaneously elevating it above the politics of its own day, "unmoored from history" like other hegemonic (fascist) practices.[16]

Hitchcock consistently rejected the deployment of historical architecture as an overt political symbol. The defeat of national socialism also did not end his condemnation of architects who used historical styles to design twentieth-century buildings. Rather, one enemy (Germany) gave way to another (the USSR) as he and other U.S. cultural actors began a coordinated strategy of resistance to communist culture—to both the megalomania of Soviet classical monuments and the instrumentalization of mass-produced prefabricated housing blocks. Cultural production on both sides of the Cold War conflict supplied a political weapon underwritten by state power, but in the U.S. this was masked by universalizing modernist rhetoric.[17] Tracing Hitchcock's postwar writings reveals how this particular fight was waged as the Cold War accelerated. Seeking to disconnect architecture from politics, Hitchcock emphasized aesthetic judgment as if it was independent of economics, class, or ideology, and of the architect as its arbiter. Paradoxically, the success of architecture as a political force in society came to reside in its aggressive refusal of party politics. Apolitical modernist architecture became the perfect vehicle for advancing imperialism-through-building, at home and abroad, throughout the years of the Cold War.[18]

Censoring the Historical Present

Hitchcock distanced both national socialist architecture and nineteenth-century building from the work of Persius and Schinkel. So have modern architects. Walter Gropius implicitly addressed national socialist appropriations of German neoclassicism in 1935: "I belong to a Prussian family of architects in which the tradition of Schinkel . . . was part of our heritage. . . . 'Respect for Tradition' does not mean the . . . . the acceptance of domination by bygone aesthetic forms."[19] Interpreting the use of period styles by national socialist architects as a return to the historicism of the late nineteenth and early twentieth centuries made national socialist building appear safely arrière garde. The *Architectural Review*, for example, called the 1937 Paris contribution "the tragedy of Germany," captioning a small photograph of the pavilion, "Germany has deliberately turned her architecture back to the time of Bismarck"—tragic in relation to the early development of modern architecture by Peter Behrens (1868–1940) and Gropius himself.[20]

Hitchcock, unusually and deeply immersed in the history of nineteenth-century architecture, carefully nuanced Gropius's critique, claiming that Germany's was a *recent* return, out of fashion more than revivalist.[21] After describing the emigration of Gropius and Ludwig Mies van der Rohe (1886–1969), he characterized German architecture as follows: "Those German architects who remained at home turned backwards in their tracks, though not very far backwards. . . . Very little of [it] deserves specific mention."[22] Affiliating the 1930s with the period 1900–1914 helped him emphasize lack of development and stylistic obsolescence.[23] Not only retrograde, national socialist building stemmed from a set of developments that were not deserving of "specific mention" because they were irretrievably flawed and aesthetically mediocre, in addition to being thoroughly outmoded. Hitchcock thus excluded it from the story altogether, as a nonorganic style incommensurate with its own historical moment.[24] Paul Mebes's influential *Um 1800*, a book that connected twentieth-century German architecture to the "revolutionary classicism" of the French revolution in France and Germany, for example, was not even mentioned in Hitchcock's compendious *Architecture: Nineteenth and Twentieth Centuries* of 1958.[25]

Hiding in the Historical Past

If postwar historians presented national socialist architecture as quaintly backward-looking, so did Nazi theorists themselves.[26] Architect and polemicist Paul Schultze-Naumburg (1869–1949) narrated a genealogy remarkably similar to that of the Neues Bauen, linking romantic classicism to national socialism by stepping backward to turn-of-the-century reform movements, and from there to architecture "around 1800." Like that of modernism, this genealogy skipped over mid- to late nineteenth-century historicism, when architects adopted revival styles to narrate building function, context, or manner of fabrication through the use of a set of established references that ranged over space and time.[27]

Yet revival styles that persisted from the nineteenth to the twentieth century clad technologically modern buildings.[28] As complex consumer products that take a long time to make, twentieth-century buildings increasingly required different orders of architectural production: aesthetic, technical, and propagandist. A highly articulated productive apparatus developed under national socialism, where historical styles related to building program (function, use), desired propaganda image, economic constraints, or all three.[29] Celebrating German ethnicity in *Heimatstil* architecture ("homeland style") was only one option from a heterogeneous stylistic mix that also included modern abstraction and monumental antiquarianism.[30] This is not nineteenth-century relativism, where building style was didactic and ethically coded, as in the work of A. W. N. Pugin. Instead, the hierarchical application of style under national socialism privileged unsubtle messaging about use, symbolization, and building economy.[31]

If arguments about style and its derivation could be debated endlessly and without conclusion throughout the first half of the twentieth century, they camouflaged an ongoing debate about relationships between architecture and technology. Here, modernists and national socialists parted company. The former projected transparency of form, use, and construction, with buildings as ostensible demonstrations of new building practices mediated by photography and graphic arts. National socialist architects, by contrast, used stylistic diversity as message carrier mediated by photography and graphic arts. For Nazi architects, technological innovation would advance an efficient building industry within local economic constraints. Construction technology and external appearance (style) belonged to different administrative realms and were not necessarily correlated, even as they coincided in buildings.

Miller Lane's important 1968 book made this claim, just as more recent studies have deepened it.[32] The integrated propaganda apparatus of the state (only possible through the systematic policy of coordination known as *Gleich-schaltung*) set media priorities for architecture and building that differed dramatically from technical priorities. The differences between propaganda needs and the requirements of useful buildings represented a newly schismatic condition that was not unique to Germany at this time. As the twentieth century passed, architecture was increasingly articulated around sophisticated demands for publicity and propaganda, in response to complex building tasks and developing technology, and as symbolic aesthetic practice. Miller Lane notes with regard to the first that "admiration for individualism and nostalgia for a hierarchical society and a preindustrial economy emerge from the party's architectural propaganda between 1930 and 1933."[33] Similarly, Hitler conflated two manners of construction that are often understood separately—that of a state and that of a work of art—so that the symbolism of architecture added yet another charge.[34] At the same time, the practical challenges of building grew more complex under the material and labor shortages that characterized wartime escalation.

Product Placement

Using various styles to sell similar consumer products was commonplace in the 1930s, whether the relevant currency was political-symbolic capital or money. We need not turn to the nineteenth century for precedents. In 1923, the year in which Henry Ford's *My Life* made its debut in Germany, Alfred P. Sloan became president of the General Motors Corporation in Detroit, which soon diversified car models in a family of brands (to include Opel from 1929). Increasing the company's consumer base, GM challenged the "purist" manufacturer of the Model T, which produced only one car model at a time until the second half of the 1920s. Sloan offered consumers automobiles in a multitude of styles and colors and at a range of prices, effectively spreading the demand for automobiles by applying stimuli. Such articulation lies at the core of successful commercial marketing.[35]

The 1920s diversification of consumer markets in Detroit and the diversification of building typologies and stylistic wrappers that occurred in Germany after 1933 share a similar phase of capitalist development with a host of other consumer products. Paul Jaskot notes how "ss architects were responding like developers and engineers everywhere to contingencies of politics, war, and material shortages (let alone labour)."[36] Another way in which national socialist builders responded to market pressures concerned working-class housing. Abandoning large-scale mass dwellings for political reasons, the state turned to single-family dwellings "on the rural side of the plant in which [laborers] work." This was not only a planning decision or a strategy of deurbanization in Nazi Germany. Putting workers on land to grow food even as they also worked full-time in factories amortized the costs of such building and muted workers' political voices.[37] New housing policy was intended to make factory workers self-sufficient through land cultivation, an economic benefit.[38] Compared with the racially selective home mortgage system sponsored by Ford Motor Company, in which monthly payments kept workers tied to their paychecks, German workers experienced different manners of social control. In both cases, architecture provided a mechanism.[39] The modernity of national socialism is well understood in relation to propaganda, building technology, cultural politics, and economic modeling. Reducing it to backward-facing antiquarianism tamed its threat, rendering the state's lethal nature familiar and easy to dismiss. Such moves disguised the equally lethal role that architecture had played, whether in accommodating prisoners in barracks, providing enclosures in which they worked to their deaths and were gassed or burned, or housing the ministers who debated the lives of others over cocktails at Wannsee Lake. But the straw man erected by Anglophone critics to account for Nazi building during the war or immediately after it was not only historically inaccurate. It also had knock-on effects.

Let us turn back to Detroit. An essay by Hitchcock on postwar U.S. architecture shows how architectural images—how architecture *as* image— migrated across geographic and political boundaries to be flexibly deployed as a political tool. Hitchcock's reference to "Nazidom" in 1947 relates the work of Detroit industrial architect Albert Kahn (1869–1942) to that of national socialist architects a decade and a half earlier. As improbable as any close comparison of these two turns out to be, made so in part because of Kahn's Judaism, his thriftiness, and his lack of formality (in building as well as in organization), the association merits attention here.

By 1947 Hitchcock was an influential voice in Anglo-American architectural history (along with Lewis Mumford, and Nikolaus Pevsner in the U.K.), co-curator of the 1932 "International Style" show and a prolific writer.

In "The Architecture of Bureaucracy and the Architecture of Genius," he compared Frank Lloyd Wright to Kahn, carefully distinguishing architecture from more prosaic building.[40] The "architecture of bureaucracy" provided a revenue stream for architectural practices; the "architecture of genius," by contrast, contributed to culture. Hitchcock's postwar campaign, of which the essay was part, further articulated a distinction that Pevsner laid down in 1943: "A bicycle shed is a building; Lincoln Cathedral is a piece of architecture."[41] Lest architects lose access to industrial and commercial building and the "bread and butter" income that such work provided, Hitchcock carefully distinguished the manner of building that sustained architects financially from that which elevated them within cultural spheres.[42] Architects might build utilitarian buildings to generate revenue for their offices; only geniuses such as Wright would build for posterity.[43] This critical scheme to safeguard professional architecture subsidized the unpredictable phase of architectural work—that of design—with more predictable tasks such as producing working drawings or supervising sites. Genius architecture was expensive; mundane work could amortize its cost. For these reasons and others, Pevsner's bipartite definition of architecture as either vernacular building or fine-art architecture was not sufficiently complex for postwar markets.

Kahn, in contrast to Wright, had contributed to modern architecture by perfecting the rapid delivery of factories, institutions, and commercial buildings. Kahn's modern architecture, shockingly different from anything coming from Europe in the 1920s, was based on a systematic reorganization of architectural work to adapt to the increasingly uncompromising demands of industrial clients. These clients were not primarily interested in aesthetics. Rather, they sought any economic advantage that might be gained over aggressive competitors in an intensely competitive market. Worker productivity (for which more carefully designed architecture that better accommodates a range of human needs might be consequential), functionality, and predictability of costs displaced aesthetics. Kahn's handful of articles and speeches testify to the degree to which he had absorbed these values while retaining a belief in the value of design despite its imperviousness to clearly measurable standards.

Kahn's work had inspired European modernists as early as the 1910s and 1920s, when his "Crystal Palace," Ford's Highland Park factory, was widely published by authors such as Gropius, Adolf Behne, and Werner Lindner. Part of a widespread "Amerikanismus," or interest in American innovations, Kahn's work was greeted as the latest technological building for large industry (figure 11.4).[44]

Abb. 115. Maschinenhaus IX der Fried. Krupp A.-G., Essen

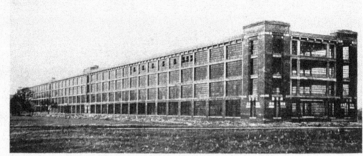

Abb. 116. Fabrik in Nordamerika

11.4 Plate illustration showing the Highland Park Old Shop, also known as the "Crystal Palace," by Albert Kahn, architect for the Ford Motor Company, 1908–10. From Werner Lindner, *Die Ingenieurbauten in ihrer Guten Gestaltung* (Berlin: Wasmuth, 1923), 110.

The raw material that Kahn provided was then crafted into "Architecture" by Gropius and others.[45] Yet, in his 1947 article, Hitchcock used the retrograde term "bureaucracy," a word associated with nineteenth-century governmental inefficiency and the rationalization of state organizations, to detail the manner in which the work of Kahn's firm could, as a function of its organization, produce undistinguished but highly competent buildings.[46] Hitchcock understood bureaucratic building as an outgrowth of the war and postwar reconstruction.[47] As European theorists signaled the need for a "new monumentality" after the war, Hitchcock instead accepted a fait accompli: that U.S. military might was based on U.S. industrial capacity. He merely tried to work around this seemingly unavoidable fact, carefully sequestering "bureaucratic" architecture from the art of building. Yet the term "bureaucratic" inadequately describes an architectural practice organized around mechanization and automation.[48] Rather than bureaucratic procedures, Kahn's office strategically adjusted standard practices.

Counterposing individual authorship with the lack of individual agency that is characteristic of bureaucracy, Hitchcock ends with a note: "The public monuments of Nazidom might serve as a warning. Moreover, England and America have their own horrible examples of twentieth-century bureaucratic monuments." The retrograde "-dom" neutralized a lethal term and a recent and very modern threat, locating it in the distant past of king*doms* or fief*doms*, even as the second sentence in the same note summons past, present, and future—"twentieth-century bureaucratic monuments."[49] Notions of applied style as distinct from organic or integrated style (such as that found in modern architecture) reject theories of dressing or cladding that were staples of steel- and concrete-framed building and of twentieth-century architectural theory, and that remained popular among practicing professionals in the U.S.

Distancing modernization from the unfolding project of modernism, Hitchcock's polemics collided with the demands of writing history or criticism, as he himself acknowledged.[50] Tunnel vision pushed "Nazidom" back into the distant past, where it could drag with it manners of building that Germany shared with other modern states, including the United States. Through such means, Hitchcock characterized Kahn's work as retrograde and obsolete, like national socialist architecture. Fred Turner convincingly relates postwar reinvestment in the perceived power of individual experience to fears of mass psychology instilled by the success of Nazi propaganda and techniques of mass persuasion.[51] Both are also part of the phase of capitalism that prevailed after World War I. Herein lies the most obvious reason to affiliate two such disparate cultural actors as Albert Speer and Albert Kahn: if you correlate them to the same general threat constituted by modernity itself, you can use one to dismiss both.

How close was Kahn's superficial stylistic eclecticism to the architecture of national socialism? Kahn's buildings were carefully calculated, reducing the quantity of material used in order to minimize cost. Stone was a cladding material attached in thin sheets to the steel frames of buildings and held by metal anchors, screws, mortar, and gravity.

The firm pioneered new building technology across a range of materials, seeking economies of scale through the use of thinner cladding, less re-

11.5 General Motors Building, Detroit, Michigan, 1923, by Albert Kahn, architect. From the Bentley Historical Library, University of Michigan. Copyright © Albert Kahn Associates.

inforcing in ferroconcrete, and less ornamentation; these were not removed entirely, but to an extent that would reduce cost while maintaining appearance. Thus rondels on many Kahn buildings remained unsculpted, like blank spots where one would typically find figurative reliefs or inscriptions. Economy was particularly important in industrial buildings, although one finds it everywhere in Kahn's practice—as in the Hatcher Library reading room at the University of Michigan, where a false barrel vault of canvas, wood, and plaster hangs from the steel trusses that span the reading room and support the floors above.

Somatic Economy

In contrast to this laboratory of reduced construction costs, the national socialist building program developed an economic model founded on slave labor from camps such as Flossenbürg and on a dearth of steel combined with plentiful masonry supplies, as Jaskot has shown.[52] Large public buildings in Germany from this time are in many cases actually load-bearing masonry buildings, an extravagance in any open-market building economy. They were economically possible only because the labor that provided the stone was cheap, if not free (requiring only that concentration camp inmates be monitored by guards and fed a minimal diet); the quarries themselves were government owned, and steel was unavailable for construction during wartime. But not only manufacture distinguishes these architectures. Whatever superficial stylistic similarities might be identified in photographs, the buildings have a different affect across the board, as Hitchcock knew well from his personal experience at Pratt and Whitney.[53] One could argue that Kahn's buildings are "background" buildings that generally don't draw sustained visual attention. Speer's buildings, by contrast, present monumental stone architecture as urban ensemble, megastructure designed to draw attention, not deflect it, and meant to constitute a public that is subservient to the will of the state. Both literally and figuratively, it is the relative *weight* of these two kinds of buildings that distinguished one from the other at the end of the 1930s, even as their images could be superficially affiliated, particularly as they vanished from the press, vilified but no longer supplied.[54]

Hitchcock, 1958

Hitchcock continued to publish after 1947, just as his frequent publishing between 1929 and 1947 was interrupted only once, when he paused to write technical manuals for aircraft engines in a building designed by Albert Kahn.[55] His 1958 *Architecture: Nineteenth and Twentieth Centuries* was a major reference work for architects and historians thirty years in the making, and it went through six editions and multiple reprints.[56] The passage cited above, on German architects after 1933, focused on Peter Behrens and constitutes most of the discussion on national socialist architecture between 1933 and 1945. Titled "Behrens and Other German Architects," the chapter includes Paul Bonatz (1877–1956), German Bestelmeyer (1874–1942), and Wilhelm Kreis (1873–1955) among those favored by the Nazi party. The same paragraph describes Oskar Kaufmann (1873–1956), who fled to Palestine in 1933, with no mention of a divergence of paths; indeed, the chapter title suggests that nothing much happened to architecture in Germany after 1933, beyond the work of a few genius creators, the most important of whom (Behrens) died in 1940.

The penultimate chapter of *Architecture*, "Architecture Called Traditional in the Twentieth Century," is as good as its word. One sentence mentions Albert Kahn before a multipage discussion of prominent British colonial architect Edwin Lutyens, a core member of the European "canon," according to consensus, even though his biggest projects were sited in British India.[57] The text explains that traditional architecture "is primarily an instance of survival; and cultural survivals are among the most difficult problems with which history has to deal. Their sluggish life, sunk in inertia and conservatism, is very different from the vitality of new developments" (392). Hitchcock thus dismisses the North American architectural scene that was ongoing when MoMA first began its campaign for modern architecture in the 1932 show; he equally mischaracterizes the construction juggernaut that engulfed Germany under Hitler.[58] The fact that Kahn's buildings were, in terms of building construction and technology, as modern as any that had theretofore been built—that historicist styles were merely draped over *technologically* modern buildings—was precluded from Hitchcock's analysis both because of events in Germany and despite them.

Modernizing Architecture

Historians hardly need question the ongoing prominence of formalism in architectural history or the inherent restrictions that formalist aesthetics impose. Yet we live with the negative consequences of positive decisions— decisions made *for* architecture, not *against* history. Traditional architecture, so called, "includes the majority of buildings designed before 1930 in most countries of the western world and a high but rapidly decreasing, proportion of those erected since," and yet its popularity did not merit sustained examination.[59] The ellipsis of national socialist architecture in Hitchcock's book is mirrored and echoed by an equal silence about what is arguably the most critical and poorly understood achievement of modern building (but not "modern architecture") in mid-twentieth-century North America: the unprecedented output of offices like Kahn's that fueled industry leading into World War II. These offices built factories, office buildings and skyscrapers, cultural institutions, and homes. By omitting such buildings from architectural history, polemicists of modernism set cultural capital apart from finance and scientific capital, erecting a barrier between culture and its sites and means.[60] Parallel exclusions of national socialist and U.S. architecture from history are striking; they may be explained in part by Hitchcock's own history.

Johnson noted, in a *Festschrift* of 1982, that "from the architect's point of view, what stands out in Russell's scholarship is his use of primary visual sources. I can bear personal witness that from his first travels in 1930, to the latest for his German Renaissance book, Russell saw every extant building he writes about."[61] Not only conscious of distinctions between load-bearing masonry and steel- or concrete-frame construction, Hitchcock was also a sophisticated reader of photographs.[62] By embracing selective formalism he erected a levee against the surge of modernization, fully aware that style was irrelevant to the juggernaut of industrial capitalism even as he opposed nineteenth-century *styles* with twentieth-century *style*. While Giedion and others explored the difficult proposition that the essential medium of architecture was space in time (and thereby, in some sense, the negation of form), Hitchcock pursued an alternative proposition.[63] For him and many others, style represented an authoritative cultural signature, the defining feature of an age—and of a personality. Lest this seem hopelessly irrelevant today, recall the working relationship between Hitchcock and Johnson, and that between Johnson and contemporary architect Peter Eisenman (b. 1932). Eisenman's influence over generations of architects should not be underestimated, in part because the progressive credentials that drape a sophisticated cultural conservatism based on architecture as elite practice camouflage that political belief far more effectively than Kahn's neoclassical styling of the steel-framed GM Building.[64]

In such a schema for architecture, it really only matters how buildings *look* in order for their value as cultural actors to be affirmed. How they are built, are inhabited, and age were within Hitchcock's purview, but primarily insofar as these affirmed decisions made during the design process. For this reason, the interchangeability of the photograph for the building is revealing. Like photographs, building style is literally superficial, accounting for building surfaces, whether inside or out, but without any necessary reference to internal organization (generally deciphered in the plan) or construction (sometimes associated with the section). The image of architecture *is* its photograph because the photograph dutifully records all of the stylistic attributes that the camera's eye can graze.[65] This tautology partly explains the agency of photography in twentieth-century architecture; today it underpins a great deal of architecture and its history.

Conclusion: No Politics in Architecture
Equals No Architecture in Politics

Hitchcock's 1947 article and his 1958 book are Cold War histories. The first used recent catastrophe to undermine interwar building in the U.S. by associating its image with wartime German architecture. Yet the so-called architecture of bureaucracy was an important part of the U.S. building industry, a key force in the development of urban and exurban landscapes of the United States and a linchpin of military-industrial power. It required careful study. Hitchcock's 1958 book left this material out of the historical picture entirely. The stripped classicism of "bureaucratic" architecture continued unabated nonetheless, in buildings whose executors cared little for architectural discourse. Hitchcock's cordon sanitaire around genius architecture protected a small percentage of building, not necessarily in the United States. By erecting it, he (and others) sought to protect professional elites, not to deploy architecture for a more democratic "surround" in the built environment.

The historian, attempting to secure agency for and yet simultaneously indemnify the architect from political responsibility, helped hand away both responsibility and agency, foreclosing a better correlation between politics and the places in which they occur. In fear of what had already happened, he (not she) removed architecture from discourse on public life and turned it into a fiction about itself.[66] Construction at scale went on unabated, carried out by those who saw buildings as machines that modulate economics, politics, form, and material for a variety of ends.[67] Architects who removed themselves ever more fully from a public discourse that they could not control contrast with working architects such as Kahn who built the fabric of U.S. industry, which was then still largely urban.

More worrying still is the notion that investing architecture in questions of style and image—not technology, economic output, use, or means for living—though intended to avoid the hubristic demonstrations of national socialism, led to similar hubris in a different register, one less immediately lethal and more successfully global. The obliteration of German architecture from historical consideration contributed to this repetition. Hannah Arendt sounded an alarm in 1950 when she wrote,

> We can no longer afford to take that which was good in the past and simply call it our heritage, to discard the bad and simply think of it as a dead load which by itself time will bury in oblivion. The subterranean stream of Western history has finally come to the surface and usurped the dig-

nity of our tradition. This is the reality in which we live. And this is why all efforts to escape, from the grimness of the present into nostalgia for a still intact past, or into the anticipated oblivion of a better future, are vain.[68]

Yet as these words were written, architects were hard at work burying the past and embracing stylistic coherence in buildings throughout the U.S. and its international territories in the 1950s and 1960s.

U.S. architects and critics celebrated high-rise glass and steel office buildings and monumental sculptural buildings designed for civic functions—as organic representations commensurate with the challenges of modern postwar life, and as fundamentally nonpolitical representations. Intentionally or not, however, these agents of economic superiority and Cold War politics at home and abroad wielded an image of stylistic coherence that was inseparable from and associated with U.S. political influence. Would stylistic heterogeneity have altered global politics? Almost certainly not. Late modern architects took then-obsolete experiments of the 1920s as the basis for a new architectural style for high-cost buildings, a style that "trickled down" through the economy of the built environment. Such consistency reinforced the interests of the state, whether through private capital (Hilton hotels, corporate office towers) or public buildings (U.S. embassies worldwide, corporate campuses, and concert halls at home). The refusal to historicize—and visualize—fascism during the immediate postwar years condemned U.S. architects to repeat its mistakes, limiting new possibilities in the present and restraining the capacity of architecture to shape political life.[69]

Notes

Epigraph: Barbara Miller Lane, *Architecture and Politics in Germany, 1918–1945* (Cambridge, MA: Harvard University Press, [1968] 1985), v.

1 I thank historian Jean Hebrard for coining the term "invisibilizing architecture."
2 Oliver Wendell Holmes, "The Stereoscope and the Stereograph," *Atlantic*, June 1859, accessed February 14, 2018, https://www.theatlantic.com/magazine/archive /1859/06/the-stereoscope-and-the-stereograph/303361.
3 See George Sylvester Viereck, ed., *A Nation Builds: Contemporary German Architecture* (New York: German Library of Information, 1940); Werner Rittich, *New German Architecture* (Berlin: Terramare, 1941); Albert Speer and Rudolf Wolters, *Neue Deutsche Baukunst* (Prag: Volk und Reich Verlag, 1943); Gerdy Troost, *Das Bauen im neuen Reich* (Bayreuth: Gauverlag, 1938). Also see Rolf Sachsse, *Die Erziehung zum Wegsehen: Fotografie im NS-Staat* (Hamburg: Philo Fine Arts, 2003); Otto Thomae, *Die Propaganda-maschinerie bildende Kunst und Öffentlilchkeits-*

arbeit im dritten Reich (Berlin: Gebr. Mann, 1978). On the traveling exhibition "Neue deutsche Baukunst," see Jörn Düwel and Niels Gutschow, *Baukunst und Nationalsozialismus: Demonstration von Macht in Europa, 1940–1943: Die Ausstellung Neue Deutsche Baukunst von Rudolf Wolters* (Berlin: DOM, 2015).

4 Robert R. Taylor, *The Word in Stone: The Role of Architecture in the National Socialist Ideology* (Berkeley: University of California Press, 1974).

5 See Nadya Bair's contribution to this volume.

6 See Claire Zimmerman, *Photographic Architecture in the 20th Century* (Minneapolis: University of Minnesota Press, 2014).

7 Terrence Riley and Steven Perrella, *The International Style: Exhibition 15 and the Museum of Modern Art* (New York: Rizzoli/CBA, 1992).

8 Henry-Russell Hitchcock, "Romantic Classicism in Germany," *American-German Review* 1, no. 1 (September 1934): 19–24; Henry-Russell Hitchcock, "Romantic Architecture of Potsdam," *International Studio* 99 (May 1931): 46–49.

9 Henry-Russell Hitchcock, "Late Baroque German Gardens," *American-German Review* I, no. IV (June 1935): 26–33; Henry-Russell Hitchcock, "The Romantic Gardens of Potsdam," *American-German Review* 2, no. 1 (September 1935): 19–24.

10 Contrast with the NS-sponsored German Library of Information (from 1936), VDA (Volksbund für das Deutschtum im Ausland, founded 1880), and Amerikadeutscher Volksbund (from 1936). German Library publications included *Facts in Review* (ed. George Sylvester Viereck), *The War in Maps 1939/40* (1941), *A Nation Builds: Contemporary German Architecture* (1940), and *Caspar David Friedrich* (1940). See M. Sayers and A. E. Kahn, *Sabotage! The Secret War against America*, 2nd ed. (New York, 1944), 61–62; and Ron Rosenbaum, *Waking to Danger: Americans and National Socialist Germany, 1933–1941* (Santa Barbara, CA: Praeger, 2010). On the VDA, see Ralph Frederic Bischoff, *Nazi Conquest through German Culture* (Cambridge, MA: Harvard University Press, 1942); on the Volksbund, see Frederick Turner, *The Democratic Surround: Multimedia and American Liberalism from World War II to the Psychedelic Sixties* (Chicago: University of Chicago Press, 2013), 18–21.

11 Barry Bergdoll, "Romantic Modernity in the 1930s. Henry-Russell Hitchcock's Architecture: Twentieth and Nineteenth Centuries?," and Paolo Scrivano, "A Thirty-Year Project: Henry-Russell Hitchcock's *Architecture: Nineteenth and Twentieth Centuries*," both in *Summerson and Hitchcock: Centenary Essays on Architectural Historiography*, ed. F. Salmon (New Haven, CT: Yale University Press, 2006), 193–208 and 171–192.

12 Serge Guilbaut, *How New York Stole the Idea of Modern Art* (Chicago: University of Chicago Press, 1984).

13 Henry-Russell Hitchcock, *Modern Architecture: Romanticism and Reintegration* (New York: Payson and Clarke, 1929); Emil Kauffmann, *Von Ledoux bis Le Corbusier* (Vienna: Passer, 1933); Fiske Kimball, "Romantic Classicism in Architecture," *Gazette des Beaux-Arts* 25 (February 1944): 95–112. Sigfried Giedion's doc-

toral dissertation, "Spätbarocker und romantischer Klassizismus" (University of Munich, 1922), covers a slightly earlier set of developments (1770–1830).

14 Matthias Schmitz, *Caspar David Friedrich: His Life and Work* (New York: German Library of Information, 1940).

15 Henry-Russell Hitchcock, "Paris 1937," *The Architectural Forum* (September 1937): 163. A monumental Soviet pavilion faced the German. J. M. Richards described the Italian Pavilion at the 1939 New York World's Fair as "a bombastic piece of showmanship, and one of the worst buildings in the Fair." James Maude Richards, *Introduction to Modern Architecture* (Harmondsworth: Penguin, 1940), 76.

16 Julia Adeney Thomas's introduction in this volume.

17 Francis Stönor Saunders, *The Cultural Cold War: The CIA and the World of Arts and Letters* (New York: New Press, 2000).

18 See Jack Masey and C. Morgan, *Cold War Confrontations: US Exhibitions and Their Role in the Cultural Cold War* (Baden: Lars Müller, 2008); Annabel Wharton, *Building the Cold War: Hilton International Hotels and Modern Architecture* (Chicago: University of Chicago, 2001); Jane Loeffler, *The Architecture of Diplomacy: Building America's Embassies* (New York: Princeton Architectural Press, 1998); Robert H. Haddow, *Pavilions of Plenty: Exhibiting American Culture Abroad in the 1950s* (Washington, DC: Smithsonian Institution Press, 1997).

19 Walter Gropius and P. Morton Shand, *The New Architecture and the Bauhaus* (London: Faber and Faber, 1935), 112.

20 "The National Pavilions," *Architectural Review* 83, no. 490 (September 1937): 110.

21 Hitchcock moved backward from his 1929 book on modern architecture to late work on the German Baroque. See the introduction and Paolo Scrivano, "A Thirty-Year Project: Henry-Russell Hitchcock's *Architecture: Nineteenth and Twentieth Centuries*," both in *Summerson and Hitchcock: Centenary Essays on Architectural Historiography*, ed. F. Salmon (New Haven, CT: Yale University Press, 2006), 171–92.

22 Henry-Russell Hitchcock, *Architecture: Nineteenth and Twentieth Centuries* (Baltimore: Penguin, 1958), 347. Also see Taylor, *The Word in Stone*. Miller Lane notes that the "um 1800" years provided key images among architects associated with the Kampfbund, but that these architects did not represent the regime after 1934: Barbara Miller Lane, *Architecture and Politics in Germany, 1918–1945* (Cambridge, MA: Harvard University Press, [1968] 1985), 167, 179–80.

23 Nazi architecture was flexibile and stylistically eclectic in part because of ambiguous policies. See Miller Lane, *Architecture and Politics*, chapter 8.

24 Hitchcock, *Modern Architecture*, 160; for an earlier rendition of a similar idea, see Nikolaus Pevsner, *Pioneers of the Modern Movement: From William Morris to Walter Gropius* (London: Faber & Faber, 1936).

25 Paul Mebes, *Um 1800: Architektur und Handwerk im letzten Jahrhundert ihrer traditionellen Entwicklung* (Munich: F. Bruckman, 1908).

26 See the "Beispiele-Gegenbeispiele" illustrated in P. Schultze-Naumburg, *Die Kul-turarbeiten*, 9 vols. (Munich: G. D. W. Callwey, 1901–1917).

27 H. Hubsch, *In welchem Stil sollen wir bauen?* (In What Style Shall We Build?) (1828) is a classic example.

28 See Gropius and Shand, *The New Architecture and the Bauhaus*, 43–44, on fights between Right and Left on this subject.

29 Winfried Nerdinger, "Baustil im Nationalsozialismus: Zwischen Klassizismus und Regionalismus," published in English as "A Hierarchy of Styles: Architec-ture between Neoclassicism and Regionalism," in *Art and Power: Europe under the Dictators 1930–45*, ed. David Elliott, Dawn Ades, Tim Benton, and Iain Boyd Whyte (London: Thames and Hudson, 1996), 322–25; and Winfried Nerdinger, ed., *Bauhaus-Moderne im National-sozialismus* (Munich: Prestel, 1993), particu-larly the chapter by Rolf Sachsse, "Kontinuitätetn, Brüche und Mißverständnisse: Bauhaus-Photographie in den dreißiger Jahren," 64–84.

30 See Miller Lane's review of Speer's *Inside the Third Reich*, in which she argues convincingly for Mesopotamian and Egyptian models being knowingly deployed despite their Semitic roots: *Journal of the Society of Architectural Historians* 32, no. 4 (December 1973): 341–46.

31 A. Tooze, *The Wages of Destruction: The Making and Breaking of the Nazi Econ-omy* (London: Penguin, 2006).

32 Taylor, *The Word in Stone*; Alex Scobie, *Hitler's State Architecture* (College Park: Pennsylvania State University Press, 1990); Nerdinger, *Bauhaus-Moderne im Na-tionalsozialismus*; Winfried Nerdinger and Katharina Blohm, *Bauen im Nation-alsozialismus: Bayern 1933–1945* (Munich: Klinkhardt & Biermann, 1993); Paul Jaskot, *The Architecture of Oppression: The ss, Forced Labor and the Nazi Monu-mental Building Economy* (New York: Routledge, 2000); also see the series *Hitlers Architekten* (Wien). On the traveling exhibition "Neue deutsche Baukunst," see Düwel and Gutschow, *Baukunst und Nationalsozialismus*.

33 Miller Lane, *Architecture and Politics in Germany*, 167.

34 "By 1933, Hitler . . . had come to think of art and politics as essentially the same. This was so, he explained at the Party Congress of 1936, because both art and the state are the products of a creative force. . . . The interpreters of this creative force were, according to Hitler, the artist on the one hand and the politician on the other. Characteristically, he often spoke of the two in almost interchangeable terms." Miller Lane, *Architecture and Politics in Germany*, 187–88, 265. Also see Corey Ross, *Media and the Making of Modern Germany* (New York: Oxford Uni-versity Press, 2008).

35 Mary Nolan, *The Transatlantic Century: Europe and America, 1890–2010* (Cam-bridge: Cambridge University Press, 2012); and Mary Nolan, *Visions of Moder-nity: American Business and the Modernization of Germany* (New York: Oxford University Press, 1994). On the GM Building, see Michael Abrahamson, "'Actual Center of Detroit': Method, Management, and Decentralization in Albert Kahn's

General Motors Building," *Journal of the Society of Architectural Historians* 77, no. 1 (March 2018): 56–76.

36 Paul Jaskot, "Building the Nazi Economy: Adam Tooze and a Cultural Critique of Hitler's Plans for War," *Historical Materialism* 22, nos. 3–4 (2014): 312–29; also see Tooze, *Wages of Destruction*.

37 G. Gray, "Highlights of a Housing Tour of Northern Europe, Part II," *Octagon*, February 1938, 15–18.

38 "The minimum of land for the new subsistence homesteads is 1250 sq. meters, every inch of which must be profitably cultivated under expert direction through the labor office—even the shade trees and the hedges must be fruit-bearing." Gray, "Highlights of a Housing Tour." Tooze notes the inadequacy of this effort in *Wages of Destruction*, 157–61. Miller Lane comments in *Architecture and Politics*, chapter 7.

39 Ford-backed mortgages required marriage, cleanliness, good dental care, and so on. See Michael McCulloch, "Building the Working City" (PhD diss., University of Michigan, 2015). Also see Mary Nolan, "America in the German Imagination," in H. Fehrenbach, *Transactions, Transgressions, Transformations: American Culture in Western Europe and Japan* (New York: Berghahn Books, 2000), 3–25.

40 Nikolaus Pevsner, editor of the *Architectural Review*, pressed Hitchcock for contributions. See correspondence files, Henry-Russell Hitchcock Papers, Archives of American Art.

41 Nikolaus Pevsner, *Outline of European Architecture* (Harmondsworth: Penguin, 1943), 1.

42 Henry-Russell Hitchcock, "The Architecture of Bureaucracy and the Architecture of Genius," *Architectural Review* 101 (January 1947): 3–6.

43 Hitchcock displeased Wright in *Modern Architecture: International Style* in 1932 and made amends in *In the Nature of Materials 1887–1941: The Buildings of Frank Lloyd Wright* (New York: Museum of Modern Art, 1942).

44 For a comprehensive summary, see Jean-Louis Cohen, *Scenes of the World to Come* (Montreal: Flammarion, 1995).

45 "Path of Kahn," www.pathofkahn.com.

46 See Max Weber, *Economy and Society: An Outline of Interpretive Sociology* (Berkeley: University of California Press, 1978), originally published in German in 1922; Michael Herzfeld, *The Social Production of Indifference: Exploring the Symbolic Roots of Western Bureaucracy* (New York: Berg, 1992); Matthew Hull, *Government of Paper: The Materiality of Bureaucracy in Urban Pakistan* (Berkeley: University of California Press, 2012). The word dates to 1818, when "French political economist Jean Claude Marie Vincent de Gournay coined the derisive term *bureaucracy*, or rule by writing desk." See Hull, *Government of Paper*, 11, accessed October 12, 2016, https://books.google.com/books?id=qoFAuc5LRHsC&lpg=PR1&pg=PA11#v=onepage&q&f=false.

47 His experience of this manner of building was gained firsthand; from 1943 to 1945

he worked in a Pratt and Whitney factory built by Kahn's firm, writing technical manuals for how to assemble aircraft engines.

48 Jayne Choi has shown how the firm's organization required constant adjustment—Kahn likened his role to that of the conductor of an orchestra, refining processes by which architectural projects were completed. See Jayne Choi, "Cybernetic Industriousness: The Production of Albert Kahn Associates, 1918–42" (unpublished manuscript, September 20, 2016).

49 Similarly, a decade earlier, "the traditionalists . . . had worked out a formula of adaptation of the styles of the past which was not too completely ludicrous; following a line very similar to that of the Romans who so generally clothed their brilliant engineering with the shopworn and vulgarized fragments of Greek architecture." Henry-Russell Hitchcock, "The Architectural Future in America," *Architectural Review* 81, no. 488 (July 1937): 1–2. For "Nazidom," the Oxford English Dictionary records five occurrences in journalistic contexts (1933, 1935, and 1941) and two in fiction (1947, 1971). Dietrich Neumann notes that Ayn Rand used the term. A cursory word search of *The Fountainhead* does not reveal its use: https://babel.hathitrust.org/cgi/pt?id=mdp.39015054079721. Accessed May 2019.

50 "From this point on the ideal objectivity of the historian . . . is inevitably colored, if not cancelled out, by the subjectivity of the critic writing of events he knew at first hand." Hitchcock, *Architecture: Nineteenth and Twentieth Centuries*, 380.

51 Turner, *The Democratic Surround*, introduction. *The Fountainhead* also manifests this fear.

52 Jaskot, "Building the Nazi Economy."

53 See the unpublished paper on industrial architecture, Hitchcock Papers, Archives of American Art.

54 See Scobie, *Hitler's State Architecture*, chapter 4.

55 See James H. Grady, "Henry-Russell Hitchcock: The First Thirty Years," *The American Association of Architectural Bibliographers Papers* 1 (1965): 1–22. See Hitchcock Papers, Archives of American Art.

56 Scrivano, "A Thirty-Year Project: Henry-Russell Hitchcock's *Architecture: Nineteenth and Twentieth Centuries*," in Salmon, ed., *Summerson and Hitchcock*, 171–92.

57 Kahn receives two other mentions: in reference to Detroit's Fisher Building and in a note on reinforced concrete.

58 Hitchcock's co-curator, Philip Johnson, was also an acknowledged anti-Semite who joined the American fascist party, hoping for a leader in first Huey Long and then Father Coughlin. William Shirer writes of Johnson as "an American fascist . . . spying for the Nazis" in *Berlin Diary* (Harmondsworth: Penguin, [1940] 1979), 213.

59 Hitchcock, *Architecture: Nineteenth and Twentieth Centuries*, 392.

60 Here, Daniel Abramson notes, "a rearguard aesthetic, stylistically, could stand in capitalism's vanguard, ideologically, precisely by reutilizing and revaluing residues and castoffs." Yet the modernization described here may call for a more nu-

anced political economy in which materials, technology, aesthetics, and social life figure prominently. See Daniel Abramson, *Obsolescence* (Chicago: University of Chicago Press, 2013), 137.

61 P. Johnson, "Preface," in Helen Searing, ed., *In Search of Modern Architecture: A Tribute to Henry-Russell Hitchcock* (Cambridge, MA: MIT Press, 1982), vii; Nigel Whiteley, "High Hopes and Universal Disappointment," in Salmon, ed., *Summerson and Hitchcock*, 324.

62 During World War II, Hitchcock applied to work at the OSS photographic library. He was assiduously careful with photographs and curated photography of buildings. See correspondence files, Henry-Russell Hitchcock Papers, Archives of American Art.

63 On Giedion's relationship to Hitchcock, see Scrivano, "A Thirty-Year Project: Henry-Russell Hitchcock's *Architecture: Nineteenth and Twentieth Centuries*," in Salmon, ed., *Summerson and Hitchcock*, 171–92.

64 Also see Peter Eisenman, *Ten Canonical Buildings 1950–2000* (New York: Rizzoli, 2008), all attributed solely to successful white male Euro-American auteurs.

65 Sachsse, *Die Erziehung zum Wegsehen*; Thomae, *Die Propaganda-maschinerie bildende Kunst und Öffentlilchkeitsarbeit im dritten Reich*.

66 Gail Day, "Manfredo Tafuri, Fredric Jameson and the Contestations of Political Memory," *Historical Materialism* 20, no. 1 (2012): 31–77, notes that Tafuri endorsed this removal. Critics such as Ada Louise Huxtable and Jane Jacobs did not.

67 For alternative approaches, see Jesse LeCavalier, *The Rule of Logistics: Walmart and the Architecture of Fulfillment* (Minneapolis: University of Minnesota Press, 2016); and Kenny Cupers, *Use Matters: An Alternative History of Architecture* (London: Routledge, 2013).

68 Hannah Arendt, *The Origins of Totalitarianism* (London: Harcourt, Brace & World, 1979), ix.

69 Alfred Roth, *"USA baut": Bildbericht der Ausstellung Moderne amerikanische Architektur* (Winterthur: Verlag Buchdruckerei, 1945); Mary Mix, *Amerikanische Architektur seit 1947* (Stuttgart: G. Hatje, 1951).

CONCLUSION

GEOFF ELEY

How should we visualize fascism today? Taken together, our essays suggest several strong arguments. More than just an assortment of cases drawn from discrete parts of the world, they show fascism's emergence in a shared global setting. By the 1930s, that setting contained multiple centers with multidirectional flows: a globality of rival imperialisms caught in the fallout of a worldwide capitalist downturn. Just as World War II far exceeded a merely European framework of clashing nation-states, so fascism also had plural and varied origins. Fascism began from East Asia as well as Europe, from Africa and the Americas, with varying success across regions. These fascisms displayed similar political dynamics, ideology, and practices and had convergent political effects. An explicitly *global* understanding is vital for our purposes.[1]

By pointing to multiple *origins*, we also stress multiple *forms*. We want to pluralize the picture, whether in the movement or the regime phases, showing the diverse starting points and trajectories of national fascisms as against the progenitive primacy of the Italian and German examples. Thus fascism sought power through stealthy maneuvers and elite-driven brokerage as well as by the full-frontal challenge of a Nazi *Machtergreifung* or Mussolini's March on Rome; by more diffuse plebiscitary appeals, as against the highly organized, party-based mobilizing of the Nazis in 1928–32; and by backdoor institutional leverage rather than through popular disorders. The absence of a mass party on the Nazi pattern does not in itself mean the absence of fascism. As our essays also show, fascism could just as frequently fail, or be successfully held at bay, rather than coming ultimately to power. In short, our range of examples reflects the convergent circumstances of political polarization and societal crisis across the globe during the interwar years, for which "fascism" then delivered the shared political language, whether as willingly embraced self-description or as a label its opponents bestowed.

We can go further. If fascism's emergence was globally dispersed, taking variable forms and multiple paths, it also settled only gradually and unevenly into generic existence. It developed cumulatively rather than unfolding from an already assembled ground of principles comparable in coherence to liberalism or conservatism and other political ideologies. "Fascism" as an everyday term preceded fascism as a category of sociopolitical analysis. But it soon named the commonalties of a variety of radical right-wing formations around the world, whose heterogeneous qualities caution against any restrictive typology of the movements that qualify or not. *First* came the loose and mobile repertoire of "fascism," borne by all of the discursive noise and visual tactics surrounding Mussolini's and similar movements, whether as viscerally unreflected sloganeering and images or as consciously chosen terminology and stagecraft by party intellectuals and strategists. Only *then* came fascism as the stabilized category of political understanding. That being the case, a broader definition seems more helpful and appropriate. Thus fascism was a brutally distinct type of politics: it wanted to silence and even kill its opponents; it preferred coercively authoritarian rule over democracy; it celebrated an aggressively exclusionary idea of the nation over a pluralism honoring difference; it presented itself in spectacles, photographs, graphics, and film as transcendently glorious, while invading every hearth and home, sitting quietly and insidiously next to fathers, mothers, and children.

Both geographically decentered and historically dynamic, this nontypological definition then becomes eminently portable, not only spatially across the globe in the early twentieth century but also across very different times, including our own today. And approaching fascism *visually* allows us to grasp that portability especially well. Historians have recently grown notably attentive to fascism's visual archive, perhaps earlier for Italy than for Germany, embracing first film and then the arts more generally, from painting and sculpture to architecture and the built environment, and now photography. Careful readings of these parts of fascism's account of itself can bring us closer to the leitmotifs of fascist ideology—to the emotional evocations and fantasies of national wholeness Julia Thomas emphasized in the introduction: from the masculinist grievances and aggressions to the "vitalist energy of youth, the comforts of naturally sanctioned belonging, and the necessity of righteous wars in a hostile world." From the visual archive we can begin to reconstruct not only the intended fields of officially executed meaning but also their limitations, the places where doubts and misgivings—nonconforming recognitions—retreat into the privacies of the self and where even passive resistance might occur. Materially and practically, in the machineries of propaganda and cultural production, moreover, visuality was essential to fascism's strategies of appeal, its drive for popular endorsement, whether before or after entry into power. The efficacy of those visual messages, Thomas argues, lay precisely in how "elusive and emotive" they were. The same dual effect—practical transmission, resonance of appeal—occurred across borders too, not just literally as fascist ideas traveled from one country or region of the world to another, but also ideologically as fascists sought to realize their own global imaginary of interconnectedness.

How should we judge fascism's ideological appeal *beyond* the elaborate orchestrations of the spectacle where treatments most easily begin? If the fascist spectacle will certainly keep both its resonance for current Far Right sympathizers and its interest for historians, the harder challenge concerns complexities of reception, whether among the immediate participants in a Nuremberg Rally or in its wider viewing and listening audiences.[2] On the one hand, the fearsome effects of fascism's founding acts of violence (in Italy in 1920–22, in Germany in 1933–34) were clear enough: the new rules of permissible behavior had a brutally intimidating effect and were explicitly sanctioned by force beneath new codes of belonging and exclusion. But, on the other hand, even as the immediate ferocity started to settle, fascist regimes moved with decisive speed and distressing success to secure popular consent. Ordinary reactions to fascism's rise or rule might well be structured psychically around "dissonance," while contrary and divergent emotions jostled uncomfortably together. Conformity and dissent, enthusiasm and misgivings, might be either managed and suppressed or consciously held apart and unthinkingly kept in play.[3] Yet, however conflicted and ambivalent the individual motivation, ordinary Japanese, Germans, and Italians—Julia Thomas's magazine readers, for example, or the viewers of Lutz Koepnick's accessible and domesticated Hitler, or Ruth Ben-Ghiat's faces in the crowd—began necessarily realigning their daily comportment, increasingly needing "to take a stance and position themselves according to new concepts and ideas."[4] The new times brought new interpellative mechanisms and expectations, new conditions for the fashioning of public and private selves, new emotional registers, new conditions of conscience.[5] Where fascists lacked equivalent control over a state—in the East Asian arenas examined by Maggie Clinton, Paul Barclay, and Ethan Mark, for example, or in Lorena Rizzo's southern Africa—their visualizing strategies still drew similar complexities of response.

How fascists visualized *this* normalizing process by translating it into tropes, techniques, and repertoires of image-making—and how privately made, commercialized, and nonfascist images then circulated inside the resulting visual economy—takes us far beyond the large-scale public machinery of the spectacle. As Thomas observes, fascism had many ways of seeking "to abolish the distance between the state and its subjects." Indeed, it was in the enjoyments, disappointments, and practicalities of quotidian life (through family, childhood, household, neighborhood, work, schooling, recreation, play, sexuality, intimate life) that ordinary subjects actually experienced the promises and affirmations fascists were claiming to supply. Imaginative use of photographic genres (magazine illustration, documentary reportage, tourism, hobbies, family albums) combined with an interpretive approach to ordinary people's lives that uses oral histories, ego documents, and the more conventional written archive can bring us closer to this subjective and experiential dimension, as a number of our essays (e.g., Ben-Ghiat, Thomas, Koepnick, Rizzo, Metton) show. For fascism's visual repertoire comprised not just the values choreographed into the imposing massed symbolics of the public spectacle—order, action, struggle, manliness, will, race, necessity of war, rebirth, the New Man. Its fantasies of nation and empire required roseate small-scale sentimentality too: the joys and comforts of domesticity, the wholesomeness of family and healthfulness of children, fecundity and motherhood, the robustness of homegrown morality, the haven of civilized privacy. In his reading of Hoffmann's Hitler portraiture, Koepnick shows these combining into an artfully engineered unity, where the transcendently heroic *public* was enhanced by the reassuringly idealized *private*.[6] This visual joining of the national to the local, the political to the domestic, in such close and mutually inciting collaboration, was a key element of fascist strength and innovation. Fascist visuality brought politics (qua war and expansionism) into conversation with intimacy, interiority, and everydayness.

In a variety of versions, this same potent duality of public aggressions and private reassurances could also be detected later. By the 1950s, once fascism and capitalist crisis were effectively decoupled, these terms were already being subtly reworked, as Nadya Bair and Claire Zimmerman each reveal: capitalist economic relations were perceived increasingly as natural and default, whereas Robert Capa's iconic antifascist photographs were depoliticized and brought down to their "human interest." But for our own time, the starkness is back: Middle Eastern and central Asian bombing offensives and drone warfare, refugee crises and massive population displacements, rampant xenophobia, anxiety about borders, and gun violence, on the one hand; fantasies of family wholeness and the healthy national body, on the other. As constitutional democracy and its rules of civility reel beneath criticism and threat while worryingly large popular constituencies and powerful interests disavow the legitimacy and entailments of pluralism and difference, the space for an aggressively right-wing politics palpably widens. Without replicating the mass parties and other features of the 1920s and 1930s, the signs are familiar: violence against enemies and opponents, coercively authoritarian rule, expansionist and exclusionary nationalism. But the conditions of political communication and exchange are now profoundly changed. Both the means and the mechanics of what a political movement can hope to accomplish have been transformed in the meantime by the bewildering extent and availability of our contemporary visual archive—not just from television, film, and the classical reservoirs of public and private photography, but now, too, from the internet and web-based digital apparatuses of image storage, circulation, and retrieval combined with smartphone technology and personally managed social media access.

This observation bridges to the second way our volume is pertinent for the present: the means of circulation and transmission per se. Of course, it was not ideas, images, and visual representations alone that traveled internationally inside the geopolitical arenas where fascists were making their history. People and things did so too. In Paul Barclay's account of the monuments and sites memorializing the dead, tourists voyaged and pilgrimaged all over East Asia for the purpose; Ethan Mark finds equally significant traffic between the colonial Dutch Indies and the Netherlands before Japanese expansionism changed the directions for such exchange. In this volume, in his account of Slovakia, a regional forecourt to the Nazis' eastward imperium, Bertrand Metton supplies cognate illustration of what that could mean—namely, the colonial circuitry of military, administrative, and economic occupation and collaboration with unfamiliar peoples that faced Germans and vice versa, in a hall of two-way mirrors described more obliquely by Nadya Bair for the Spanish Civil War and its rival fascist and left-wing interventions.[7] Using biographical studies of the central European emigration to southern Africa, Lorena Rizzo shows another way in which people and their ideas traveled, as her two women photographers, Ilse Steinhoff and Anneliese Scherz, reenacted subtle translations of fascist visuality.[8]

In the earlier twentieth century, the global resonance of fascist ideas both presumed and required a new mass-mediated public sphere. This made possible previously unimagined speed and quality of access to varieties of images and ideas originating elsewhere—through new visual and print technologies (illustrated magazines, advertising, cinema, photography), gramophone records and radio broadcasting, commercial entertainments, and new patterns of consumption. Mussolini's larger-than-life international popularity in the mid-1920s, reaching "veritable boom" proportions country by country, supplies one compelling illustration of this.[9] Whether in the eye-catchingly modernist graphic design described by Maggie Clinton, in poster and pamphlet illustrations, or in the conventions of newspaper and magazine photography, fascist imagery traveled thickly into global circulation. The resulting iconographies, visual tropes, and narrative patterns helped shape how fascist political formations would be perceived in the future. By means of repetition, accumulation, and interarticulation, such visual languages solidified the political narratives fascists needed in order to drive their messages home—narratives of national wholeness, of heroic and armored masculinity, of familial health and female fecundity, of youthful vigor, of racialized community, of militantly demonizing rejection of the Jewish and Bolshevik enemies. Given the transnational circuits of influence and indebtedness, such images helped vitally compose the layered ideological corpus that movements and regimes elsewhere would be able to raid.

These same processes become replicated across time. Postwar movements of the Far Right, presently far less inhibited than ever before and with apparently increasing support in many parts of the world, fish freely in this deep reservoir of iconography, signs, and associations transmitted from an earlier past, netting much material—badges, insignia, uniforms, symbols, slogans, forms of action—that is instantly usable for styling themselves inside a recognizably fascist tradition. Sometimes these movements claim indigenous descent (worryingly so in Hungary, Poland, and elsewhere); at other times they cleave vicariously to the Nazi or Italian precursors. In the United States a topography of neo-Nazi, white supremacist, militia-styled, and "Alt-Right" activism can be mapped in this way through its networks, writings, and websites, thereby disclosing a visual repertoire selectively continuous with the 1930s.[10] Moreover, if the past delivers a serviceable resource in this fashion, it is also more readily retrievable. With the dramatic reconfiguration of publicness that has been underway since the 1990s, the fascist proclivity for appropriating and repurposing imagery—its distinctive counter aesthetic of "undisciplined eclecticism," mobile symbolics, and aggressive negations, as Thomas explains it—flourishes but now presents itself differently. Presaged by the global diffusion of television since the 1960s, followed by the mass spread of fax machines, computers, and the early forms of the internet, the startling rapidity of new electronic communications, digital techniques, and information technologies—DVDs, cable and satellite TV, laptops, cell phones, Skype, streaming, smartphones, social media—now allows not only novel forms of web-based organizing but also incomparably easier access. Increasingly under this new dispensation, *violence* means not just physically harming and murdering opponents, but also coercively overriding democratic civility and its constitutional safeguards. It no longer relies as much on street fighting, pitched confrontations, and spectacular displays of massed force. It operates, rather, via verbal onslaughts, internet trolling, instantly transmitted and reproduced visual incitements, and all the other virtual means of displaced but no less brutal assaultiveness. This very differently constituted visual landscape, made dramatically apparent in the instantaneous global simultaneity of the spectacle of 9/11, requires its own terms of analysis. We can certainly see definite continuities from the 1930s: repetitions of tropes and repertoires and familiar patterns of rhetoric, including the masculine nation, the soldierly nation, the rageful nation, the misogynist nation, the racialized and racially armored nation, and so forth. But the contents and coordinates of contemporary visuality equally clearly diverge, not least in their globally spatialized dimensions. Events in one place become instantly transmitted to watchers in another, meanings are deceptively graspable, distance shrinks. This volume offers a casebook for recognizing and situating these lineaments of contiguity and difference.

Notes

1   Taking an avowedly global approach to fascism remains uncommon. Among the thirty-one essays in *The Oxford Handbook of Fascism* (Oxford: Oxford University Press, 2009), edited by Richard J. B. Bosworth, for example, Rikki Kerstin's chapter on Japan (526–44) is the only extra-European discussion, whereas Robert O. Paxton's key treatment of "Comparisons and Definitions" (547–65) remains

resolutely European. Broadly the same applies to the recent works of António Costa Pinto, *The Nature of Fascism Revisited* (New York: Columbia University Press, 2012); António Costa Pinto, ed., *Rethinking the Nature of Fascism: Comparative Perspectives* (Houndmills, U.K.: Palgrave Macmillan, 2011); Daniel Woodley, *Fascism and Political Theory: Critical Perspectives on Fascist Ideology* (London: Routledge, 2010); Aristotle A. Kallis, ed., *The Fascism Reader* (London: Routledge, 2003); and Constantin Iordachi, ed., *Comparative Fascist Studies: New Perspectives* (London: Routledge, 2010). David D. Roberts, *Fascist Interactions: Proposals for a New Approach to Fascism and Its Era, 1919–1945* (New York: Berghahn Books, 2016), does consider Japan, but only as an occasional foil to the primary European cases. Another impressive anthology, Arnd Bauerkämper and Grzegorz Rossoliński-Liebe, eds., *Fascism without Borders: Transnational Connections and Cooperation between Movements and Regimes in Europe from 1918 to 1945* (New York: Berghahn Books, 2017), is explicitly European from the outset. Two rare monographic exceptions would be Reto Hofmann, *The Fascist Effect: Japan and Italy, 1915–1952* (New York: Columbia University Press, 2015); and Federico Finchelstein, *Transatlantic Fascism: Ideology, Violence, and the Sacred in Argentina and Italy, 1919–1945* (Durham, NC: Duke University Press, 2010).

2 Intimations from contemporary political life are plentiful enough, sometimes very directly, as in the staging of Donald Trump's 2016 campaign rallies (e.g., his descent from the skies to address crowds in airport hangars) or in the organizing of a white supremacist torchlight procession. Hollywood has for decades drawn on the imagery of plebiscitary and charismatic acclamation exemplified by long-established readings of the Nuremberg Rallies and Leni Reifenstahl's *Triumph of the Will*. Examples range from *Privilege* (Peter Watkins, 1967) and *Network* (Sidney Lumet, 1976) to *The Hunger Games* trilogy (Gary Ross, 2012; Francis Lawrence, 2013 and 2014–15) and *Money Monster* (Jodie Foster, 2016). Among literary versions of this syndrome, my own essay in this volume (chapter 3) opens with Don DeLillo's novel *White Noise* (New York: Penguin, 1985).

3 See Mary Fulbrook, *Dissonant Lives: Generations and Violence through the German Dictatorships* (Oxford: Oxford University Press, 2011).

4 Kathryn Sederberg, "The 1930s in Nazi Germany as Seen through Diaries," in a review of Janosch Steuwer, *"Ein Dritter Reich, wie ich es auffasse": Politik, Gesellschaft und privates Leben in Tagebüchern 1933–1939* (Göttingen: Wallstein, 2017), published on H-German in H-Net Online, January 2018, www.h-net.org/reviews/showrev.php?id=50185/.

5 See Claudia Koonz, *The Nazi Conscience* (Cambridge, MA: Harvard University Press, 2003).

6 See also Despina Stratigakos, *Hitler at Home* (New Haven, CT: Yale University Press, 2015).

7 Elsewhere Metton explores the role of hiking and youth movements during the later 1930s and 1940s in mapping the European imaginary of a Nazi-dominated New Order: Bertrand Metton, "From the Popular Front to the Eastern Front:

Youth Movements, Travel, and Fascism in France, 1933–1945" (PhD diss., University of Michigan, 2015), and "Nazi Europe and the Atlantic Wall: On Spatial Theory and the Wartime Fascist Worldview," unpublished. Also Ruth Ben-Ghiat, *Italian Fascism's Empire Cinema* (Bloomington: Indiana University Press, 2015); Stephanie Malia Hom, *The Beautiful Country: Tourism and the Impossible State of Destination Italy* (Toronto: University of Toronto Press, 2015); and Stephanie Malia Hom, "Empires of Tourism: Travel and Rhetoric in Italian Colonial Libya and Albania, 1911–1943," *Journal of Tourism History* 4, no. 3 (2012): 281–300.

8 For the transnational circulation of fascist ideas, see Benjamin G. Martin, *The Nazi-Fascist New Order for European Culture* (Cambridge, MA: Harvard University Press, 2016); Johannes Dafinger, "The Nazi 'New Europe': Transnational Concepts of a Fascist and *Völkisch* Order for the Continent," in Bauerkämper and Rossoliński-Liebe, eds., *Fascism without Borders*, 264–87; Roel Vande Winkel and David Welch, eds., *Cinema and the Swastika: The International Expansion of Third Reich Cinema* (Houndmills, U.K.: Palgrave Macmillan, 2011).

9 Hofmann, *Fascist Effect*, 38. See also Adam Tooze, "When We Loved Mussolini," *New York Review of Books*, August 18, 2016, 55–56; John P. Diggins, *Mussolini and Fascism: The View from America* (Princeton, NJ: Princeton University Press, 1972); Simonetta Falasca-Zamponi, *Fascist Spectacle: The Aesthetics of Power in Mussolini's Italy* (Berkeley: University of California Press, 1997), 50–55.

10 For the growing literature surveying this scene, see Alexander Reid Ross, *Against the Fascist Creep* (Chico, CA: AK Press, 2017); Mark Bray, *Antifa: The Anti-Fascist Handbook* (Brooklyn, NY: Melville House, 2017); David Neiwert, *Alt-America: The Rise of the Radical Right in the Age of Trump* (London: Verso, 2017); Vegas Tenold, *Everything You Love Will Burn: Inside the Rebirth of White Nationalism in America* (New York: Nation Books, 2018).

BIBLIOGRAPHY

Abel, Jonathan E. *Redacted: The Archives of Censorship in Transwar Japan*. Berkeley: University of California Press, 2012.

Abrahamson, Michael. "'Actual Center of Detroit': Method, Management, and Decentralization in Albert Kahn's General Motors Building." *Journal of the Society of Architectural Historians* 77, no. 1 (March 2018): 56–76.

Abramson, Daniel. *Obsolescence*. Chicago: University of Chicago Press, 2013.

Achilles, Manuela. "With a Passion for Reason: Celebrating the Constitution in Weimar Germany." *Central European History* 43, no. 4 (2010): 666–89.

Allert, Tilman. *The Hitler Salute: On the Meaning of a Gesture*. London: Picador, 2009.

Antliff, Mark. "Fascism, Modernism, and Modernity." *The Art Bulletin* 84, no. 1 (2002): 148–69.

Arendt, Hannah. *The Origins of Totalitarianism*. London: Harcourt, Brace and World, 1979. Accessed July 20, 2017. https://archive.org/details/ArendtHannah TheOriginsOfTotalitarianism1979/.

Asahi Shimbun Company. *Media, Propaganda and Politics in 20th-Century Japan*, translated by Barak Kushner. London: Bloomsbury Academic, 2010.

Aschheim, Steven E. "Introduction." In *What History Tells: George L. Mosse and the Culture of Modern Europe*. Edited by Stanley G. Payne, David J. Sorkin, and John S. Tortorice, 3–22. Madison: University of Wisconsin Press, 2004.

Atkins, E. Taylor. *Primitive Selves: Koreana in the Japanese Colonial Gaze, 1910–1945*. Berkeley: University of California Press, 2010.

Aumont, Jean. *Du visage au cinéma*. Paris: Editions de l'Etoile, 1992.

Baer, Ulrich. *Spectral Evidence: The Photography of Trauma*. Cambridge, MA: MIT Press, 2002.

Baranowski, Shelley. *Nazi Empire: German Colonialism and Imperialism from Bismarck to Hitler*. Cambridge: Cambridge University Press, 2010.

Baranowski, Shelley. *Strength through Joy: Consumerism and Mass Tourism in the Third Reich*. Cambridge: Cambridge University Press, 2004.

Baranowski, Shelley. "Strength through Joy: Tourism and National Integration in the Third Reich." In *Being Elsewhere: Tourism, Consumer Culture, and Identity in Modern Europe and North America*. Edited by Shelley Baranowski and Eileen Furlough, 213–36. Ann Arbor: University of Michigan Press, 2001.

Barclay, Paul. *Outcasts of Empire: Japan's Rule on Taiwan's "Savage Border,"* *1874–1945.* Berkeley: University of California Press, 2017.

Barrera, Giuliana. "Mussolini's Colonial Race Laws and State-Settler Relations in Africa Orientale Italiana (1935–1941)." *Journal of Modern Italian Studies* 8 (2003): 425–43.

Bärsch, Claus-Ekkehard. *Die politische Religion des Nationalsozialismus. Die religiöse Dimension des NS-Ideologie in den Schriften von Dietrich Eckert, Joseph Goebbels, Adolf Rosenberg und Adolf Hitler.* Munich: W. Fink, 1998.

Barthes, Roland. *Camera Lucida: Reflections on Photography,* translated by Richard Howard. New York: Hill and Wang, 1981.

Barthes, Roland. *La Chambre claire: Note sur la photographie.* Paris: Cahiers du Cinéma/Seuil, 1980.

Barthes, Roland. "Visages et figures," *Esprit* 2–4 (July 1953): 1–11.

Bathrick, David. "Making a National Family with the Radio: The Nazi Wunschkonzert." *Modernism/Modernity* 4, no. 1 (January 1997): 115–27.

Bauerkämper, Arnd, and Grzegorz Rossoliński-Liebe, eds. *Fascism without Borders: Transnational Connections and Cooperation between Movements and Regimes in Europe from 1918 to 1945.* New York: Berghahn Books, 2017.

Ben-Ghiat, Ruth. "Envisioning Modernity: Desire and Discipline in the Italian Fascist Film." *Critical Inquiry* 23, no. 1 (autumn 1996): 109–44.

Ben-Ghiat, Ruth. *Italian Fascism's Empire Cinema.* Bloomington: Indiana University Press, 2015.

Ben-Ghiat, Ruth, and Mia Fuller, eds. *Italian Colonialism.* New York: Palgrave Macmillan, 2005.

Benjamin, Walter. "The Work of Art in the Age of Its Technological Reproducibility." In *Selected Writings, Vol. 4: 1938–1940.* Edited by Howard Eiland and Michael Jennings, 251–83. Cambridge, MA: Harvard University Press, 2003.

Benjamin, Walter. "The Work of Art in the Age of Mechanical Reproduction." In Walter Benjamin, *Illuminations.* Edited and with an introduction by Hannah Arendt, 219–53. London: Collins/Fontana, 1973.

Berezin, Mabel. *Making the Fascist Self: The Political Culture of Interwar Italy.* Ithaca, NY: Cornell University Press, 1997.

Bergdoll, Barry. "Romantic Modernity in the 1930s. Henry-Russell Hitchcock's Architecture: Twentieth and Nineteenth Centuries?" In *Summerson and Hitchcock: Centenary Essays on Architectural Historiography.* Edited by Frank Salmon. New Haven, CT: Yale University Press, 2006.

Berger, John. "Understanding a Photograph." In *Classic Essays on Photography,* 291–94. Edited by Alan Trachtenberg. New Haven, CT: Leete's Island Books, 1980.

Berger, John. *Ways of Seeing.* New York: Penguin, 1972.

Berman, Marshall. *All That Is Sold Melts into Air: The Experience of Modernity.* London: Verso, 1983.

Bird, David S. *Nazi Dreamtime: Australian Enthusiasts for Hitler's Germany.* London: Anthem Press, 2013.

Bischoff, Ralph Frederic. *Nazi Conquest through German Culture*. Cambridge, MA: Harvard University Press, 1942.

Bix, Herbert P. *Hirohito and the Making of Modern Japan*. New York: Harper Perennial, 2001.

Blackbourn, David, and Geoff Eley. *The Peculiarities of German History: Bourgeois Society and Politics Nineteenth-Century History*. Oxford: Oxford University Press, 1984.

Bosworth, Richard J. B., ed. *The Oxford Handbook of Fascism*. Oxford: Oxford University Press, 2009.

Bray, Mark. *Antifa: The Anti-Fascist Handbook*. Brooklyn, NY: Melville House, 2017.

Brennen, Bonnie, and Hanno Hardt, eds. *Picturing the Past: Media, History and Photography*. Urbana: University of Illinois Press, 1999.

Brogini Künzi, Guilia. *Italien und der Abessinienkrieg 1935/36*. Paderborn: Ferdinand Schöningh, 2006.

Brothers, Caroline. *War and Photography: A Cultural History*. London: Routledge, 1997.

Buck, David. "Railway City and National Capital: Two Faces of the Modern in Changchun." In *Remaking the Chinese City: Modernity and National Identity, 1900–1950*. Edited by Joseph W. Esherick, 65–89. Honolulu: University of Hawai'i Press, 1999.

Calvin, Andrew. "Delineating a Fascist Aesthetic? Boundary Transgression and the Nazi Degenerate Art Exhibition." Paper presented at the Visualizing Fascism Workshop, University of Michigan, Ann Arbor, MI, June 2016.

Campbell, Ian. *The Addis Ababa Massacre*. London: Hurst, 2017.

Canali, Mauro. *Le spie del regime*. Bologna: Il Mulino, 2004.

Canning, Kathleen. "Introduction: Weimar Subjects/Weimar Publics: Rethinking the Political Culture of Germany in the 1920s." In *Weimar Subjects/Weimar Publics: Rethinking the Political Culture of Germany in the 1920s*. Edited by Kathleen Canning, Kerstin Barndt, and Kristin McGuire, 1–28. New York: Berghahn Books, 2010.

Canning, Kathleen. "The Politics of Symbols, Semantics, and Sentiments in the Weimar Republic." *Central European History* 43, no. 4 (2010): 567–80.

Capa, Robert. *Death in the Making*. New York: Covici-Friede, 1938.

Caplan, Jane. "Politics, Religion, and Ideology: A Comment on Wolfgang Hardtwig." *Bulletin of the German Historical Institute* (Washington, DC) 28 (spring 2001): 28–36.

Carroll, Peter N., and James D. Fernandez. *Facing Fascism: New York and the Spanish Civil War*. New York: Museum of the City of New York and New York University Press, 2007.

Carter, Erica. *Dietrich's Ghosts: The Sublime and the Beautiful in Third Reich Film*. London: British Film Institute, 2004.

Cartier-Bresson, Henri. *Henri Cartier-Bresson: The Mind's Eye: Writings on Photography and Photographers*. New York: Aperture, 2005.

Cather, Kirsten. *The Art of Censorship in Post War Japan*. Honolulu: University of Hawai'i Press, 2012.

Chen. *Zhongguo dianying shiye* [The Chinese Film Industry]. Shanghai: Chenbao she, 1933.

Choi, Jayne. "Cybernetic Industriousness: The Production of Albert Kahn Associates, 1918–42." Unpublished manuscript, 2016.

Clark, Catherine E. "Capturing the Moment, Picturing History: Photographs of the Liberation of Paris." *American Historical Review* 121, no. 3 (2016): 824–60.

Clark, T. J. *Image of the People: Gustave Courbet and the 1848 Revolution*. Berkeley: University of California Press, 1973.

Clarke, Peter. "The Century of the Hedgehog: The Demise of Political Ideologies in the Twentieth Century." In *The Future of the Past: Big Questions in History*. Edited by Peter Martland, 113–126. London: Pimlico, 2002.

Clinton, Maggie. "Ends of the Universal: Chinese Fascism and the League of Nations on the Eve of World War II." *Modern Asian Studies* 48, no. 6 (2014): 1740–68.

Clinton, Maggie. *Revolutionary Nativism: Fascism and Culture in China, 1925–1937*. Durham, NC: Duke University Press, 2017.

Clossey, Luke, and Nicholas Guyatt. "It's a Small World after All: The Wider World in the Historians' Peripheral Vision." *Perspectives on History* (May 2013). Accessed August 22, 2014. http://www.historians.org/publications-and-directories /perspectives-on-history.

Cohen, Aaron J. "Long Ago and Far Away: War Monuments, Public Relations, and the Memory of the Russo-Japanese War in Russia, 1907–14." *The Russian Review* 69 (July 2010): 388–411.

Cohen, Jean-Louis. *Scenes of the World to Come*. Montreal: Flammarion, 1995.

Conrad, Sebastian, and Sorcha O'Hagan. *German Colonialism: A Short History*. Cambridge: Cambridge University Press, 2011.

Corner, Paul. "Collaboration, Complicity, and Evasion under Italian Fascism." In *Everyday Life in Mass Dictatorship*. Edited by Alf Lüdtke, 75–93. New York: Palgrave, 2016.

Crew, David. "The Pathologies of Modernity: Detlev Peukert on Germany's Twentieth Century." *Social History* 17, no. 2 (1992): 319–28.

Crowley, James B. *Japan's Quest for Autonomy: National Security and Foreign Policy, 1930–1938*. Princeton, NJ: Princeton University Press, 1966.

Culver, Annika A. *Glorify the Empire: Japanese Avant-Garde Propaganda in Manchukuo*. Vancouver, BC, Canada: University of British Columbia Press, 2013.

Cupers, Kenny. *Use Matters: An Alternative History of Architecture*. London: Routledge, 2013.

Dafinger, Johannes. "The Nazi 'New Europe': Transnational Concepts of a Fascist and *Völkisch* Order for the Continent." In *Fascism without Borders: Transnational Connections and Cooperation between Movements and Regimes in Europe from 1918 to 1945*. Edited by Arnd Bauerkämper and Grzegorz Rossoliński-Liebe, 264–87. New York: Berghahn Books, 2017.

Dahm, Bernhard. *History of Indonesia in the Twentieth Century*. London: Praeger, 1971.

Dale, Richard. "Reconfiguring White Ethnic Power in Colonial Africa: The German Community in Namibia, 1923–1950." *Nationalism and Ethnic Politics* 7, no. 2 (2001): 75–94.

Dalle Vacche, Angela. *The Body in the Mirror*. Princeton, NJ: Princeton University Press, 1992.

Day, Gail. "Manfredo Tafuri, Fredric Jameson and the Contestations of Political Memory." *Historical Materialism* 20, no. 1 (2012): 31–77.

de Baecque, Antoine. *Camera Historica: The Century in Cinema*. New York: Columbia University Press, 2012.

de Felice, Renzo. *Mussolini il Duce: Gli anni del consenso 1929–1935*. Turin: Einaudi, 2007.

Delage, Christian, and Vincent Guigueno. *Le historien et le film*. Paris: Gallimard, 2004.

Del Boca, Angelo, ed. *I gas di Mussolini*. Rome: Editori Riuniti, 2007.

DeLillo, Don. *White Noise*. New York: Penguin, 1985.

Deng Yuanzhong. *Guomindang hexin zhuzhi zhenxiang: Lixingshe, Fuxingshe, yu suowei "Lanyishe" de yanbian yu chengzhang* [The Truth about the Guomindang's Core Organizations: The Forceful Action Society, the Renaissance Society, and the So-Called "Blue Shirts"]. Taipei: Lianjing, 2000.

Denison, Edward, and Guangyu Ren. *Ultra-Modernism: Architecture and Modernity in Manchuria*. Hong Kong: Hong Kong University Press, 2016.

Didi-Huberman, Georges. *Images malgré tout*. Paris: Les Édition de Minuit, 2003.

Diggins, John P. *Mussolini and Fascism: The View from America*. Princeton, NJ: Princeton University Press, 1972.

Doane, Mary Ann. "The Close Up: Scale and Detail in the Cinema." *Differences* 14 (2003): 89–111.

Domon, Ken. "Hōdō mango, 3." *Foto Times* 17, no. 10 (October 1940): 50–52.

Domon, Ken. "Hōdō mango, 4." *Foto Times* 17, no. 11 (November 1940): 44–46.

Domon, Ken. "Taigai senden zasshi ron" [A Discussion of International Propaganda Magazines]. *Nihon hyōron* 18 (September 1943): 62–66.

Dower, John W. "Japanese Cinema Goes to War." In *Japan in War and Peace: Selected Essays*, 33–54. New York: New Press, 1993.

Dower, John W. "Throwing off Asia III." *Visualizing Cultures*. Cambridge, MA: Massachusetts Institute of Technology, 2008. Accessed February 11, 2018. http://visualizingcultures.mit.edu.

Dower, John W., Anne Nishimura Morse, Jacqueline Atkins, and Frederic Sharf. *The Brittle Decade: Visualizing Japan in the 1930s*. Boston: Boston Museum of Fine Arts, 2012.

Drea, Edward J. *Japan's Imperial Army: Its Rise and Fall, 1853–1945*. Lawrence: University of Kansas Press, 2009.

Driscoll, Mark. *Absolute Erotic, Absolute Grotesque: The Living, Dead, and Undead in Japan's Imperialism, 1895–1945*. Durham, NC: Duke University Press, 2010.

Dubow, Saul. "Afrikaner Nationalism, Apartheid and the Conceptualization of Race." *Journal of African History* 33, no. 2 (1992): 209–37.

Durica, Milan. *Dejiny Slovenska a Slovákov.* Kosice: Pressko, 1995.

Du Toit, Marijke. "Blank Verbeeld, or the Incredible Whiteness of Being: Amateur Photography and Afrikaner Nationalist Historical Narrative." *Kronos* 27 (2001): 77–113.

Duus, Peter, and Daniel I. Okimoto. "Fascism and the History of Pre-War Japan: The Failure of a Concept." *Journal of Asian Studies* 39, no. 1 (November 1979): 65–79.

Düwel, Jörn, and Niels Gutschow. *Baukunst und Nationalsozialismus: Demonstration von Macht in Europa, 1940–1943: Die Ausstellung Neue Deutsche Baukunst von Rudolf Wolters.* Berlin: DOM Publishers, 2015.

Earhart, David C. *Certain Victory: Images of World War II in the Japanese Media.* Armonk, NY: M. E. Sharpe, 2008.

Eberhardt, Martin. *Zwischen Nationalsozialismus und Apartheid. Die deutsche Bevölkerungsgruppe Südwestafrikas 1915–1965.* Berlin: Lit, 2005.

Ebner, Michael, Kate Ferris, and Josh Arthurs, eds. *Everyday Life in Fascist Italy.* London: Palgrave, 2017.

Edwards, Elizabeth. *Raw Histories: Photographs, Anthropology and Museums.* Oxford: Berg, 2001.

Eley, Geoff. *A Crooked Line: From Cultural History to the History of Society.* Ann Arbor: University of Michigan Press, 2005.

Eley, Geoff. "Empire, Ideology, and the East: Thoughts on Nazism's Spatial Imaginary." In *Nazism as Fascism: Violence, Ideology, and the Ground of Consent in Germany, 1930–1945,* 131–55. London: Routledge, 2013.

Eley, Geoff. *Nazism as Fascism: Violence, Ideology, and the Ground of Consent in Germany 1930–1945.* London: Routledge, 2013.

Eley, Geoff. "What Produces Fascism: Pre-Industrial Traditions or a Crisis of the Capitalist State?" In *From Unification to Nazism: Reinterpreting the German Past.* Edited by Geoff Eley, 254–82. London: Allen and Unwin, 1986.

Eman Hiromichi. *Manshū jinjō shōgaku sahōsho.* Dalian: Zaiman Nihon kyōikukai kyōkasho henshū-bu, 1940.

Erbaggio, Pier Luigi. "Writing Mussolini: Il Duce's Biographies on Paper and on Screen, 1922–1935." PhD diss., Department of Romance Languages and Literatures, University of Michigan, 2016.

Erjavec, Aleš, ed. *Aesthetics Revolutions and Twentieth-Century Avant-Garde Movements.* Durham, NC: Duke University Press, 2015.

Evans, Jessica, and Stuart Hall, eds. *Visual Culture: The Reader.* Thousand Oaks, CA: Sage, 1999.

Evans, Richard J. *The Third Reich in Power 1933–1939.* New York: Penguin, 2005.

Falasca-Zamponi, Simonetta. *Fascist Spectacle: The Aesthetics of Power in Mussolini's Italy.* Berkeley: University of California Press, 1997.

"Fascist Temporalities." Special issue, *Journal of Modern European History* 13 (2015).

Favre, Sisto. "Film di guerra." *Lo Schermo,* June 1943.

Felak, James. *At the Price of the Republic: Hlinka's Slovak People's Party, 1929–1939.* Pittsburgh: University of Pittsburgh Press, 1993.

Fernández, Horacio. *Photobooks Spain 1905–1977.* Madrid: Museo Nacional Centro de Arte Reina Sofía, 2014.

Ferris, Kate. *Everyday Life in Fascist Venice.* London: Palgrave, 2012.

Ferro, Marc. *Cinema and History,* translated by N. Greene. Detroit: Wayne State University Press, 1988. Originally published as *Cinéma et histoire.* Paris: Denoël, 1977.

Finchelstein, Federico. *Transatlantic Fascism: Ideology, Violence, and the Sacred in Argentina and Italy, 1919–1945.* Durham, NC: Duke University Press, 2010.

Fletcher, W. Miles, III. "The Fifteen-Year War." In *A Companion to Japanese History.* Edited by William M. Tsutsui, 241–62. Hoboken, NJ: Wiley-Blackwell, 2009.

Föllmer, Moritz, and Rüdiger Graf, eds. *Die "Krise" der Weimarer Republic: Zur Kritik eines Deutungsmusters.* Frankfurt: Campus, 2005.

Foster, Jeremy. "'Land of Contrasts' or 'Home We Have Always Known'? The SAR&H and the Imaginary Geography of White South African Nationhood, 1920–1930." *Journal of Southern African Studies* 29, no. 3 (2003): 657–80.

Fritzsche, Peter. "Did Weimar Fail?" *Journal of Modern History* 68, no. 3 (1996): 629–56.

Fritzsche, Peter. "Historical Time and Future Experience in Postwar Germany." In *Ordnungen in der Krise: Zur politischen Kulturgeschichte Deutschlands 1900–1933.* Edited by Wolfgang Hardtwig, 141–64. Munich: Oldenbourg, 2007.

Fritzsche, Peter. "Landscape of Danger, Landscape of Design: Crisis of Modernism in Weimar Germany." In *Dancing on the Volcano: Essays on the Culture of the Weimar Republic.* Edited by Thomas W. Kniesche and Stephen Brockmann, 29–46. Columbus, SC: Camden House, 1994.

Fritzsche, Peter. *A Nation of Fliers: German Aviation and the Popular Imagination.* Cambridge, MA: Harvard University Press, 1992.

Fujitani, Takashi. *Splendid Monarchy: Power and Pageantry in Modern Japan.* Berkeley: University of California Press, 1998.

Fulbrook, Mary. *Dissonant Lives: Generations and Violence through the German Dictatorships.* Oxford: Oxford University Press, 2011.

Fuller, Mia. *Moderns Abroad: Architecture, Cities, and Italian Imperialism.* New York: Routledge, 2003.

Furlong, Patrick J. "The National Party of South Africa: A Transnational Perspective." In *New Perspectives on the Transnational Right.* Edited by M. Durham and M. Power, 67–84. New York: Palgrave Macmillan, 2010.

Gates, Lisa. "Of Seeing Otherness: Leni Riefenstahl's African Photographs." In *The Imperialist Imagination: German Colonialism and Its Legacy.* Edited by Sara Friedrichsmeyer, Sara Lennox, and Susanne Zantop, 233–46. Ann Arbor: University of Michigan Press, 1998.

Gentile, Emilio. *Politics as Religion.* Princeton, NJ: Princeton University Press, 2006.

Gentile, Emilio. "A Professional Dwelling: The Origin and Development of the Concept of Fascism in Mosse's Historiography." In *What History Tells: George L. Mosse and the Culture of Modern Europe*. Edited by Stanley G. Payne, David J. Sorkin, and John S. Tortorice, 47–62. Madison: University of Wisconsin Press, 2004.

Gentile, Emilio. *The Sacralization of Politics in Fascist Italy*. Cambridge, MA: Harvard University Press, 1996.

Germer, Andrea. "Artists and Wartime Agency: Natori Yōnosuke—A Japanese Riefenstahl?" *Contemporary Japan* 24, no. 1 (2012): 21–50.

Germer, Andrea. "Visible Cultures, Invisible Politics: Propaganda in the Magazine *Nippon Fujin*, 1942–1945." *Japan Forum* 25, no. 4 (2013): 505–39.

Germer, Andrea. "Visual Propaganda in Wartime East Asia—The Case of Natori Yōnosuke." *The Asia-Pacific Journal* 9, no. 20 (2011). https://apjjf.org/2011/9/20/Andrea-Germer/3530/article.html.

Geyer, Martin. "'Die Gleichzeitigkeit des Ungleichzeitigen': Zeitsemantik und die Suche nach Gegenwart in der Weimarer Republik." In *Ordnungen in der Krise. Zur politischen Kulturgeschichte Deutschlands 1900–1933*. Edited by Wolfgang Hardtwig, 165–87. Munich: Oldenbourg, 2007.

Geyer, Michael. "The Militarization of Europe (1914–1945)." In *The Militarization of the Western World*. Edited by John Gillis. New Brunswick: Rutgers University Press, 1989.

Gibson, James William. *The Perfect War: Technowar in Vietnam*. Boston: Atlantic Monthly Press, 1986.

Giedion, Sigfried. "Spätbarocker und romantischer Klassizismus." PhD diss., University of Munich, 1922.

Giliomee, Hermann. "The Making of the Apartheid Plan, 1929–48." *Journal of Southern African Studies* 29, no. 2 (2003): 373–92.

Gillis, John, ed. *The Militarization of the Western World*. New Brunswick, NJ: Rutgers University Press, 1989.

Gordon, Andrew. *Labor and Imperial Democracy in Prewar Japan*. Berkeley: University of California Press, 1991.

Gordon, Andrew. *A Modern History of Japan: From Tokugawa Times to the Present*. New York: Oxford University Press, 2009.

Goto-Jones, Christopher. *Political Philosophy in Japan: Nishida, the Kyoto School and Co-Prosperity*. New York: Routledge, 2005.

Goto-Jones, Christopher. *Re-Politicising the Kyoto School as Philosophy*. New York: Routledge, 2008.

Gough, Maria. "Back in the USSR: John Heartfield, Gustav Klucis, and the Medium of Soviet Propaganda." *New German Critique* 107/36, no. 2 (2009): 133–83.

Grady, James H. "Henry-Russell Hitchcock: The First Thirty Years." *The American Association of Architectural Bibliographers Papers* I (1965): 1–22.

Graf, Rüdiger. "Either-Or: The Narrative of Crisis in Weimar Germany and Historiography." *Central European History* 43, no. 4 (2010): 592–615.

Graf, Rüdiger. *Die Zukunft der Weimarer Republik. Krisen und Zukunftsaneignungen in Deutschland 1918–1933*. Munich: Oldenbourg, 2008.

Gray, G. "Highlights of a Housing Tour of Northern Europe, Part II." *Octagon*, February 1938, 15–18.

Griffin, Roger, ed. *Fascism, Totalitarianism, and Political Religion*. London: Routledge, 2005.

Griffin, Roger. *A Fascist Century*. Palgrave: London, 2008.

Griffin, Roger. *Modernism and Fascism: The Sense of a Beginning under Mussolini and Hitler*. London: Palgrave Macmillan, 2007.

Griffin, Roger. *The Nature of Fascism*. London: Routledge, 1993.

Griffin, Roger. "Withstanding the Rush of Time: The Prescience of Mosse's Anthropological View of Fascism." In *What History Tells: George L. Mosse and the Culture of Modern Europe*. Edited by Stanley G. Payne, David J. Sorkin, and John S. Tortorice, 110–33. Madison: University of Wisconsin Press, 2004.

Gropius, Walter, and P. Morton Shand. *The New Architecture and the Bauhaus*. London: Faber and Faber, 1935.

Gruber, Helmut. "History of the Austrian Working Class: Unity of Scholarship and Practice." *International Labor and Working-Class History* 24 (fall 1983): 50–52.

Guerin, Frances. *Through Amateur Eyes: Film and Photography in Nazi Germany*. Minneapolis: University of Minnesota Press, 2012.

Guilbaut, Serge. *How New York Stole the Idea of Modern Art*. Chicago: University of Chicago Press, 1984.

Gundle, Stephen. *Mussolini's Dream Factory*. New York: Berghahn Books, 2012.

Gundle, Stephen, Christopher Duggan, and Giuliana Pieri, eds. *The Cult of the Duce*. Manchester: Manchester University Press, 2013.

Haddow, Robert H. *Pavilions of Plenty: Exhibiting American Culture Abroad in the 1950s*. Washington, DC: Smithsonian Institution Press, 1997.

Hanscom, Christopher P., and Dennis Washburn, eds. *The Affect of Difference: Representations of Race in East Asian Empire*. Honolulu: University of Hawaiʻi Press, 2016.

Harada Keiichi. "Irei no seijigaku." In *Nichiro sensō sutadiizu*. Edited by Komori Yōichi and Narita Ryūichi, 219–33. Tokyo: Kinokuniya shoten, 2004.

Hardtwig, Wolfgang. "Political Religion in Modern Germany: Reflections on Nationalism, Socialism, and National Socialism." *Bulletin of the German Historical Institute* (Washington, DC) 28 (spring 2001): 3–27.

Harootunian, Harry D. "Comment on Professor Matsumoto's 'Introduction.'" *Journal of Social and Political Ideas in Japan* 5, nos. 2–3 (1967): 315–330.

Harootunian, Harry D. *History's Disquiet: Modernity, Cultural Practice, and the Question of Everyday Life*. New York: Columbia University Press, 2000.

Harootunian, Harry D. *Overcome by Modernity: History, Culture, and Community in Interwar Japan*. Princeton, NJ: Princeton University Press, 2000.

Hedinger, Daniel. "The Spectacle of Global Fascism: The Italian Blackshirt Mission to Japan's Asian Empire." *Modern Asian Studies* 51, no. 6 (2017): 1999–2034.

Hedinger, Daniel. "Universal Fascism and Its Global Legacy: Italy's and Japan's Entangled History in the Early 1930s." *Fascism* 2 (2013): 141–60.

Herz, Rudolf. *Hoffmann and Hitler: Fotografie als Medium des Führer-Mythos*. Munich: Klinkhardt and Biermann, 1994.

Herzfeld, Michael. *The Social Production of Indifference: Exploring the Symbolic Roots of Western Bureaucracy*. New York: Berg, 1992.

High, Peter B. *The Imperial Screen: Japanese Film Culture in the Fifteen Years' War, 1931–1945*. Madison: University of Wisconsin Press, 2003.

Hishikari Takashi. *Chūreitō monogatari*. Tokyo: Dōwa shūnju, 1942.

Hitchcock, Henry-Russell. "The Architecture of Bureaucracy and the Architecture of Genius." *Architectural Review* 101 (January 1947): 3–6.

Hitchcock, Henry-Russell. "The Architectural Future in America." *Architectural Review* 81, no. 488 (July 1937): 1–2.

Hitchcock, Henry-Russell. *In the Nature of Materials 1887–1941: The Buildings of Frank Lloyd Wright*. New York: Museum of Modern Art, 1942.

Hitchcock, Henry-Russell. "Late Baroque German Gardens," *American-German Review* 1, no. 4 (June 1935): 26–33.

Hitchcock, Henry-Russell. *Modern Architecture: Romanticism and Reintegration*. New York: Payson and Clarke, 1929.

Hitchcock, Henry-Russell. "Paris 1937." *Architectural Forum* (September 1937): 163.

Hitchcock, Henry-Russell. "Romantic Architecture of Potsdam." *International Studio* 99 (May 1931): 46–49.

Hitchcock, Henry-Russell. "Romantic Classicism in Germany." *American-German Review* 1, no. 1 (September 1934): 19–24.

Hitchcock, Henry-Russell. "The Romantic Gardens of Potsdam," *American-German Review* 2, no. 1 (September, 1935): 19–24.

Hoffmann, Heinrich. *Hitler Was My Friend*, translated by R. H. Stevens. London: Burke, 1955.

Hoffmann, Heinrich. *Hitler wie ihn keiner kennt: 100 Bilddokumente aus dem Leben des Führers*. Berlin: Zeitgeschichte-Verlag, 1941.

Hofmann, Reto. *The Fascist Effect: Japan and Italy, 1915–1952*. New York: Columbia University Press, 2015.

Hofmann, Reto, and Daniel Hedinger, eds. "Axis Empires: Towards a Global History of Fascist Imperialism." Special issue, *Journal of Global History* 12, part 2 (July 2017).

Holmes, Oliver Wendell. "The Stereoscope and the Stereograph." *Atlantic*, June 1859. Accessed February 14, 2018. https://www.theatlantic.com/magazine/archive/1859/06/the-stereoscope-and-the-stereograph/303361.

Hom, Stephanie Malia. *The Beautiful Country: Tourism and the Impossible State of Destination Italy*. Toronto: University of Toronto Press, 2015.

Hom, Stephanie Malia. "Empires of Tourism: Travel and Rhetoric in Italian Colonial Libya and Albania, 1911–1943." *Journal of Tourism History* 4, no. 3 (2012): 281–300.

Hotta, Eri. *Japan 1941: Countdown to Infamy*. New York: Alfred A. Knopf, 2013.

Hull, Matthew. *Government of Paper: The Materiality of Bureaucracy in Urban Pakistan*. Berkeley: University of California Press, 2012.

Hüppauf, Bernd. "Emptying the Gaze: Framing Violence through the Viewfinder." *New German Critique* 72 (1997): 3–44.

Iaccio, Pasquale. *Cinema e storia*. Naples: Liguori, 1988.

Ikegami Shirō. "Tennō to shashin" [The Emperor and Photography]. *Shashin Tenbō* 1, no. 1 (January 1947): 30–34.

Ina Nobuo. "Nihonteki shashin geijustu no kakuritsu e, 1" [Toward the Establishment of Japanese-Style Photographic Art, I]. *Camera Art* 12, no. 5 (November, 1940): 193–195.

Ina Nobuo. "Nihonteki shashin geijutsu no kakuritsu e, 2" [Toward the Establishment of Japanese Photographic Art, 2]. *Camera Art* 12, no. 6 (December 1940): 248–258.

Ina Nobuo. "Shin taisei ni okeru shashinka no ninmu" [The Duty of Photographers in the New Order]. *Camera Art* 12, no. 3 (September 1940): 85–89.

Iordachi, Constantin, ed. *Comparative Fascist Studies: New Perspectives*. London: Routledge, 2010.

Iyob, Ruth. "*Madamismo* and Beyond: The Construction of Eritrean Women." *Nineteenth Century Contexts* 22, no. 2 (2000): 217–38.

Jackson, Anna. "Art Deco in East Asia." In *Art Deco 1930–1939*. Edited by Charlotte Benton, Tim Benton, and Ghislaine Wood, 371–81. Boston: Bullfinch Press, 2003.

Janos, Andrew. *East Central Europe in the Modern World*. Berkeley: University of California Press, 2000.

Japanese Delegation to the League of Nations. *The Manchurian Question: Japan's Case in the Sino-Japanese Dispute as Presented before the League of Nations*. Geneva: League of Nations, 1933.

Jaskot, Paul. *The Architecture of Oppression: The ss, Forced Labor and the Nazi Monumental Building Economy*. New York: Routledge, 2000.

Jaskot, Paul. "Building the Nazi Economy: Adam Tooze and a Cultural Critique of Hitler's Plans for War." *Historical Materialism* 22, nos. 3–4 (2014): 312–29.

Jaskot, Paul B. "Heinrich Himmler and the Nuremberg Party Rally Grounds: The Interest of the ss in the German Building Economy." In *Art, Culture, and Media under the Third Reich*. Edited by Richard A. Etlin, 230–56. Chicago: University of Chicago Press, 2002.

Jay, Martin. "Can Photographs Lie? Reflections on a Perennial Anxiety." *Critical Studies* 2 (2016): 6–19.

Jünger, Ernst. "Photography and the 'Second Consciousness': An Excerpt from 'On Pain,'" translated by Joel Agee. In *Photography in the Modern Era: European Documents and Critical Writings, 1913–1940*. Edited by Christopher Phillips, 207–10. New York: Metropolitan Museum of Art/Aperture, 1989.

Kallis, Aristotle A., ed. *The Fascism Reader*. London: Routledge, 2003.

Kamenec, Ivan. *Slovensky Štát*. Prague: Anomal, 1992.

Kamenec, Ivan. *Tragédia Politika, Knaza a Človeka*. Bratislava: Archa, 1998.

Kantorowicz, Ernst H. *The King's Two Bodies: A Study in Mediaeval Political Theology*. Princeton, NJ: Princeton University Press, 1958.

Kasza, Gregory J. "Fascism from Above: Japan's Kakushin Right in Comparative Perspective." In *Fascism outside Europe*. Edited by Stein Ugelvik Larsen, 1–46. Boulder, CO: Social Science Monographs, 2001.

Kasza, Gregory J. *The State and the Mass Media in Japan 1918–1945*. Berkeley: University of California Press, 1988.

Kater, Michael. *Hitler Youth*. Cambridge, MA: Harvard University Press, 2004.

Kauffmann, Emil. *Von Ledoux bis Le Corbusier*. Vienna: Passer, 1933.

Kern, Stephen. *The Culture of Time and Space, 1880–1918*. Cambridge, MA: Harvard University Press, 1983.

Kershaw, Ian. *Hitler 1889–1936: Hubris*. New York: Norton, 1998.

Kershaw, Ian. *Hitler 1936–1945: Nemesis*. New York: Norton, 2000.

Kersten, Rikki. "Japan." In *The Oxford Handbook of Fascism*. Edited by R. J. B. Bosworth, 526–44. Oxford: Oxford University Press, 2009.

Kikuchi, Yuko, ed. *Refracted Modernity: Visual Culture and Identity in Colonial Taiwan*. Honolulu: University of Hawai'i Press, 2007.

Kimball, Fiske. "Romantic Classicism in Architecture." *Gazette des Beaux-Arts* 25 (February 1944): 95–112.

Kimura, Masato, and Tosh Minohara. *Tumultuous Decade: Empire Society, and Diplomacy in 1930s Japan*. Toronto: University of Toronto Press, 2013.

Kinmonth, Earl H. "The Mouse That Roared: Saitō Takao, Conservative Critic of Japan's 'Holy War' in China." *Journal of Japanese Studies* 25 (1999): 331–60.

Kishi Toshihiko. *Manshūkoku no bijuaru-media: Postā, ehagaki, kitte*. Tokyo: Yoshikawa Kōbunkan, 2010.

Kita Ikki. *Kita Ikki Chosaku shū*. Tokyo: Misuzu Shobō, 1959.

Kitchen, Martin. *Speer: Hitler's Architect*. New Haven, CT: Yale University Press, 2015.

Knight, Michael, and Dany Chan. *Shanghai: Art of the City*. San Francisco: Asian Art Museum, 2010.

Koepnick, Lutz. *The Dark Mirror: German Cinema between Hitler and Hollywood*. Berkeley: University of California Press, 2002.

Koepnick, Lutz. "Face/Off: Hitler and Weimar Political Photography." In *Visual Culture in Twentieth-Century Germany: Text as Spectacle*. Edited by Gail Finney, 214–34. Bloomington: Indiana University Press, 2006.

Koepnick, Lutz. "Fascist Aesthetics Revisited." *modernism/modernity* 6 (1999): 51–73.

Koepnick, Lutz. "Photographs and Memories." *South Central Review* 21, no. 1 (spring 2004): 94–129.

Koepnick, Lutz. *Walter Benjamin and the Aesthetics of Power*. Lincoln: University of Nebraska Press, 1999.

Koga, Yukiko. *Inheritance of Loss: China, Japan, and the Political Economy of Redemption after Empire*. Chicago: University of Chicago Press, 2016.

Koonz, Claudia. *The Nazi Conscience*. Cambridge, MA: Harvard University Press, 2003.

Kracauer, Siegfried. *From Caligari to Hitler: A Psychological History of the German Film*. Princeton, NJ: Princeton University Press, 1966

Kracauer, Siegfried. *The Mass Ornament: Weimar Essays*, edited by Thomas Y. Levin. Cambridge, MA: Harvard University Press, 2005.

Krautwurst, Udo Rainer. "Tales of the 'Land of Stories': Settlers and Anti-modernity in German Colonial Discourses on German South West Africa, 1884–1914." PhD diss., University of Connecticut, 1997.

Kushnar, Barack. *The Thought War: Japanese Imperial Propaganda*. Honolulu: University of Hawai'i Press, 2006.

Kuwabara Kineo. *Manshu Shōwa ju-go nen* [Manchuria in Shōwa 15 (1940)]. Tokyo: Shōbunsha, 1974.

Landy, Marcia. *Cinematic Uses of the Past*. Minneapolis: University of Minnesota Press, 1996.

Langbehn, Volker, and Mohammad Salama, eds. *German Colonialism: Race, the Holocaust, and Postwar Germany*. New York: Columbia University Press, 2011.

Lattuada, Alberto. *Occhio quadrato* (1941). Reprinted in Piero Berengo Gardin, ed., *Alberto Lattuada fotografo*. Florence: Alinari, 1982.

Lavin, Maud, and Matthew Teitelbaum, ed. *Montage and Modern Life, 1919–1942*. Cambridge, MA: MIT Press, 1992.

Lebrun, Bernard, and Michel Lefebvre. *Robert Capa: The Paris Years, 1933–1954*. New York: Abrams, 2011.

LeCavalier, Jesse. *The Rule of Logistics: Walmart and the Architecture of Fulfillment*. Minneapolis: University of Minnesota Press, 2016.

Lee, Leo Ou-fan. *Shanghai Modern: The Flowering of a New Urban Culture in China, 1930–1945*. Cambridge, MA: Harvard University Press, 1999.

Le Houérou, Fabienne. *L'épopée des soldats de Mussolini en Abyssinie, 1935–1936*. Paris: L'Harmattan, 1994.

Lethen, Helmut. *Cool Conduct: The Culture of Distance in Weimar Germany*, translated by Don Reneau. Berkeley: University of California Press, 2002.

Lockyer, Angus. "Expo Fascism? Ideology, Representation, Economy." In *The Culture of Japanese Fascism*. Edited by Alan Tansman, 276–95. Durham, NC: Duke University Press, 2009.

Loeffler, Jane. *The Architecture of Diplomacy: Building America's Embassies*. New York: Princeton Architectural Press, 1998.

Luckert, Steven, and Susan Bachrach, eds. *The State of Deception: The Power of Nazi Propaganda*. Washington, DC: U.S. Holocaust Memorial Museum, 2011.

Lüdtke, Alf, ed. *Everyday Life in Mass Dictatorship*. New York: Palgrave, 2016.

Luzzato, Sergio. *The Body of Il Duce*. New York: Metropolitan Books, 2005.

Madar, Chase. "23-F." *London Review of Books*, September 8, 2011, 30–31.

Maffei, Nicolas P. "The Search for an American Design Aesthetic: From Art Deco to Streamlining." In *Art Deco 1930–1939*. Edited by Charlotte Benton, Tim Benton, and Ghislaine Wood, 361–69. Boston: Bullfinch Press, 2003.

Mann, Michael. *Fascists*. Cambridge: Cambridge University Press, 2004.

Marino, Natalia, and Valerio Marino, *Ovra a Cinecittà*. Turin: Bollati Boringhieri, 2005.

Mark, Ethan. *The Japanese Occupation of Java in the Second World War: A Transnational History*. London: Bloomsbury, 2018.

Mark, Ethan. "Translator's Introduction." In *Grassroots Fascism: The War Experience of the Japanese People*. Edited by Yoshimi Yoshiaki, translated by Ethan Mark, 1–39. New York: Columbia University Press, 2015.

Martin, Benjamin G. *The Nazi-Fascist New Order for European Culture*. Cambridge, MA: Harvard University Press, 2016.

Maruyama, Masao. "The Ideology and Dynamics of Japanese Fascism." In *Thought and Behavior in Modern Japanese Politics*. Edited by Ivan Morris, 24–83. London: Oxford University Press, 1969.

Maruyama, Masao. " Theory and Psychology of Ultra-nationalism." In *Modern Japanese Politics*. Edited and translated by Ivan Morris, 1–24. Oxford: Oxford University Press, [1963] 1969.

Masey, Jack, and C. Morgan, *Cold War Confrontations: US Exhibitions and Their Role in the Cultural Cold War*. Baden: Lars Müller, 2008.

Matsumura, Janice. *More Than a Momentary Nightmare: The Yokohama Incident and Wartime Japan*. Ithaca, NY: Cornell University Press, 1998.

McCulloch, Michael. "Building the Working City." PhD diss., University of Michigan, 2015.

Mebes, Paul. *Um 1800: Architektur und Handwerk im letzten Jahrhundert ihrer traditionellen Entwicklung*. Munich: F. Bruckman, 1908.

Mendelson, Jordana. *Documenting Spain: Artists, Exhibition Culture. and the Modern Nation, 1929–1939*. University Park: Pennsylvania State University Press, 2005.

Mendelson, Jordana. *Revistas y Guerra, 1936–1939*. Madrid: Museo Nacional Centro de Arte Reina Sofía, 2007.

Merleau-Ponty, Maurice. *Phenomenology of Perception*, translated by Colin Smith. London: Routledge and Kegan Paul, 1965.

Metton, Bertrand. "From the Popular Front to the Eastern Front: Youth Movements, Travel, and Fascism in France, 1933–1945." PhD diss., University of Michigan, 2015.

Metton, Bertrand. "Nazi Europe and the Atlantic Wall: On Spatial Theory and the Wartime Fascist Worldview." Forthcoming.

Mignone, Gian Giacomo. *The United States and Fascist Italy: The Rise of American Finance in Europe*, translated by Molly Tambor. Cambridge: Cambridge University Press, 2015.

Milla, Michal. *Hlinkova Mládež, 1938–1945*. Bratislava: Ústav Pamäti Národa, 2008.

Miller, Frank O. *Minobe Tatsukichi: Interpreter of Constitutionalism in Japan*. Berkeley: University of California Press, 1965.

Miller Lane, Barbara. *Architecture and Politics in Germany, 1918–1945*. Cambridge, MA: Harvard University Press, [1968] 1985.

Miller Lane, Barbara. Review of Albert Speer, *Inside the Third Reich. Journal of the Society of Architectural Historians* 32, no. 4 (December 1973): 341–46.

Mimura, Janis. *Planning for Empire: Reform Bureaucrats and the Japanese Wartime State*. Ithaca, NY: Cornell University Press, 2011.

Minick, Scott, and Jiao Ping. *Chinese Graphic Design in the Twentieth Century*. London: Thames and Hudson, 2010.

Minobe Tatsukichi. *Kenpō kōwa* [Lectures on the Constitution]. Tokyo: Yūhikaku Shobō, 1921.

Mirzoeff, Nicholas. *The Right to Look: A Counterhistory of Visuality*. Durham, NC: Duke University Press, 2011.

Mishra, Pankaj. *Age of Anger: A History of the Present*. New York: Farrar, Strauss and Giroux, 2017.

Mitter, Rana. *Forgotten Ally: China's World War II, 1937–1945*. Boston: Houghton Mifflin Harcourt, 2013.

Monbukagakushō, ed. *Chūtō chiri ni*. Tokyo: Chūtō gakkō kyōkasho kabushiki kaisha, 1944.

Monbukagakushō, ed. *Chūtō chiri san*. Tokyo: Chūtō gakkō kyōkasho kabushiki kaisha, 1945.

Moore, Bob, and Kent Federowich, eds. *The British Empire and Italian Prisoners of War, 1940–1947*. New York: Palgrave, 2002.

Mosse, George L. *The Fascist Revolution: Toward a General Theory of Fascism*. New York: Howard Fertig, 1999.

Mosse, George L. *Masses and Man: Nationalist and Fascist Perceptions of Reality*. New York: Howard Fertig, 1980.

Mosse, George L. *The Nationalization of the Masses: Political Symbolism and Mass Movements in Germany from the Napoleonic Wars through the Third Reich*. New York: Meridian, 1977.

Moyd, Michelle R. *Violent Intermediaries: African Soldiers, Conquest, and Everyday Colonialism in German East Africa*. Columbus: Ohio University Press, 2014.

Mussolini, Benito. "La mobilitazione generale. Discorso del 2 ottobre 1935." In *Scritti e discorsi*, vol. 9, 217–20. Milan: Hoepli, 1935.

Nagahara, Hiromu. *Japan's Pop Era: Music in the Making of Middle-Class Society*. Cambridge, MA: Harvard University Press, 2017.

Naranch, Bradley, and Geoff Eley, eds. *German Colonialism in a Global Age*. Durham, NC: Duke University Press, 2015.

"The National Pavilions." *Architectural Review* 83, no. 490 (September 1937): 110.

Neiwert, David. *Alt-America: The Rise of the Radical Right in the Age of Trump*. London: Verso, 2017.

Neocleous, Mark. *Fascism*. Buckingham, U.K.: Open University Press, 1997.

Nerdinger, Winfried. "A Hierarchy of Styles: Architecture between Neoclassicism and Regionalism." In *Art and Power: Europe under the Dictators 1930–45*. Edited by David Elliott, Dawn Ades, Tim Benton, and Iain Boyd Whyte, 322–25. London: Thames and Hudson, 1996.

Nerdinger, Winfried, ed. *Bauhaus-Moderne im National-sozialismus*. Munich: Prestel, 1993.

Nishizawa Yasuhiko. *Nihon shokuminchi kenchikuron*. Nagoya: Nagoya Daigaku shuppankai, 2008.

Nolan, Mary. "America in the German Imagination." In *Transactions, Transgressions, Transformations: American Culture in Western Europe and Japan*. Edited by H. Fehrenbach, 3–25. New York: Berghahn Books, 2000.

Nolan, Mary. *The Transatlantic Century: Europe and America, 1890–2010*. Cambridge: Cambridge University Press, 2012.

Nolan, Mary. *Visions of Modernity: American Business and the Modernization of Germany*. New York: Oxford University Press, 1994.

Pan, Lynn. *Shanghai Style: Art and Design between the Wars*. San Francisco: Long River Press, 2008.

Passerini, Luisa. *Fascism in Popular Memory*. Cambridge: Cambridge University Press, 1987.

Passerini, Luisa. *Mussolini immaginario*. Rome: Laterza, 1991.

Paxton, Robert O. *The Anatomy of Fascism*. New York: Vintage Books, 2005.

Paxton, Robert O. "Comparisons and Definitions." In *The Oxford Handbook of Fascism*. Edited by Richard J. B. Bosworth, 547–65. Oxford: Oxford University Press, 2009.

Payne, Stanley G. "Fascisms, Nazism, and Japanism." *International History Review* 6, no. 2 (May 1984): 265–76.

Payne, Stanley G. *A History of Fascism 1914–1945*. Madison: University of Wisconsin Press, 1995.

Peattie, Mark. "The Dragon's Seed: Origins of the War." In *The Battle for China: Essays on the Military History of the Sino-Japanese War of 1937–1945*. Edited by Mark Peattie, Edward Drea, and Hans Van de Ven, 48–78. Stanford, CA: Stanford University Press, 2011.

Pennington, Lee K. *Causalities of War: Wounded Japanese Servicemen and the Second World War*. Ithaca, NY: Cornell University Press, 2015.

Person, John D. "Between Patriotism and Terrorism: The Policing of Nationalist Movements in 1930s Japan." *Journal of Japanese Studies* 43, no. 2 (2017): 289–318.

Peukert, Detlev J. K. *Inside Nazi Germany: Conformity, Opposition, and Racism in Everyday Life*. London: Batsford, 1987.

Peukert, Detlev J. K. *Max Webers Diagnose der Moderne*. Göttingen: Vandenhoeck and Ruprecht, 1989.

Peukert, Detlev J. K. *The Weimar Republic: The Crisis of Classical Modernity*. New York: Hill and Wang, 1989.

Pevsner, Nikolaus. *Outline of European Architecture*. Harmondsworth: Penguin, 1943.

Phillips, Richard T. "'A Picturesque but Hopeless Resistance': Rehe in 1933." *Modern Asian Studies* 42, no. 4 (2008): 733–50.

Pickowicz, Paul, Kuiyi Shen, and Yingjin Zhang, eds. *Liangyou: Kaleidoscopic Modernity and the Shanghai Global Metropolis, 1926–1945.* Leiden: Brill, 2013.

Pinto, António Costa. *The Nature of Fascism Revisited.* New York: Columbia University Press, 2012.

Pinto, António Costa, ed. *Rethinking the Nature of Fascism: Comparative Perspectives.* Houndmills, U.K.: Palgrave Macmillan, 2011.

Ponzio, Alessio. *Shaping the New Man: Youth Training Regimes in Fascist Italy and Nazi Germany.* Madison: University of Wisconsin Press, 2015.

Poole, Deborah. *Vision, Race, and Modernity: A Visual Economy of the Andean Image World.* Princeton, NJ: Princeton University Press, 1997.

Preston, Paul. *The Spanish Holocaust: Inquisition and Extermination in Twentieth Century Spain.* New York: Norton and Simon, 2012.

Rabinbach, Anson G. "The Aesthetics of Production in the Third Reich." *Journal of Contemporary History* 11, no. 4 (1976): 43–74.

"Racconto (di C. Malaparte). Il corpo straziato di Mussolini a Piazzale Loreto e la folla sudicia." Barbaridllo.it, July 20, 2017. http://www.barbadillo.it/67636-il -racconto-di-c-malaparte-il-corpo-straziato-di-mussolini-a-piazzale-loreto-e -la-folla-sudicia/

Reichel, Peter. *Der schöne Schein des Dritten Reiches. Faszination und Gewalt des Faschismus.* Munich: Carl Hanser Verlag, 1992.

Rentschler, Eric. *The Ministry of Illusion: Nazi Cinema and Its Afterlife.* Cambridge, MA: Harvard University Press, 1996.

Reynolds, Jonathan M. "Imperial Diet Building, National Identity." In *Culture of Japanese Fascism.* Edited by Alan Tansman, 254–75. Durham, NC: Duke University Press, 2009.

Richards, James Maude. *Introduction to Modern Architecture.* Harmondsworth: Penguin, 1940.

Rieger, Bernhard. *The People's Car: A Global History of the Volkswagen Beetle.* Cambridge, MA: Harvard University Press, 2013.

Riley, Terrence, and Steven Perrella. *The International Style: Exhibition 15 and the Museum of Modern Art.* New York: Rizzoli/CBA, 1992.

Rittich, Werner. *New German Architecture.* Berlin: Terramare, 1941.

Roberts, David D. *Fascist Interactions: Proposals for a New Approach to Fascism and Its Era, 1919–1945.* New York: Berghahn Books, 2016.

Rochat, Giorgio. *Le guerre italiane, 1935–1943.* Turin: Einaudi, 2005.

Rochat, Giorgio. "The Italian Air Force in the Ethiopian War (1935–36)." In *Italian Colonialism.* Edited by Ruth Ben-Ghiat and Mia Fuller, 37–46. New York: Palgrave Macmillan, 2005.

Rosenbaum, Ron. *Waking to Danger: Americans and National Socialist Germany, 1933–1941.* Santa Barbara, CA: Praeger, 2010.

Rosenfeld, Gavriel D. *Munich and Memory: Architecture, Monuments, and the Legacy of the Third Reich.* Berkeley: University of California Press, 2000.

Rosenstone, Robert. *Revisioning History: Film and the Construction of a New Past.* Princeton, NJ: Princeton University Press, 1995.

Ross, Alexander Reid. *Against the Fascist Creep.* Chico, CA: AK Press, 2017.

Ross, Corey. *Media and the Making of Modern Germany.* New York: Oxford University Press, 2008.

Rossol, Nadine. *Performing the Nation in Interwar Germany: Sport, Spectacle, and Political Symbolism, 1926–36.* Houndmills, U.K.: Palgrave Macmillan, 2010.

Rossol, Nadine. "Performing the Nation: Sport, Spectacles, and Aesthetics in Germany, 1926–36." *Central European History* 43, no. 4 (2010): 616–38.

Roth, Alfred. *"USA baut": Bildbericht der Ausstellung Moderne amerikanische Architektur.* Winterthur: Verlag Buchdruckerei, 1945.

Ruoff, Kenneth J. *Imperial Japan at Its Zenith: The Wartime Celebration of the Empire's 2,600th Anniversary.* Ithaca, NY: Cornell University Press, 2010.

Saaler, Sven, and Christopher W. A. Szpilman, eds. *Pan-Asianism: A Documentary History*, volumes 1 and 2. Lanham, MD: Rowman and Littlefield, 2011.

Sachsse, Rolf. *Die Erziehung zum Wegsehen: Fotografie im NS-Staat.* Hamburg: Philo Fine Arts, 2003.

Sachsse, Rolf. "Kontinuitäten, Brüche und Mißverständnisse: Bauhaus-Photographie in den dreißiger Jahren." In *Bauhaus-Moderne im National-sozialismus.* Edited by Winfried Nerdinger, 64–84. Munich: Prestel, 1993.

Sandler, Willeke. "Deutsche Heimat in Afrika: Colonial Revisionism and the Construction of Germanness through Photography." *Journal of Women's History* 25, no. 1 (2013): 37–61.

Saunders, Francis Stonor. *The Cultural Cold War: The CIA and the World of Arts and Letters.* New York: New Press, 1999.

Schmitt, Carl. *Staat, Bewegung, Volk: Die Dreigliederung der politischen Einheit.* Hamburg: Hanseatische Verlagsanstalt, 1933.

Schmitz, Matthias. *Caspar David Friedrich: His Life and Work.* New York: German Library of Information, 1940.

Schmölders, Claudia. *Hitler's Face: The Biography of an Image*, translated by Adrian Daub. Philadelphia: University of Pennsylvania Press, 2009.

Schnapp, Jeffrey T. *Staging Fascism: 18 BL and the Theater of Masses for Masses.* Stanford, CA: Stanford University Press, 1996.

Schneider, Axel, and Daniel Woolf, eds. *Oxford History of Historical Writing*, volume 5. Oxford: Oxford University Press, 2011.

Schultze-Naumburg, P. *Die Kulturarbeiten*, 9 volumes. Munich: Calwey, 1901–1917.

Schwartz, Margaret. *Dead Matter: The Meaning of Iconic Corpses.* Minneapolis: University of Minnesota Press, 2015.

Scobie, Alex. *Hitler's State Architecture.* College Park: Pennsylvania State University Press, 1990.

Scrivano, Paolo. "A Thirty-Year Project: Henry-Russell Hitchcock's *Architecture: Nineteenth and Twentieth Centuries.*" In *Summerson and Hitchcock: Centenary*

Essays on Architectural Historiography. Edited by F. Salmon. New Haven, CT: Yale University Press, 2006.

Searing, Helen, ed. *In Search of Modern Architecture: A Tribute to Henry-Russell Hitchcock.* Cambridge, MA: MIT Press, 1982.

Sederberg, Kathryn. "The 1930s in Nazi Germany as Seen through Diaries." Review of Janosch Steuwer, *"Ein Dritter Reich, wie ich es auffasse": Politik, Gesellschaft und privates Leben in Tagebüchern 1933–1939.* Göttingen: Wallstein, 2017. H-German in H-Net Online, January 2018. www.h-net.org/reviews/showrev.php?id=50185/.

Shen, Vivian. *The Origins of Left-Wing Cinema in China, 1932–1937.* New York: Routledge, 2005.

Shillony, Ben-Ami. *Revolt in Japan: The Young Officers and the February 26, 1936 Incident.* Princeton, NJ: Princeton University Press, 1973.

Shimada Toshihiko. "Designs on North China, 1933–1937." In *Japan's Road to the Pacific War: The China Quagmire.* Edited by James Morley, 11–230. New York: Columbia University Press, 1983.

Shimazu, Naoko. *Japanese Society at War: Death, Memory and the Russo-Japanese War.* Cambridge: Cambridge University Press, 2009.

Shirer, William. *Berlin Diary.* Harmondsworth, U.K.: Penguin, [1940] 1979.

Shu, Zhao. "CC de kuozhang huodong" ["The CC Clique's Expanded Activities"]. In *CC Neimu* [*The Inside Story of the CC Clique*]. Edited by Chai Fu. Beijing: Zhongguo wenshi chubanshe, 1988.

Sims, Richard. *Japanese Political History since the Meiji Renovation 1868–2000.* New York: Palgrave, 2001.

Simson, Howard. *The Social Origins of Afrikaner Fascism and Its Apartheid Policy.* Stockholm: Almqvist and Wiksell International, 1980.

Sokolovič, Peter. *Hlinková Garda, 1938–1945.* Bratislava: Ústav Pamäti Národa, 2009.

Sontag, Susan. "Fascinating Fascism." In *Under the Sign of Saturn: Essays*, 73–105. New York: Farrar, Straus and Giroux, 1980. Originally published in the *New York Review of Books*, February 6, 1975.

Sorlin, Pierre. *The Film in History.* Totowa, NJ: Barnes and Noble, 1980.

Spector, Scott. "Was the Third Reich Movie-Made? Interdisciplinarity and the Reframing of 'Ideology.'" *American Historical Review* 106, no. 2 (2001): 482–83.

Speer, Albert, and Rudolf Wolters. *Neue Deutsche Baukunst.* Prag: Volk und Reich Verlag, 1943.

Starl, Timm. *Knipser: Die Bildgeschichte der privaten Fotografie in Deutschland und Österreich von 1880 bis 1980.* Munich: Koehler and Amelang, 1995.

Steigmann-Gall, Richard. *The Holy Reich: Nazi Conceptions of Christianity, 1919–1945.* Cambridge: Cambridge University Press, 2004.

Steimatsky, Noa. *The Face on Film.* Oxford: Oxford University Press, 2017.

Stoler, Ann Laura. *Carnal Knowledge and Imperial Power.* Berkeley: University of California Press, 2002.

Stoler, Ann Laura. "Introduction: 'The Rot Remains': From Ruins to Ruination." In *Imperial Debris: On Ruins and Ruination*. Edited by Ann Laura Stoler. Durham, NC: Duke University Press, 2013.

Stoler, Ann Laura. "Sexual Affronts and Racial Frontiers: European Identities and the Cultural Politics of Exclusion." *Comparative Studies in Society and History* 34, no. 3 (July 1992): 514–51.

Strang, G. Bruce, ed. *Collision of Empires*. London: Routledge, 2013.

Stratigakos, Despina. *Hitler at Home*. New Haven, CT: Yale University Press, 2015.

Switzer, Les, ed. *South Africa's Alternative Press: Voices of Protest and Resistance, 1880–1960*. Cambridge: Cambridge University Press, 1997.

Szpilman, Christopher W. A. "Fascist and Quasi-Fascist Ideas in Interwar Japan, 1918–1941." In *Japan in the Fascist Era*. Edited by Bruce Reynolds, 73–106. London: Palgrave, 2004.

Szpilman, Christopher W. A. "The Yūzonsha's 'War Cry,' 1920." In *Pan-Asianism: A Documentary History: Volume 2*. Edited by Sven Saaler and Christopher W. A. Szpilman, 55–62. Lanham, MD: Rowman and Littlefield, 2011.

Tabata Shūichirō. *Boku no Manshū ryokōki*. Tokyo: Jidō tosho shuppansha, 1944.

Tachibana, Takashi. "The Aftermath of the Emperor-Organ Incident: The Tōdai Faculty of Law," translated by Richard H. Minear. *The Asia-Pacific Journal* 11, 9, no. 1 (March 4, 2013): 1–21.

Taiheiyō sensō kenkyūkai, ed. *"Shashin shuhō" ni miru senjika no Nihon*. Tokyo: Sekai bunkasha, 2011.

Takenaka, Akiko. "Architecture for Mass-Mobilization." In *The Culture of Japanese Fascism*. Edited by Alan Tansman, 235–53. Durham, NC: Duke University Press, 2009.

Takenaka, Akiko. *Yasukuni Shrine: History, Memory, and Japan's Unending Postwar*. Honolulu: University of Hawai'i Press, 2015.

Tang, Xiaobing. *Origins of the Chinese Avant-Garde: The Modern Woodcut Movement*. Berkeley: University of California Press, 2007.

Tankha, Brij. *Kita Ikki and the Making of Modern Japan: A Vision of Empire*. Folkestone, Kent, U.K.: Global Oriental, 2006.

Tansman, Alan. *The Aesthetics of Japanese Fascism*. Berkeley: University of California Press, 2009.

Tansman, Alan, ed. *The Culture of Japanese Fascism*. Durham, NC: Duke University Press, 2009.

Taylor, Robert R. *The Word in Stone: The Role of Architecture in the National Socialist Ideology*. Berkeley: University of California Press, 1974.

Tenold, Vegas. *Everything You Love Will Burn: Inside the Rebirth of White Nationalism in America*. New York: Nation Books, 2018.

Thies, Jochen. "Nazi Architecture: a Blueprint for World Domination: The Last Aims of Adolf Hitler." In *Nazi Propaganda: The Power and the Limitations*. Edited by David Welch, 45–64. London: CroomHelm, 1983.

Thomae, Otto. *Die Propaganda-maschinerie bildende Kunst und Öffentlilchkeitsarbeit im dritten Reich*. Berlin: Gebr. Mann, 1978.

Thomas, Julia Adeney. "The Cage of Nature: Modernity's History in Japan." *History and Theory* 40, no. 1 (February 2001): 16–36.

Thomas, Julia Adeney. "The Evidence of Sight." Theme issue, "Photography and Historical Interpretation." *History and Theory* 48 (December 2009): 151–68.

Thomas, Julia Adeney. "Power Made Visible: Photography and Postwar Japan's Elusive Reality." *Journal of Asian Studies* 67, no. 2 (May 2008): 365–94.

Thomas, Julia Adeney. *Reconfiguring Modernity: Concepts of Nature in Japanese Political Ideology*. Berkeley: University of California Press, 2001.

Thomas, Julia Adeney. "Why Do Only Some Places Have History? Japan, the West, and the Geography of the Past." *Journal of World History* 28, no. 2 (June 2017): 187–218.

Till, Karen E. *The New Berlin: Memory, Politics, Place*. Minneapolis: University of Minnesota Press, 2005.

Tohmatsu, Haruo. "From the Manchurian Incident to Japan's Withdrawal from the League of Nations." In *Fifteen Lectures: Road to the Pacific War in Recent Historiography*. Edited by Tsutsui Kiyotada, 83–104. Tokyo: Japan Publishing Industry Foundation for Culture, 2016.

Tooze, Adam. *The Wages of Destruction: The Making and Breaking of the Nazi Economy*. London: Penguin, 2006.

Tooze, Adam. "When We Loved Mussolini." *New York Review of Books*, August 18, 2016, 55–56.

Trevor-Roper, Hugh. "The Phenomenon of Fascism." In. *Fascism in Europe*. Edited by Stuart Woolf, 3–25. London: Methuen, 1981.

Troost, Gerdy. *Das Bauen im neuen Reich*. Bayreuth, 1938.

Tseng, Alice Y. "Domon Ken's Murōji." Special issue, "Pictures and Things: Bridging Visual and Material Culture in Japan." *Impressions* 30 (March 2009): 114–18.

Tsutsui Kiyotada, ed. *Fifteen Lectures on Showa Japan: Road to the Pacific War in Recent Historiography*, translated by Noda Makito and Paul Narum. Tokyo: Japan Publishing Industry Foundation for Culture, 2016.

Turner, Frederick. *The Democratic Surround: Multimedia and American Liberalism from World War II to the Psychedelic Sixties*. Chicago: University of Chicago Press, 2013.

Umbach, Maiken. "Selfhood, Place, and Ideology in German Photo Albums, 1933–1945." *Central European History* 48 (2015): 335–65.

Umland, Andreas. "Diachronic and Cross-Cultural Comparison: Toward a Better Understanding of International Fascism." *Fascism* 1 (2012): 62–63.

Vande Winkel, Roel, and David Welch, eds. *Cinema and the Swastika: The International Expansion of Third Reich Cinema*. Houndmills, U.K.: Palgrave Macmillan, 2011.

van Leeuwen, Lizzie. *Ons Indisch Erfgoed: Zestig jaar strijd om cultuur en identiteit*. Amsterdam: Bert Bakker, 2008.

Vanvugt, Ewald. "Beknopte iconologie van de koloniale sculptuur in Amsterdam." In *Pluriform Amsterdam: Essays*. Edited by Irene van Eerd and Berne Hermes, 174–75. Amsterdam: University of Amsterdam Press, 1998.

Viereck, George Sylvester, ed. *A Nation Builds: Contemporary German Architecture*. New York: German Library of Information, 1940.

Viereck, George Sylvester, ed. *The War in Maps 1939/40*. New York: German Library of Information, 1941.

Virilio, Paul. *Vitesse et Politique: Essai de Dromologie*. Paris: Galilée, 1977.

Vnuk, František. *Mat' Svoj Štát Znamená Život*. Bratislava: Slovensky Ustav, 1991.

Vondung, Klaus. *Magie und Manipulation: Ideologischer Kult und politische Religion des Nationalsozialismus*. Göttingen: Vandenhoeck and Ruprecht, 1994.

von Moltke, Johannes. *The Curious Humanist: Siegfried Kracauer in America*. Berkeley: University of California Press, 2016.

Wald, Alan. *American Night: The Literary Left in the Era of the Cold War*. Chapel Hill: University of North Carolina Press, 2014.

Wald, Alan. *Trinity of Passion: The Literary Left and the Antifascist Crusade*. Chapel Hill: University of North Carolina Press, 2007.

Walther, Daniel Joseph. *Creating Germans Abroad: Cultural Policies and Settler Identities in Namibia*. Athens: Ohio University Press, 2002.

Ward, James M. "People Who Deserve It: Jozef Tiso and the Presidential Exemption." *Nationalities Papers* 30, no. 4 (August 2002): 571–601.

Ward, James M. *Priest, Politician, Collaborator: Josef Tiso and the Making of Fascist Slovakia*. Ithaca, NY: Cornell University Press, 2013.

Ward, Max. "Displaying the World View of Japanese Fascism." *Critical Asian Studies* 47, no. 3 (2015): 414–39.

Watt, Lori. *When Empire Comes Home: Repatriation and Reintegration in Postwar Japan*. Cambridge, MA: Harvard University Asia Center, 2009.

Weber, Max. *Economy and Society: An Outline of Interpretive Sociology*. Edited by Guenther Roth and Claus Wittich. Berkeley: University of California Press, 1978.

Welch, David. "Nazi Propaganda and the *Volksgemeinschaft*: Constructing a People's Community." *Journal of Contemporary History* 39, no. 2 (2004): 213–38.

Werneburg, Brigitte. "Die veränderte Welt: Der gefährliche anstelle des entscheidenden Augenblicks: Ernst Jüngers Überlegungen zur Fotografie." *Fotogeschichte* 51 (1994): 51–67.

Wharton, Annabel. *Building the Cold War: Hilton International Hotels and Modern Architecture*. Chicago: University of Chicago Press, 2001.

Whelan, Richard. *Robert Capa: A Biography*. New York: Alfred A. Knopf, 1985.

Willoughby-Herard, Tiffany. *Waste of a White Skin: The Carnegie Corporation and the Racial Logic of White Vulnerability*. Berkeley: University of California Press, 2015.

Wilson, Sandra. "The Russo-Japanese War and Japan: Politics, Nationalism and Historical Memory." In *The Russo-Japanese War in Cultural Perspective, 1904–05*. Edited by David Wells and Sandra Wilson, 160–93. New York: St. Martin's, 1999.

Winkler, Heinrich August. "Vom Mythos der *Volksgemeinschaft.*" *Archiv für Sozial-geschichte* 17 (1977): 484–90.

Wohl, Robert. *The Spectacle of Flight: Aviation and the Western Imagination.* New Haven, CT: Yale University Press, 2005.

Wollen, Peter. "Modern Times: Cinema/Americanism/The Robot." In *Raiding the Icebox: Reflections on Twentieth-Century Culture*, 35–71. London: Verso, 1993.

Wollen, Peter. *Paris Hollywood: Writings on Film.* London: Verso, 2002.

Wollen, Peter. *Paris Manhattan: Writings on Art.* London: Verso, 2004.

Woodley, Daniel. *Fascism and Political Theory: Critical Perspectives on Fascist Ideology.* London: Routledge, 2010.

Xiao, Zhiwei. "Constructing a New National Culture: Film Censorship and Issues of Cantonese Dialect, Superstition, and Sex in the Nanjing Decade." In *Cinema and Urban Culture in Shanghai, 1922–1943.* Edited by Yingjin Zhang. Stanford, CA: Stanford University Press, 1999.

Yang, Kuisong, *Guomindang de "lian gong" yu "fangong"* [*Koumintang: Unity with Communists and Anti-Communism*]. Beijing: Shehuikexue wenxian chubanshe, 2008.

Yiping, Wu. "Kangzhan shiqi Zhongguo Guomindang de wenyi zhengce jiqi yunzuo" ["The Literature and Art Policy of the Kuomintang, 1937–1945"]. PhD diss., National Chengchi University, 2009.

Yokoyama Atsuo. "Nihon gun ga chūgoku ni kensetsushita jūsan-ki no chūreitō." *Nihon kenkyū* 49 (2014): 57–116.

Yoshiaki, Yoshimi. *Grassroots Fascism: The War Experience of the Japanese People*, translated by Ethan Mark. New York: Columbia University Press, 2015.

Young, Louise. *Japan's Total Empire: Manchuria and the Culture of Wartime Imperialism.* Berkeley: University of California Press, 1998.

Young, Louise. "When Fascism Met Empire in Japanese-Occupied Manchuria." *Journal of Global History* 12 (2017): 274–96.

Zachariah, Benjamin. "Global Fascisms and the *Volk*: The Framing of Narratives and the Crossing of Lines." *South Asia: Journal of South Asian Studies* 38, no. 4 (2015): 608–12.

Zagarrio, Vito. *L'immagine del fascism.* Rome: Bulzoni, 2009.

Zahra, Tara. *Kidnapped Souls: National Indifference and the Battle for Children and the Bohemian Lands, 1900–1948.* Ithaca, NY: Cornell University Press, 2011.

Zexiang, Xu. "Ruhe jianshe Zhongguo minzu wenhua" ["How to Construct China's National Culture"]. *Zhongguo jianshe xiehui huibao* [*Periodical of the Chinese Cultural Construction Association*] 1, no. 4 (1934): 22–24.

Zimmerman, Claire. "Albert Kahn in the Second Industrial Revolution." *AA Files* 75 (December 2017): 28–44.

Zimmerman, Claire. *Photographic Architecture in the 20th Century.* Minneapolis: University of Minnesota Press, 2014.

CONTRIBUTORS

NADYA BAIR is a postdoctoral associate at Yale University's Digital Humanities Lab. Her book project, *The Decisive Network: Magnum Photos and the Postwar Image Market,* examines how photo agencies shaped global visual culture and the business of picture supply after World War II. Bair's articles have appeared in the journals *History of Photography* and *American Art,* and in the edited volume *Getting the Picture: The Visual Culture of the News.* She received her PhD in Art History from the University of Southern California.

PAUL D. BARCLAY is a professor and head of the History Department at Lafayette College in Easton, Pennsylvania. He is the general editor of the digital repository East Asia Image Collection (https://dss.lafayette.edu/collections/east-asia-image-collection/) and author of *Outcasts of Empire: Japanese Rule on Taiwan's "Savage Border" 1874–1945* (2018). Barclay's research has received support from the National Endowment from the Humanities, the Social Science Research Council, the Japanese Council for the Promotion of Science, and the Taiwan Ministry of Foreign Affairs.

RUTH BEN-GHIAT is a professor of history and Italian studies at New York University. She writes about fascism, authoritarian regimes, war, and propaganda for academic and general audiences. Her latest book is the award-winning *Italian Fascism's Empire Cinema* (2015).

MAGGIE CLINTON is an associate professor of history at Middlebury College in Middlebury, Vermont. Her first book, *Revolutionary Nativism: Fascism and Culture in China, 1925–1937,* was published by Duke University Press in 2017. She is currently pursuing a master's degree in social work at Columbia University.

GEOFF ELEY is the Karl Pohrt Distinguished University Professor of Contemporary History at the University of Michigan, where he has taught since 1979. He taught previously at the University of Cambridge (1975–79) and received a PhD from the University of Sussex (1974). His earliest works were *Reshaping the German Right: Radical Nationalism and Political Change after Bismarck* (1980, 1991) and (with David Blackbourn) *The Peculiarities of German History* (1980, 1984). More recent books include *Forging Democracy: A History of the Left in Europe, 1850–2000* (2002); *A Crooked Line: From Cultural History to the History of Society* (2005); *The Future of Class in*

History (with Keith Nield, 2007); and *Nazism as Fascism: Violence, Ideology, and the Ground of Consent in Germany, 1930–1945* (2013). He was coeditor of *German Colonialism in a Global Age* (2014) and *German Modernities from Wilhelm to Weimar: A Contest of Futures* (2016). He is writing a general history of Europe in the twentieth century and a new study of the German Right titled *Genealogies of Nazism: Conservatives, Radical Nationalists, Fascists in Germany, 1860–1930.*

LUTZ KOEPNICK is the Gertrude Conaway Vanderbilt Professor of German, Cinema, and Media Arts at Vanderbilt University in Nashville, Tennessee. Koepnick has published widely on film, media theory, visual culture, new media aesthetic, and intellectual history from the nineteenth to the twenty-first century. He is the author of the recent books *The Long Take: Contemporary Art Cinema and the Wondrous* (2017); *Michael Bay: World Cinema in the Age of Populism* (2017); and *On Slowness: Toward an Aesthetic of the Contemporary* (2014).

ETHAN MARK is an associate professor of modern Japanese and Asian history at Leiden University, the Netherlands. He is author of *Japan's Occupation of Java in the Second World War: A Transnational History* (2018) and of essays published in the *American Historical Review* and the *Journal of Asian Studies.* His annotated translation of Yoshimi Yoshiaki's *Grassroots Fascism: The War Experience of the Japanese People* was published by Columbia University Press in 2015.

BERTRAND METTON teaches modern European history at Rutgers University in New Brunswick, New Jersey, and world history at the City University of New York, Queens College. He received his PhD in anthropology and history from the University of Michigan, Ann Arbor. His book project entitled "Hitler's Europe: A Fascist Spatial Revolution," examines the role fascist and Nazi conceptions of Europe played in reshaping the spatial imaginary and ideology of fascism during World War II.

LORENA RIZZO is a historian of southern Africa (Namibia and South Africa) with a special interest in visual history. She's the co-chair of the African Studies Center, University of Basel and an associate fellow at the Hutchins Center, Harvard University. Among her publications are *Gender and Colonialism: A History of Kaoko in North-western Namibia, 1870s–1950* (2012); "Rethinking Empire in Southern Africa," published in the *Journal of Southern African Studies* in 2015 (cowritten with Dag Henrichsen, Giorgio Miescher, and Ciraj Rassool); "Gender and Visuality: Identification Photographs, Respectability and Personhood in Colonial Southern Africa in the 1920s and 1930s," published in *Gender and History* in 2014; and "The Elephant Shooting: Colonial Law and Indirect Rule in Kaoko, North-western Namibia, 1920s and 1930s," published in the *Journal of African History* in 2007. Her book entitled *Photography and History in Colonial Southern Africa: Shades of Empire* will be published by Routledge & WITS University Press in 2019.

JULIA ADENEY THOMAS is in the History Department at the University of Notre Dame. She received the American Historical Association's John K. Fairbank Prize for *Reconfiguring Modernity: Concepts of Nature in Japanese Political Ideology* and the Berkshire Conference of Women Historians' Best Article of the Year Award for "Photography, National Identity, and the 'Cataract of Times': Wartime Images and the Case of Japan," published in the *American Historical Review*. Two collaborative books, *Japan at Nature's Edge: The Environmental Context of a Global Power* (with Ian J. Miller and Brett L. Walker) and *Rethinking Historical Distance* (with Mark Salber Phillips and Barbara Caine) consider theory, history, and the environment. Forthcoming work includes *The Anthropocene* with Mark Williams and Jan Zalasiewicz (Polity, 2020). She is currently completing *The Historian's Task in the Anthropocene* for Princeton University Press.

CLAIRE ZIMMERMAN is an associate professor at the University of Michigan, author of *Photographic Architecture in the Twentieth Century* (2014), and coeditor of *Neo-avant-garde and Postmodern: Postwar Architecture in Britain and Beyond* (2010). Recent and forthcoming essays include "Reading the (Photographic) Evidence," in the *Journal of the Society of Architectural Historians* (2017); "Albert Kahn in the Second Machine Age," in *Architectural Association Files* (2017); and "The Cost of Architecture," a coedited special issue of *Grey Room* (2018). Current projects include a historical analysis of the impact of U.S. industrialization on architecture through the Kahn family of Detroit, and continuing work on the impact of photographic architecture on producers and users of buildings worldwide.

INDEX

Page numbers in italics refer to figures.

CPSIA information can be obtained
at www.ICGtesting.com
Printed in the USA
LVHW020038170620
658145LV00021B/2312